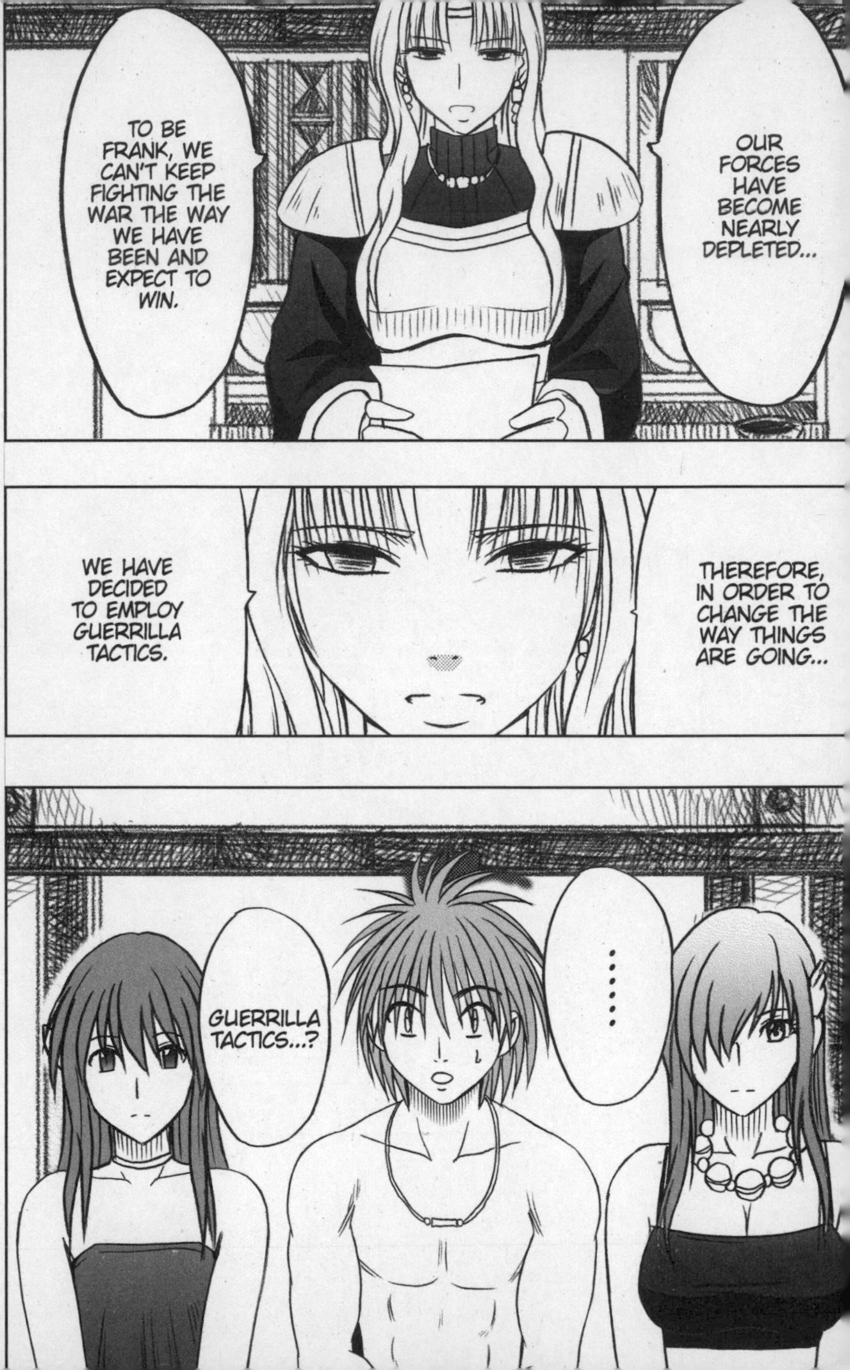
OUR FORCES HAVE BECOME NEARLY DEPLETED...
TO BE FRANK, WE CAN'T KEEP FIGHTING THE WAR THE WAY WE HAVE BEEN AND EXPECT TO WIN.
THEREFORE, IN ORDER TO CHANGE THE WAY THINGS ARE GOING...
WE HAVE DECIDED TO EMPLOY GUERRILLA TACTICS.
.....
GUERRILLA TACTICS...?

Part 2

CHAPTER 17

CHAINS

DISC 1

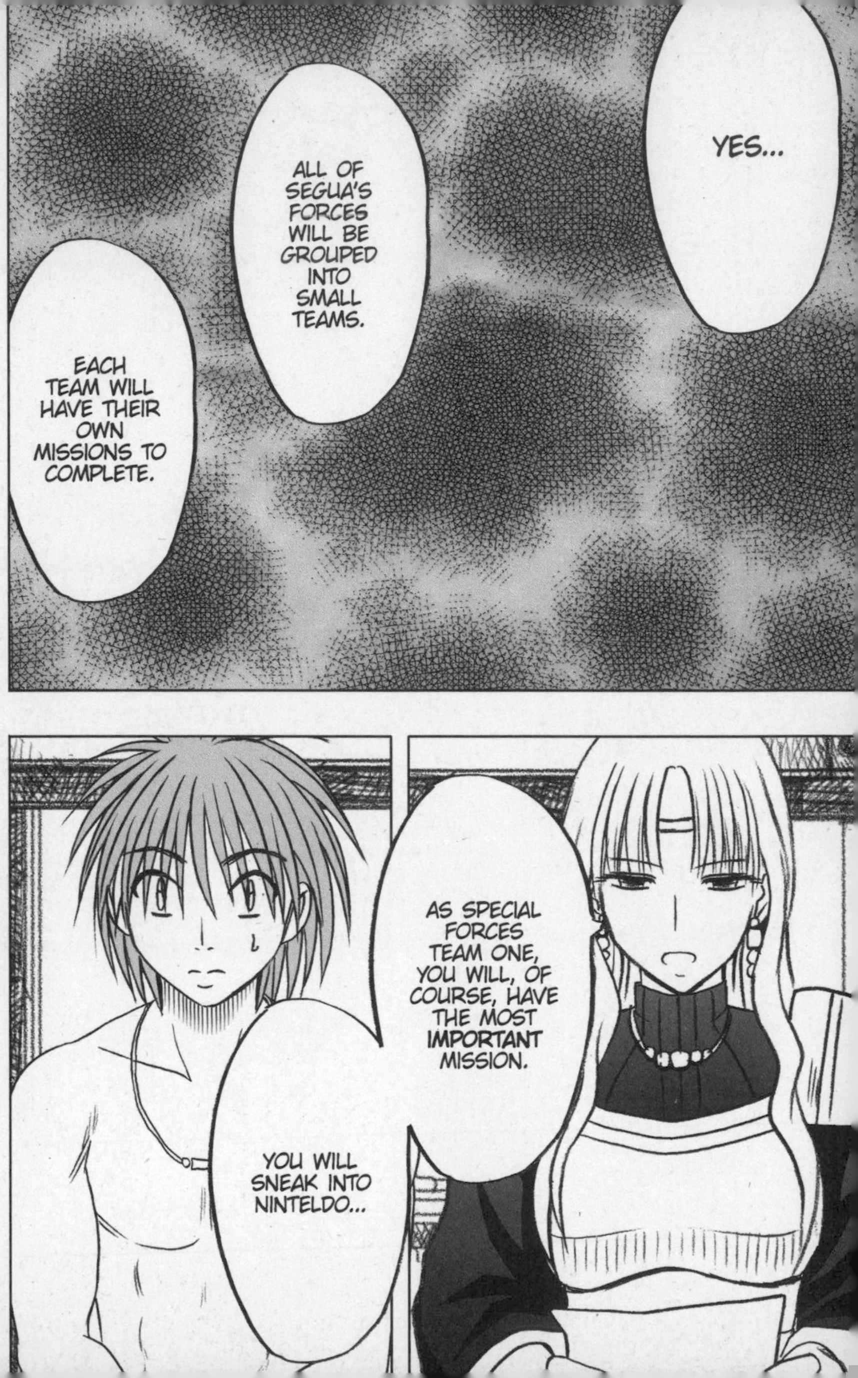
YES...
ALL OF SEGUA'S FORCES WILL BE GROUPED INTO SMALL TEAMS.
EACH TEAM WILL HAVE THEIR OWN MISSIONS TO COMPLETE.
AS SPECIAL FORCES TEAM ONE, YOU WILL, OF COURSE, HAVE THE MOST IMPORTANT MISSION.
YOU WILL SNEAK INTO NINTELDO...

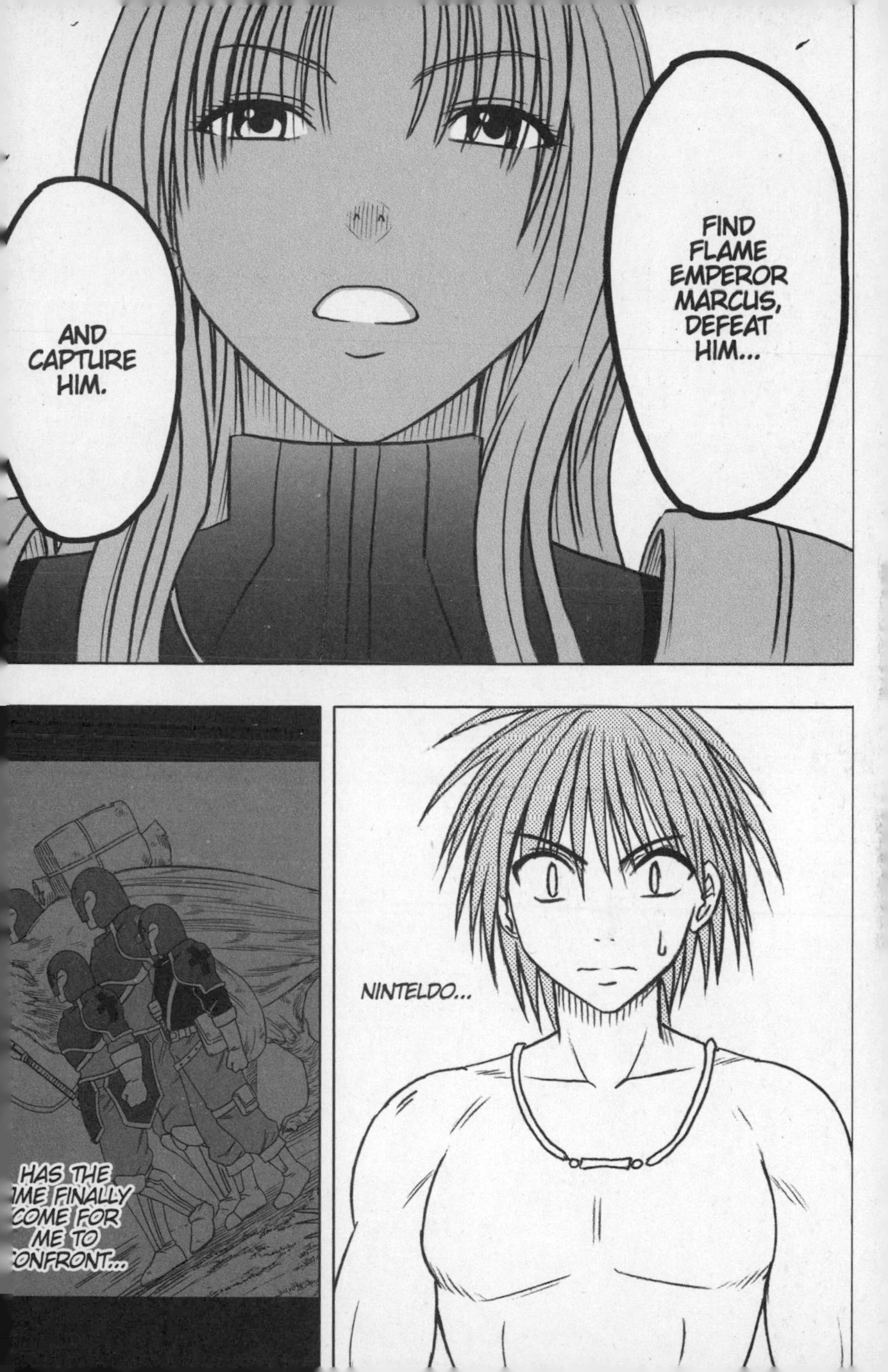
FIND FLAME EMPEROR MARCUS, DEFEAT HIM...
AND CAPTURE HIM.
NINTELDO...
HAS THE IME FINALLY COME FOR ME TO ONFRONT...

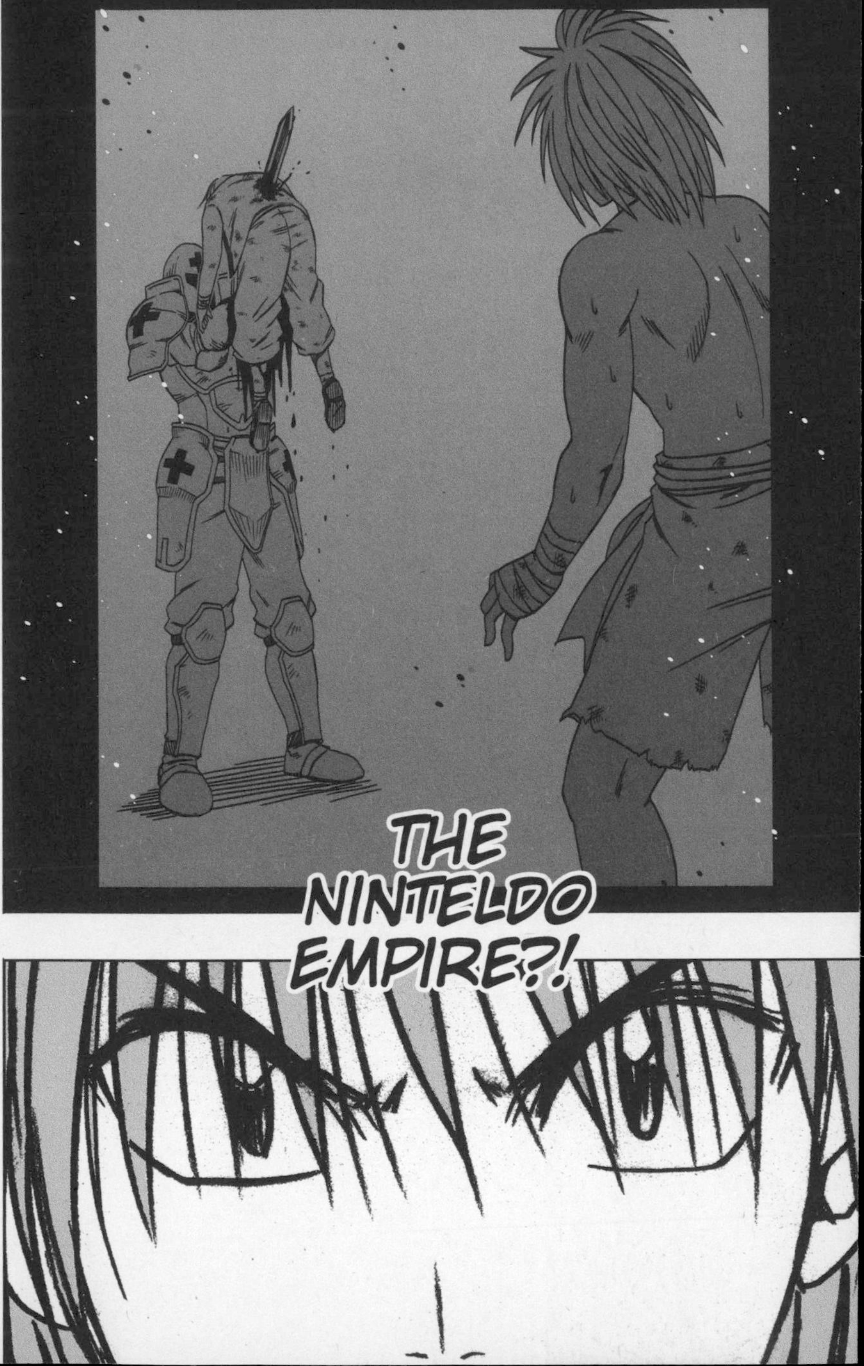
THE NINTELDO EMPIRE?!

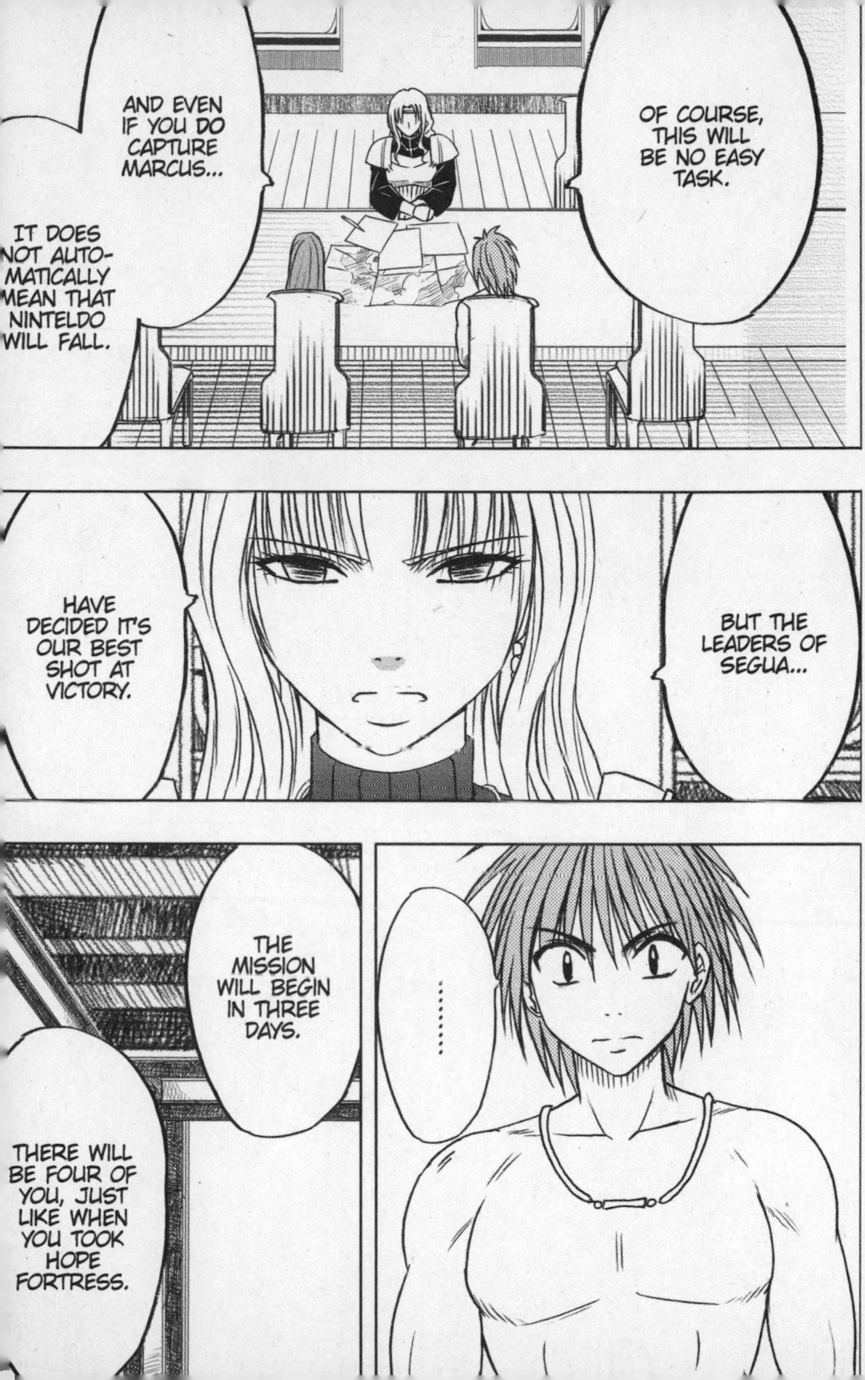
OF COURSE, THIS WILL BE NO EASY TASK.
AND EVEN IF YOU DO CAPTURE MARCUS...
IT DOES NOT AUTO-MATICALLY MEAN THAT NINTELDO WILL FALL.
BUT THE LEADERS OF SEGUA...
HAVE DECIDED IT'S OUR BEST SHOT AT VICTORY.
......
THE MISSION WILL BEGIN IN THREE DAYS.
THERE WILL BE FOUR OF YOU, JUST LIKE WHEN YOU TOOK HOPE FORTRESS.

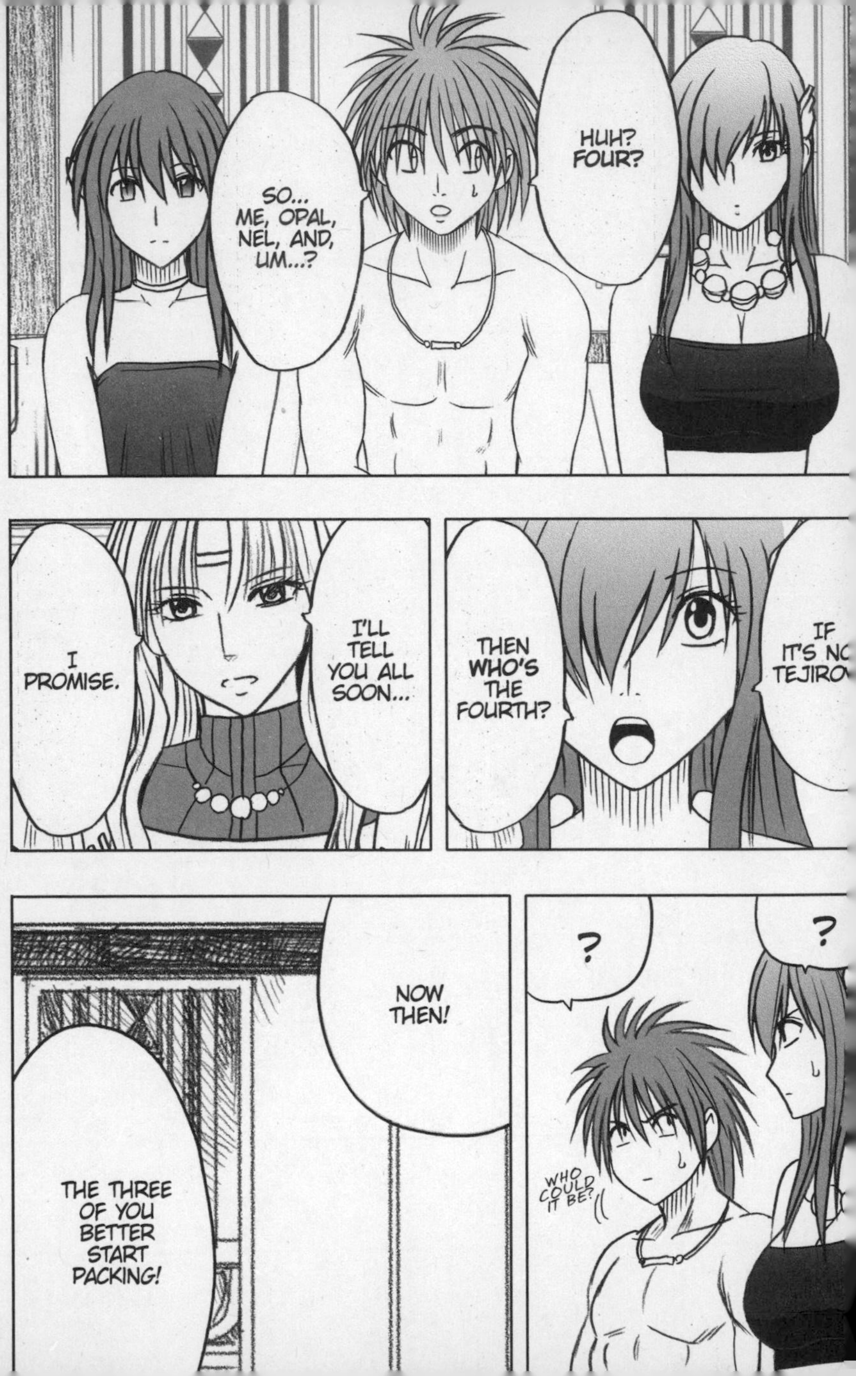
HUH? FOUR?
SO... ME, OPAL, NEL, AND, UM...?
IF IT'S NO TEJIRO
THEN WHO'S THE FOURTH?
I'LL TELL YOU ALL SOON...
I PROMISE.
?
?
WHO COULD IT BE?
NOW THEN!
THE THREE OF YOU BETTER START PACKING!

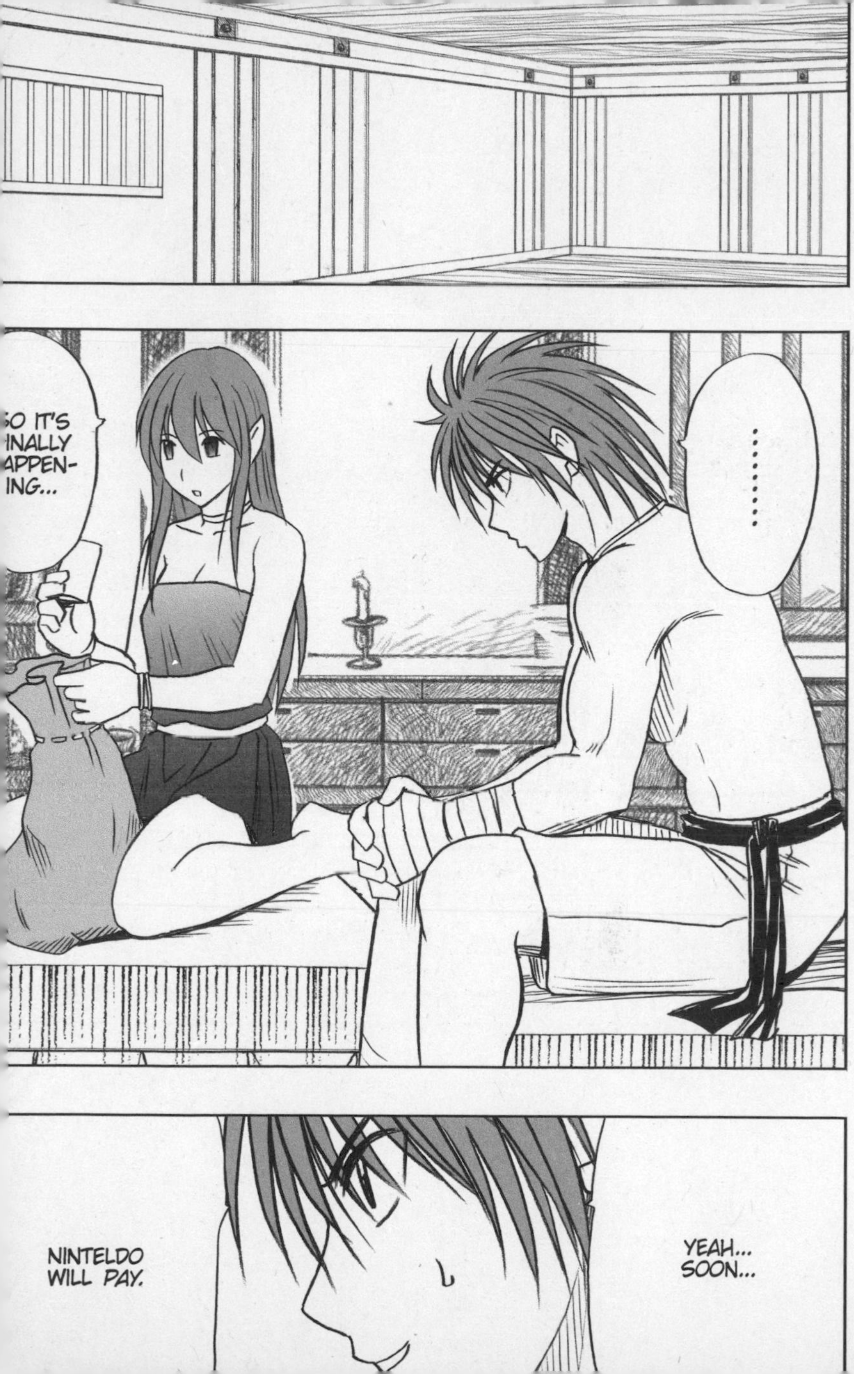
......
SO IT'S FINALLY HAPPEN-ING...
YEAH... SOON...
NINTELDO WILL PAY.

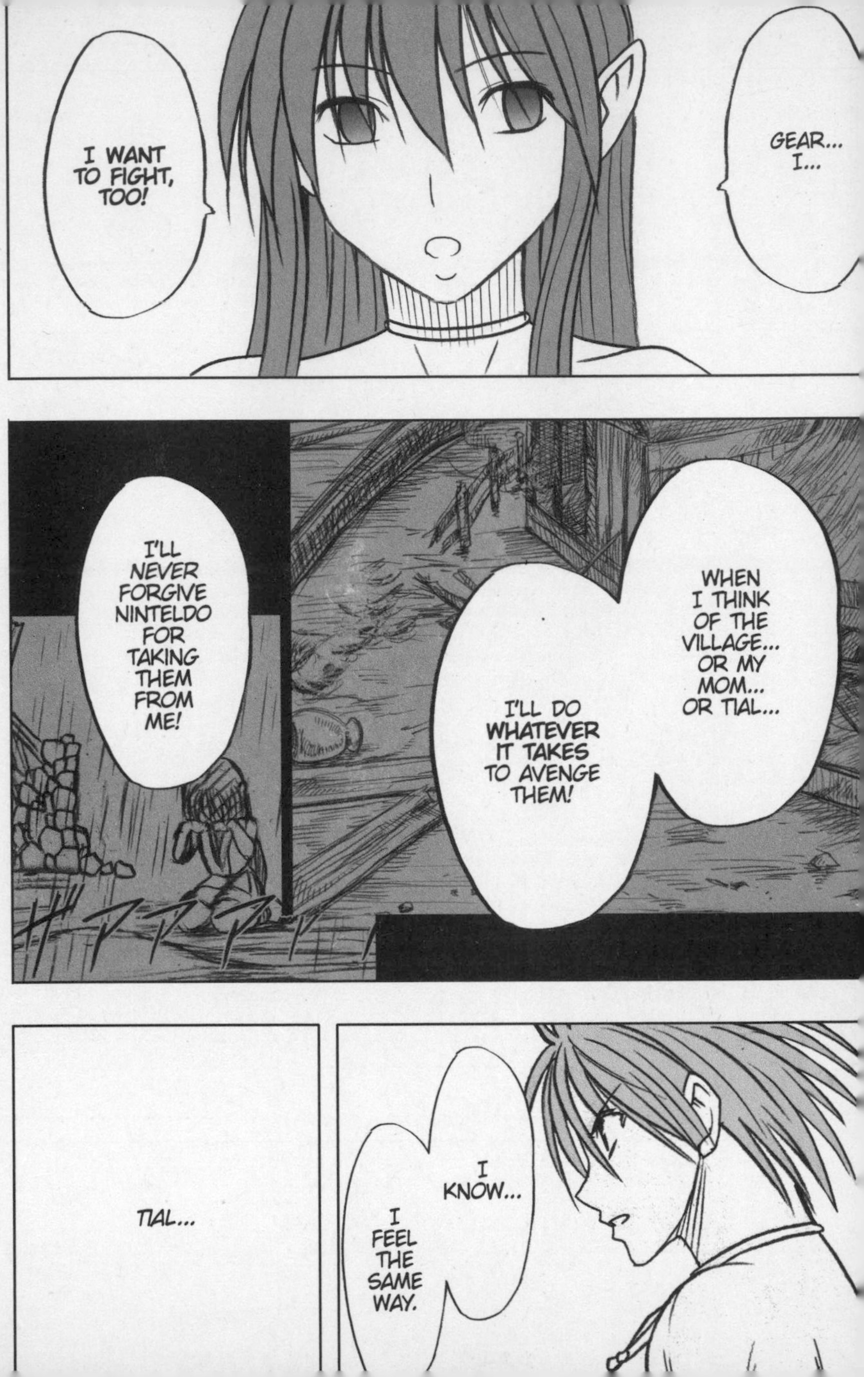
GEAR... I...
I WANT TO FIGHT, TOO!
WHEN I THINK OF THE VILLAGE... OR MY MOM... OR TIAL...
I'LL DO WHATEVER IT TAKES TO AVENGE THEM!
I'LL NEVER FORGIVE NINTELDO FOR TAKING THEM FROM ME!
I KNOW...
I FEEL THE SAME WAY.
TIAL...

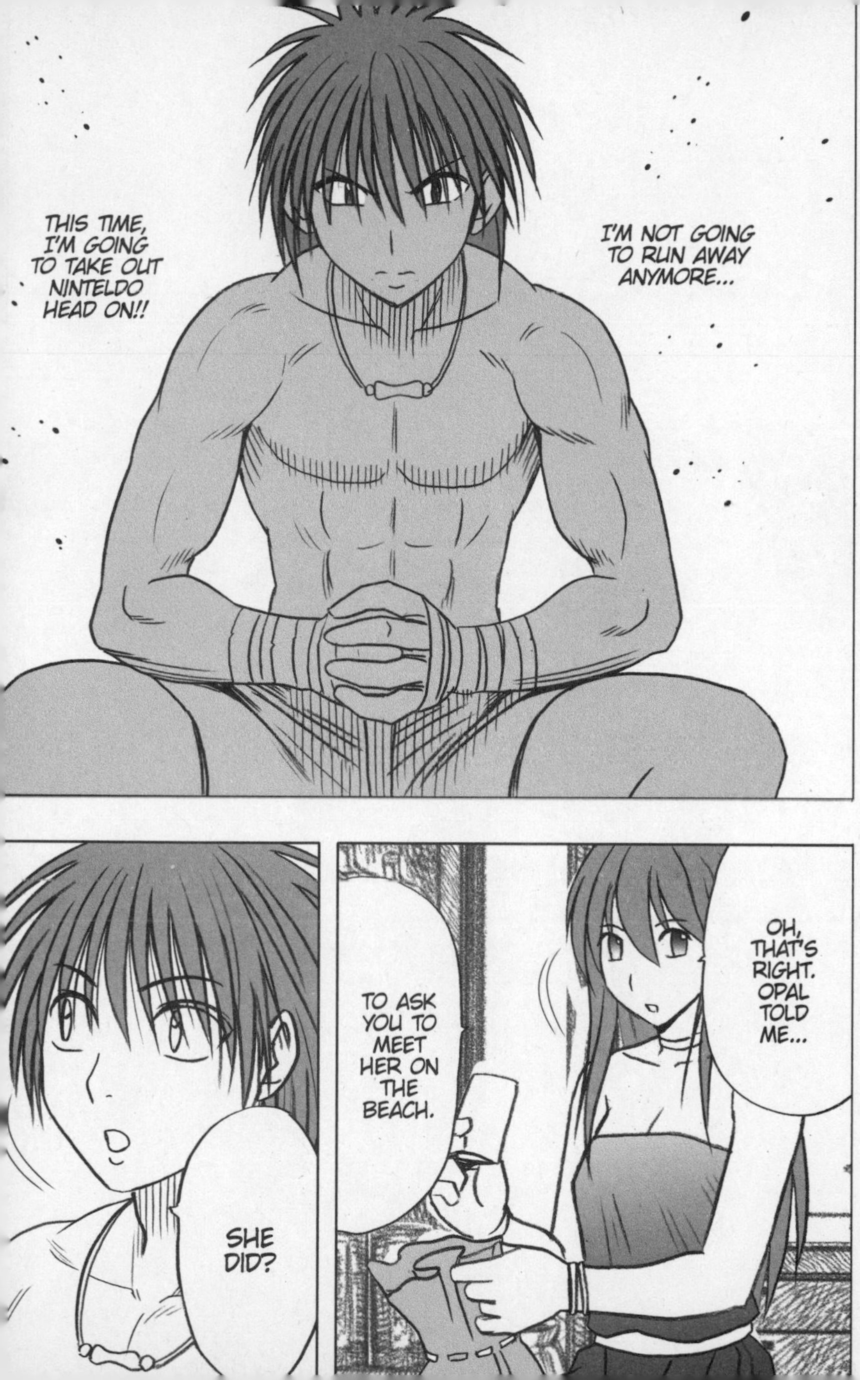
I'M NOT GOING TO RUN AWAY ANYMORE...
THIS TIME, I'M GOING TO TAKE OUT NINTELDO HEAD ON!!
OH, THAT'S RIGHT. OPAL TOLD ME...
TO ASK YOU TO MEET HER ON THE BEACH.
SHE DID?

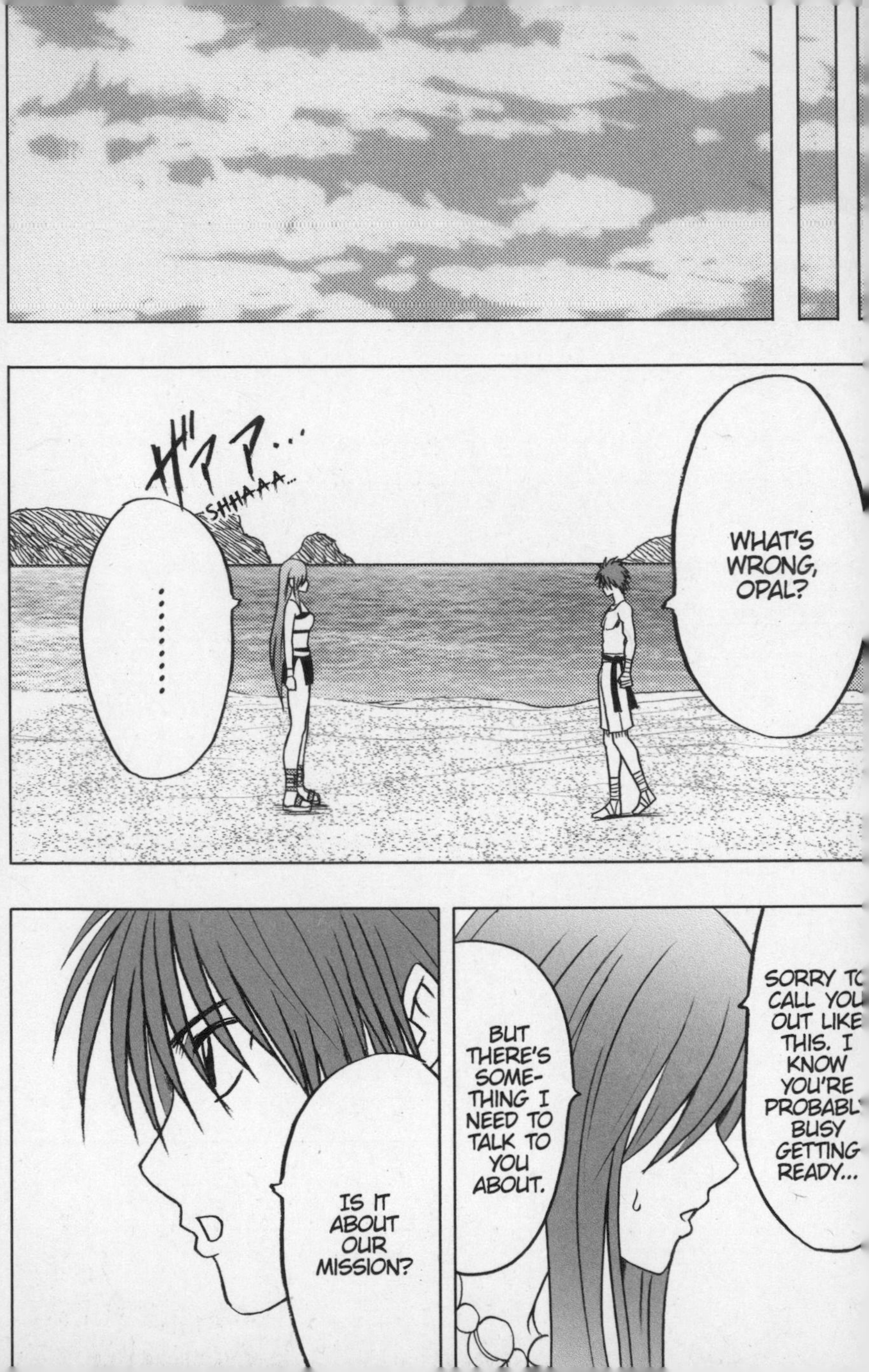
WHAT'S WRONG, OPAL?
ザァア…
SHHAAA...
......
SORRY TO CALL YOU OUT LIKE THIS. I KNOW YOU'RE PROBABLY BUSY GETTING READY...
BUT THERE'S SOME-THING I NEED TO TALK TO YOU ABOUT.
IS IT ABOUT OUR MISSION?

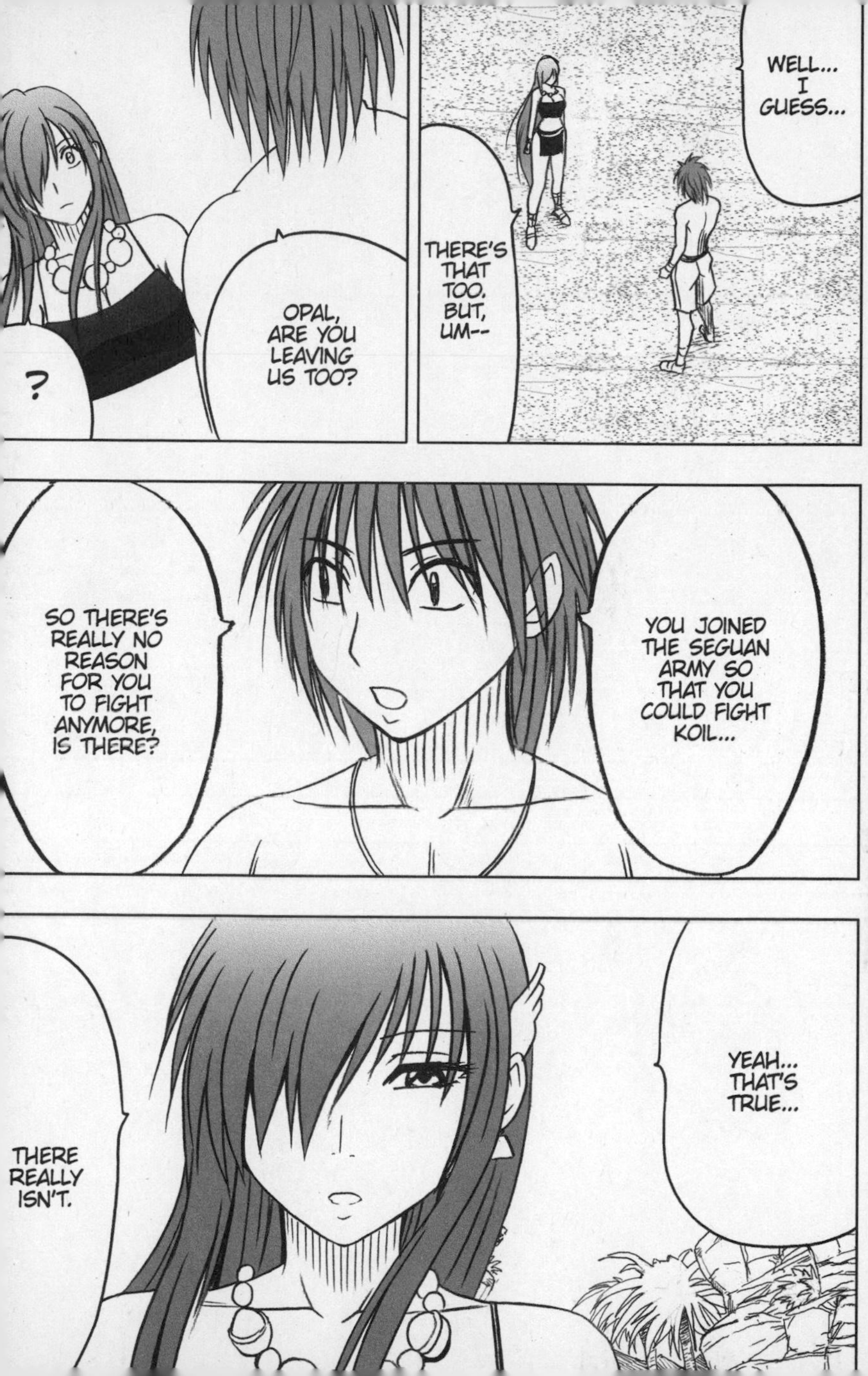

WELL... I GUESS...
THERE'S THAT TOO. BUT, UM--
OPAL, ARE YOU LEAVING US TOO?
?
YOU JOINED THE SEGUAN ARMY SO THAT YOU COULD FIGHT KOIL...
SO THERE'S REALLY NO REASON FOR YOU TO FIGHT ANYMORE, IS THERE?
YEAH... THAT'S TRUE...
THERE REALLY ISN'T.

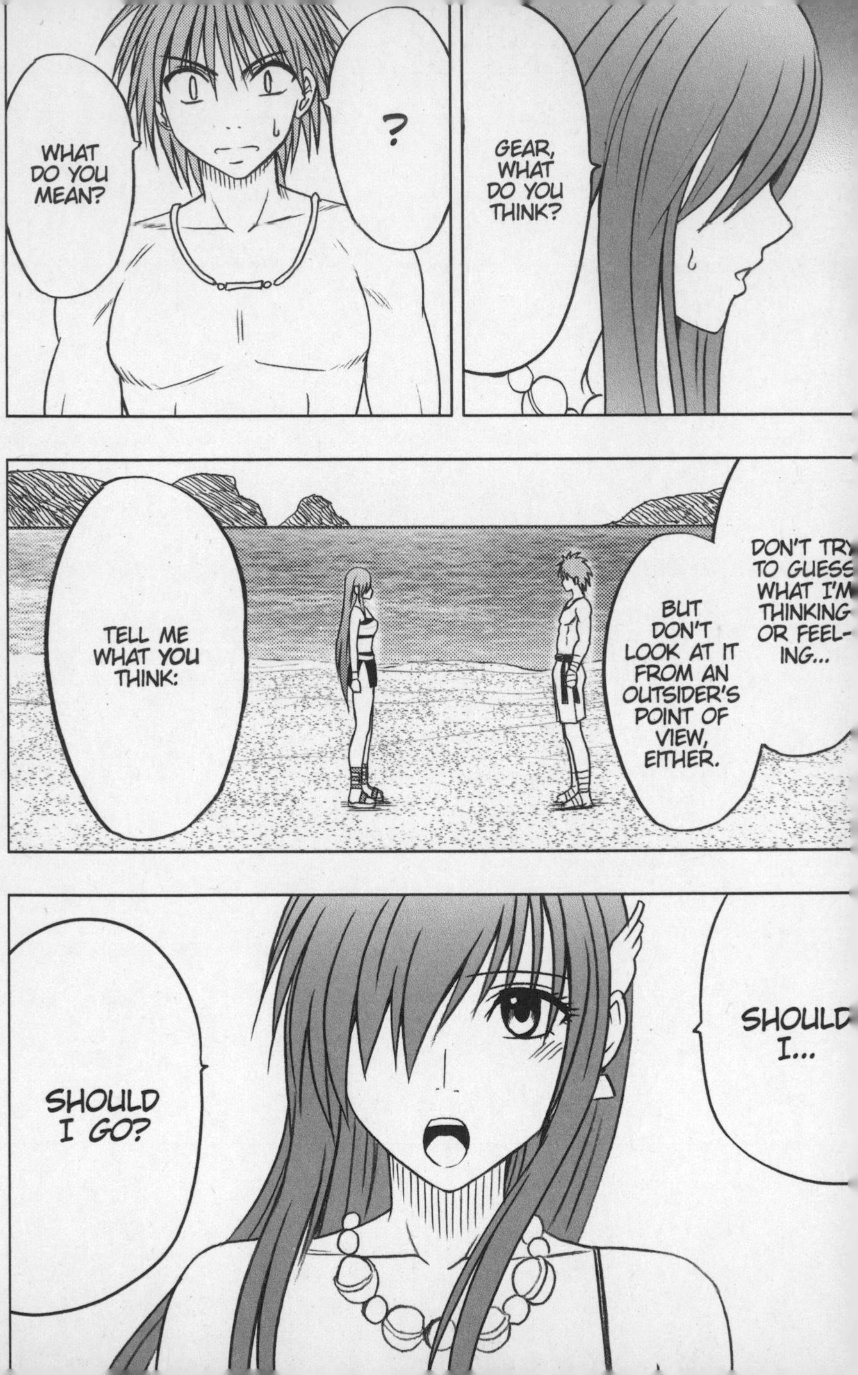
GEAR, WHAT DO YOU THINK?
?
WHAT DO YOU MEAN?
DON'T TRY TO GUESS WHAT I'M THINKING OR FEEL-ING...
BUT DON'T LOOK AT IT FROM AN OUTSIDER'S POINT OF VIEW, EITHER.
TELL ME WHAT YOU THINK:
SHOULD I...
SHOULD I GO?

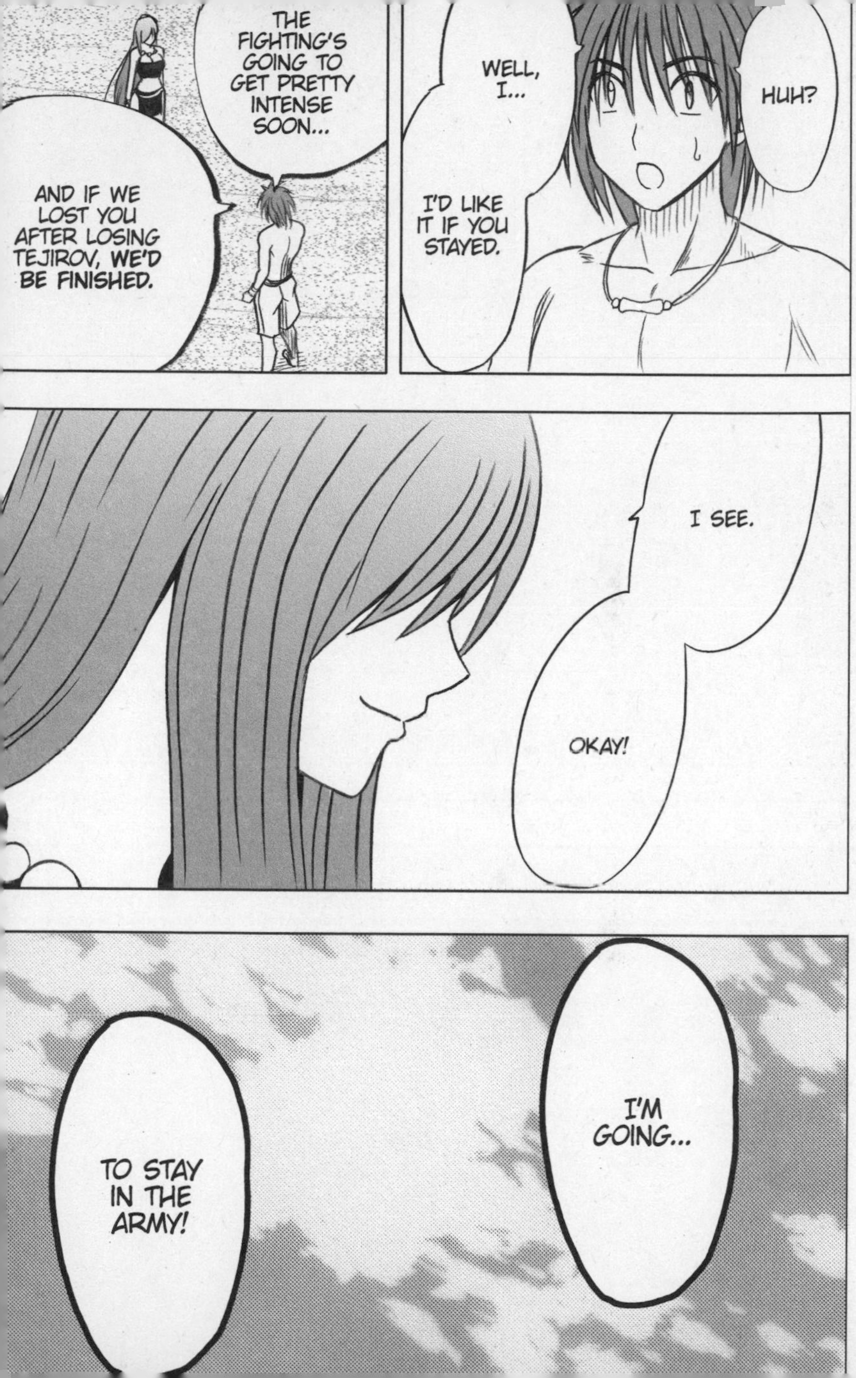
HUH?
WELL, I...
I'D LIKE IT IF YOU STAYED.
THE FIGHTING'S GOING TO GET PRETTY INTENSE SOON...
AND IF WE LOST YOU AFTER LOSING TEJIROV, WE'D BE FINISHED.
I SEE.
OKAY!
I'M GOING...
TO STAY IN THE ARMY!

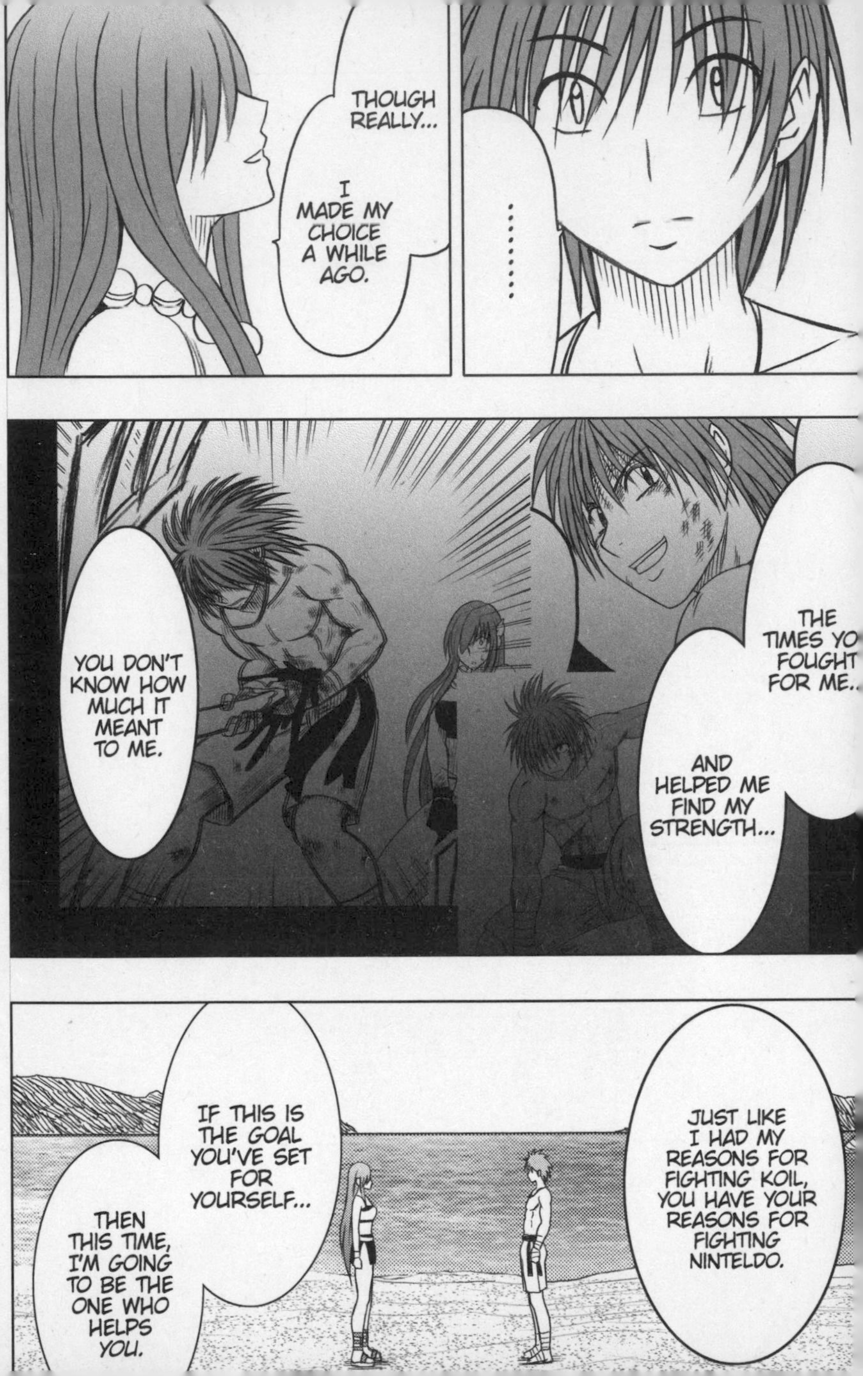
......
THOUGH REALLY...
I MADE MY CHOICE A WHILE AGO.
THE TIMES YO FOUGHT FOR ME..
AND HELPED ME FIND MY STRENGTH...
YOU DON'T KNOW HOW MUCH IT MEANT TO ME.
JUST LIKE I HAD MY REASONS FOR FIGHTING KOIL, YOU HAVE YOUR REASONS FOR FIGHTING NINTELDO.
IF THIS IS THE GOAL YOU'VE SET FOR YOURSELF...
THEN THIS TIME, I'M GOING TO BE THE ONE WHO HELPS YOU.

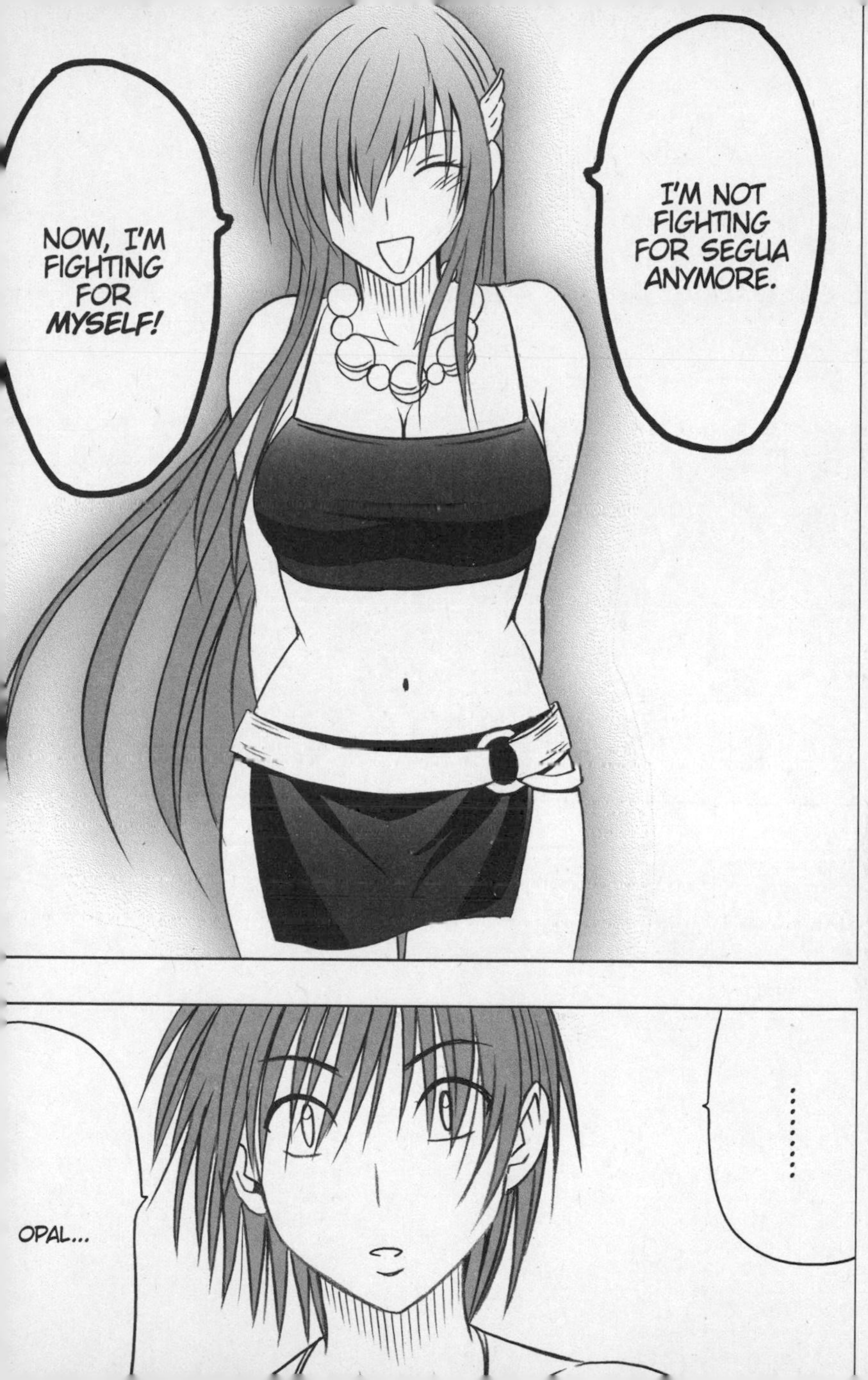
I'M NOT FIGHTING FOR SEGUA ANYMORE.
NOW, I'M FIGHTING FOR MYSELF!
....
OPAL...

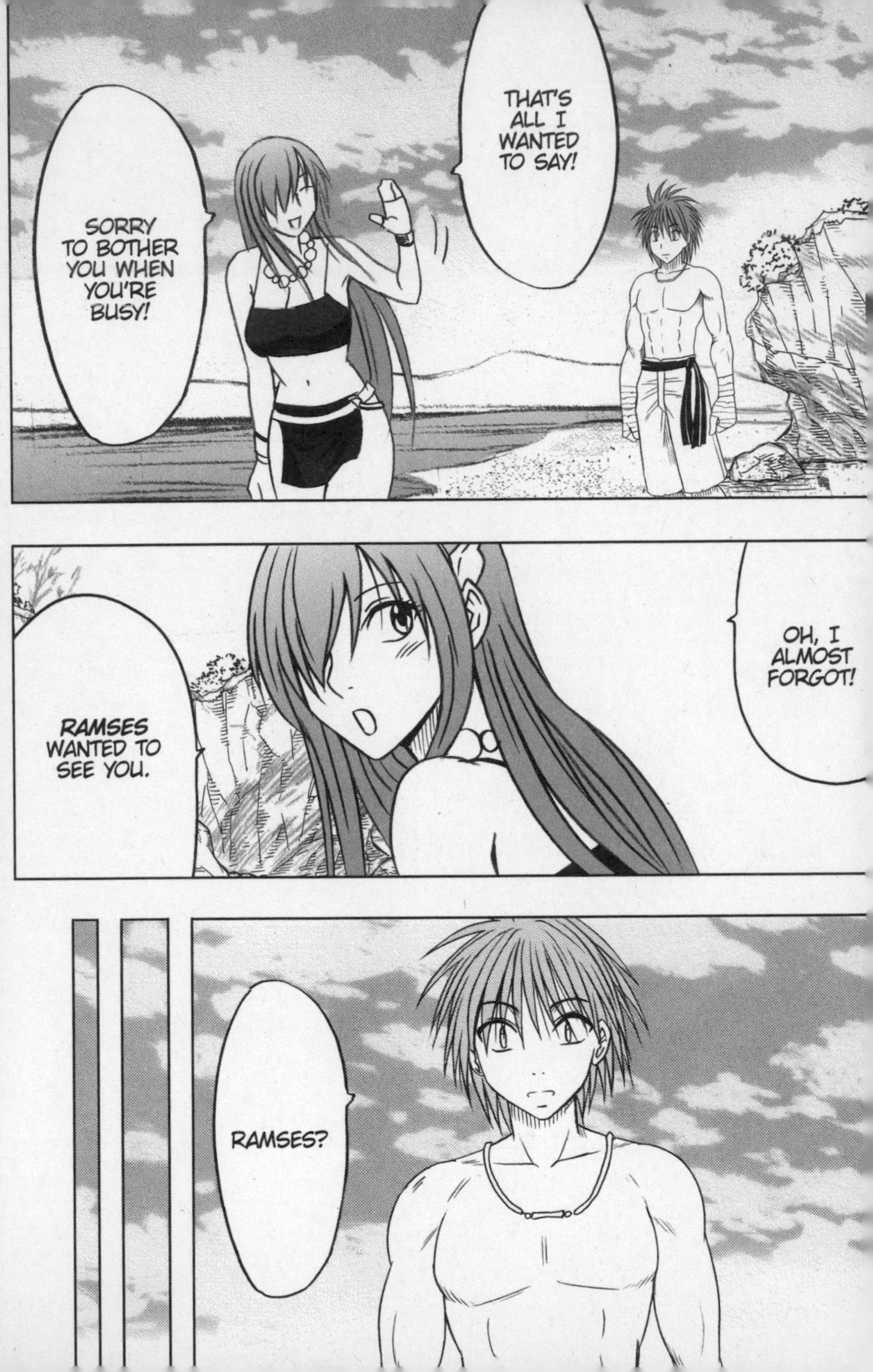
THAT'S ALL I WANTED TO SAY!
SORRY TO BOTHER YOU WHEN YOU'RE BUSY!
OH, I ALMOST FORGOT!
RAMSES WANTED TO SEE YOU.
RAMSES?

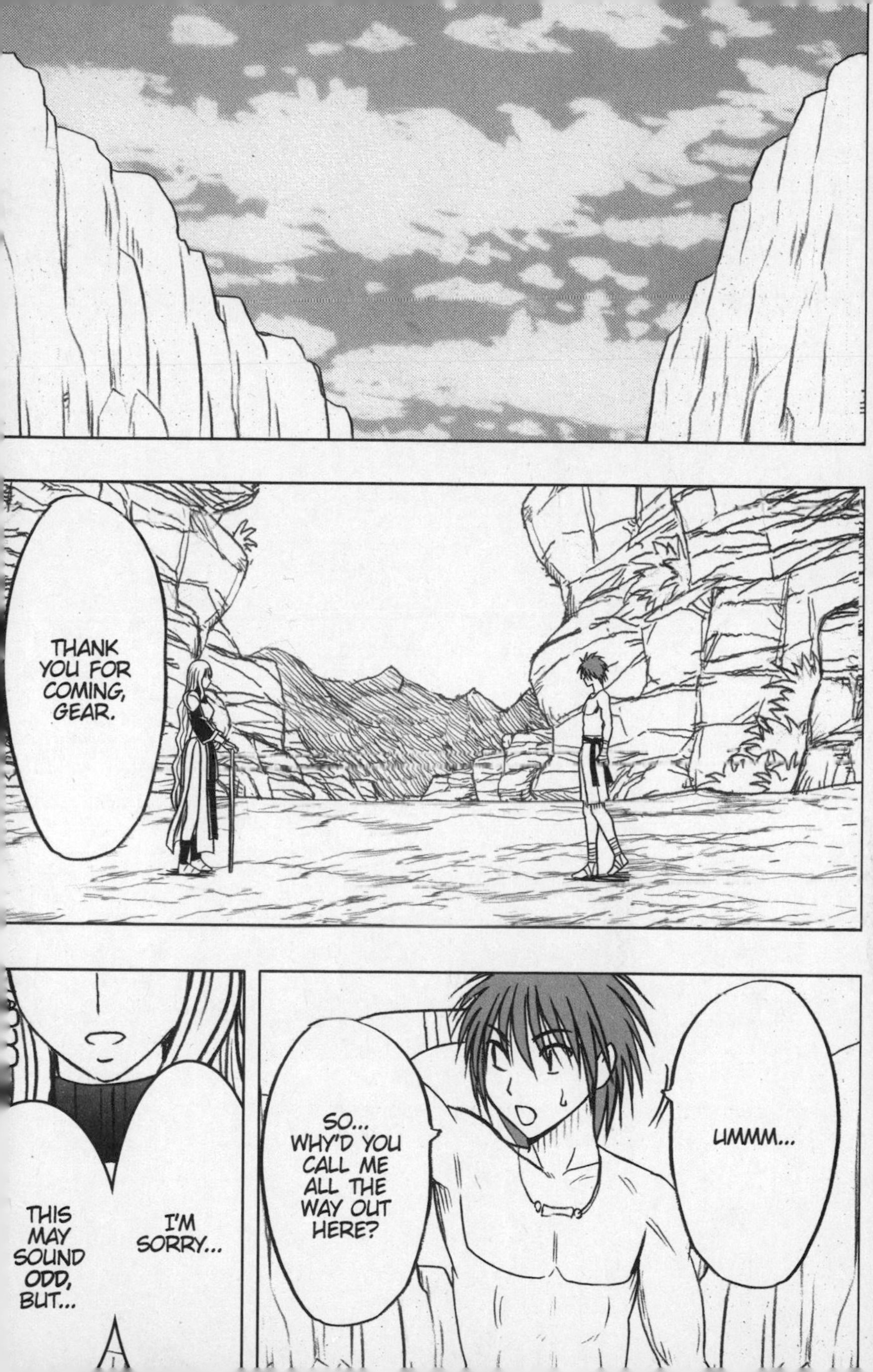
THANK YOU FOR COMING, GEAR.
UMMM...
SO... WHY'D YOU CALL ME ALL THE WAY OUT HERE?
I'M SORRY...
THIS MAY SOUND ODD, BUT...

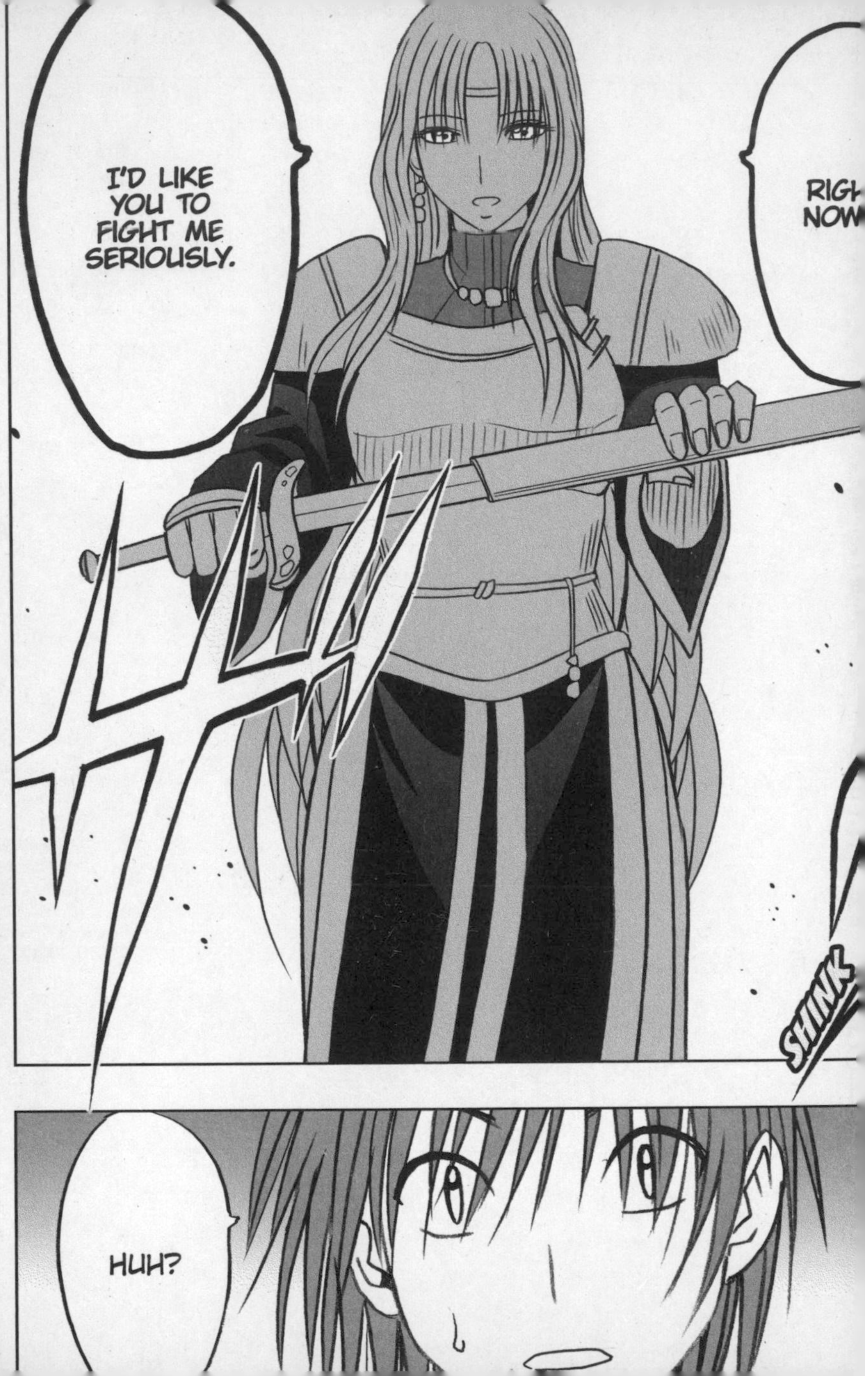
RIGH NOW
I'D LIKE YOU TO FIGHT ME SERIOUSLY.
SHINK
HUH?

Part 2
CHAPTER 17

CHAINS

DISC 2

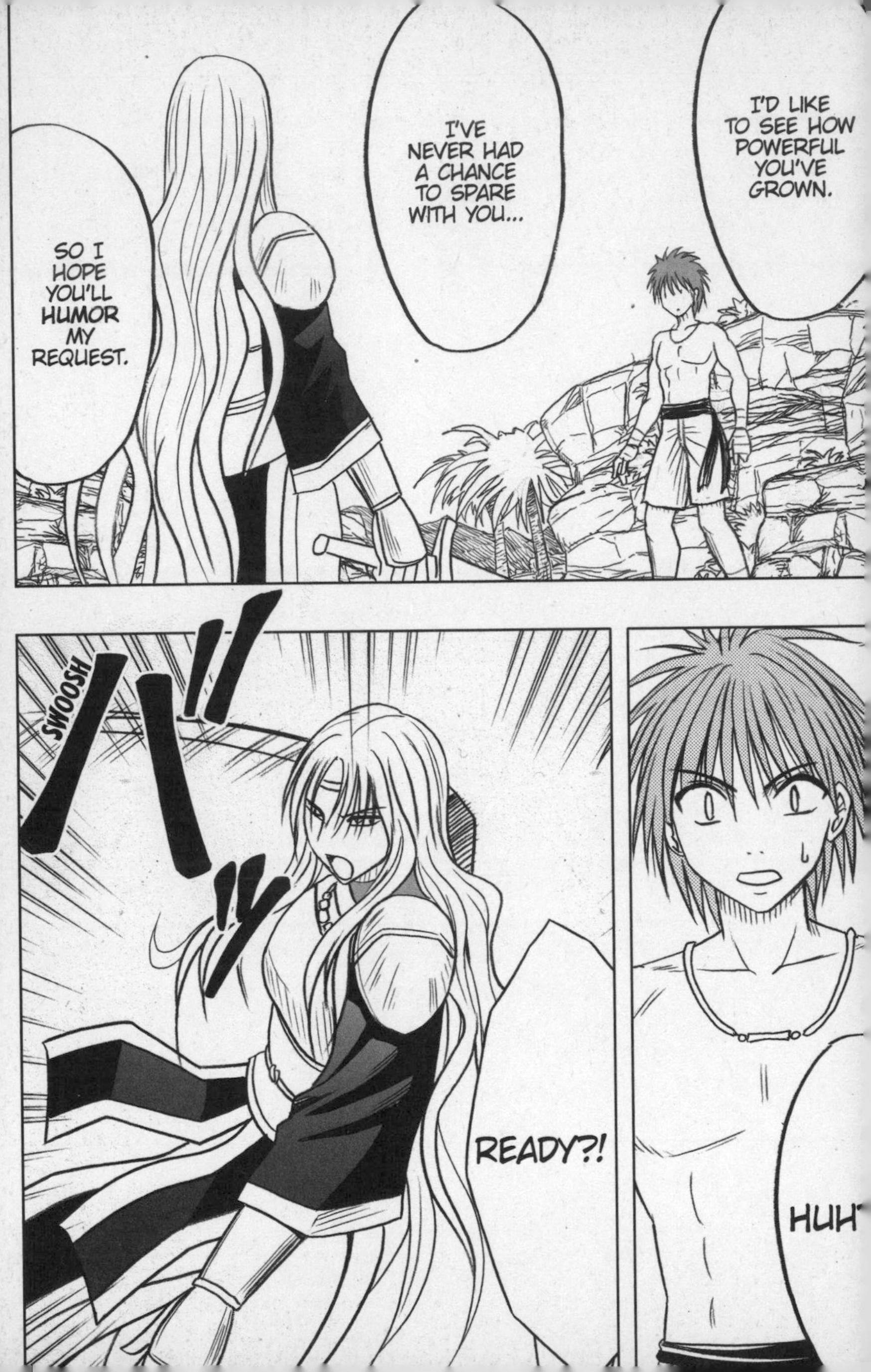
I'D LIKE TO SEE HOW POWERFUL YOU'VE GROWN.
I'VE NEVER HAD A CHANCE TO SPARE WITH YOU...
SO I HOPE YOU'LL HUMOR MY REQUEST.
HUH
SWOOSH
READY?!

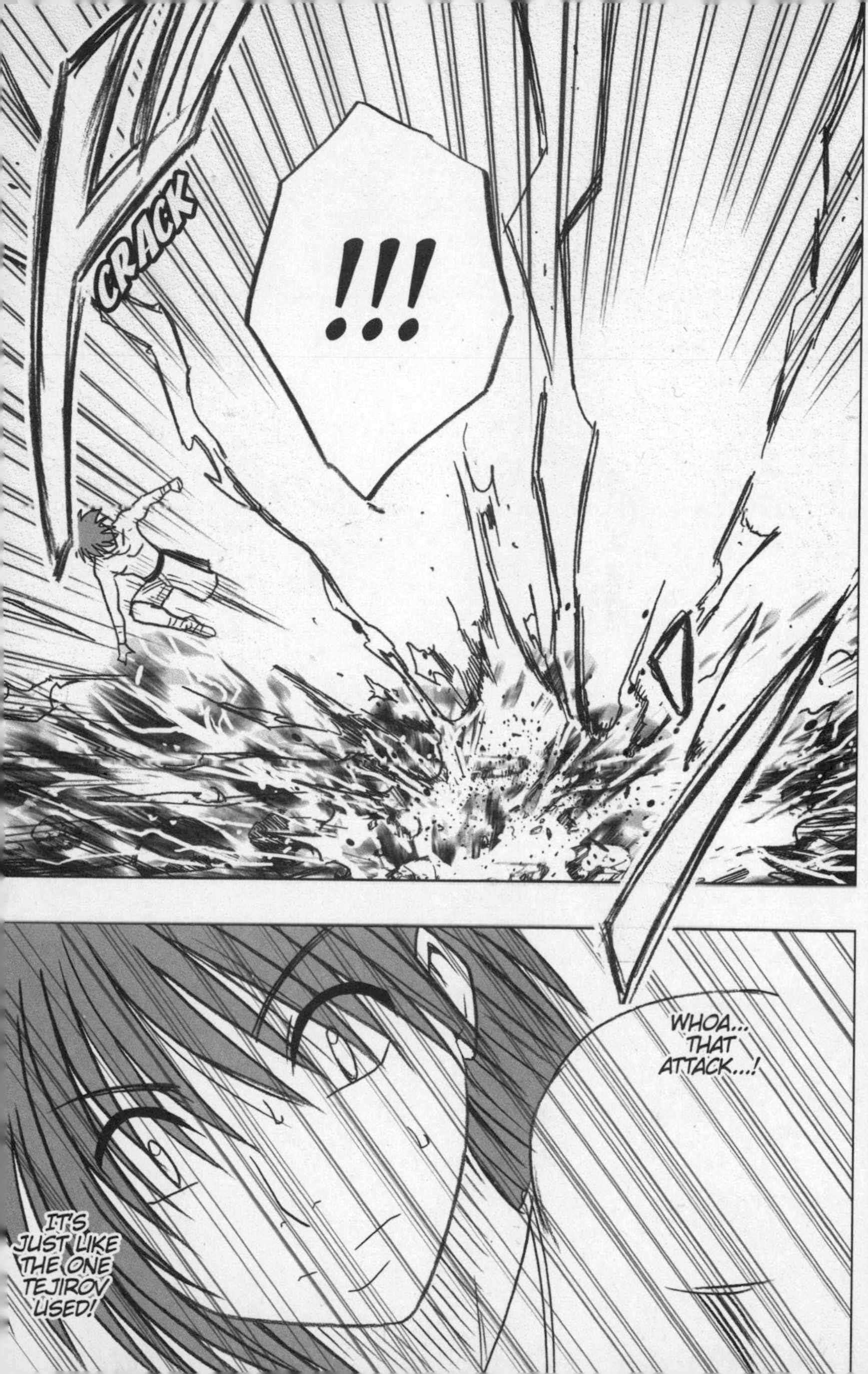
!!!
CRACK
WHOA... THAT ATTACK...!
IT'S JUST LIKE THE ONE TEJIROV USED!

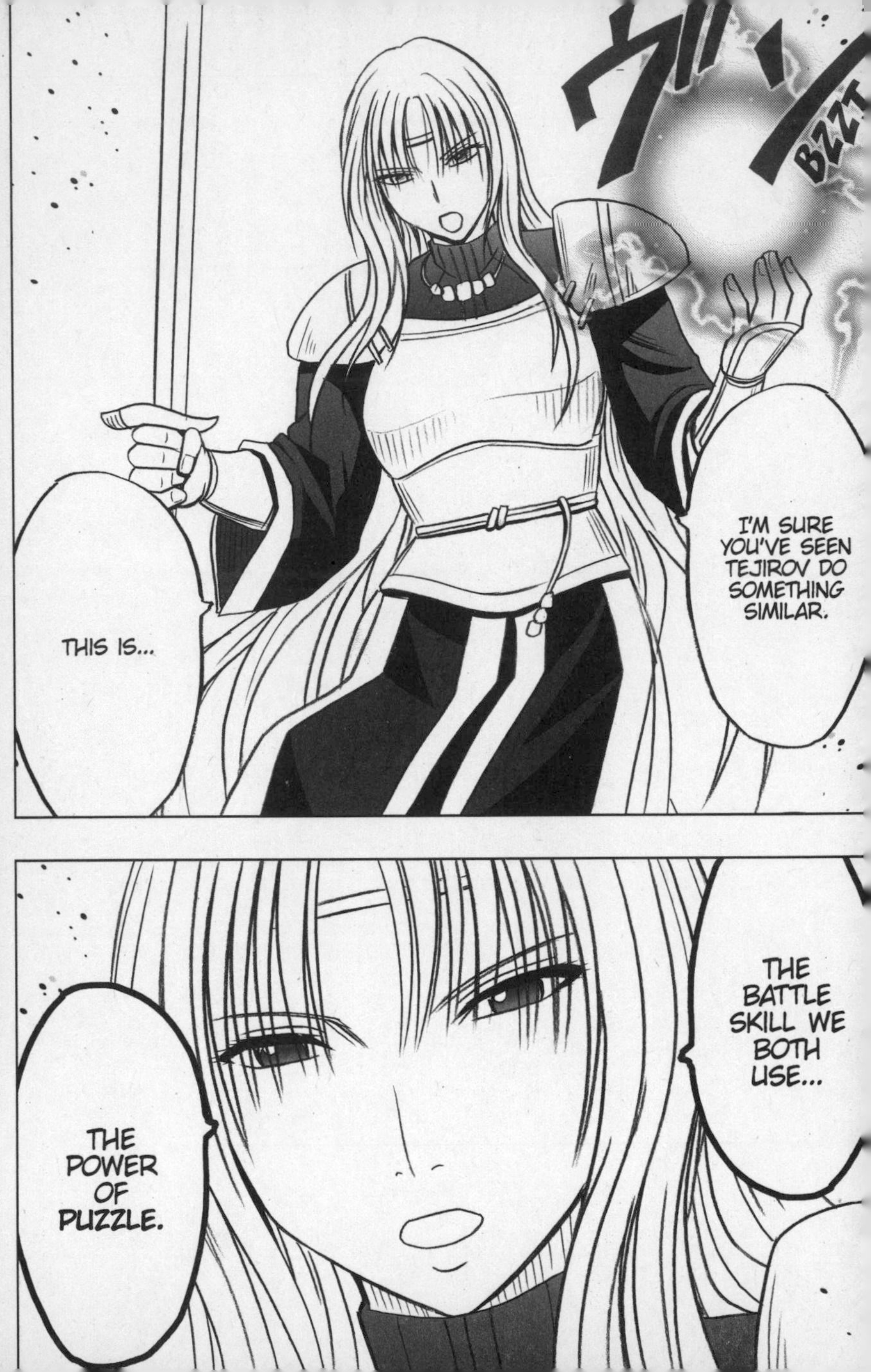
BZZT
I'M SURE YOU'VE SEEN TEJIROV DO SOMETHING SIMILAR.
THIS IS...
THE BATTLE SKILL WE BOTH USE...
THE POWER OF PUZZLE.

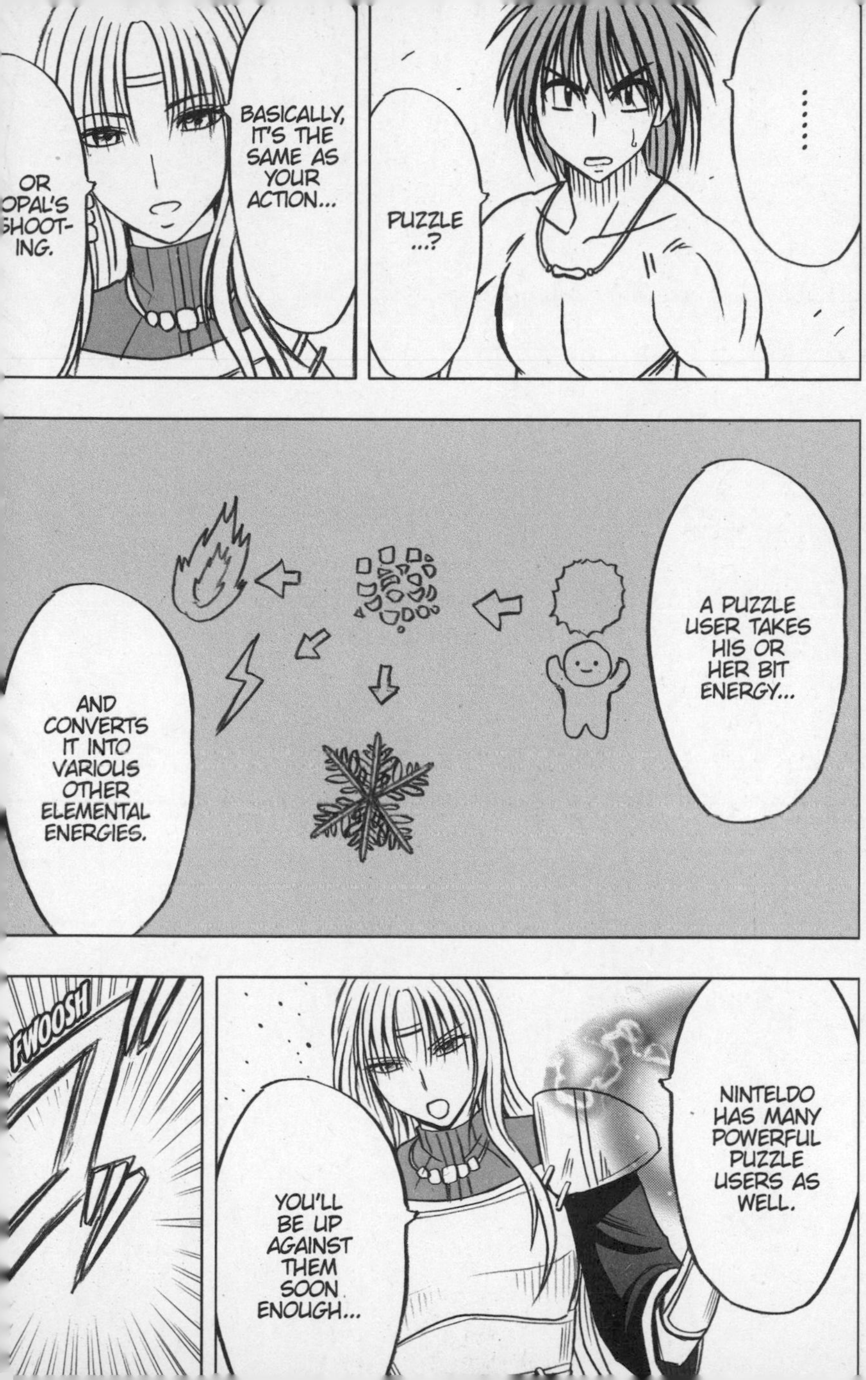
......
PUZZLE ...?
BASICALLY, IT'S THE SAME AS YOUR ACTION...
OR OPAL'S SHOOTING.
A PUZZLE USER TAKES HIS OR HER BIT ENERGY...
AND CONVERTS IT INTO VARIOUS OTHER ELEMENTAL ENERGIES.
NINTELDO HAS MANY POWERFUL PUZZLE USERS AS WELL.
YOU'LL BE UP AGAINST THEM SOON ENOUGH...
FWOOSH

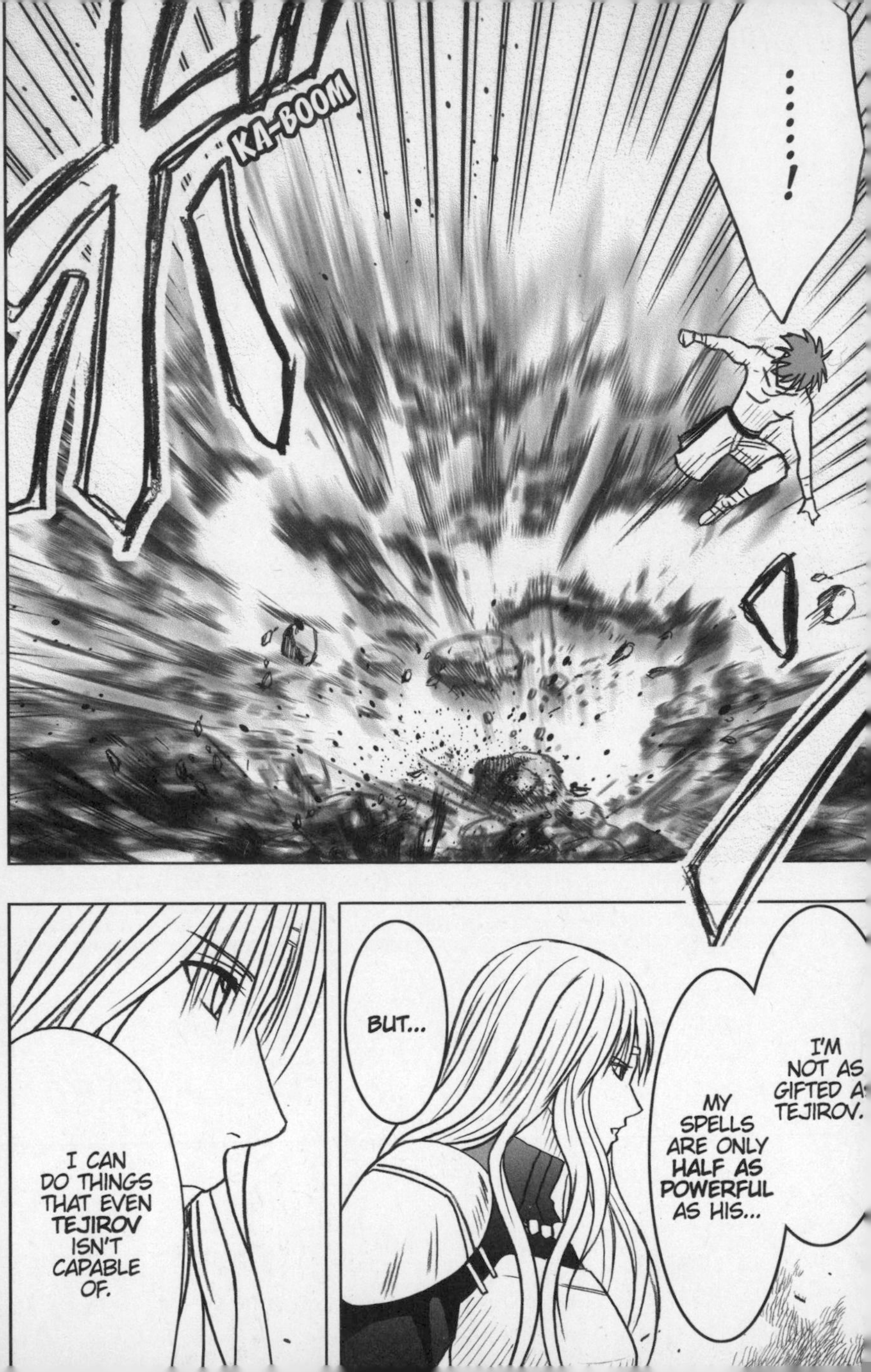
......!
KA-BOOM
I'M NOT AS GIFTED A TEJIROV.
MY SPELLS ARE ONLY HALF AS POWERFUL AS HIS...
BUT...
I CAN DO THINGS THAT EVEN TEJIROV ISN'T CAPABLE OF.

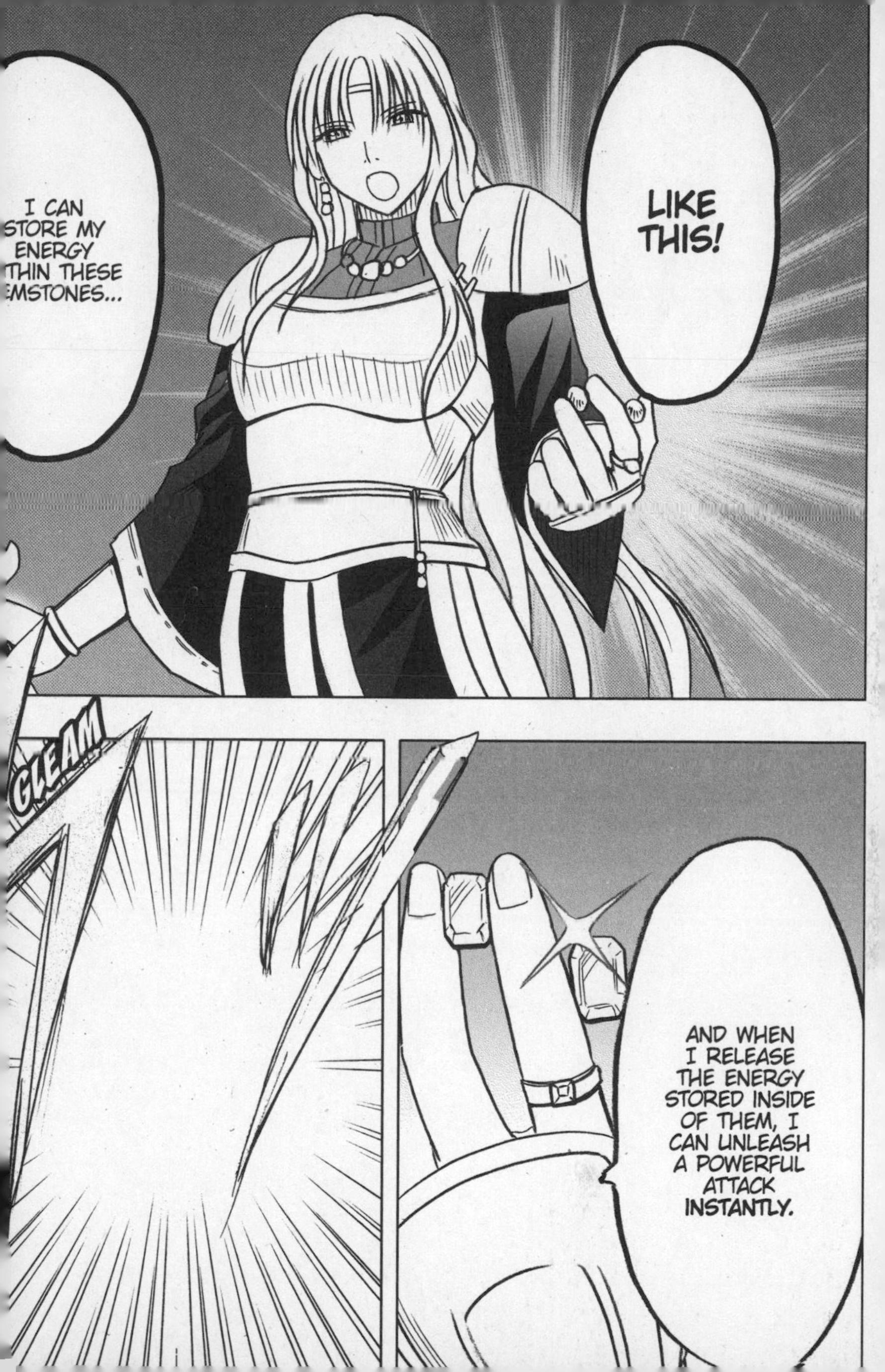
I CAN STORE MY ENERGY THIN THESE EMSTONES...
LIKE THIS!
AND WHEN I RELEASE THE ENERGY STORED INSIDE OF THEM, I CAN UNLEASH A POWERFUL ATTACK INSTANTLY.
GLEAM

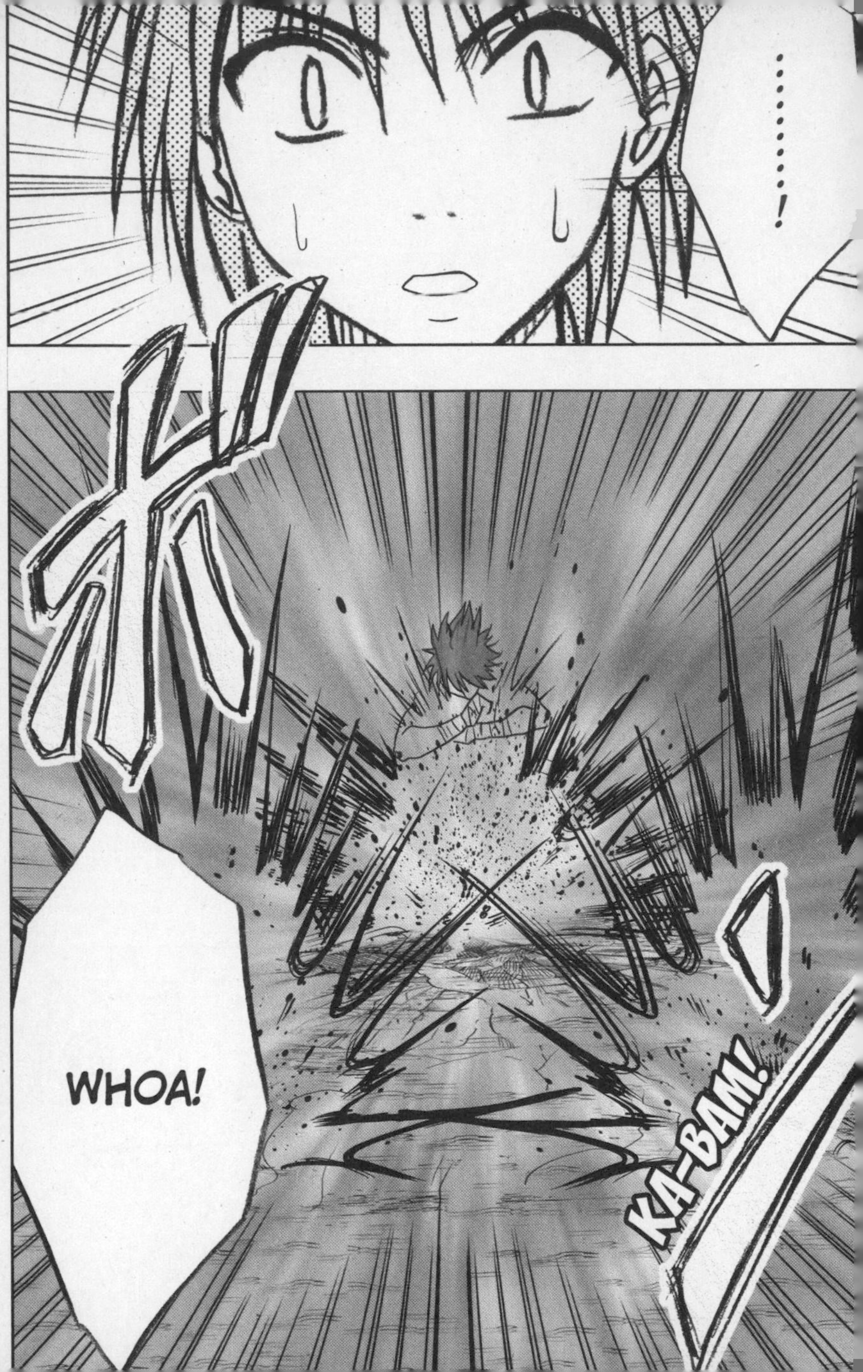

......!
KA-BAM!
WHOA!

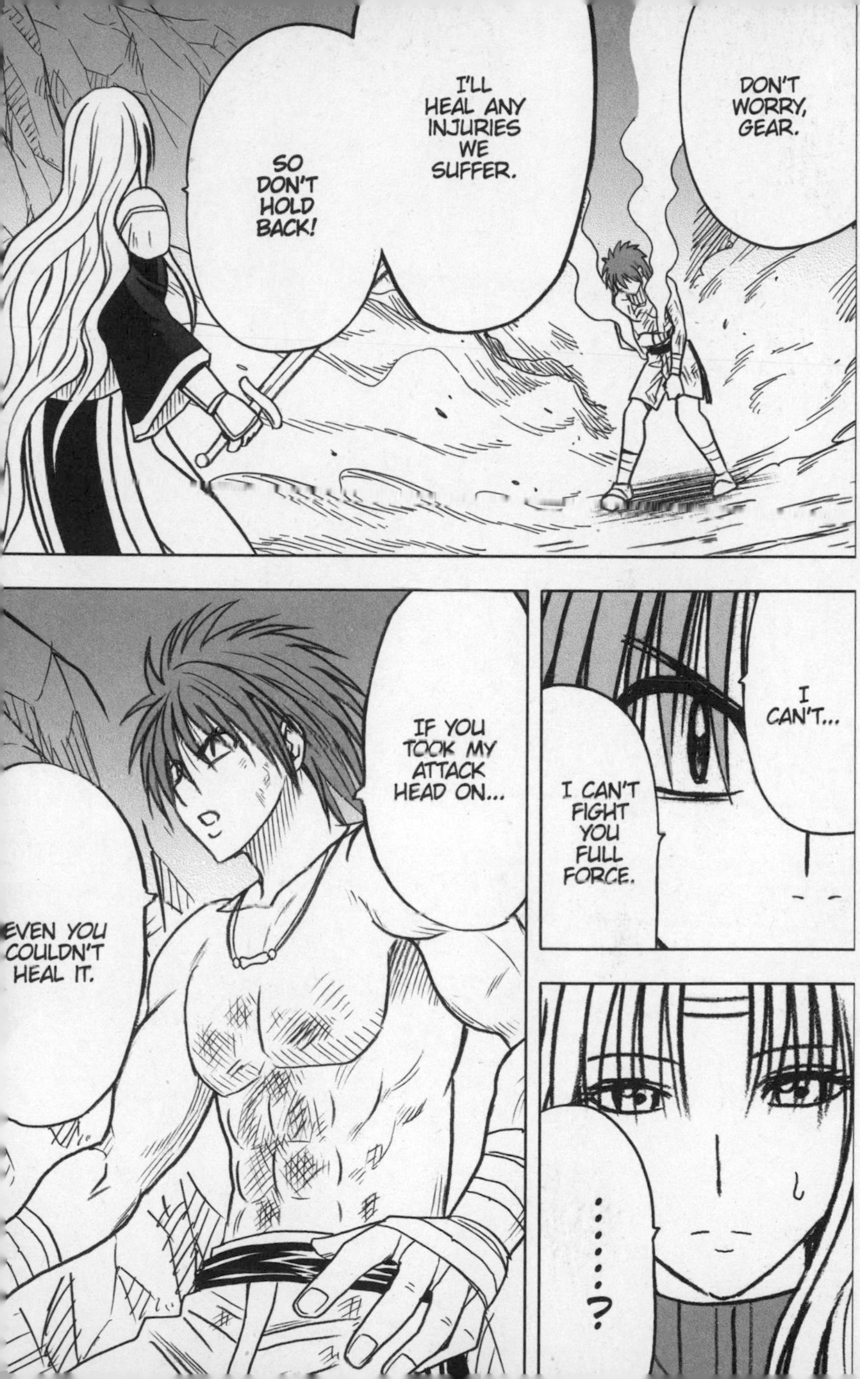
DON'T WORRY, GEAR.
I'LL HEAL ANY INJURIES WE SUFFER.
SO DON'T HOLD BACK!
I CAN'T...
I CAN'T FIGHT YOU FULL FORCE.
......?
IF YOU TOOK MY ATTACK HEAD ON...
EVEN YOU COULDN'T HEAL IT.

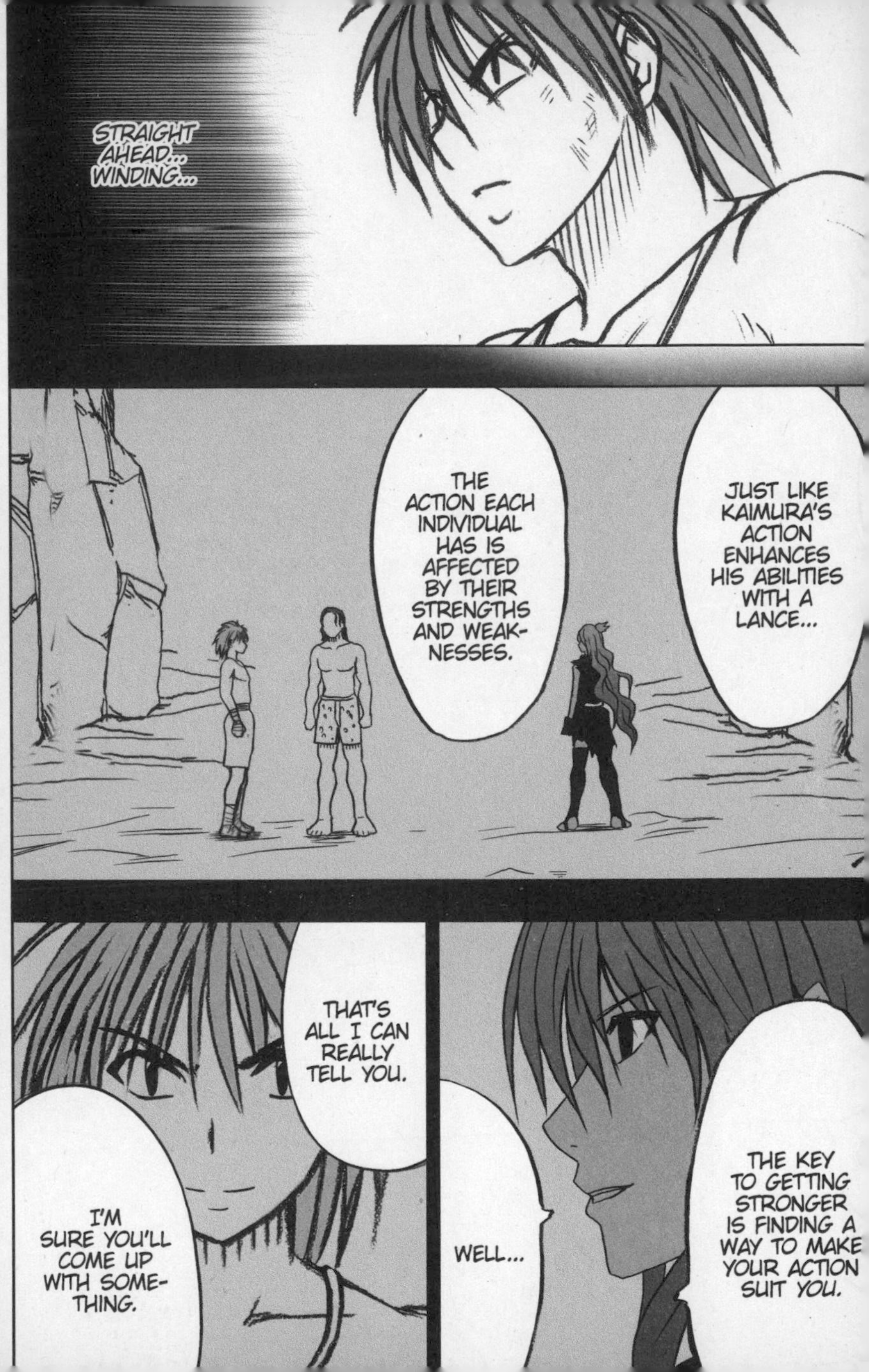

STRAIGHT AHEAD... WINDING...
JUST LIKE KAIMURA'S ACTION ENHANCES HIS ABILITIES WITH A LANCE...
THE ACTION EACH INDIVIDUAL HAS IS AFFECTED BY THEIR STRENGTHS AND WEAK-NESSES.
THE KEY TO GETTING STRONGER IS FINDING A WAY TO MAKE YOUR ACTION SUIT YOU.
WELL...
THAT'S ALL I CAN REALLY TELL YOU.
I'M SURE YOU'LL COME UP WITH SOME-THING.

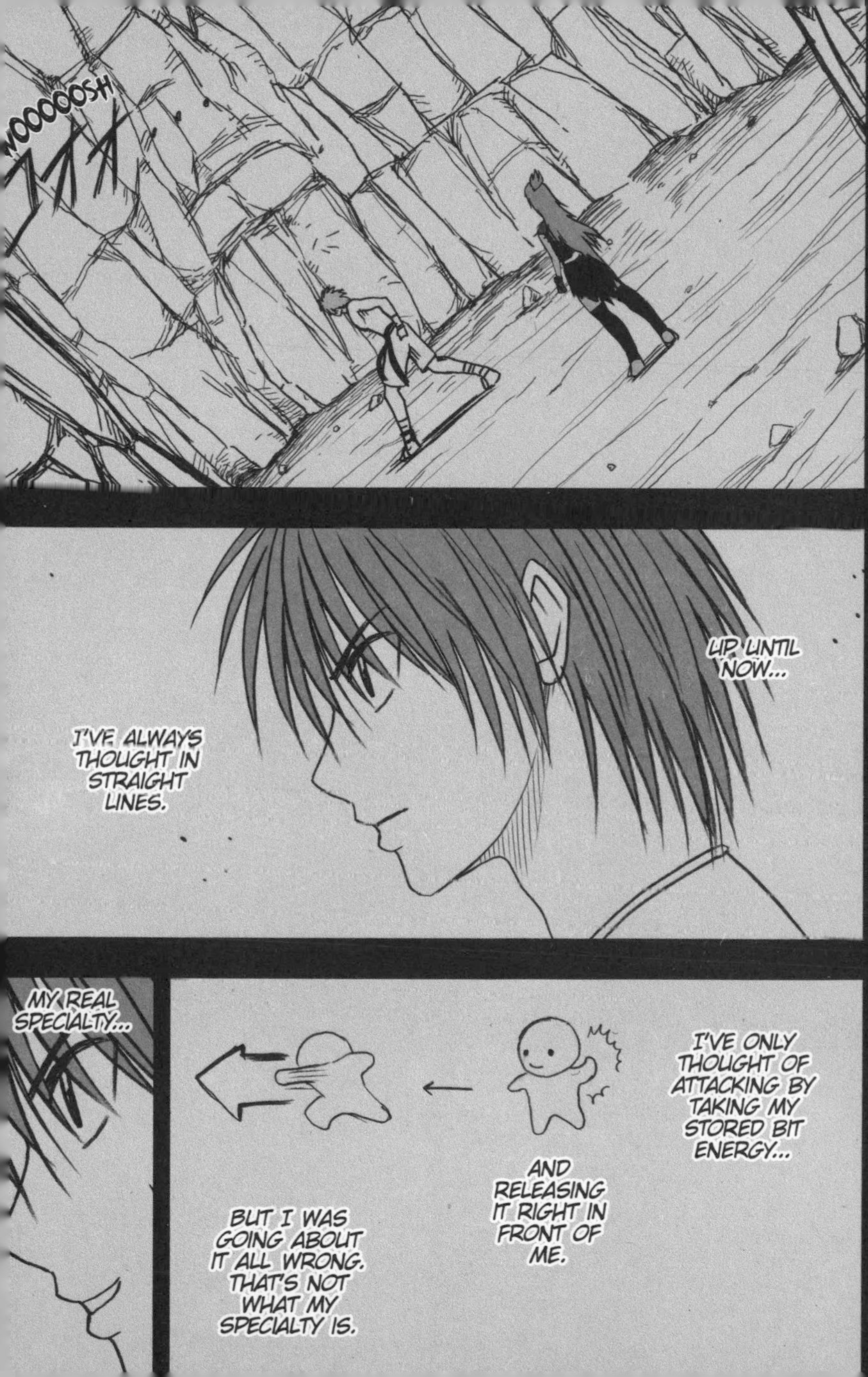
WOOOOOOSH
UP UNTIL NOW...
I'VE ALWAYS THOUGHT IN STRAIGHT LINES.
I'VE ONLY THOUGHT OF ATTACKING BY TAKING MY STORED BIT ENERGY...
AND RELEASING IT RIGHT IN FRONT OF ME.
BUT I WAS GOING ABOUT IT ALL WRONG. THAT'S NOT WHAT MY SPECIALTY IS.
MY REAL SPECIALTY...

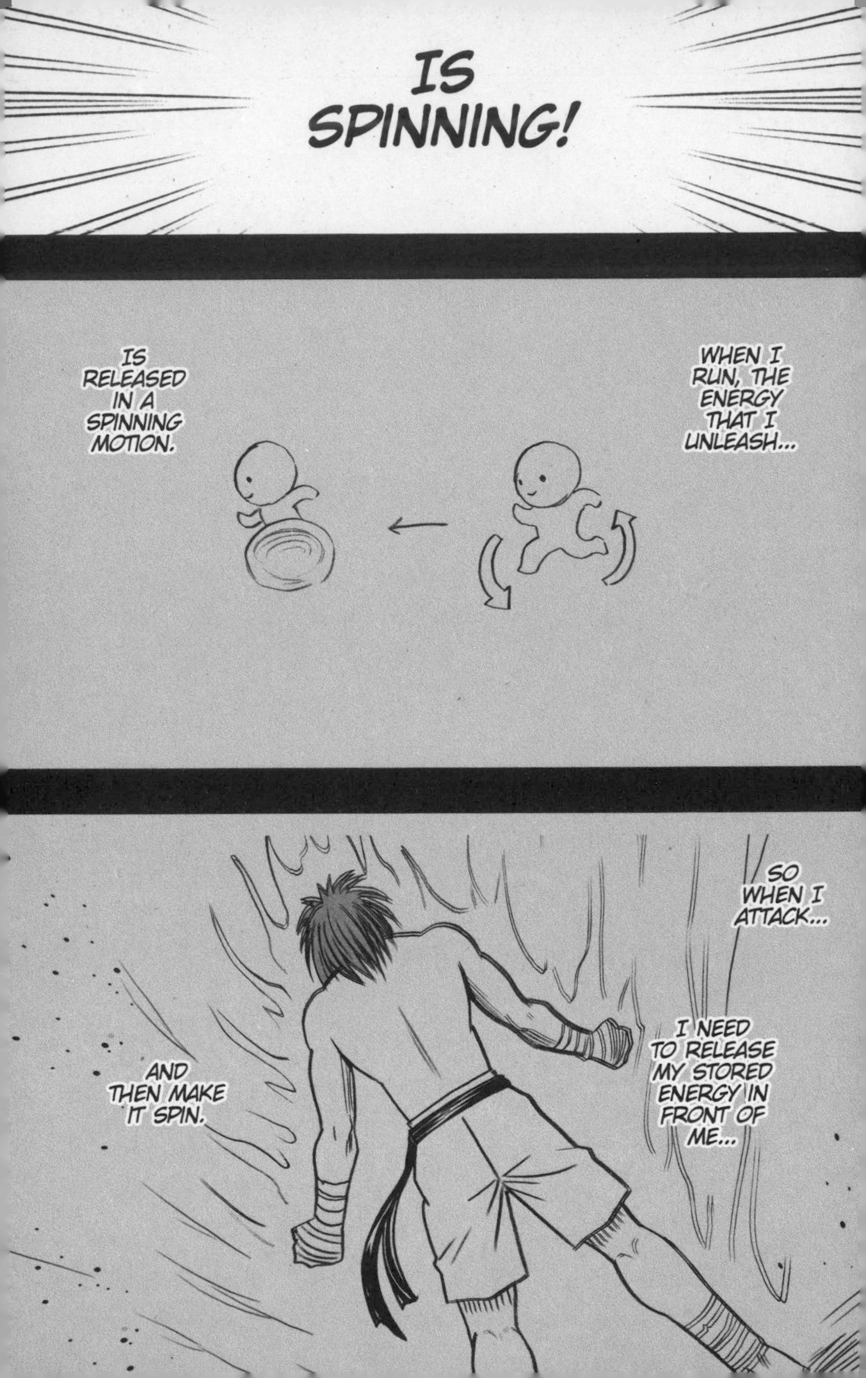
IS SPINNING!
WHEN I RUN, THE ENERGY THAT I UNLEASH...
IS RELEASED IN A SPINNING MOTION.
SO WHEN I ATTACK...
I NEED TO RELEASE MY STORED ENERGY IN FRONT OF ME...
AND THEN MAKE IT SPIN.

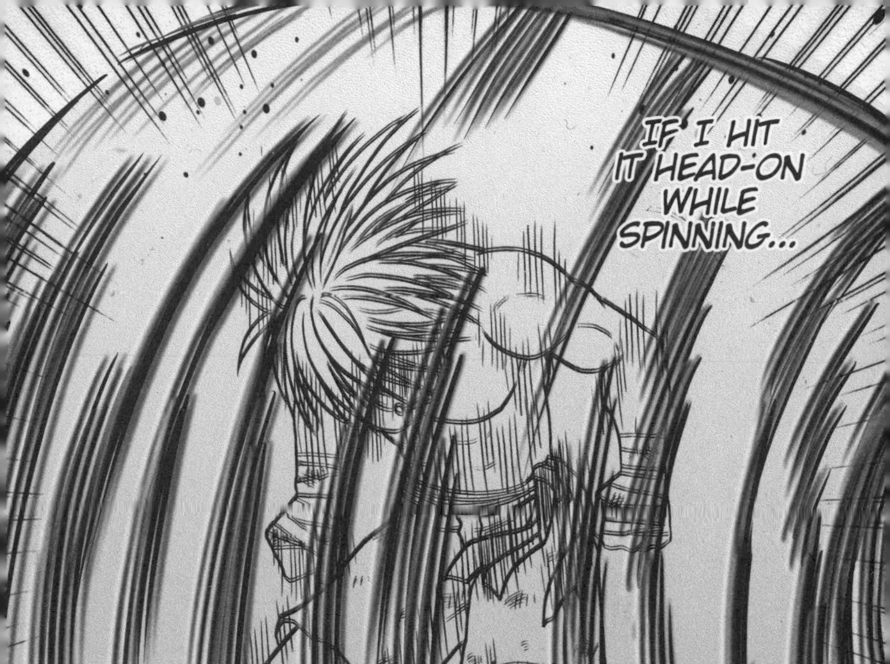
IF I HIT IT HEAD-ON WHILE SPINNING...
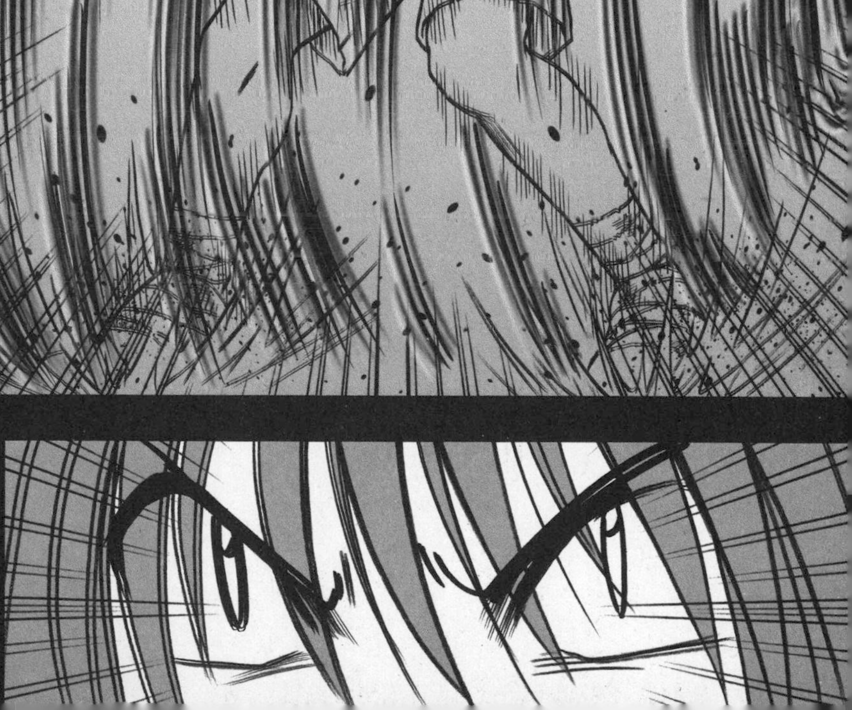

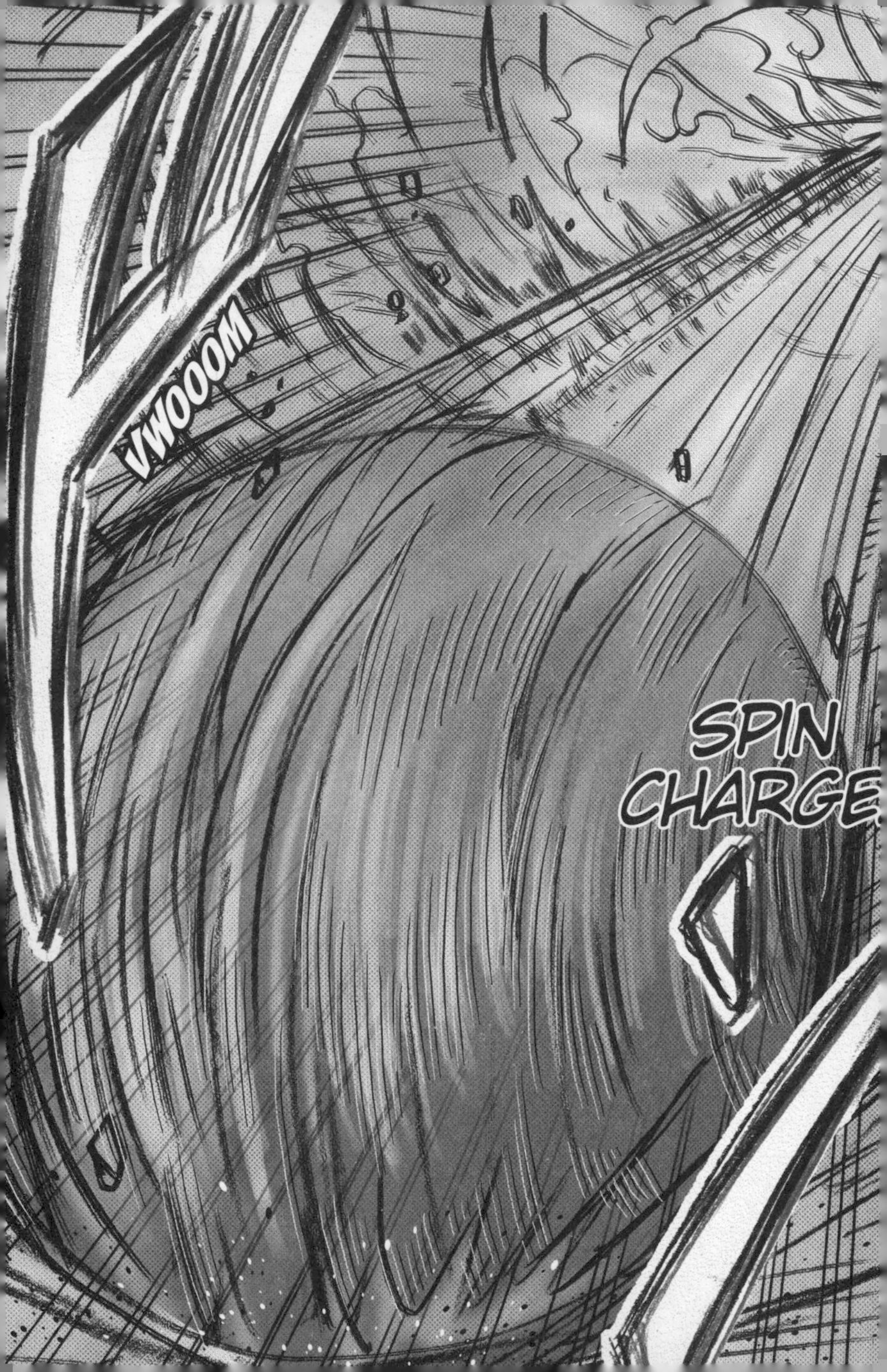
SPIN CHARGE
VWOOOM

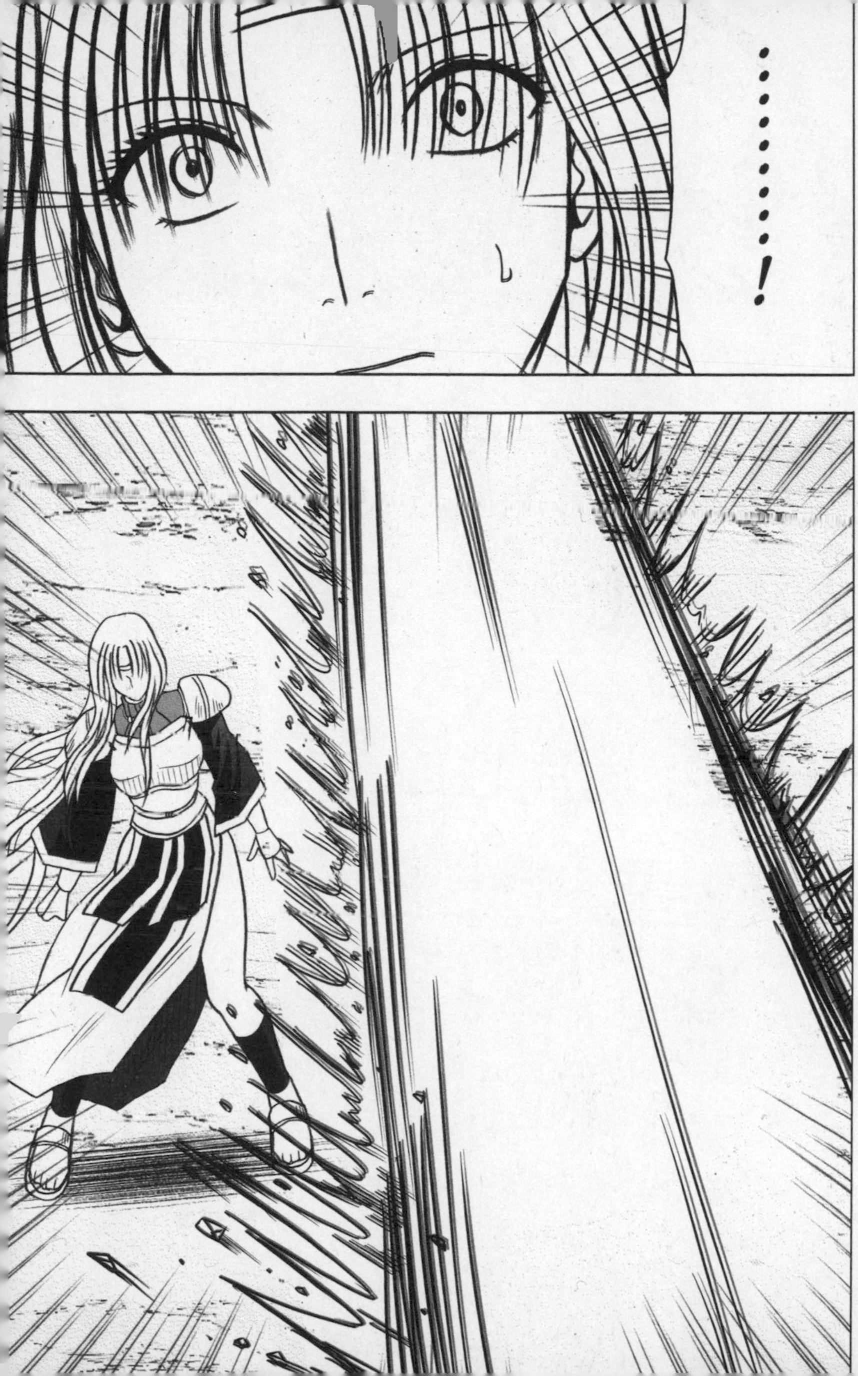
.........!

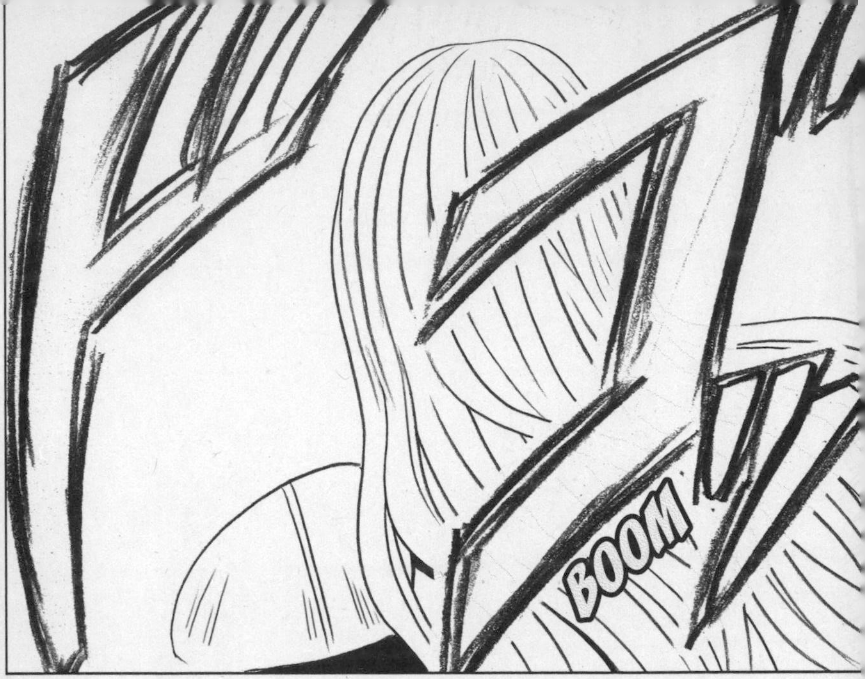
BOOM
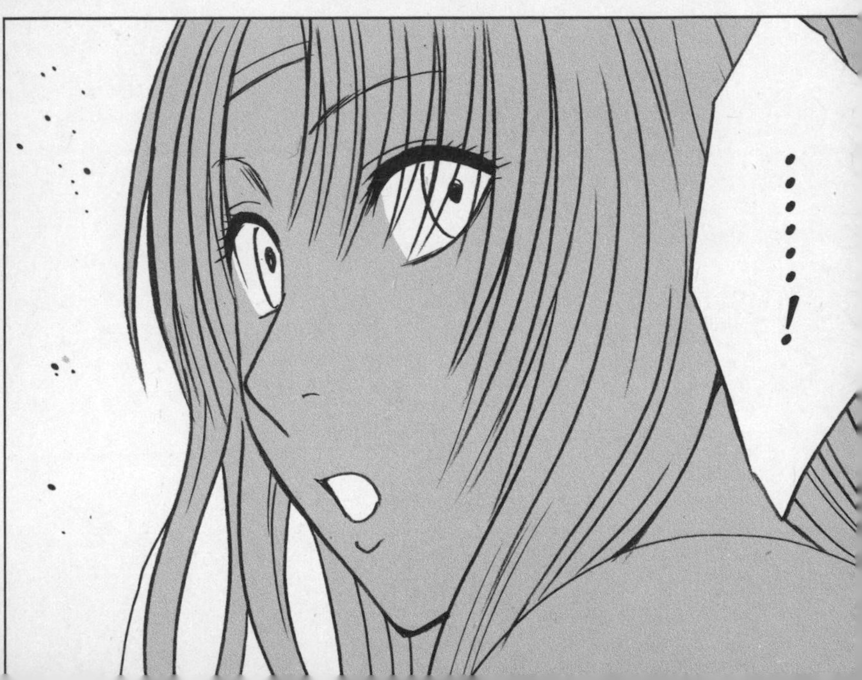
......!

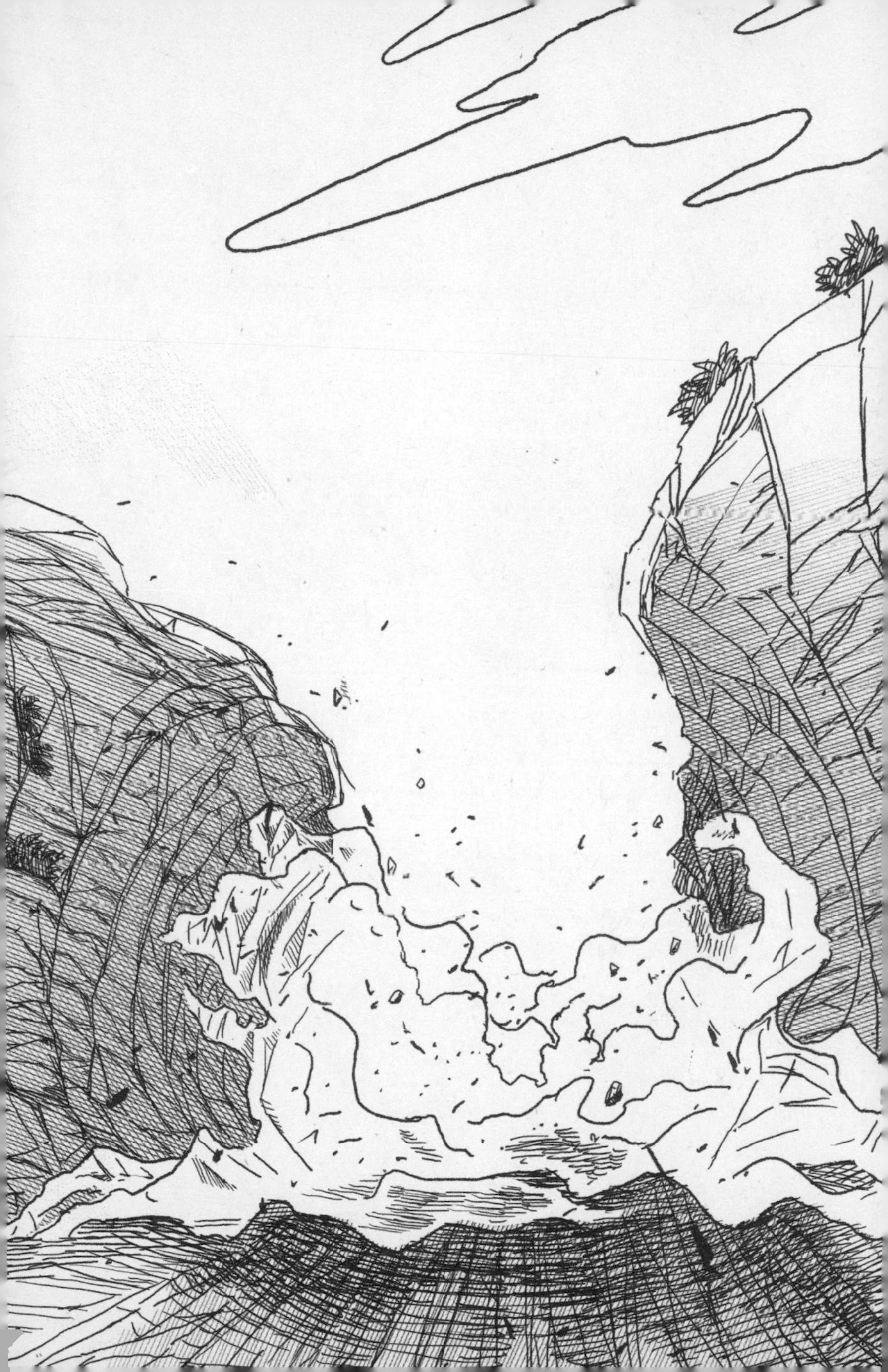

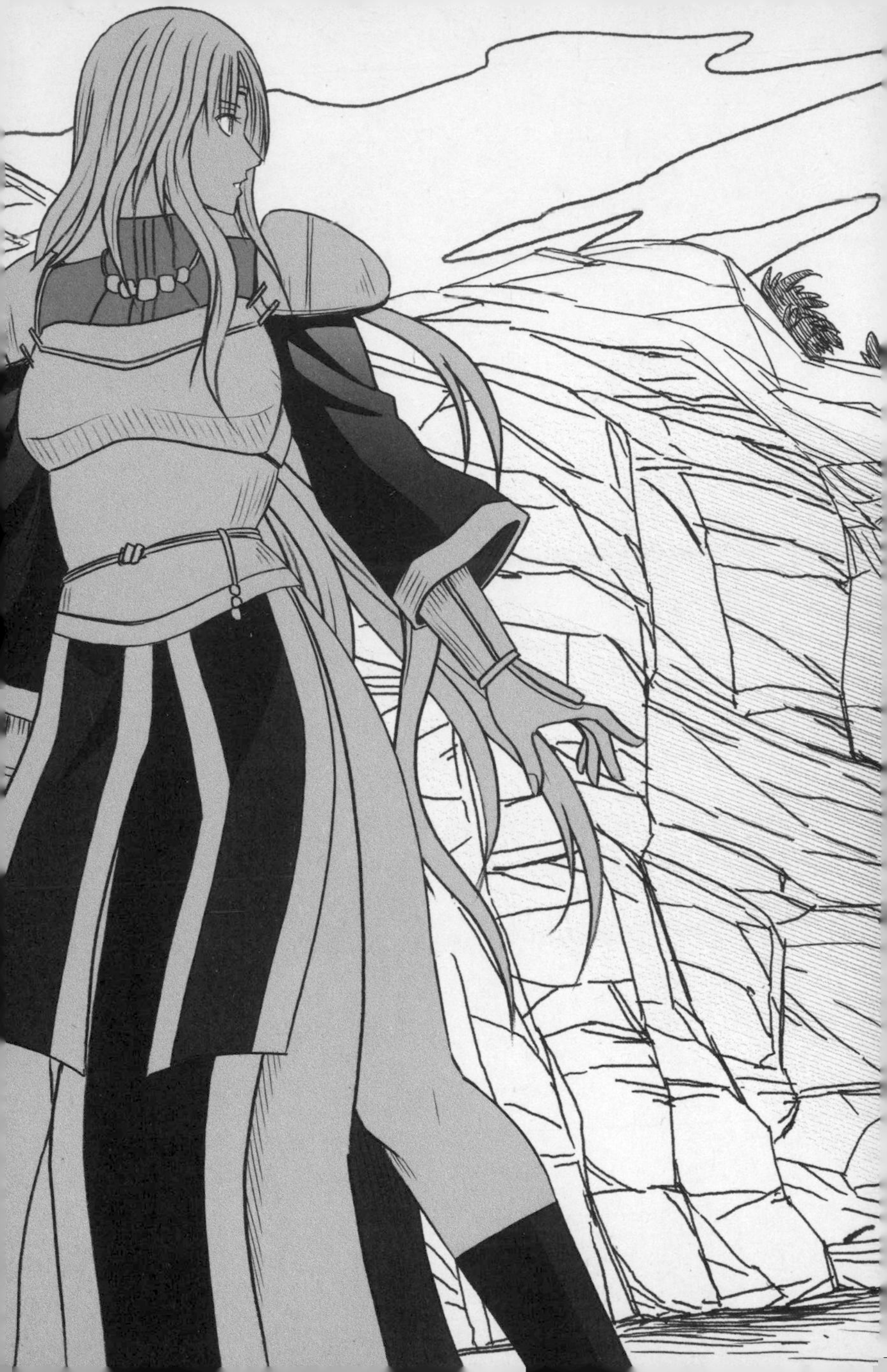

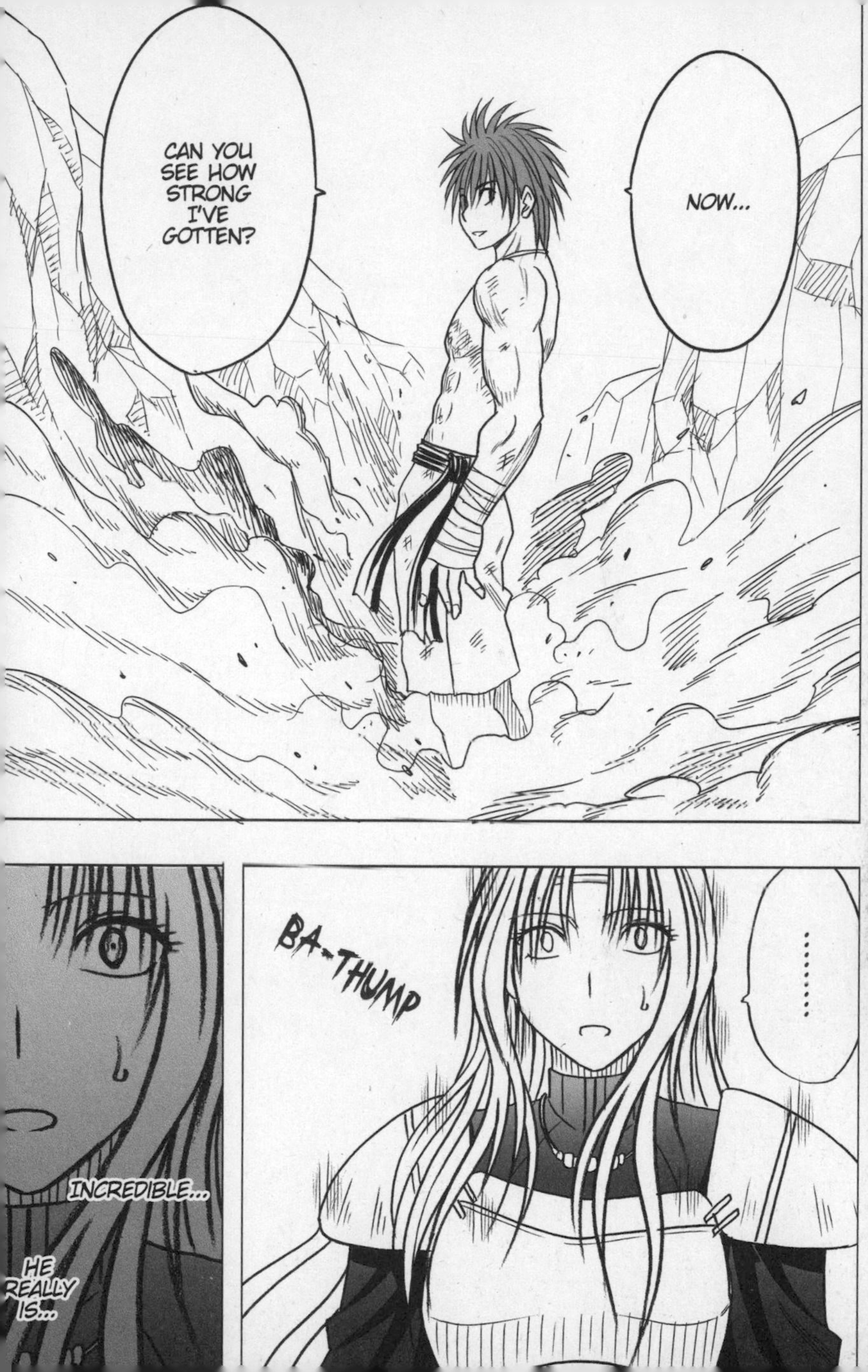
NOW...
CAN YOU SEE HOW STRONG I'VE GOTTEN?
......
BA-THUMP
INCREDIBLE...
HE REALLY IS...

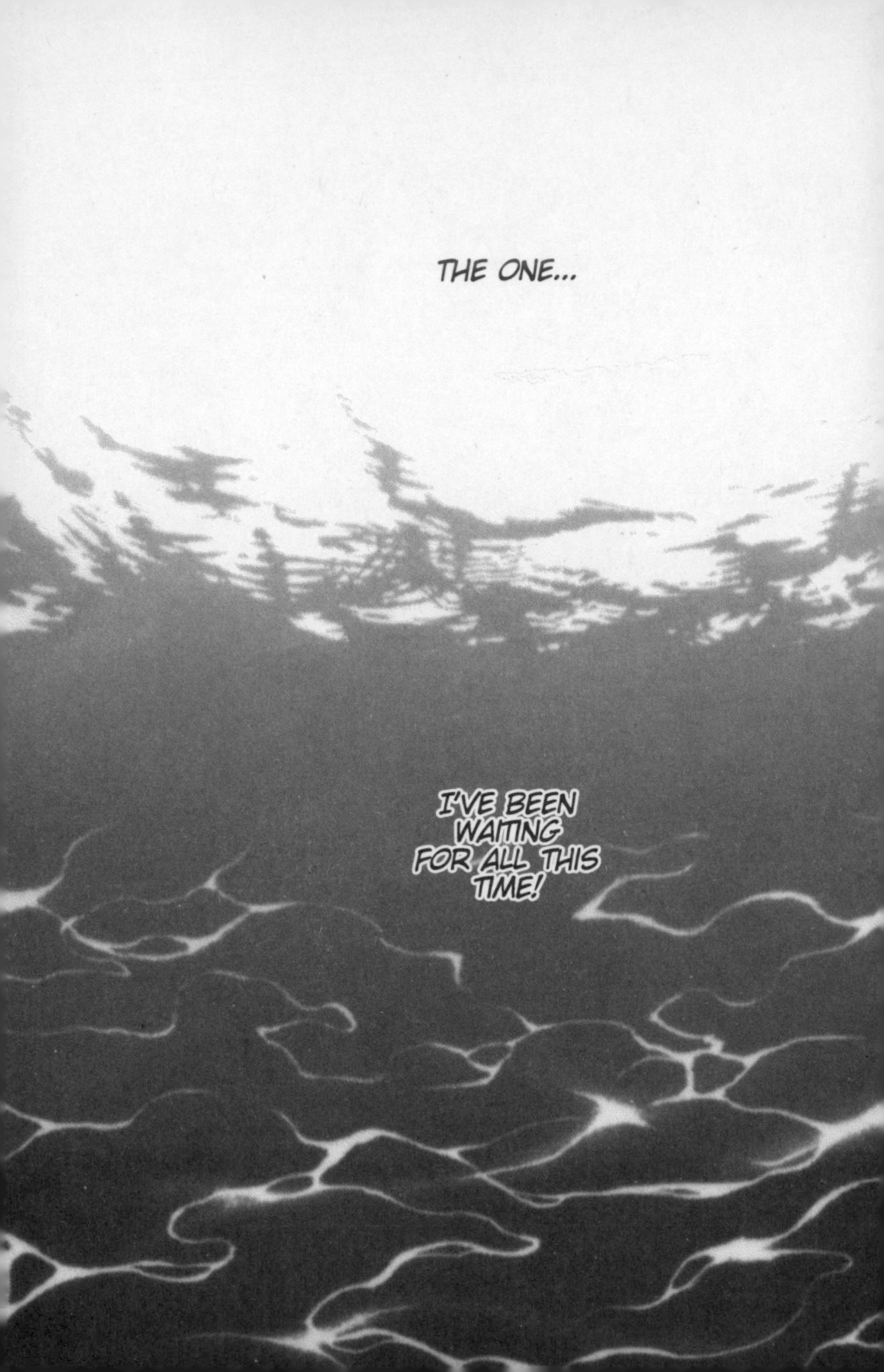
THE ONE...
I'VE BEEN WAITING FOR ALL THIS TIME!

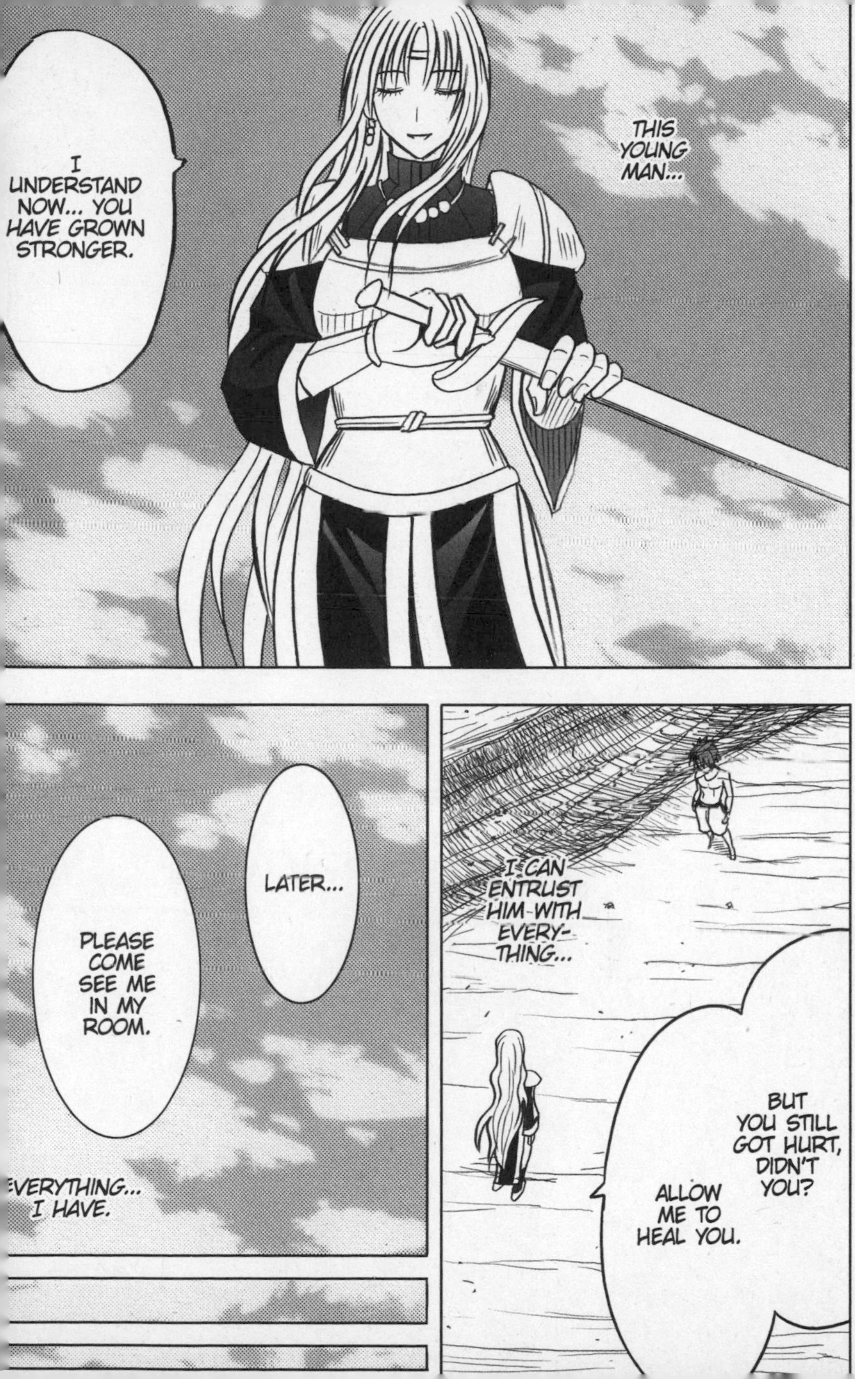
THIS YOUNG MAN...
I UNDERSTAND NOW... YOU HAVE GROWN STRONGER.
I CAN ENTRUST HIM WITH EVERYTHING...
BUT YOU STILL GOT HURT, DIDN'T YOU?
ALLOW ME TO HEAL YOU.
LATER...
PLEASE COME SEE ME IN MY ROOM.
EVERYTHING... I HAVE.

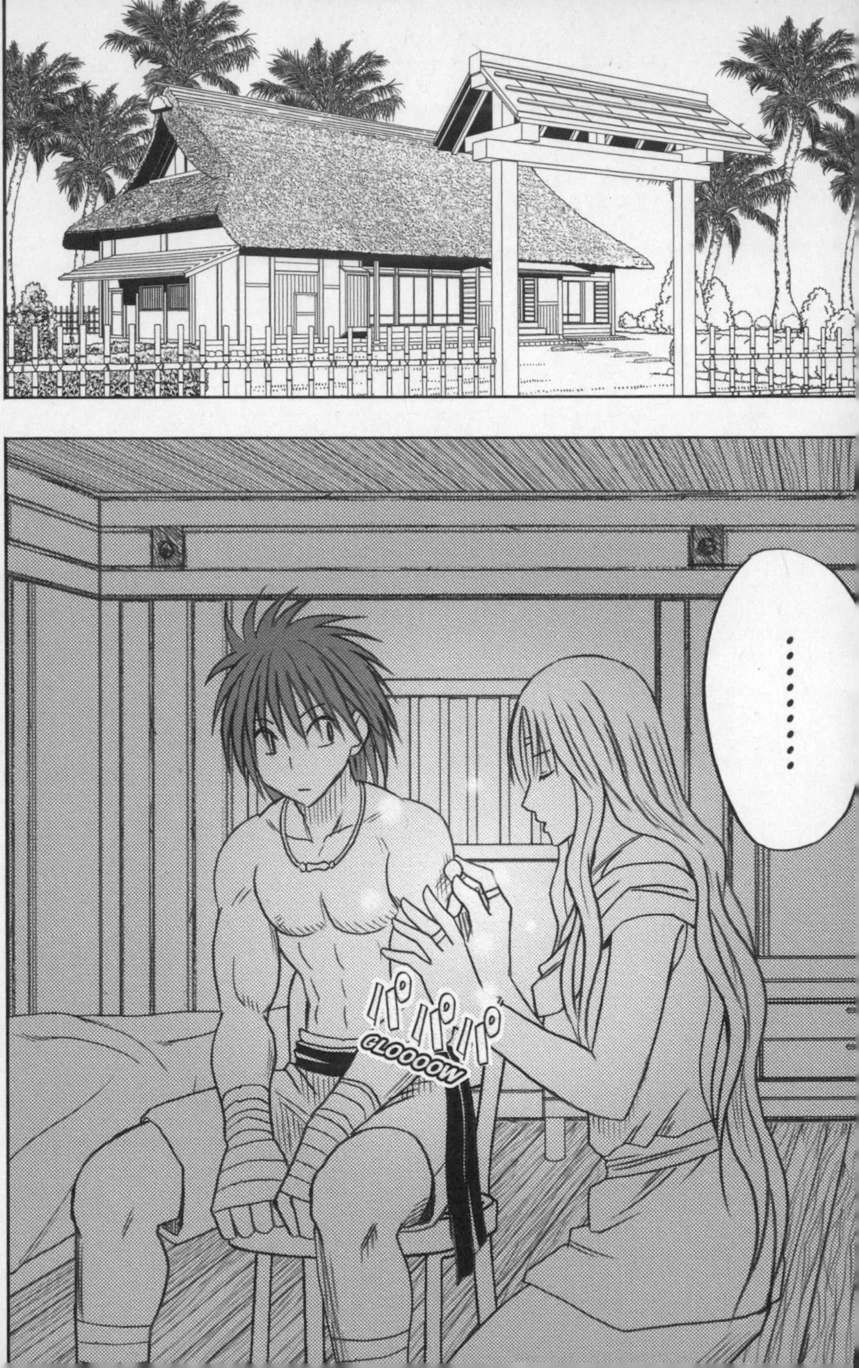
……
パパパパ
GLOOOOW

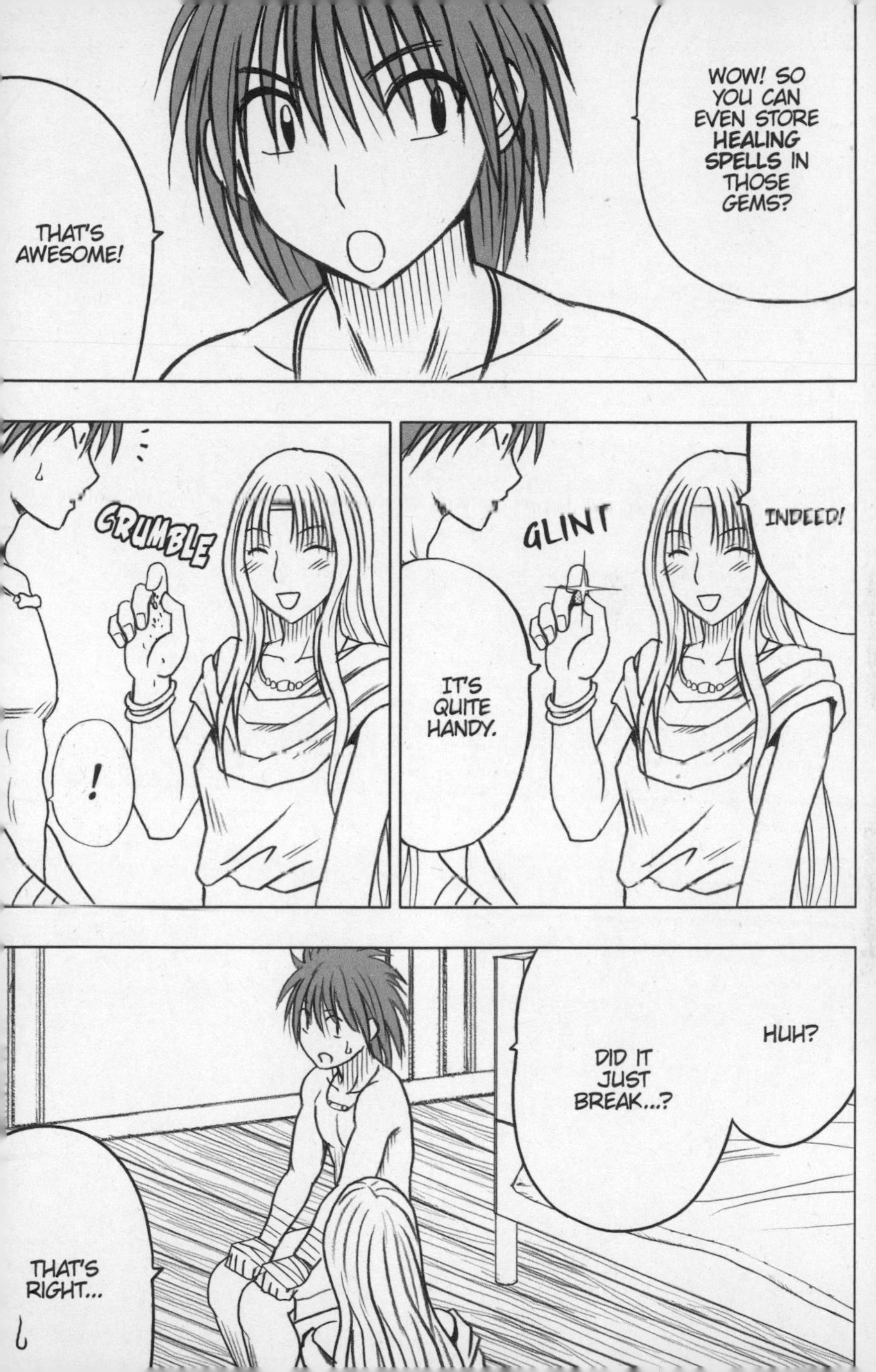
WOW! SO YOU CAN EVEN STORE HEALING SPELLS IN THOSE GEMS?
THAT'S AWESOME!
INDEED!
GLINT
IT'S QUITE HANDY.
CRUMBLE
!
HUH?
DID IT JUST BREAK...?
THAT'S RIGHT...

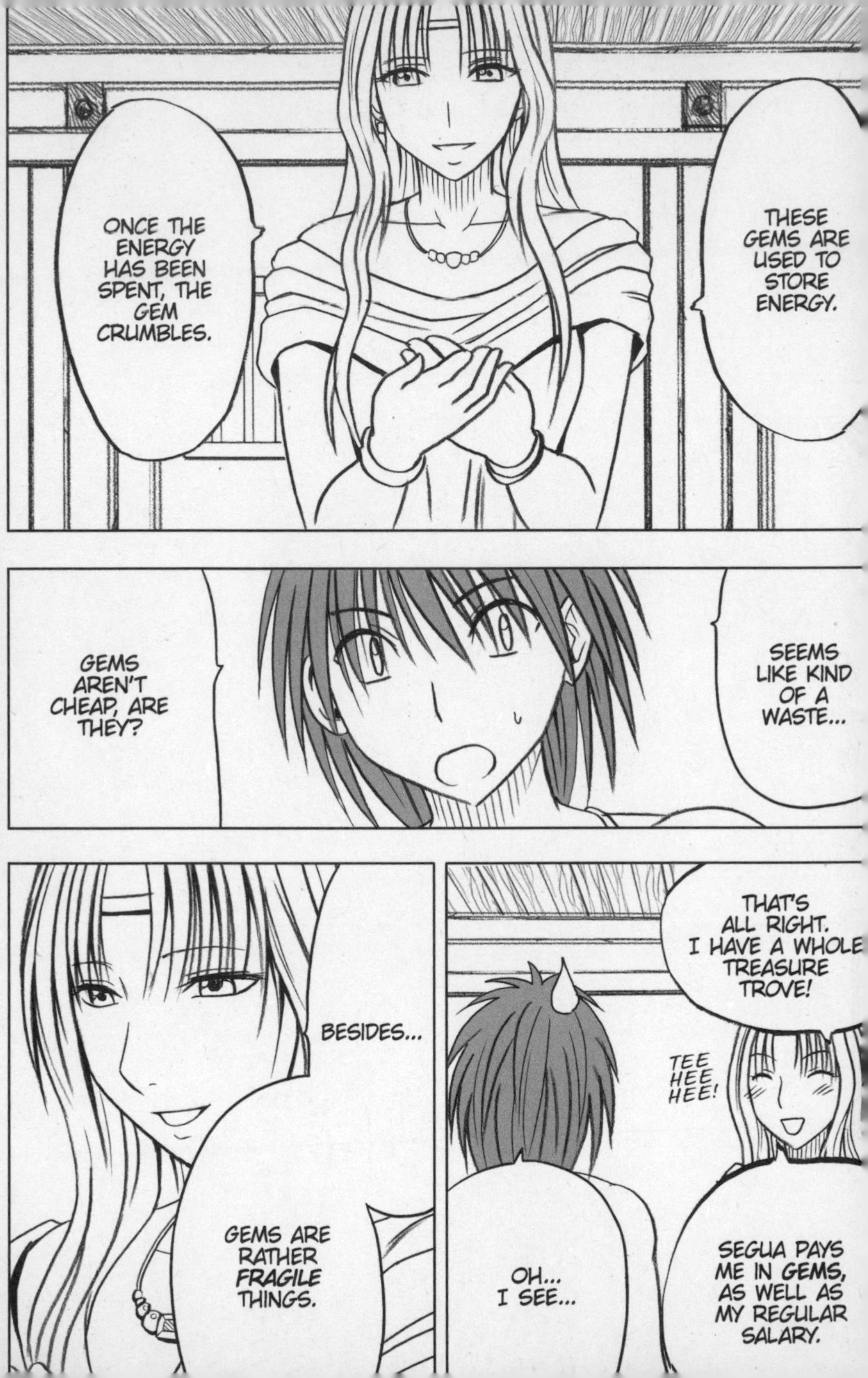
THESE GEMS ARE USED TO STORE ENERGY.
ONCE THE ENERGY HAS BEEN SPENT, THE GEM CRUMBLES.
SEEMS LIKE KIND OF A WASTE...
GEMS AREN'T CHEAP, ARE THEY?
THAT'S ALL RIGHT. I HAVE A WHOLE TREASURE TROVE!
TEE HEE HEE!
SEGUA PAYS ME IN GEMS, AS WELL AS MY REGULAR SALARY.
OH... I SEE...
BESIDES...
GEMS ARE RATHER *FRAGILE* THINGS.

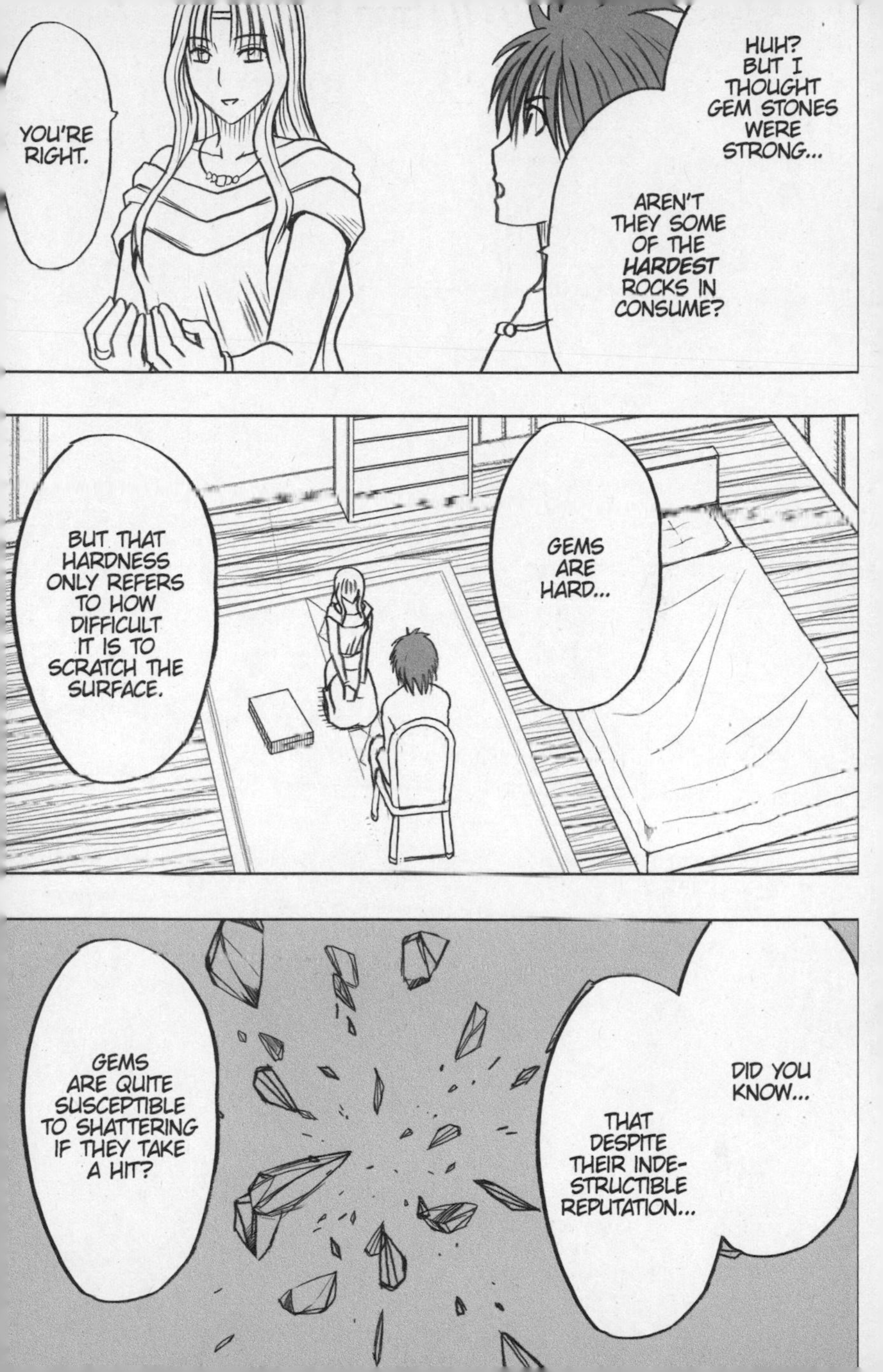
HUH? BUT I THOUGHT GEM STONES WERE STRONG...
AREN'T THEY SOME OF THE *HARDEST* ROCKS IN CONSUME?
YOU'RE RIGHT.
GEMS ARE HARD...
BUT THAT HARDNESS ONLY REFERS TO HOW DIFFICULT IT IS TO SCRATCH THE SURFACE.
DID YOU KNOW...
THAT DESPITE THEIR INDE-STRUCTIBLE REPUTATION...
GEMS ARE QUITE SUSCEPTIBLE TO SHATTERING IF THEY TAKE A HIT?

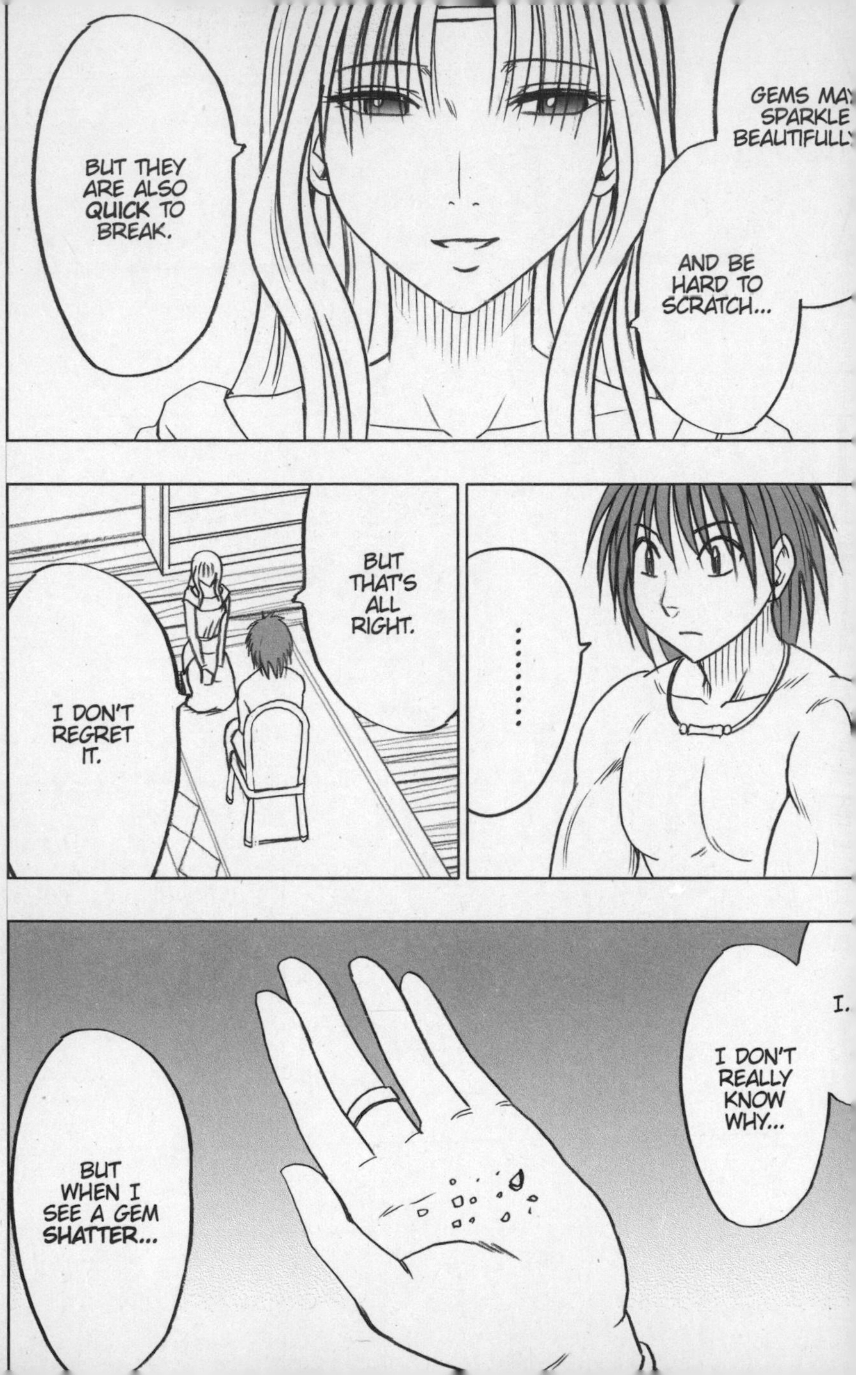

GEMS MA
SPARKLE
BEAUTIFULL
AND BE HARD TO SCRATCH...
BUT THEY ARE ALSO QUICK TO BREAK.
......
BUT THAT'S ALL RIGHT.
I DON'T REGRET IT.
I.
I DON'T REALLY KNOW WHY...
BUT WHEN I SEE A GEM SHATTER...

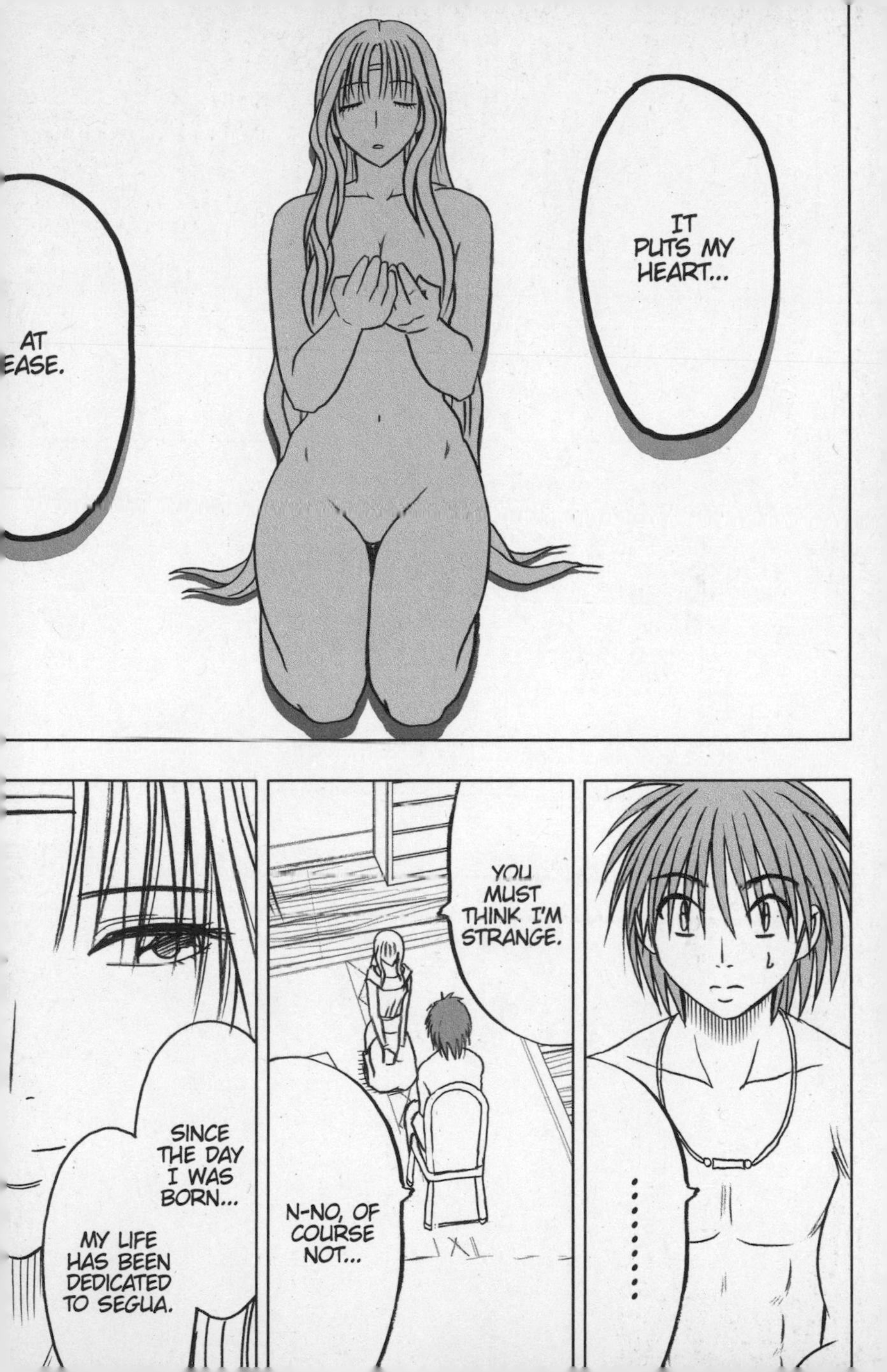
IT PUTS MY HEART...
AT EASE.
....
YOU MUST THINK I'M STRANGE.
N-NO, OF COURSE NOT...
SINCE THE DAY I WAS BORN...
MY LIFE HAS BEEN DEDICATED TO SEGUA.

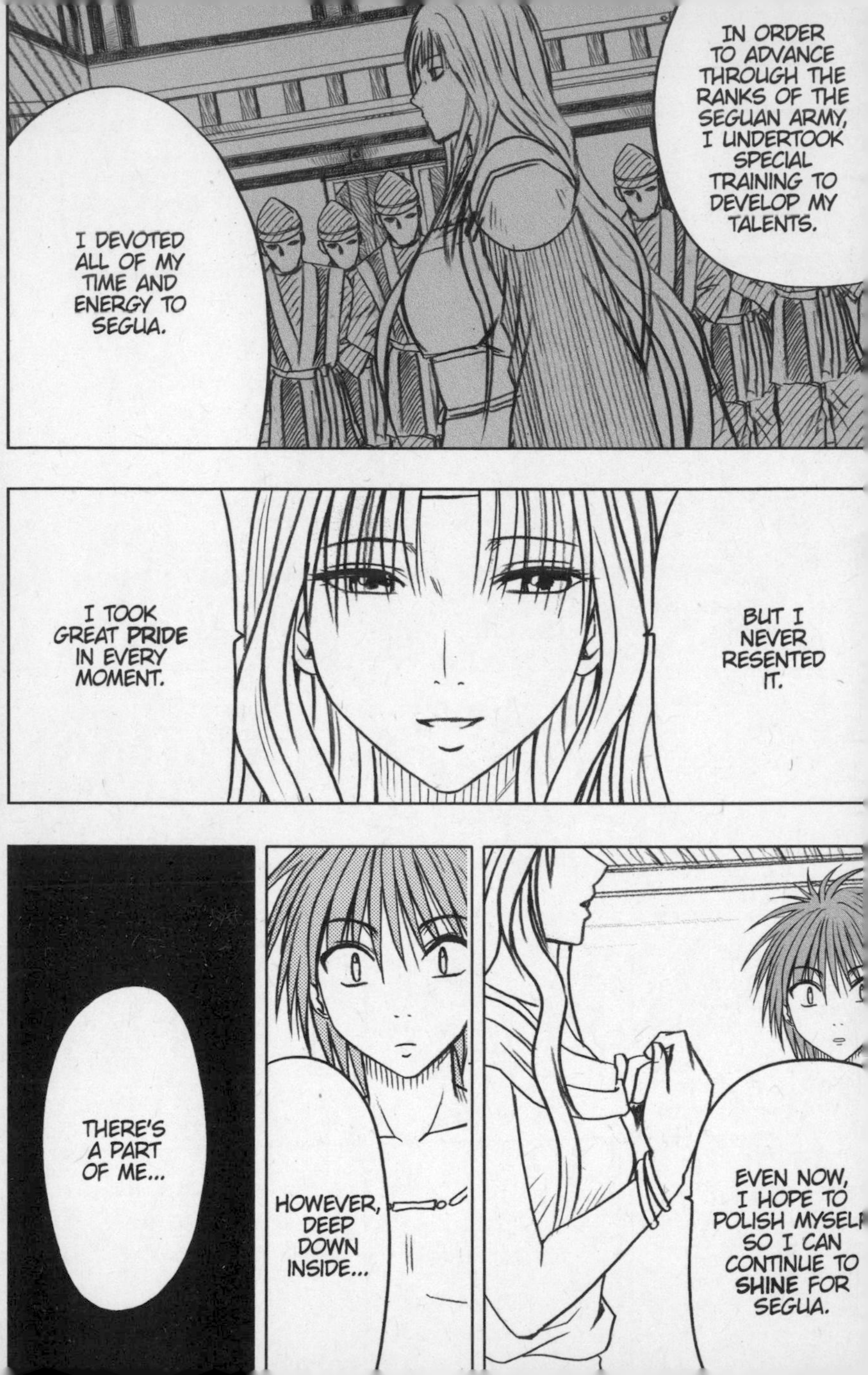
IN ORDER TO ADVANCE THROUGH THE RANKS OF THE SEGUAN ARMY, I UNDERTOOK SPECIAL TRAINING TO DEVELOP MY TALENTS.
I DEVOTED ALL OF MY TIME AND ENERGY TO SEGUA.
BUT I NEVER RESENTED IT.
I TOOK GREAT PRIDE IN EVERY MOMENT.
EVEN NOW, I HOPE TO POLISH MYSELF SO I CAN CONTINUE TO SHINE FOR SEGUA.
HOWEVER, DEEP DOWN INSIDE...
THERE'S A PART OF ME...

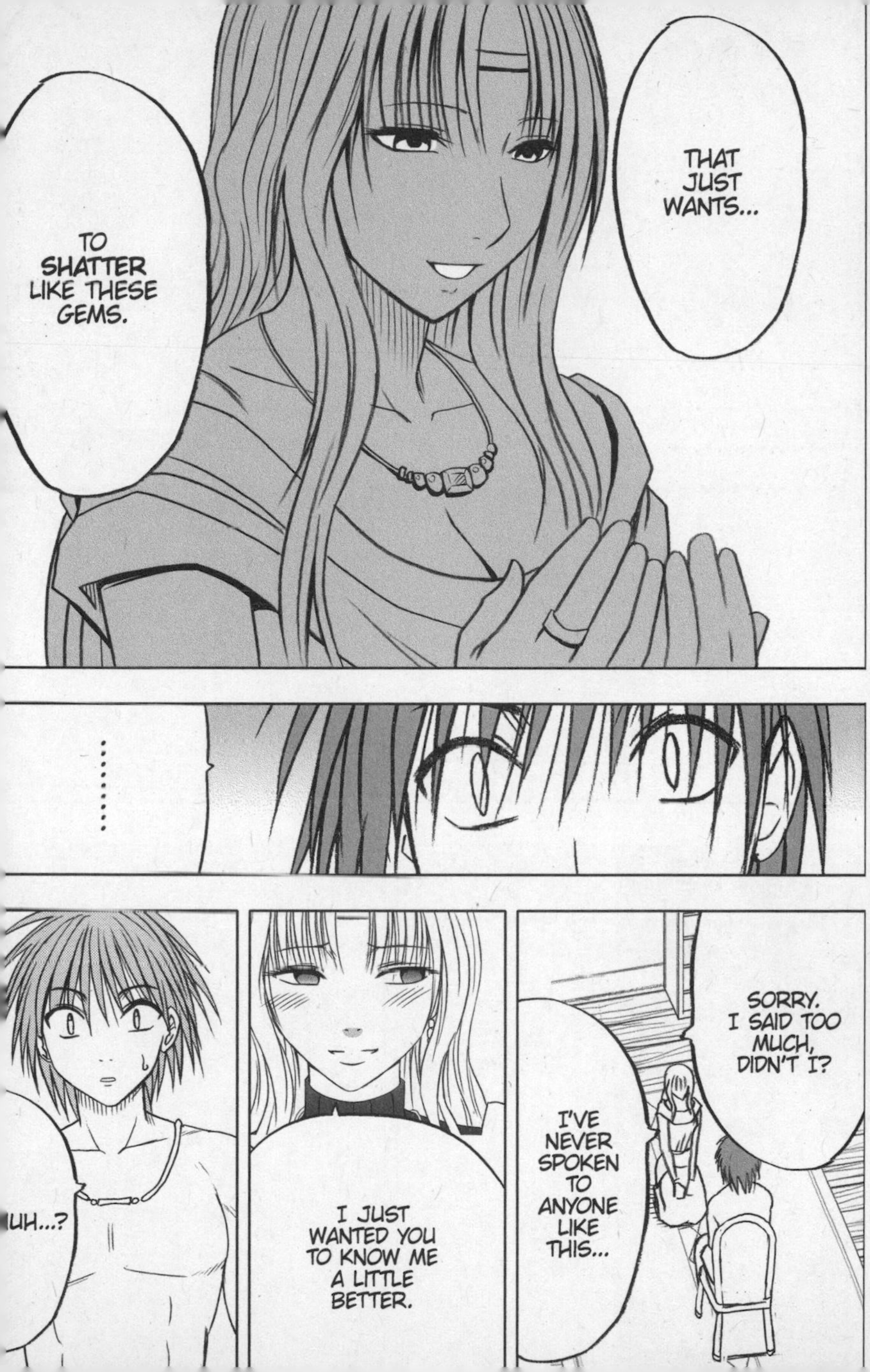
THAT JUST WANTS...
TO SHATTER LIKE THESE GEMS.
......
SORRY. I SAID TOO MUCH, DIDN'T I?
I'VE NEVER SPOKEN TO ANYONE LIKE THIS...
I JUST WANTED YOU TO KNOW ME A LITTLE BETTER.
UH...?

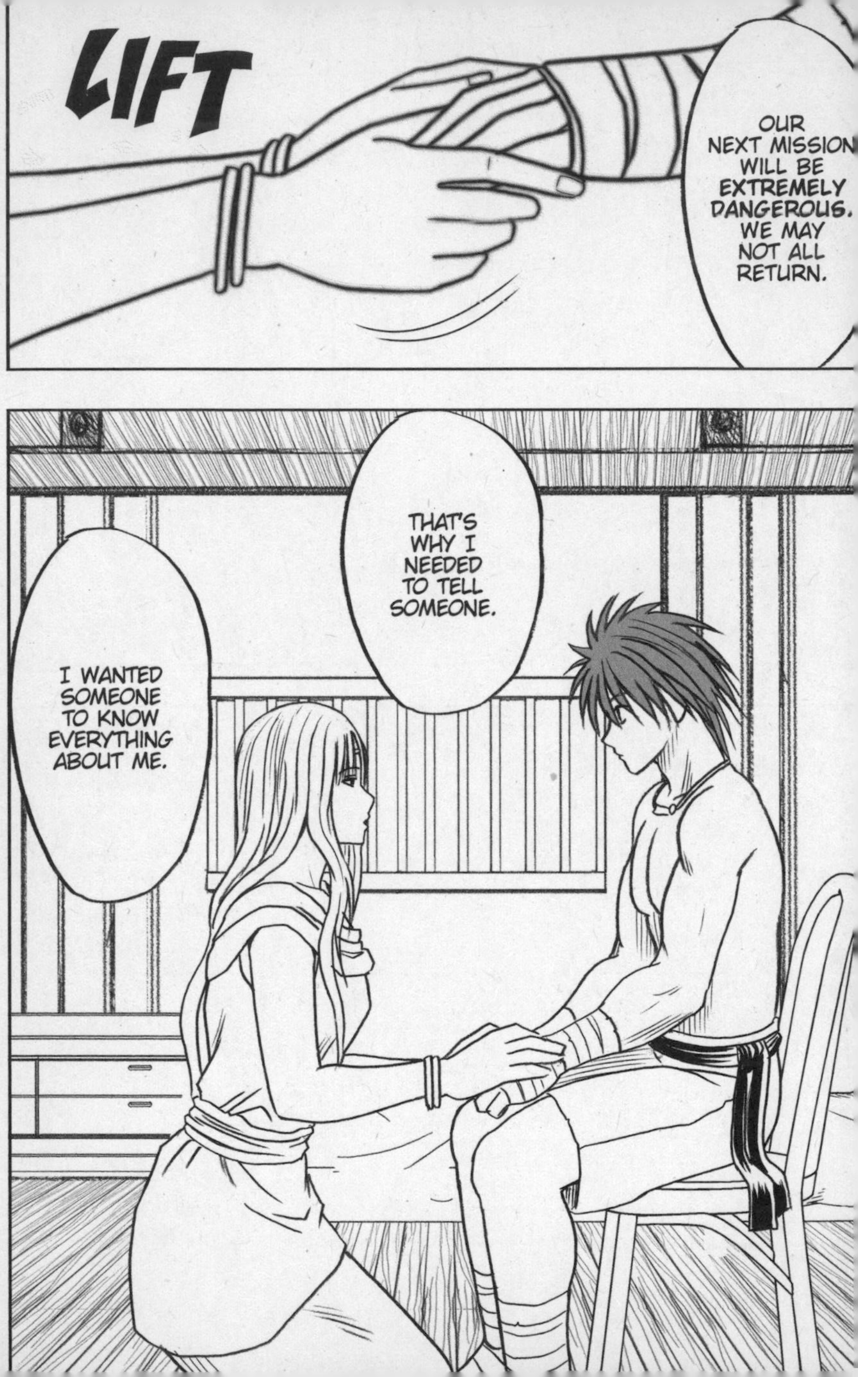
OUR NEXT MISSION WILL BE EXTREMELY DANGEROUS. WE MAY NOT ALL RETURN.
LIFT
THAT'S WHY I NEEDED TO TELL SOMEONE.
I WANTED SOMEONE TO KNOW EVERYTHING ABOUT ME.

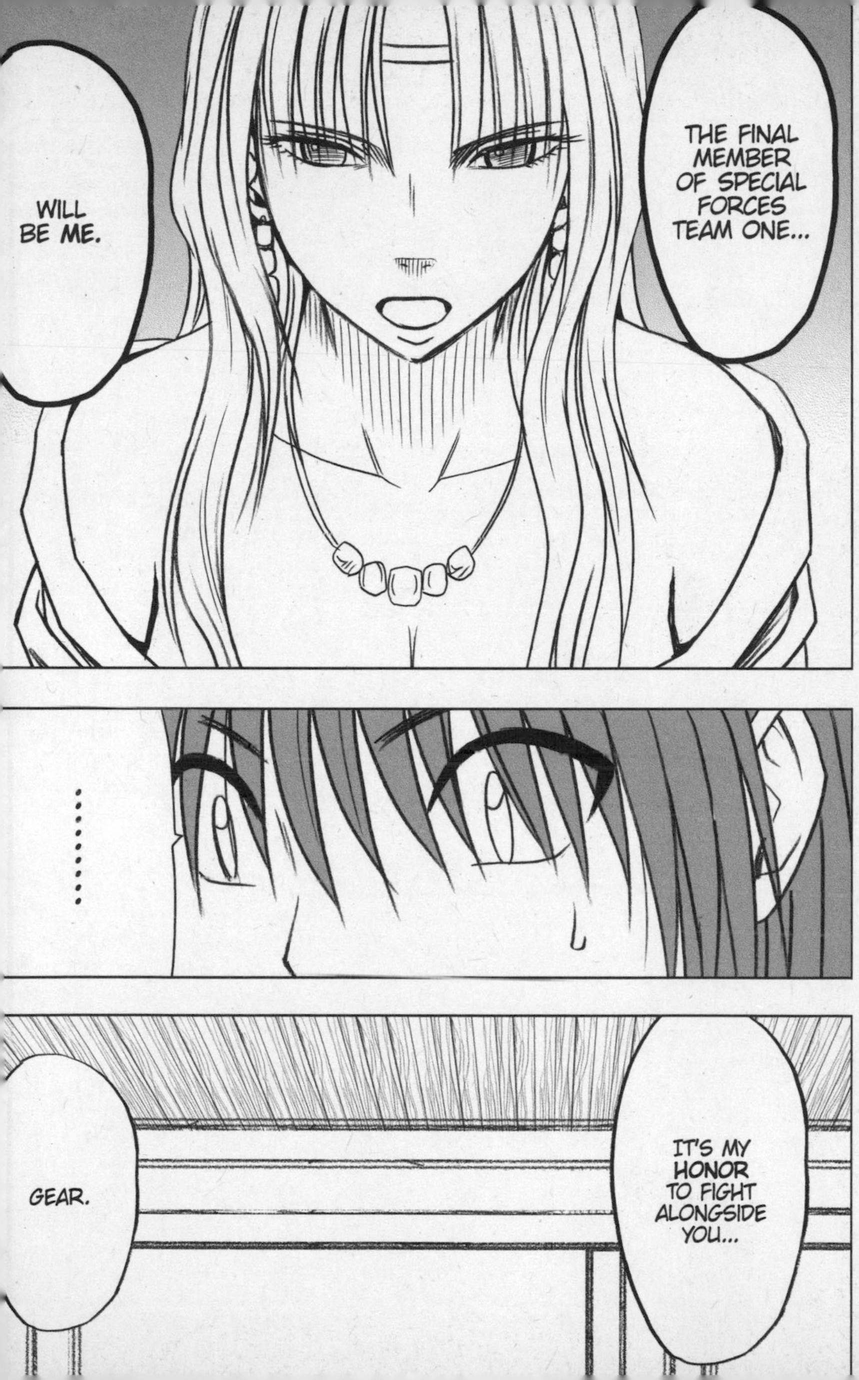
THE FINAL MEMBER OF SPECIAL FORCES TEAM ONE...
WILL BE ME.
....
IT'S MY HONOR TO FIGHT ALONGSIDE YOU...
GEAR.

Bonus Comic

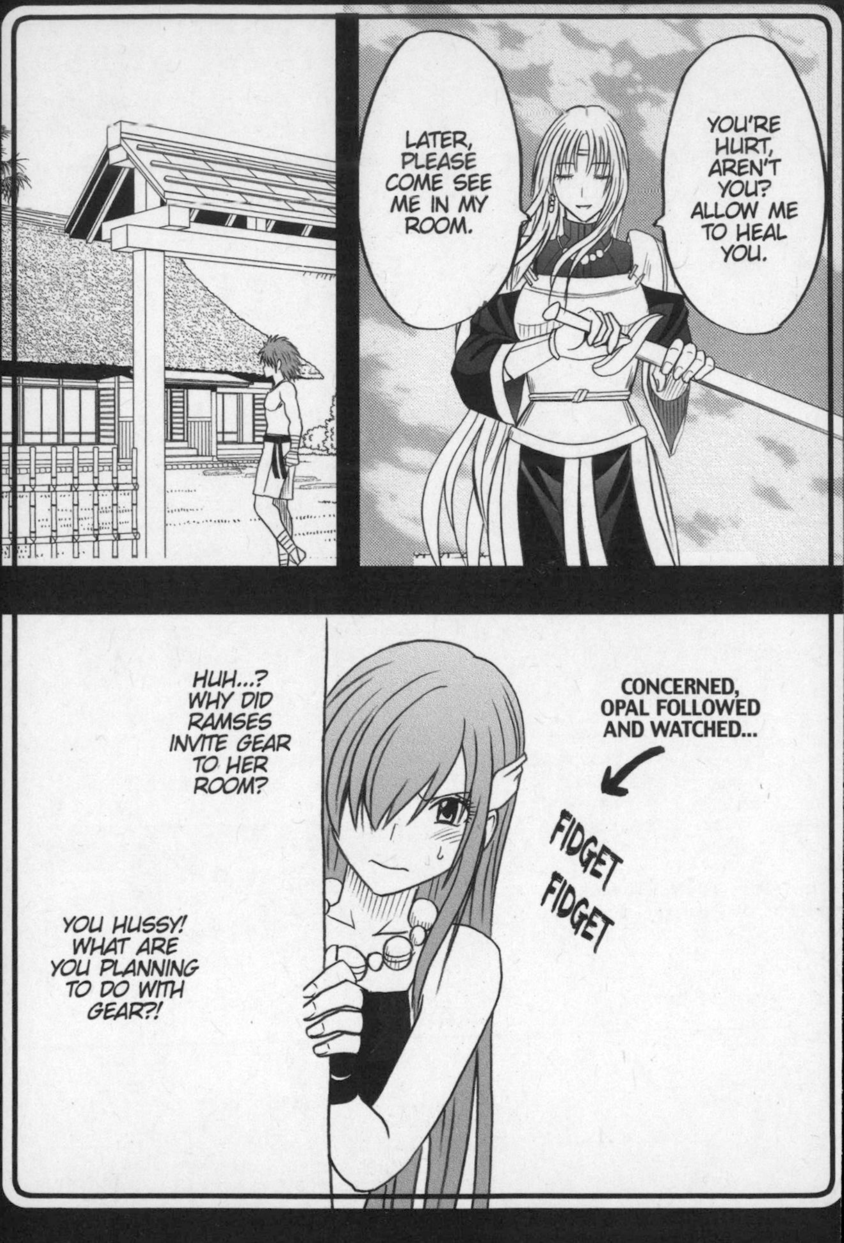
YOU'RE HURT, AREN'T YOU? ALLOW ME TO HEAL YOU.
LATER, PLEASE COME SEE ME IN MY ROOM.
CONCERNED, OPAL FOLLOWED AND WATCHED...
FIDGET FIDGET
HUH...? WHY DID RAMSES INVITE GEAR TO HER ROOM?
YOU HUSSY! WHAT ARE YOU PLANNING TO DO WITH GEAR?!

Perusing Video Game History

ON THE EDGE OF THE BLUE WORLD

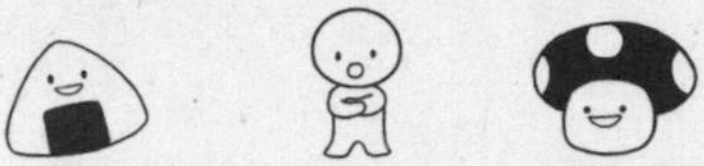

Dr. Onigiri **Mr. Why** **Prof. Mushroom**

Today's Topic

COLUMNS

Mr. Why: Hello, everyone! Just like in the previous volumes, the Doctor, the Professor, and I are going to chat a little bit about video games and their history. As always, please keep in mind that this has nothing to do with the main story of the manga in any way.

Dr. Onigiri: Hello! I'm Dr. Onigiri! Whenever you feel like savoring the feeling of achievement, have some onigiri!

Prof. Mushroom: Thanks for having me. I'm Professor Mushroom. If you want to grow up big and strong, mushrooms are the best thing to eat!

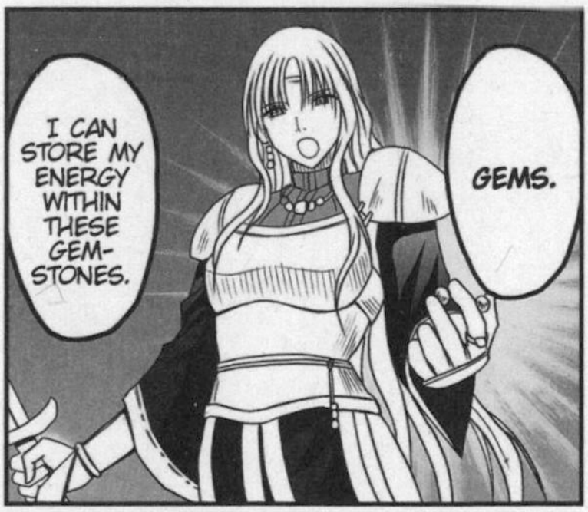
GEMS.
I CAN STORE MY ENERGY WITHIN THESE GEM-STONES.

Segua's best puzzle user, Ramses. She can store energy in gems and make them explode.

Dr. Onigiri: Today we're going to talk about a game that we touched on a little bit back in volume 1, but now we're going to talk about in more detail. That game is *Columns* by Sega. Like *Tetris* and *Magical Drop*, it is a falling block puzzle game.
However, it is considered the first of this genre to have the element of "chains."

Prof. Mushroom: Using gems to instantly destroy gems of the same color when you got a chain was a lot of fun!

Dr. Onigiri: There's nothing like the thrill of storing up your gems to the limit then breaking them all in one big chain. That was awesome, and new too!

Mr. Why: Sega sure has a lot of games that give you a rush, don't they?

Dr. Onigiri: You're right! In the original *Sonic the Hedgehog*, Sonic could use his Super Sonic Spin Attack to roll into a ball and speed through obstacles. That made it a really fun platformer, and one that only got better when they introduced the Spin Dash in the sequel. Sega made a lot of fun action games.

Prof. Mushroom: Nintendo had thrilling games too. *The Legend of Zelda* is one such game that comes to mind.

Mr. Why: Oh? Really?

To Be Continued...

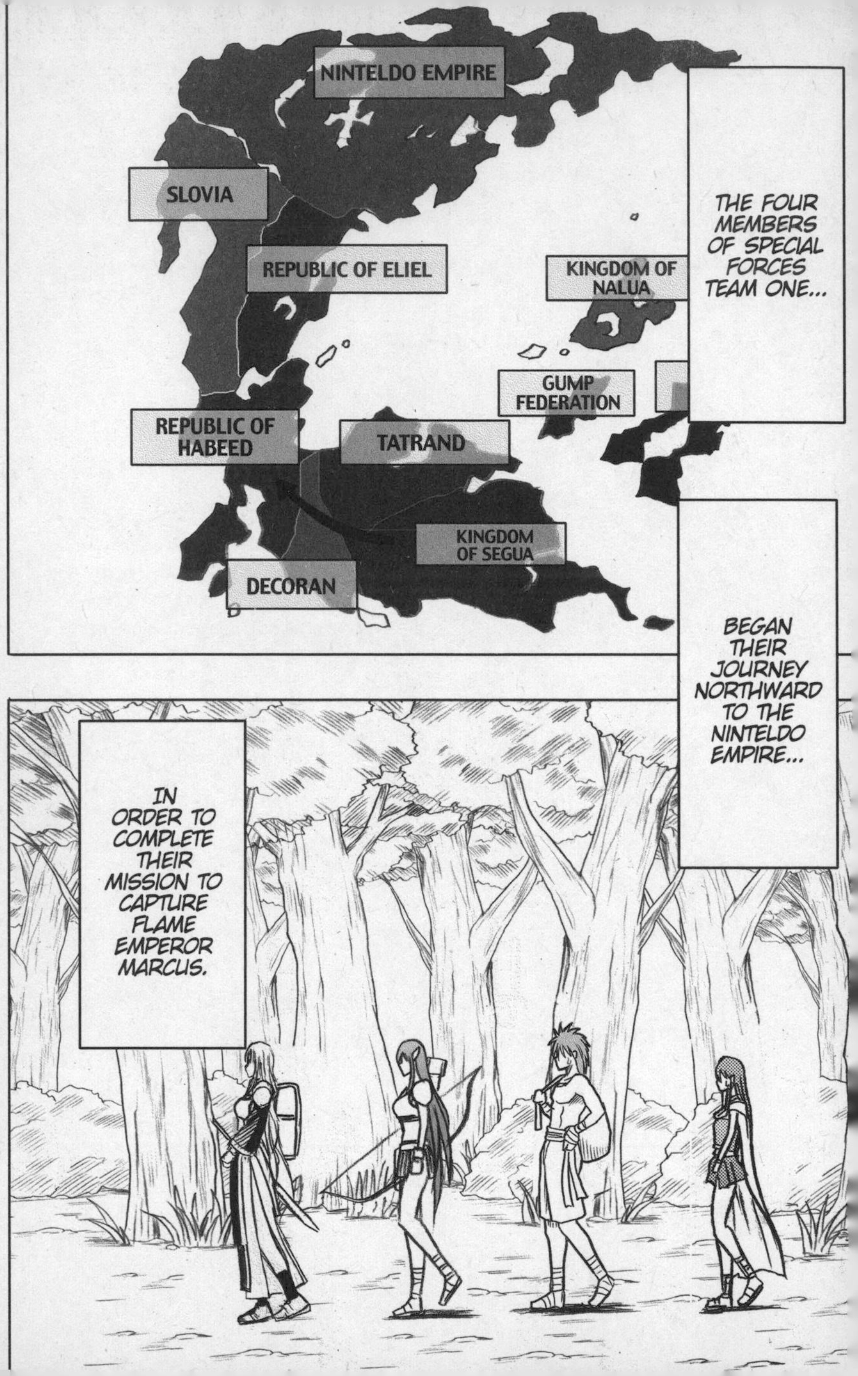
THE FOUR MEMBERS OF SPECIAL FORCES TEAM ONE...
NINTELDO EMPIRE
KINGDOM OF NALUA
SLOVIA
REPUBLIC OF ELIEL
GUMP FEDERATION
TATRAND
REPUBLIC OF HABEED
KINGDOM OF SEGUA
DECORAN
BEGAN THEIR JOURNEY NORTHWARD TO THE NINTELDO EMPIRE...
IN ORDER TO COMPLETE THEIR MISSION TO CAPTURE FLAME EMPEROR MARCUS.

Part 2

CHAPTER 18

HEART CONTAINER

DISC 1

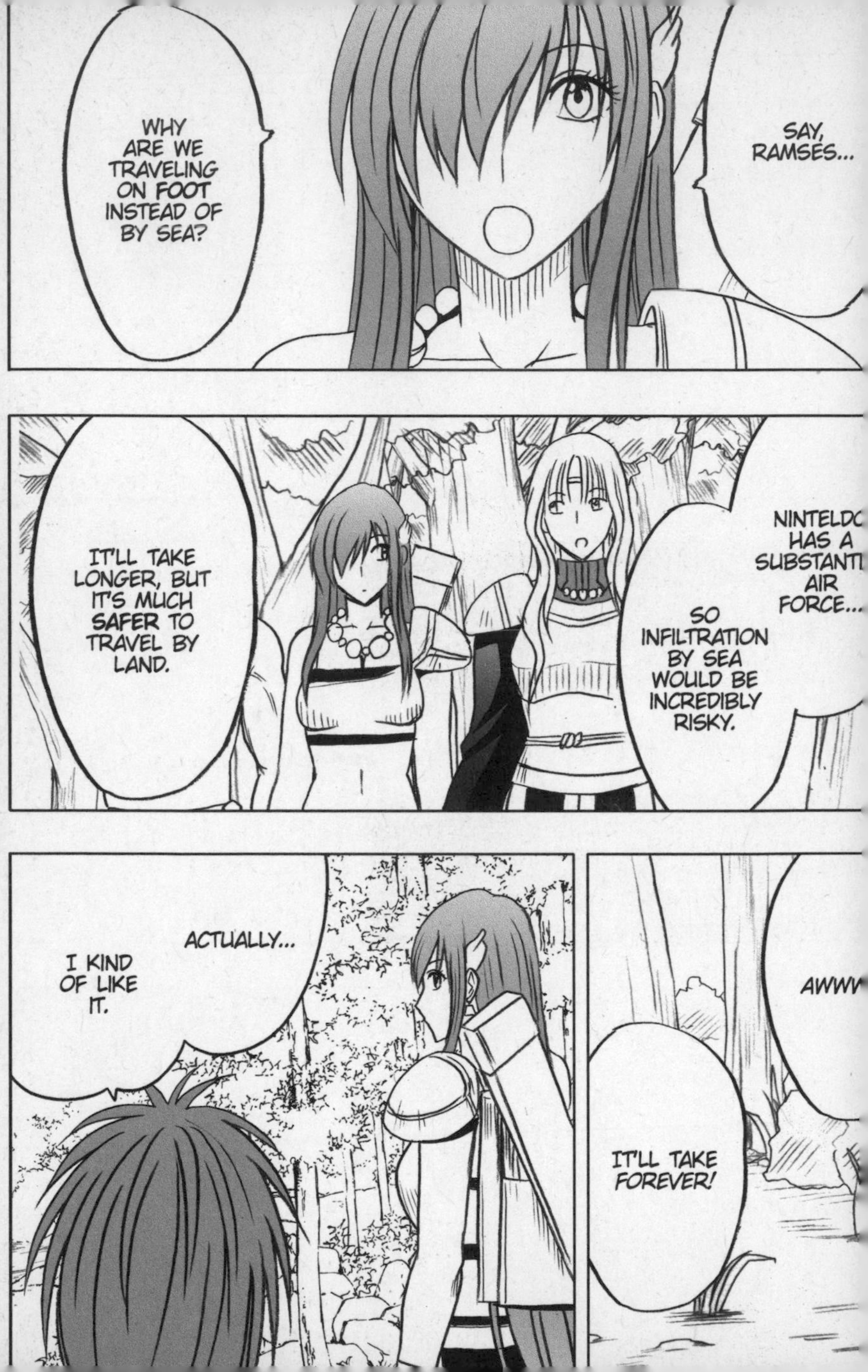
SAY, RAMSES...
WHY ARE WE TRAVELING ON FOOT INSTEAD OF BY SEA?
NINTELD HAS A SUBSTANT AIR FORCE...
SO INFILTRATION BY SEA WOULD BE INCREDIBLY RISKY.
IT'LL TAKE LONGER, BUT IT'S MUCH SAFER TO TRAVEL BY LAND.
AWW
IT'LL TAKE FOREVER!
ACTUALLY...
I KIND OF LIKE IT.

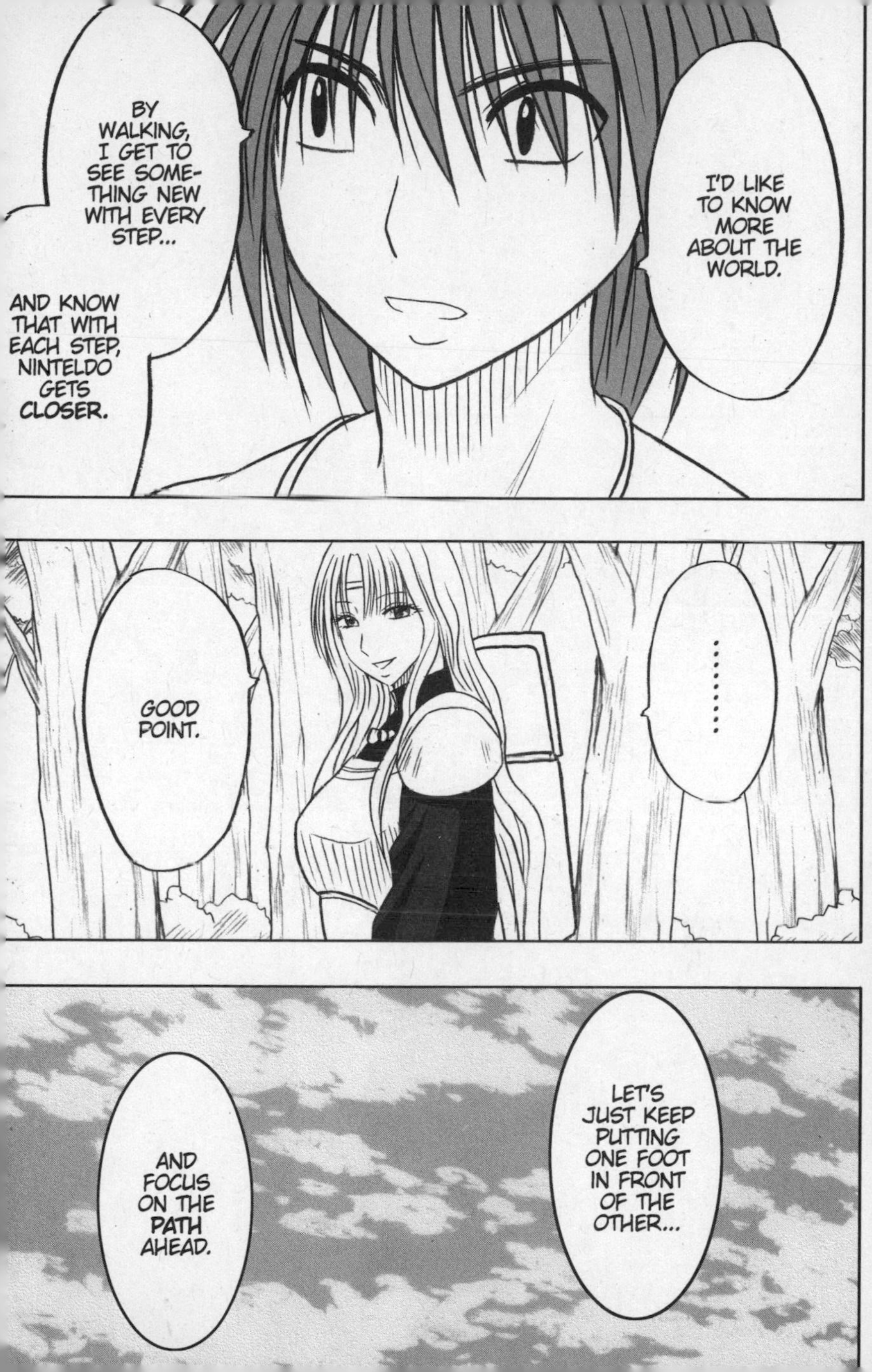
I'D LIKE TO KNOW MORE ABOUT THE WORLD.
BY WALKING, I GET TO SEE SOME-THING NEW WITH EVERY STEP...
AND KNOW THAT WITH EACH STEP, NINTELDO GETS CLOSER.
......
GOOD POINT.
LET'S JUST KEEP PUTTING ONE FOOT IN FRONT OF THE OTHER...
AND FOCUS ON THE PATH AHEAD.

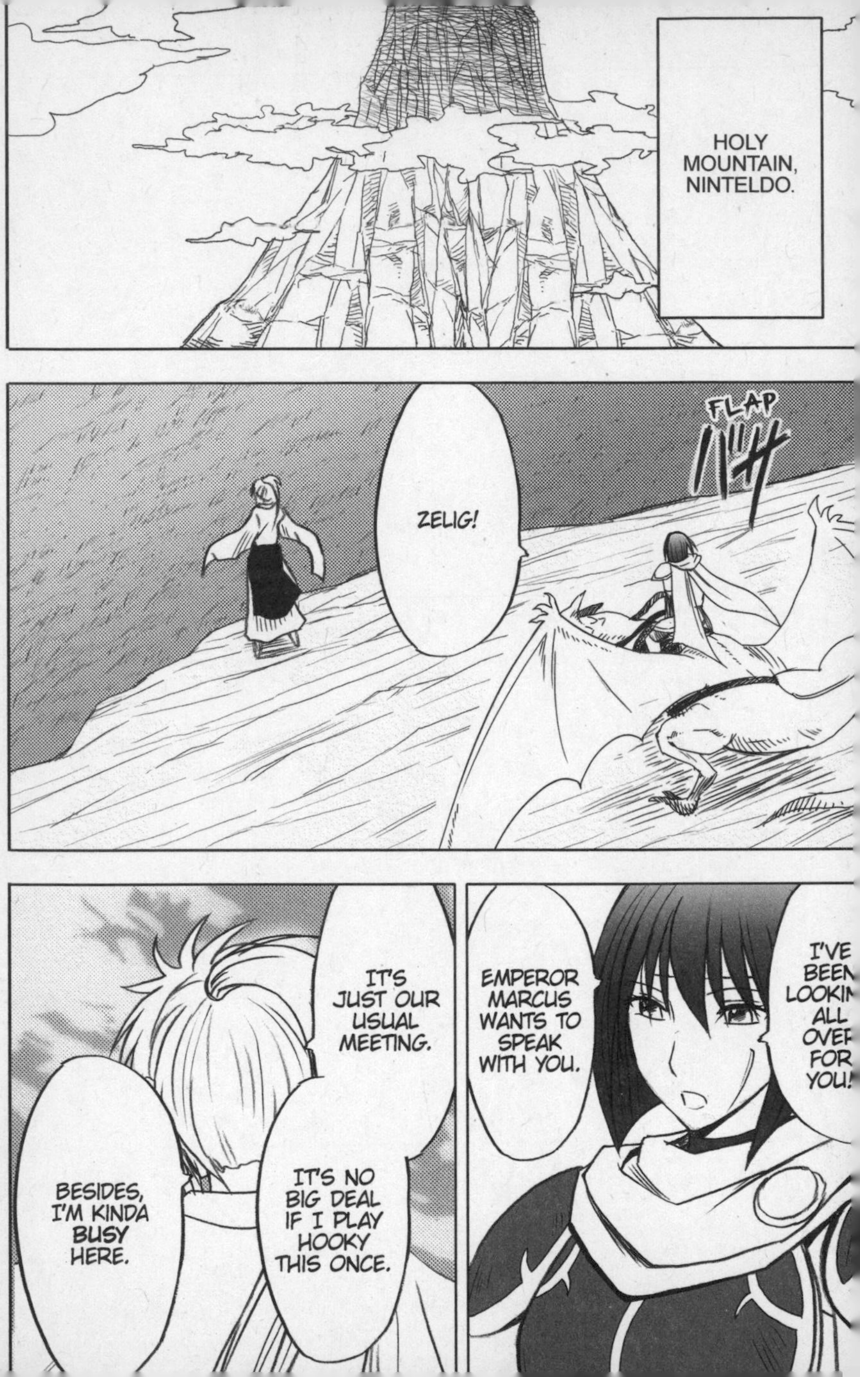
HOLY MOUNTAIN, NINTELDO.
FLAP
ZELIG!
I'VE BEEN LOOKIN ALL OVER FOR YOU!
EMPEROR MARCUS WANTS TO SPEAK WITH YOU.
IT'S JUST OUR USUAL MEETING.
IT'S NO BIG DEAL IF I PLAY HOOKY THIS ONCE.
BESIDES, I'M KINDA BUSY HERE.

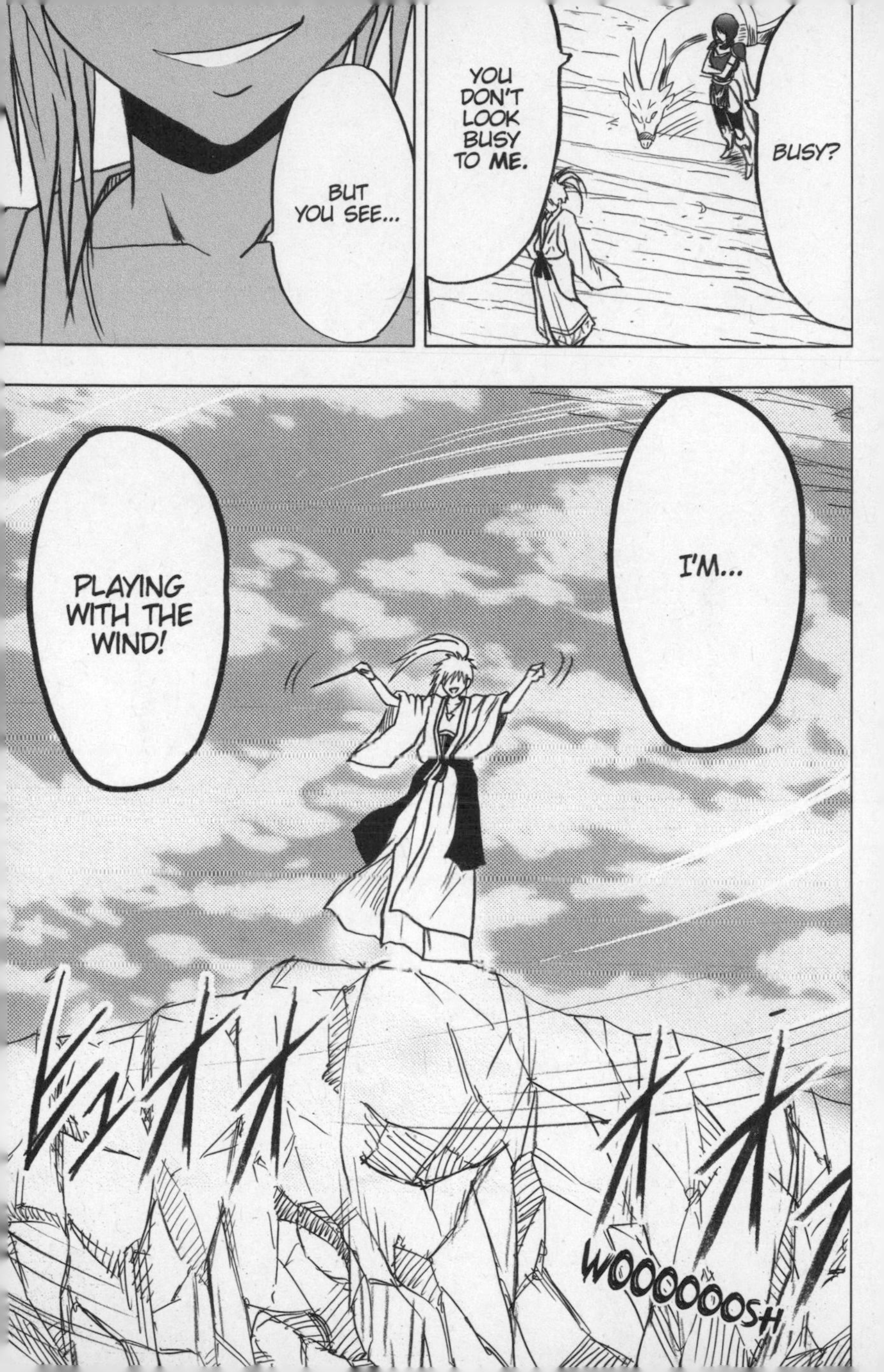
BUSY?
YOU DON'T LOOK BUSY TO ME.
BUT YOU SEE...
I'M...
PLAYING WITH THE WIND!
WOOOOOOSH

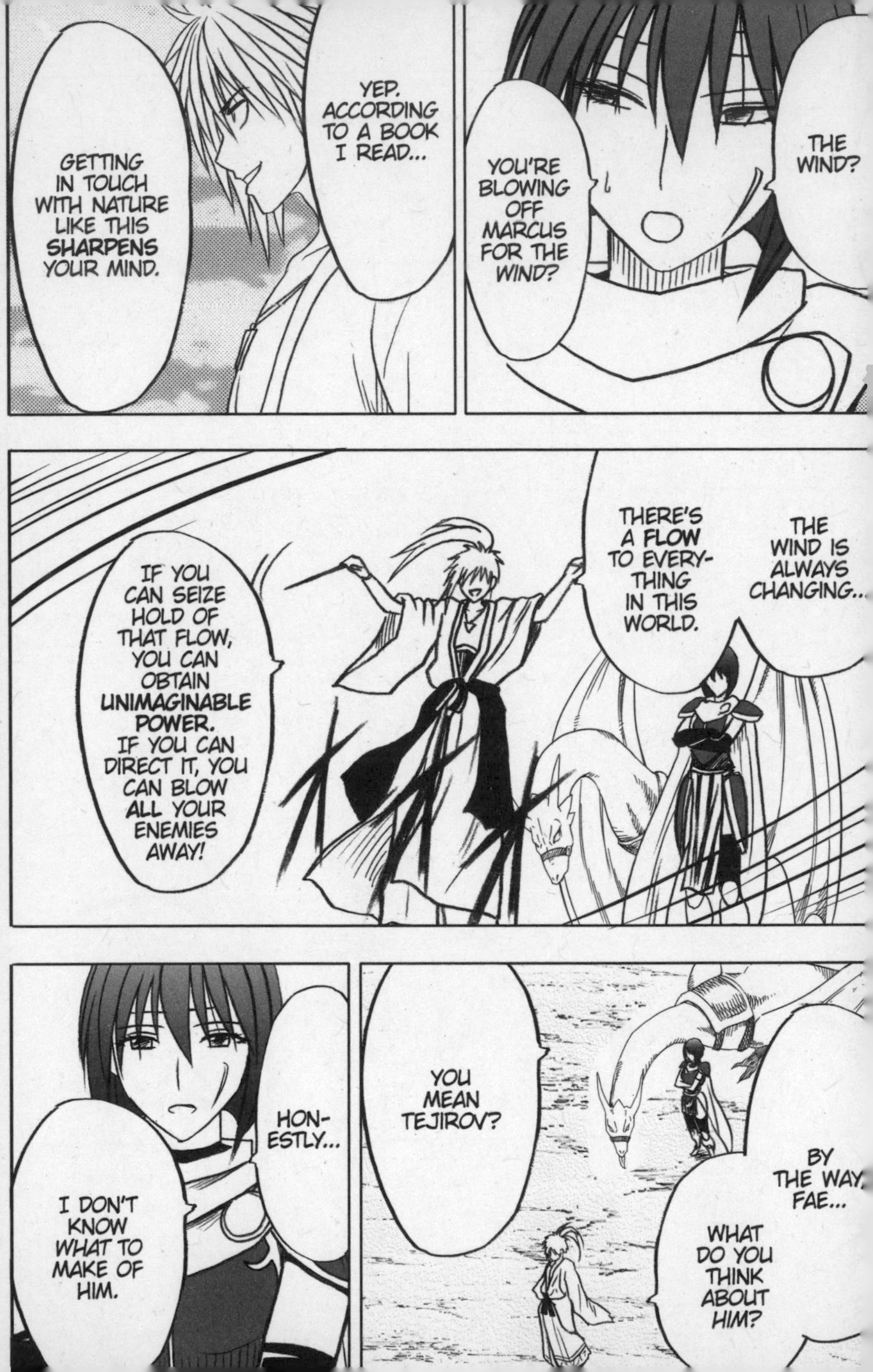
THE WIND?
YOU'RE BLOWING OFF MARCUS FOR THE WIND?
YEP. ACCORDING TO A BOOK I READ...
GETTING IN TOUCH WITH NATURE LIKE THIS **SHARPENS** YOUR MIND.
THE WIND IS ALWAYS CHANGING...
THERE'S A **FLOW** TO EVERY-THING IN THIS WORLD.
IF YOU CAN SEIZE HOLD OF THAT FLOW, YOU CAN OBTAIN **UNIMAGINABLE POWER.** IF YOU CAN DIRECT IT, YOU CAN BLOW **ALL** YOUR ENEMIES AWAY!
BY THE WAY, FAE...
WHAT DO YOU THINK ABOUT HIM?
YOU MEAN TEJIROV?
HON-ESTLY...
I DON'T KNOW WHAT TO MAKE OF HIM.

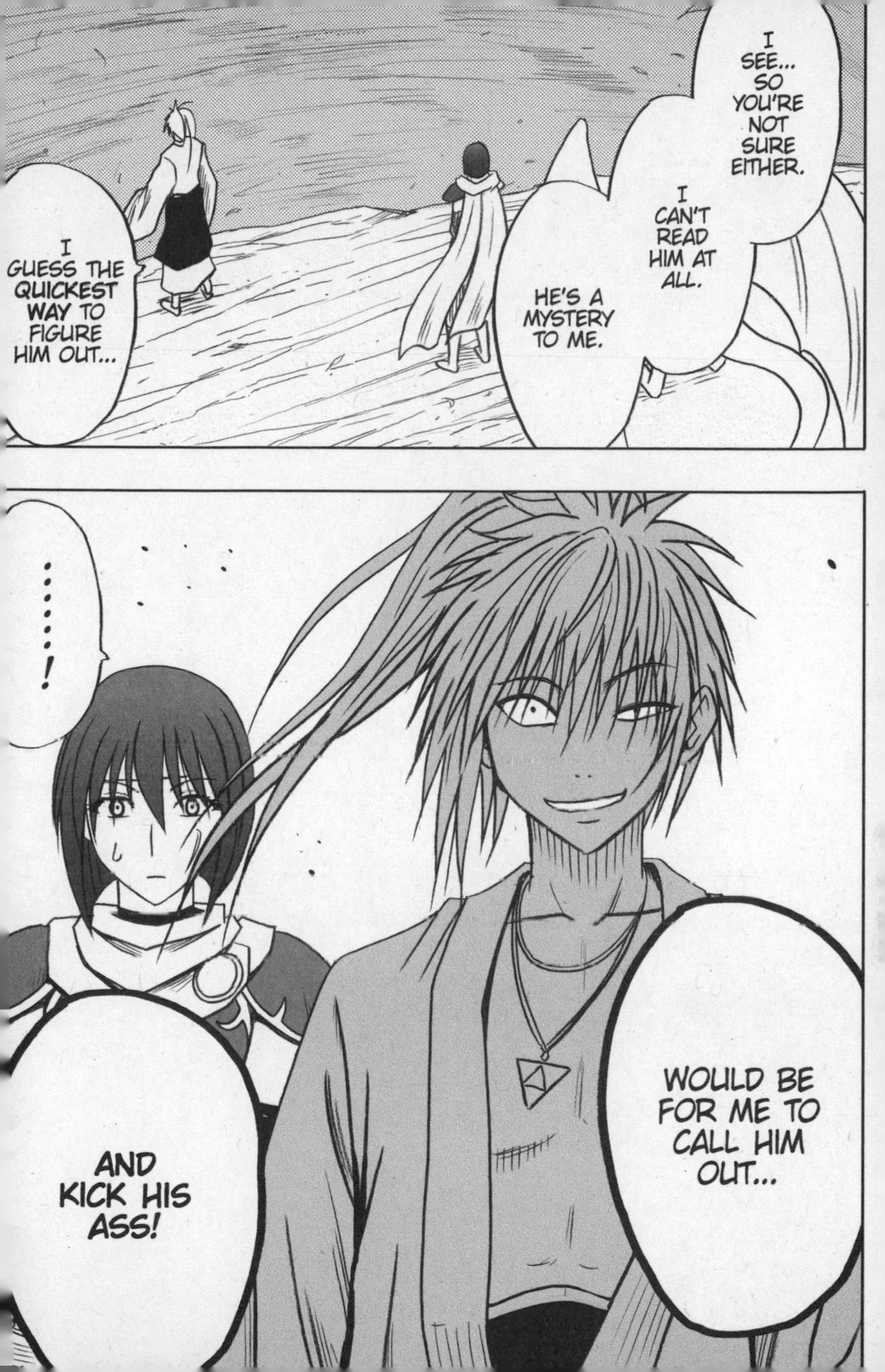
I SEE... SO YOU'RE NOT SURE EITHER.
I CAN'T READ HIM AT ALL.
HE'S A MYSTERY TO ME.
I GUESS THE QUICKEST WAY TO FIGURE HIM OUT...
WOULD BE FOR ME TO CALL HIM OUT...
AND KICK HIS ASS!
......!

WAIT A MINUTE! TEJIROV IS OUR ALLY...

EMPEROR MARCUS HAS STRICTLY FORBIDDEN FIGHTING AMONGST OURSELVES.

YEAH, YEAH.

"KICK HIS ASS" AS IN A FIST FIGHT, OR ANYTHING LIKE THAT.

I DON'T MEAN...

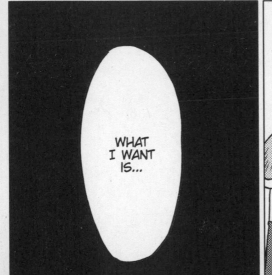

WHAT I WANT IS...

...?

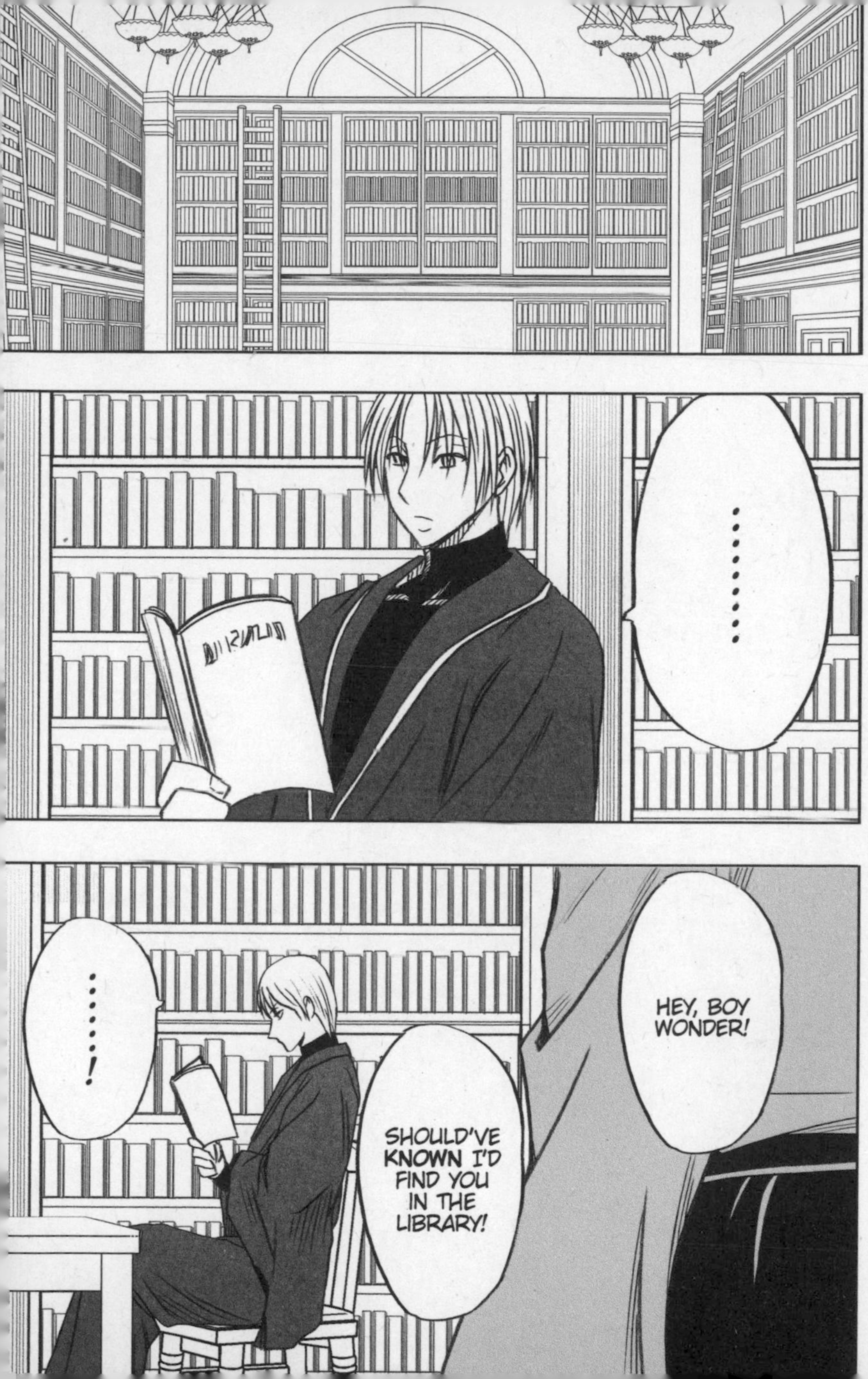
......
HEY, BOY WONDER!
SHOULD'VE KNOWN I'D FIND YOU IN THE LIBRARY!
......!

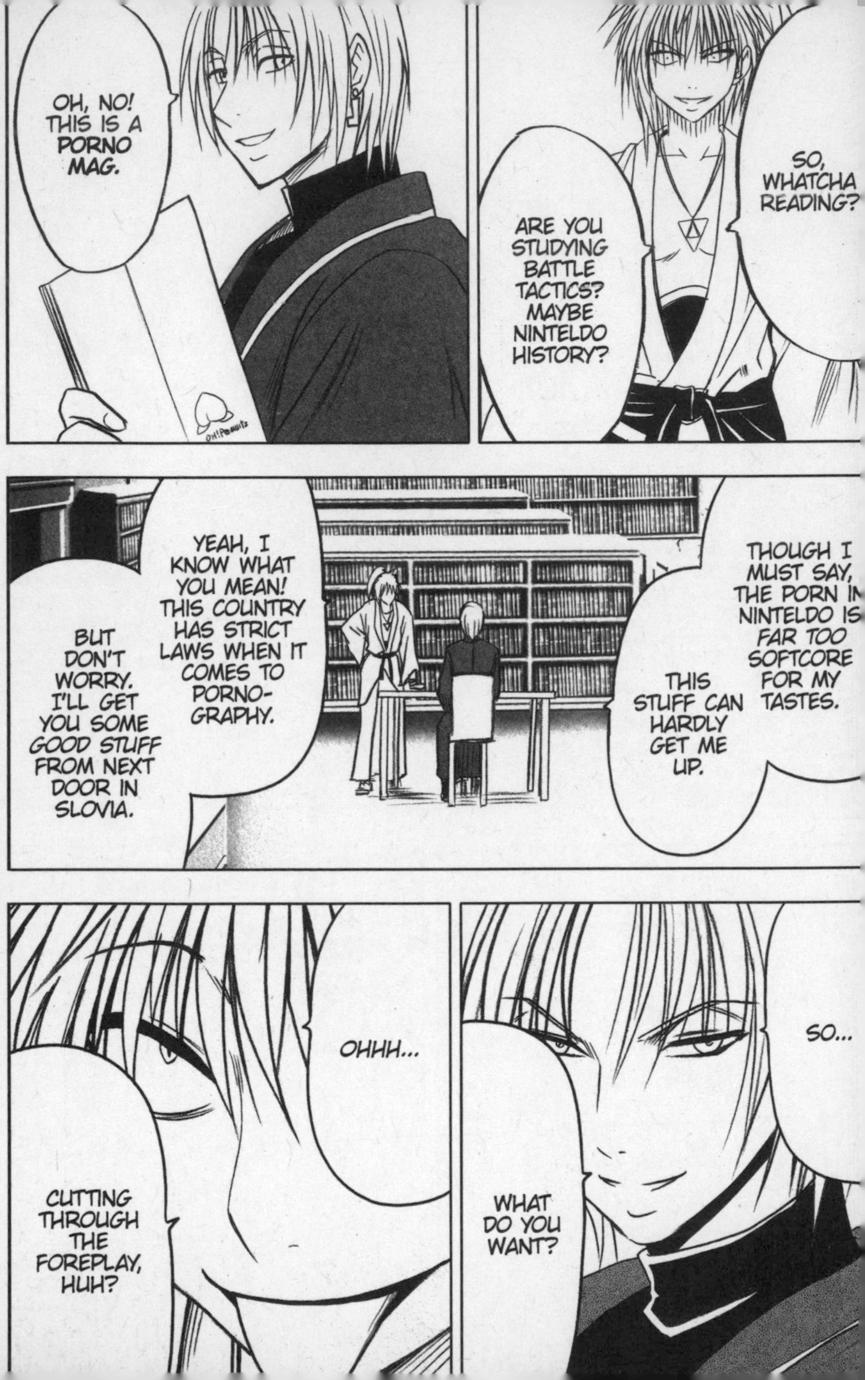
SO, WHATCHA READING?
ARE YOU STUDYING BATTLE TACTICS? MAYBE NINTELDO HISTORY?
OH, NO! THIS IS A PORNO MAG.
THOUGH I MUST SAY, THE PORN IN NINTELDO IS FAR TOO SOFTCORE FOR MY TASTES.
THIS STUFF CAN HARDLY GET ME UP.
YEAH, I KNOW WHAT YOU MEAN! THIS COUNTRY HAS STRICT LAWS WHEN IT COMES TO PORNOGRAPHY.
BUT DON'T WORRY. I'LL GET YOU SOME GOOD STUFF FROM NEXT DOOR IN SLOVIA.
SO...
WHAT DO YOU WANT?
OHHH...
CUTTING THROUGH THE FOREPLAY, HUH?

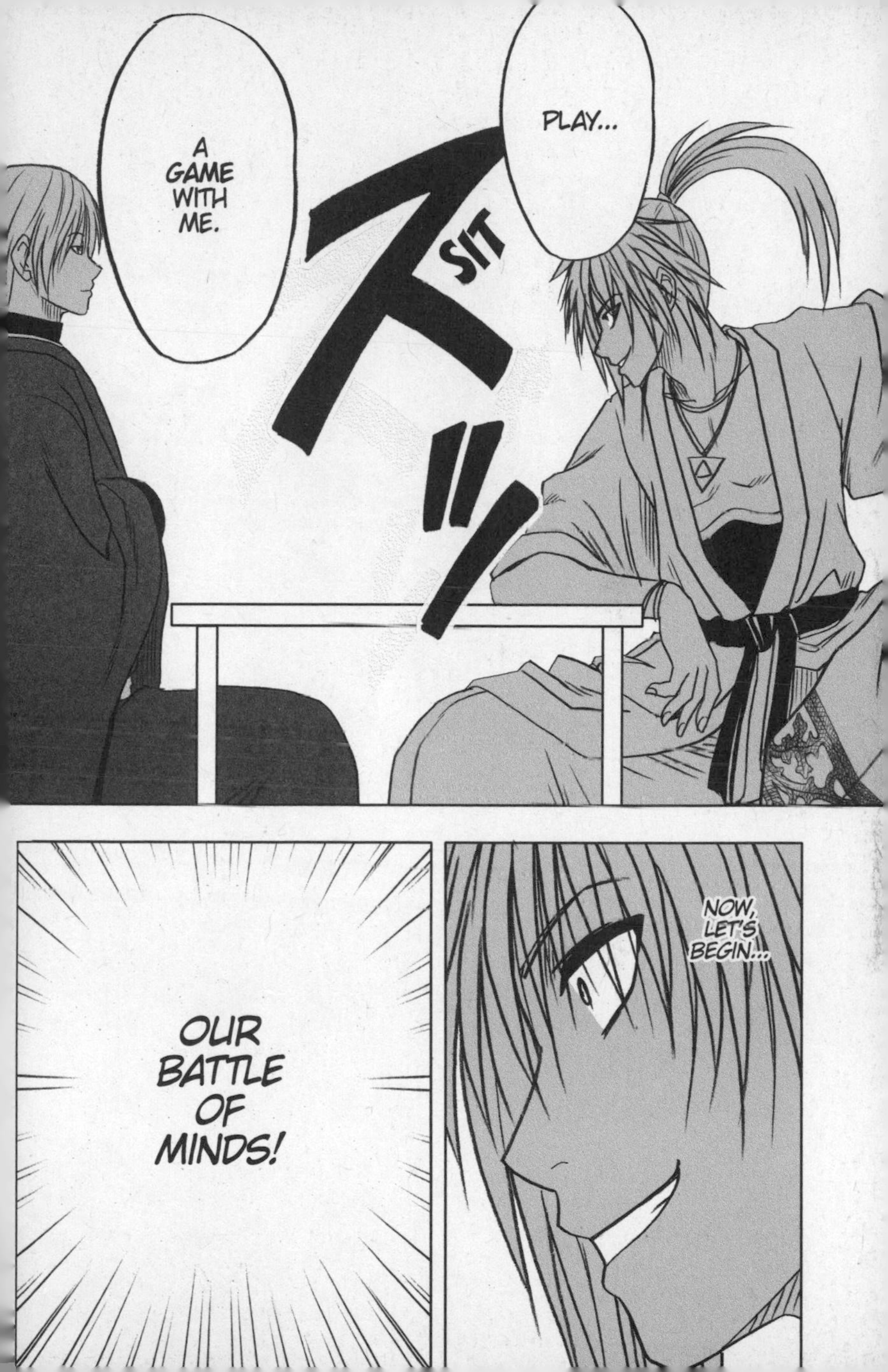
PLAY...
A GAME WITH ME.
SIT
NOW, LET'S BEGIN...
OUR BATTLE OF MINDS!

HEART CONTAINER

DISC 2

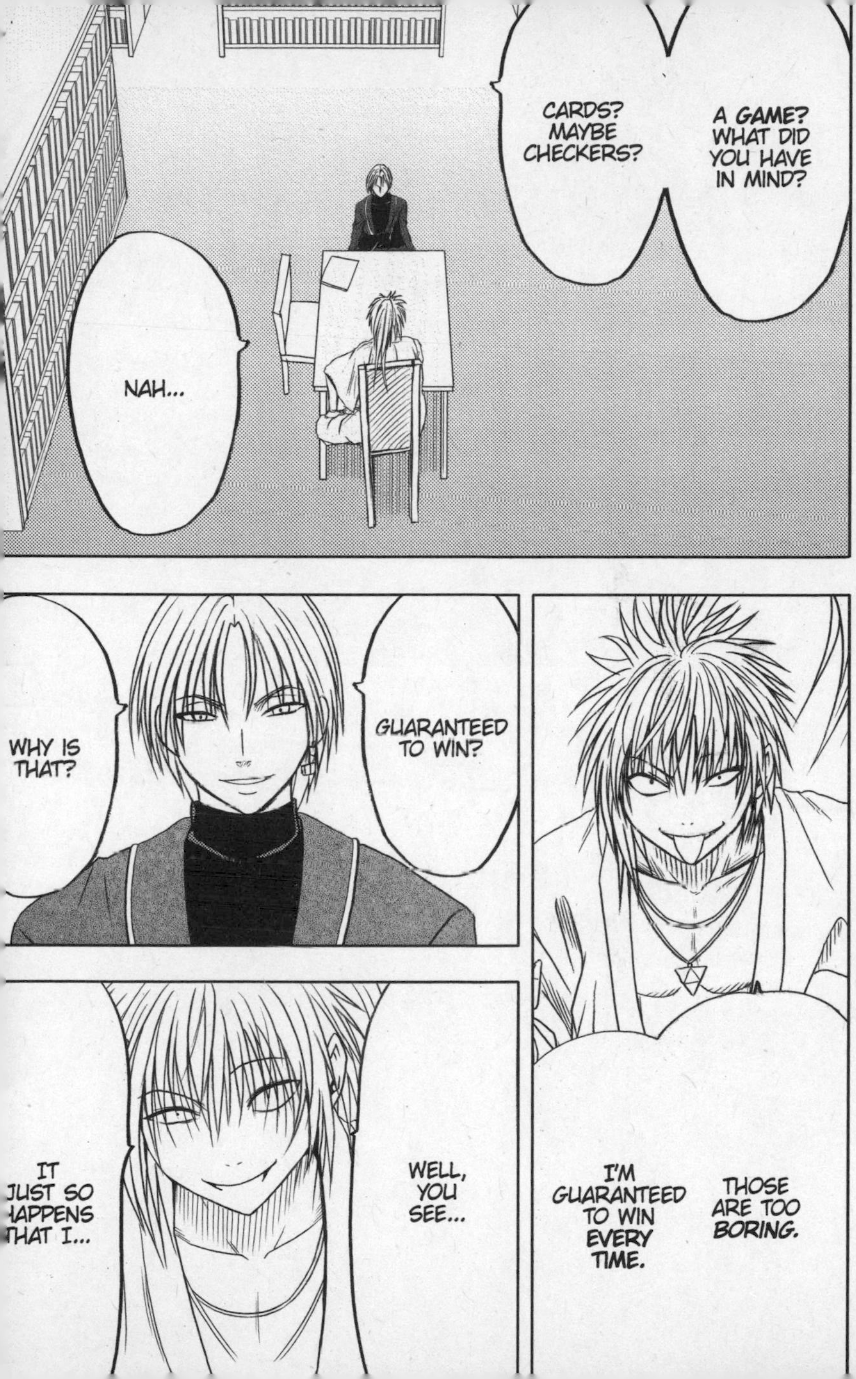
A GAME? WHAT DID YOU HAVE IN MIND?
CARDS? MAYBE CHECKERS?
NAH...
THOSE ARE TOO BORING.
I'M GUARANTEED TO WIN EVERY TIME.
GUARANTEED TO WIN?
WHY IS THAT?
WELL, YOU SEE...
IT JUST SO HAPPENS THAT I...

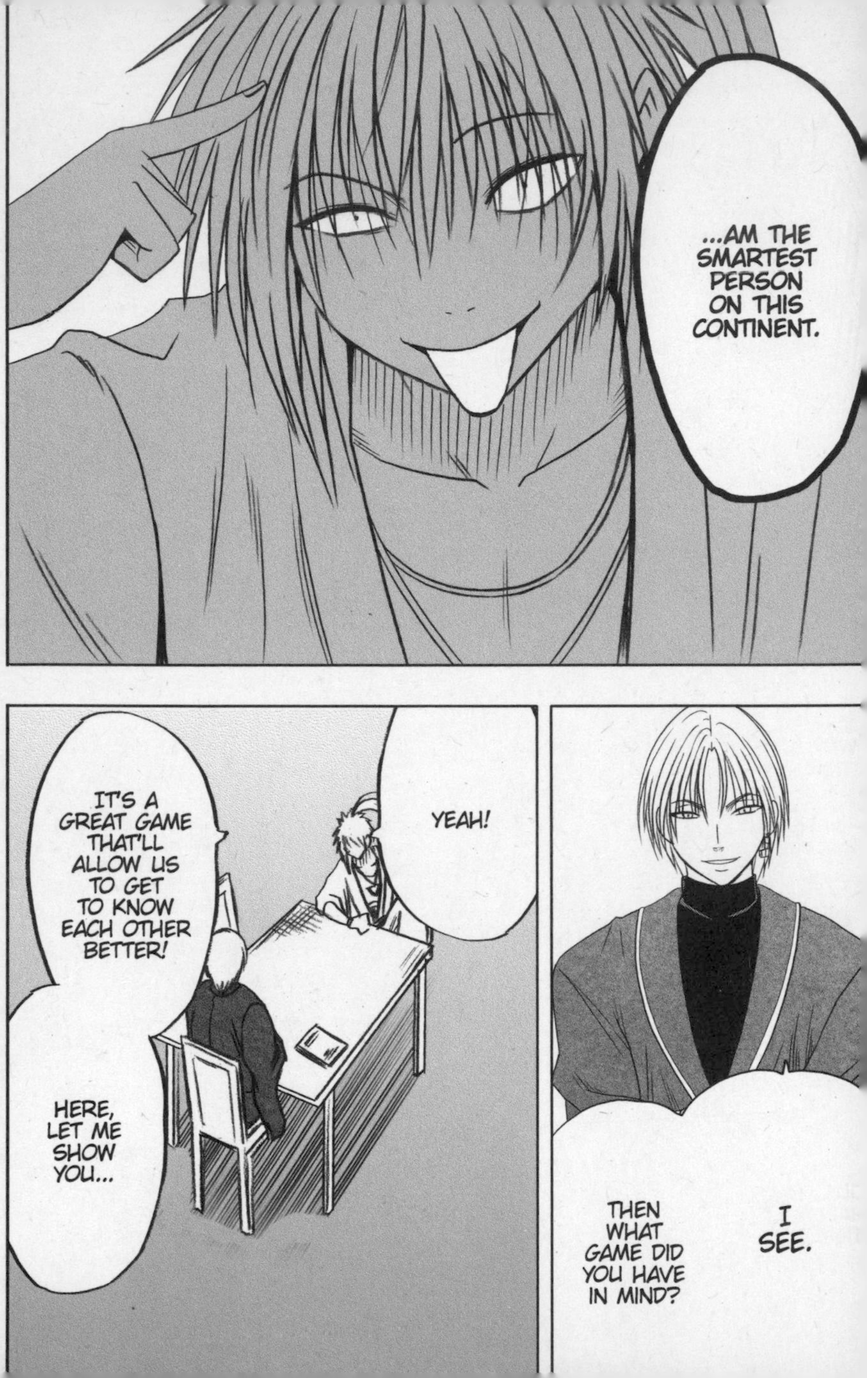
...AM THE SMARTEST PERSON ON THIS CONTINENT.
I SEE.
THEN WHAT GAME DID YOU HAVE IN MIND?
YEAH!
IT'S A GREAT GAME THAT'LL ALLOW US TO GET TO KNOW EACH OTHER BETTER!
HERE, LET ME SHOW YOU...

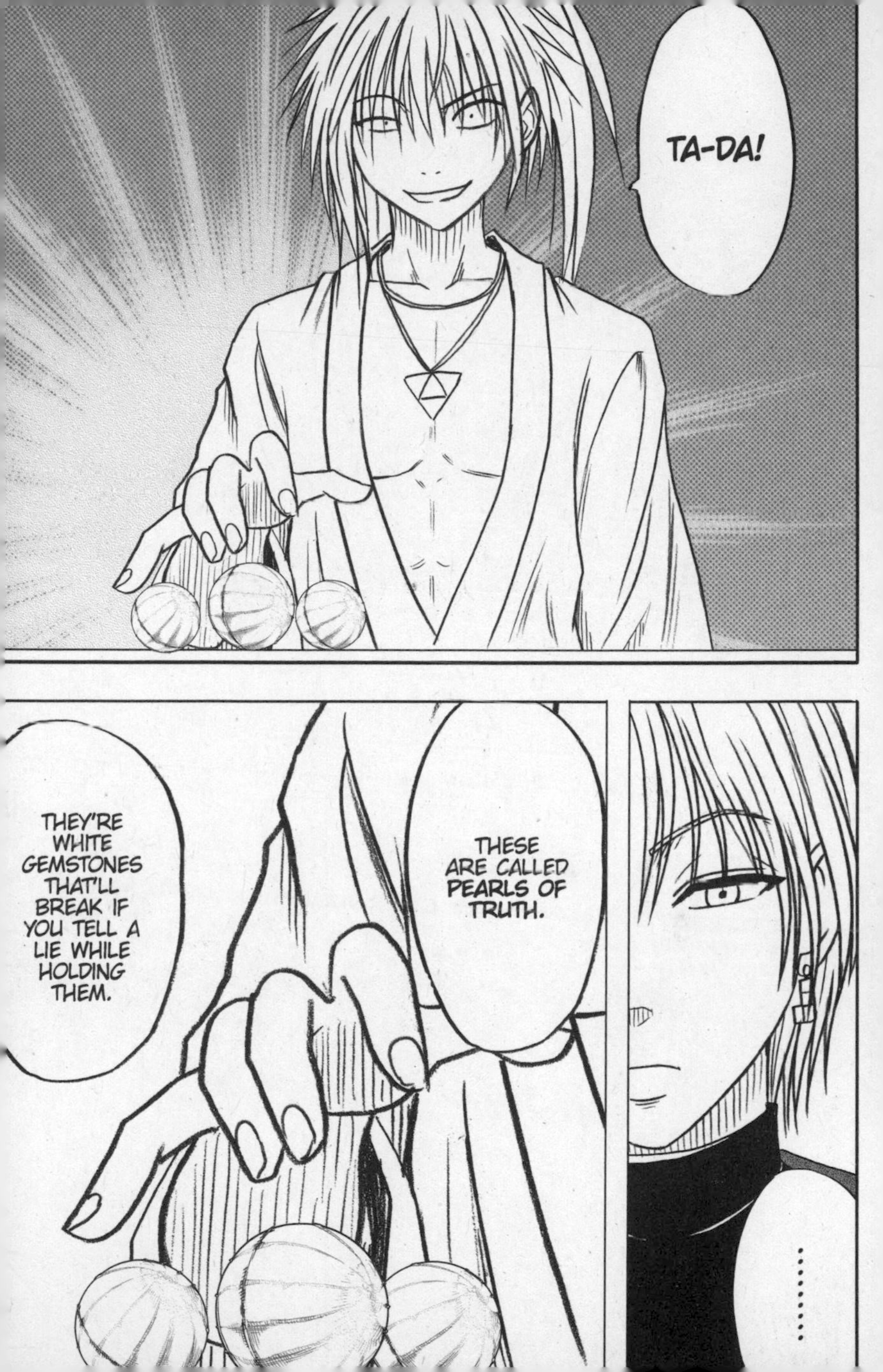
TA-DA!
......
THESE ARE CALLED PEARLS OF TRUTH.
THEY'RE WHITE GEMSTONES THAT'LL BREAK IF YOU TELL A LIE WHILE HOLDING THEM.

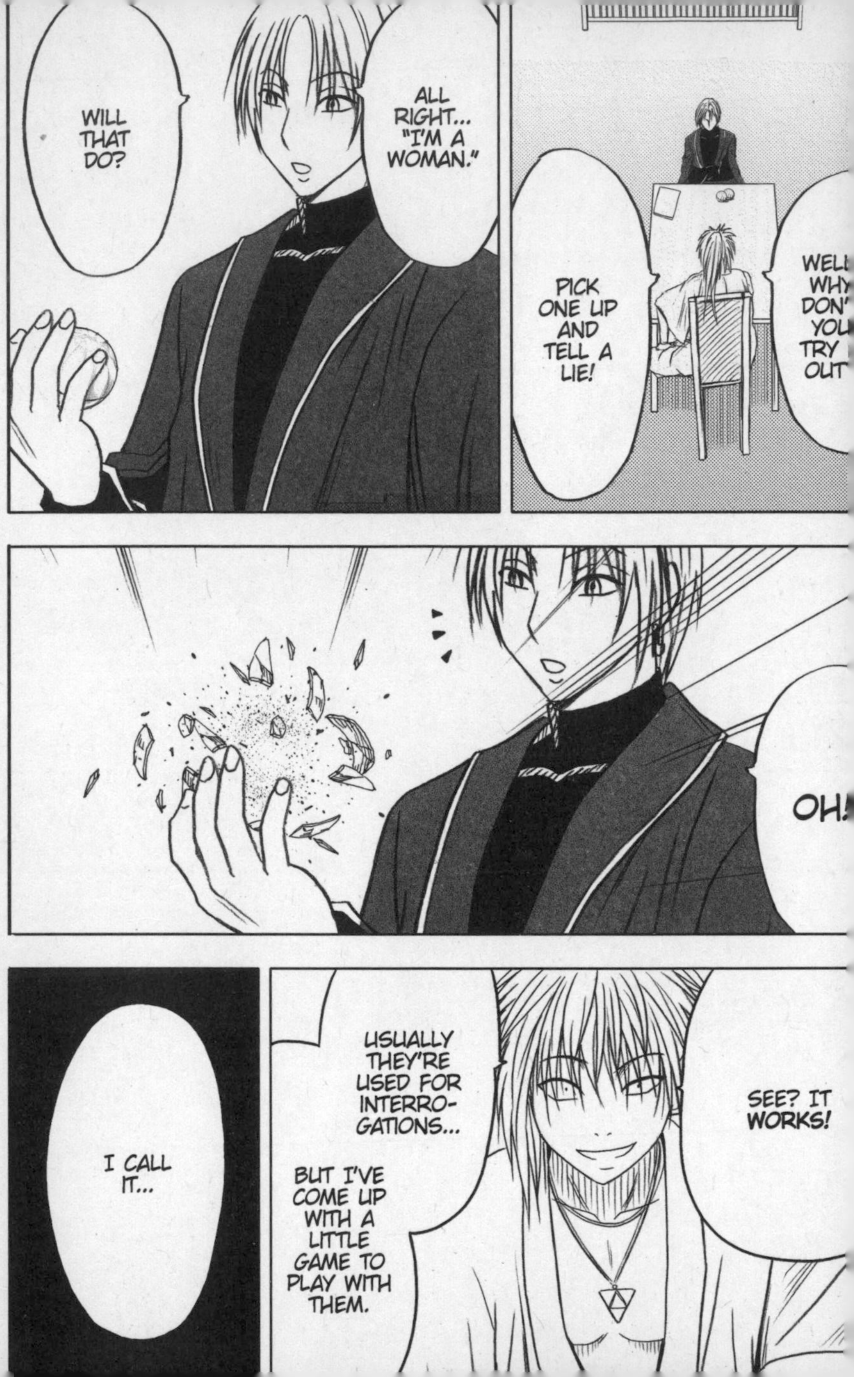
WELL WHY DON' YOU TRY OUT
PICK ONE UP AND TELL A LIE!
ALL RIGHT... "I'M A WOMAN."
WILL THAT DO?
OH!
SEE? IT WORKS!
USUALLY THEY'RE USED FOR INTERROGATIONS...
BUT I'VE COME UP WITH A LITTLE GAME TO PLAY WITH THEM.
I CALL IT...

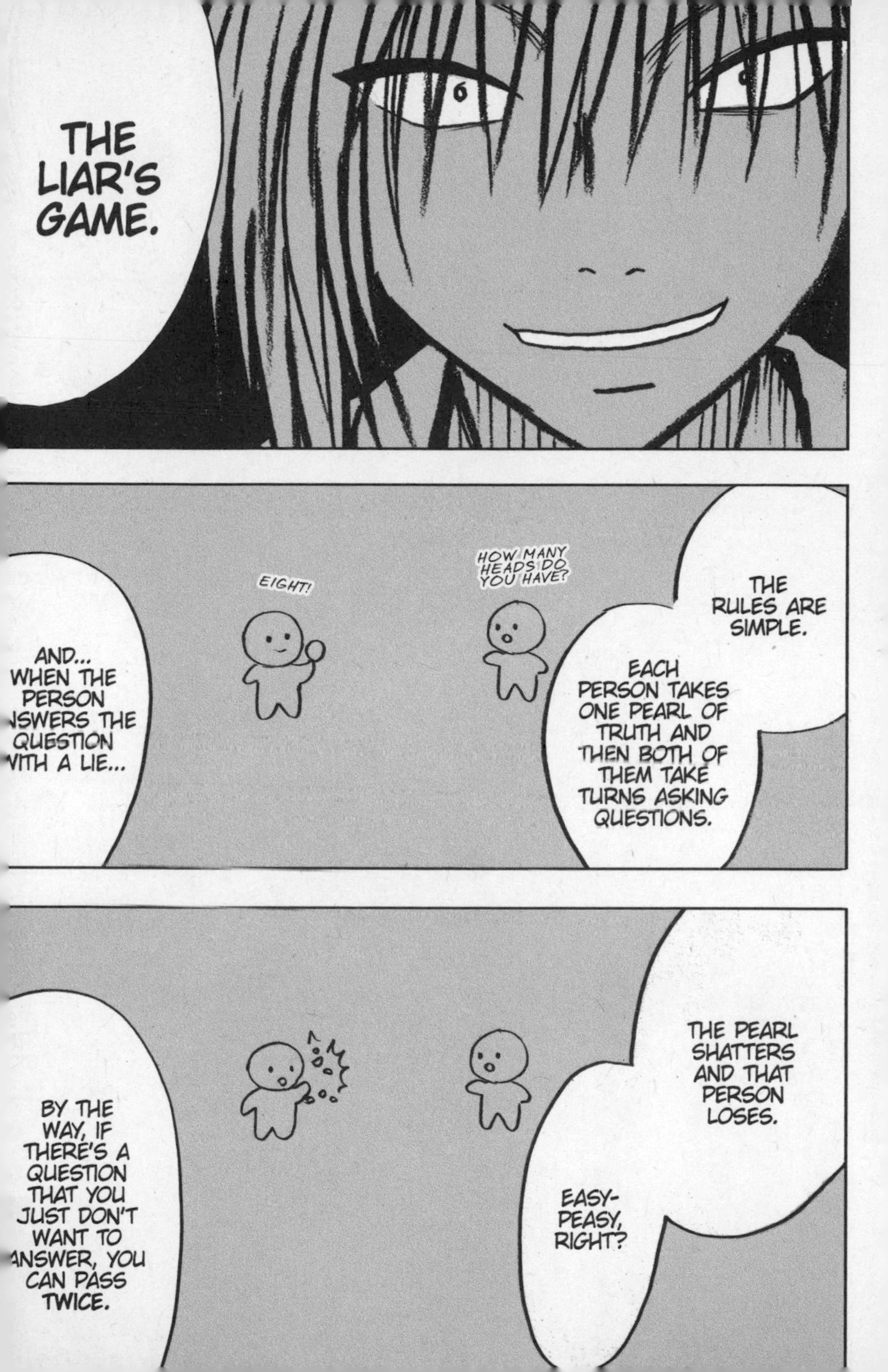
THE LIAR'S GAME.
THE RULES ARE SIMPLE.
EACH PERSON TAKES ONE PEARL OF TRUTH AND THEN BOTH OF THEM TAKE TURNS ASKING QUESTIONS.
HOW MANY HEADS DO YOU HAVE?
EIGHT!
AND... WHEN THE PERSON NSWERS THE QUESTION VITH A LIE...
THE PEARL SHATTERS AND THAT PERSON LOSES.
EASY-PEASY, RIGHT?
BY THE WAY, IF THERE'S A QUESTION THAT YOU JUST DON'T WANT TO NSWER, YOU CAN PASS TWICE.

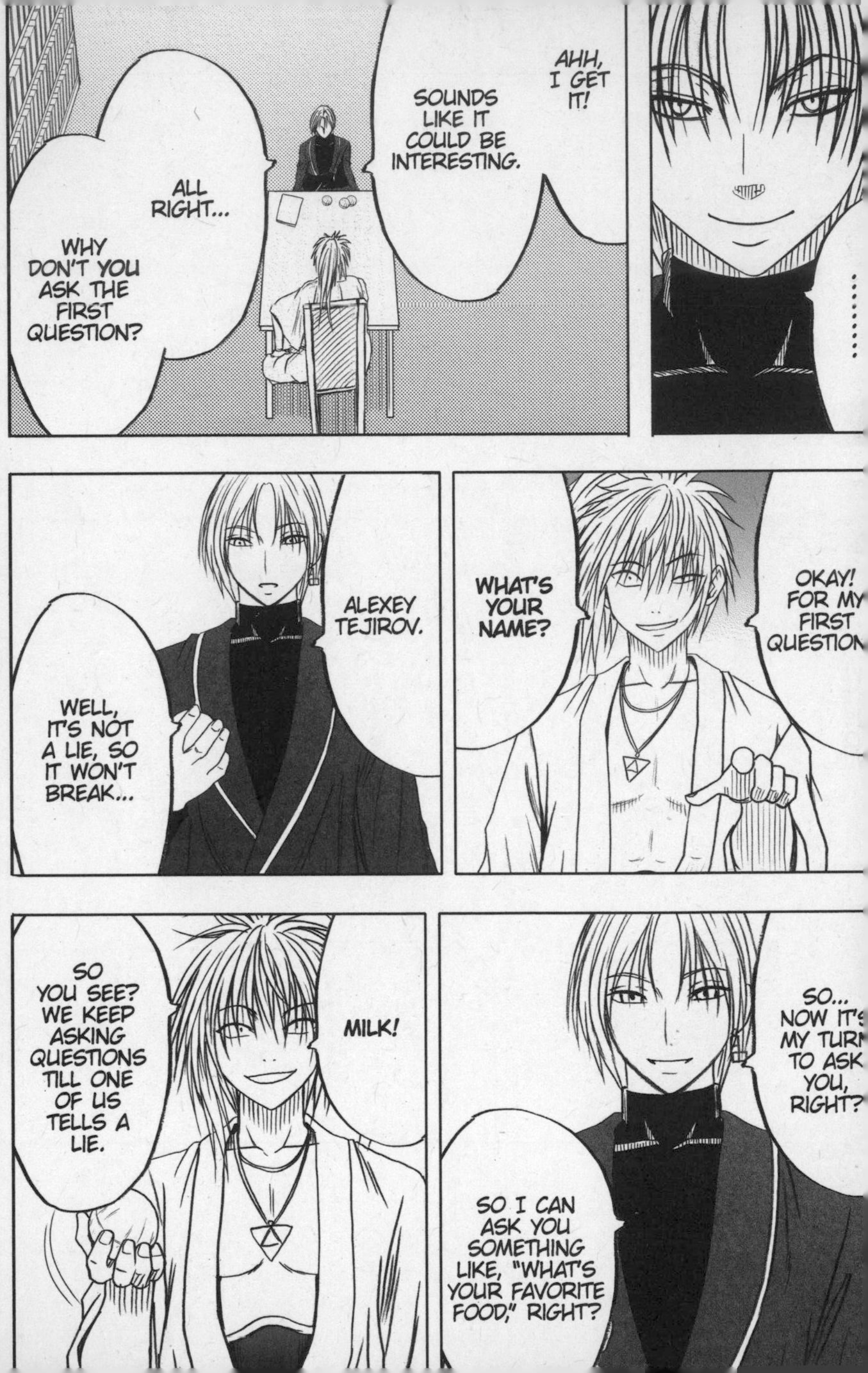
......
AHH, I GET IT!
SOUNDS LIKE IT COULD BE INTERESTING.
ALL RIGHT...
WHY DON'T YOU ASK THE FIRST QUESTION?
OKAY! FOR MY FIRST QUESTION
WHAT'S YOUR NAME?
ALEXEY TEJIROV.
WELL, IT'S NOT A LIE, SO IT WON'T BREAK...
SO... NOW IT'S MY TURN TO ASK YOU, RIGHT?
SO I CAN ASK YOU SOMETHING LIKE, "WHAT'S YOUR FAVORITE FOOD," RIGHT?
MILK!
SO YOU SEE? WE KEEP ASKING QUESTIONS TILL ONE OF US TELLS A LIE.

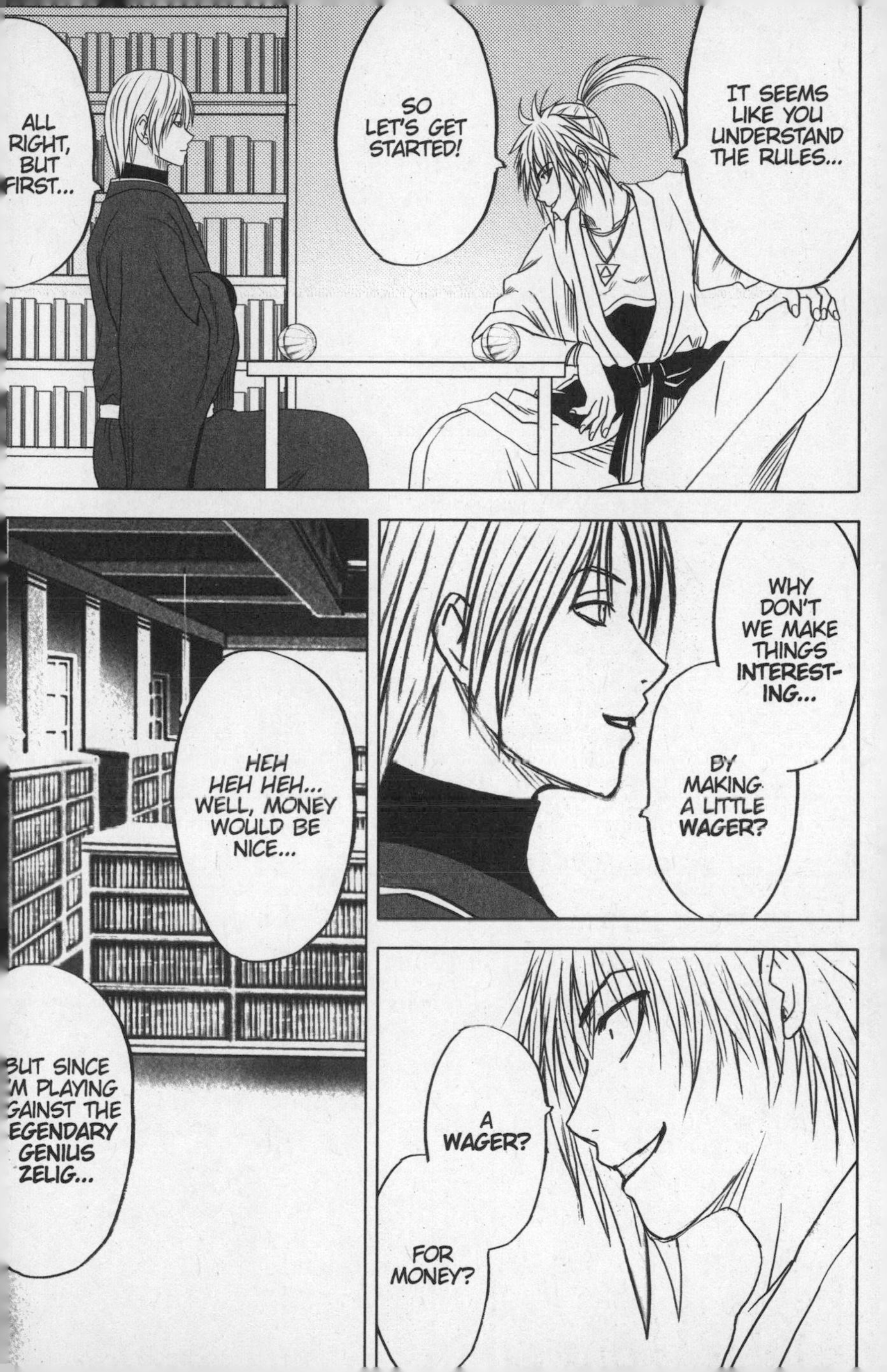
IT SEEMS LIKE YOU UNDERSTAND THE RULES...
SO LET'S GET STARTED!
ALL RIGHT, BUT FIRST...
WHY DON'T WE MAKE THINGS INTEREST-ING...
BY MAKING A LITTLE WAGER?
A WAGER?
FOR MONEY?
HEH HEH HEH... WELL, MONEY WOULD BE NICE...
BUT SINCE 'M PLAYING GAINST THE EGENDARY GENIUS ZELIG...

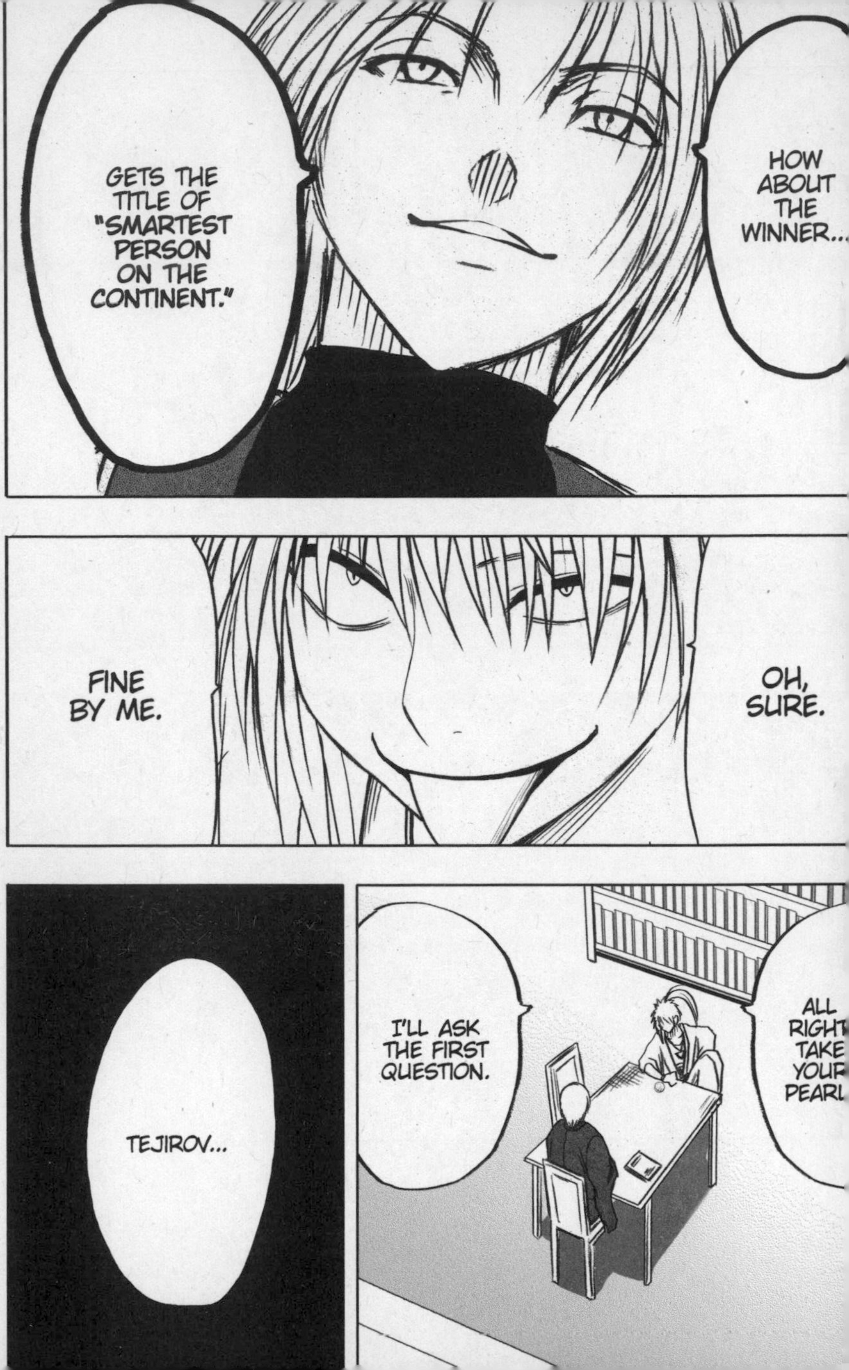
HOW ABOUT THE WINNER...
GETS THE TITLE OF "SMARTEST PERSON ON THE CONTINENT."
OH, SURE.
FINE BY ME.
ALL RIGHT TAKE YOUR PEARL
I'LL ASK THE FIRST QUESTION.
TEJIROV...

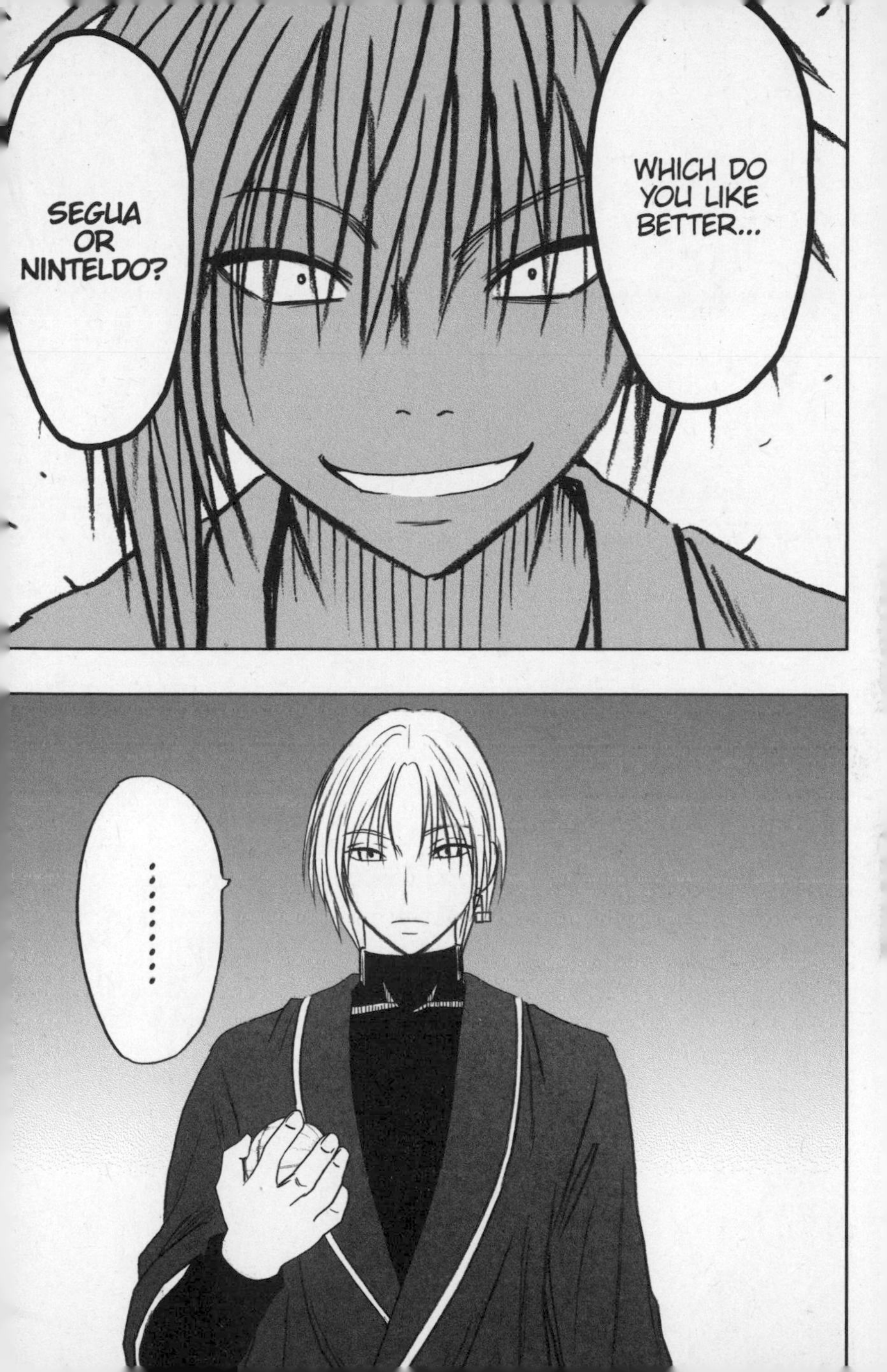
WHICH DO YOU LIKE BETTER...
SEGUA OR NINTELDO?
....

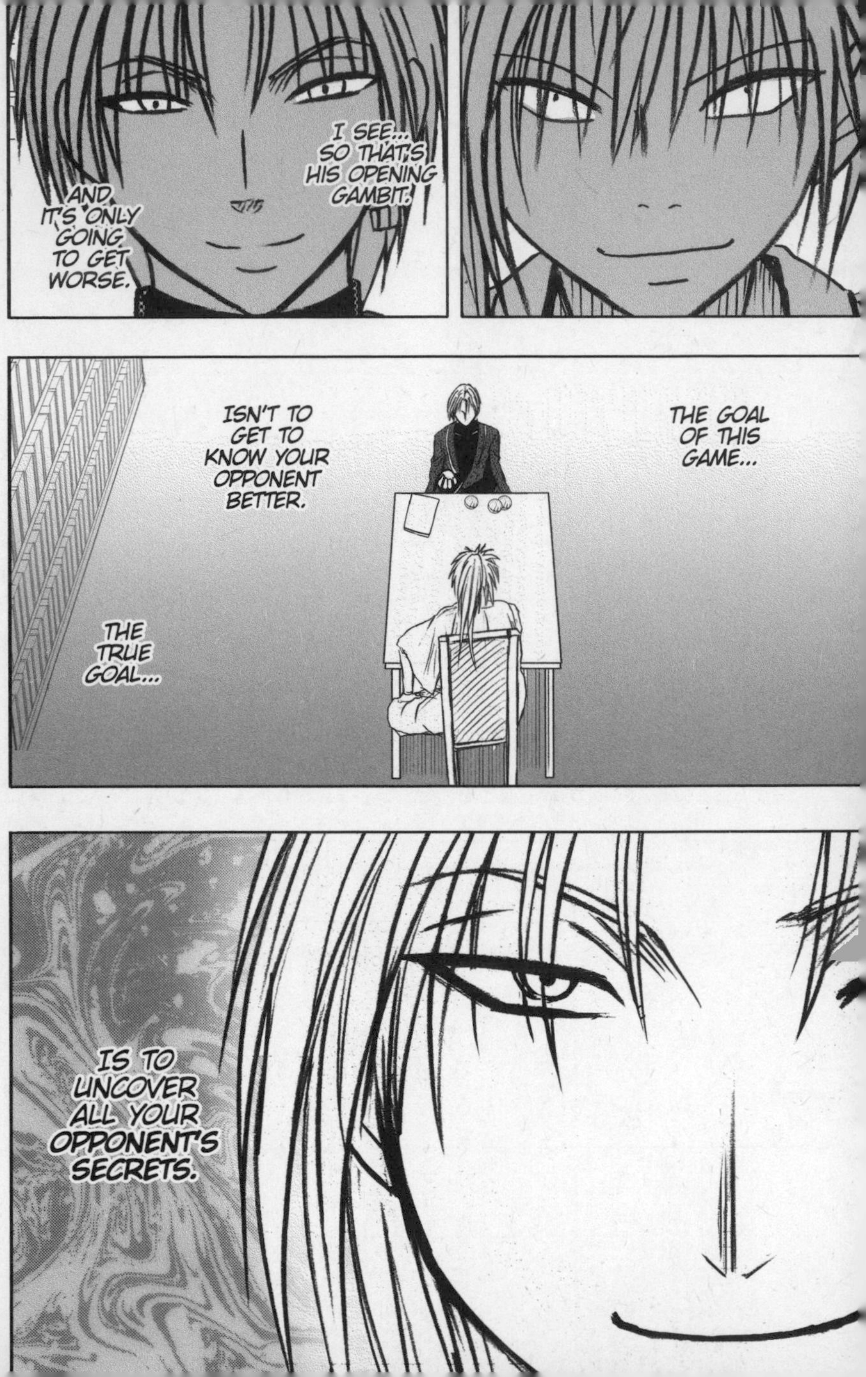
I SEE... SO THAT'S HIS OPENING GAMBIT.
AND IT'S ONLY GOING TO GET WORSE.
THE GOAL OF THIS GAME...
ISN'T TO GET TO KNOW YOUR OPPONENT BETTER.
THE TRUE GOAL...
IS TO UNCOVER ALL YOUR OPPONENT'S SECRETS.

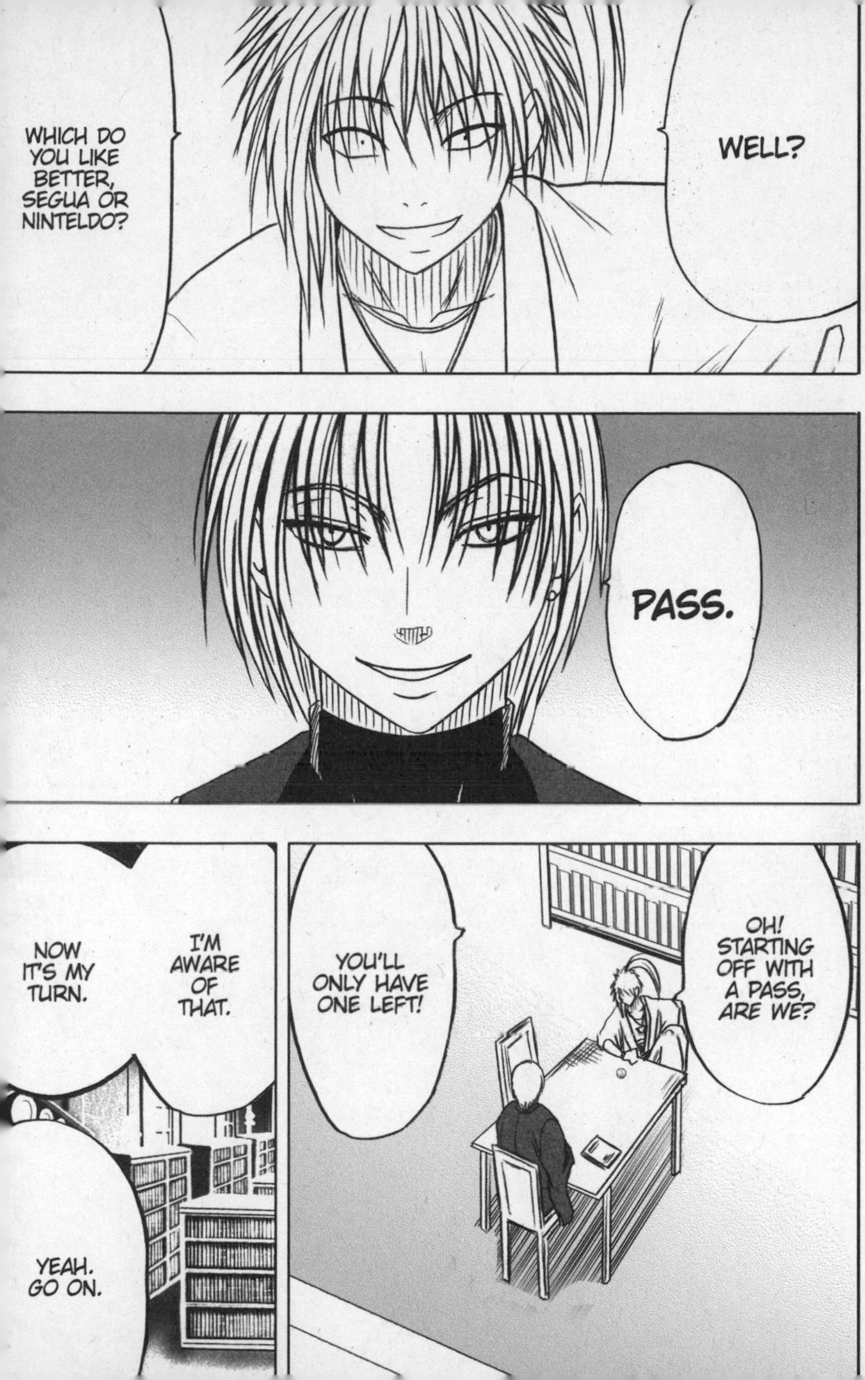
WELL?
WHICH DO YOU LIKE BETTER, SEGUA OR NINTELDO?
PASS.
OH! STARTING OFF WITH A PASS, ARE WE?
YOU'LL ONLY HAVE ONE LEFT!
I'M AWARE OF THAT.
NOW IT'S MY TURN.
YEAH. GO ON.

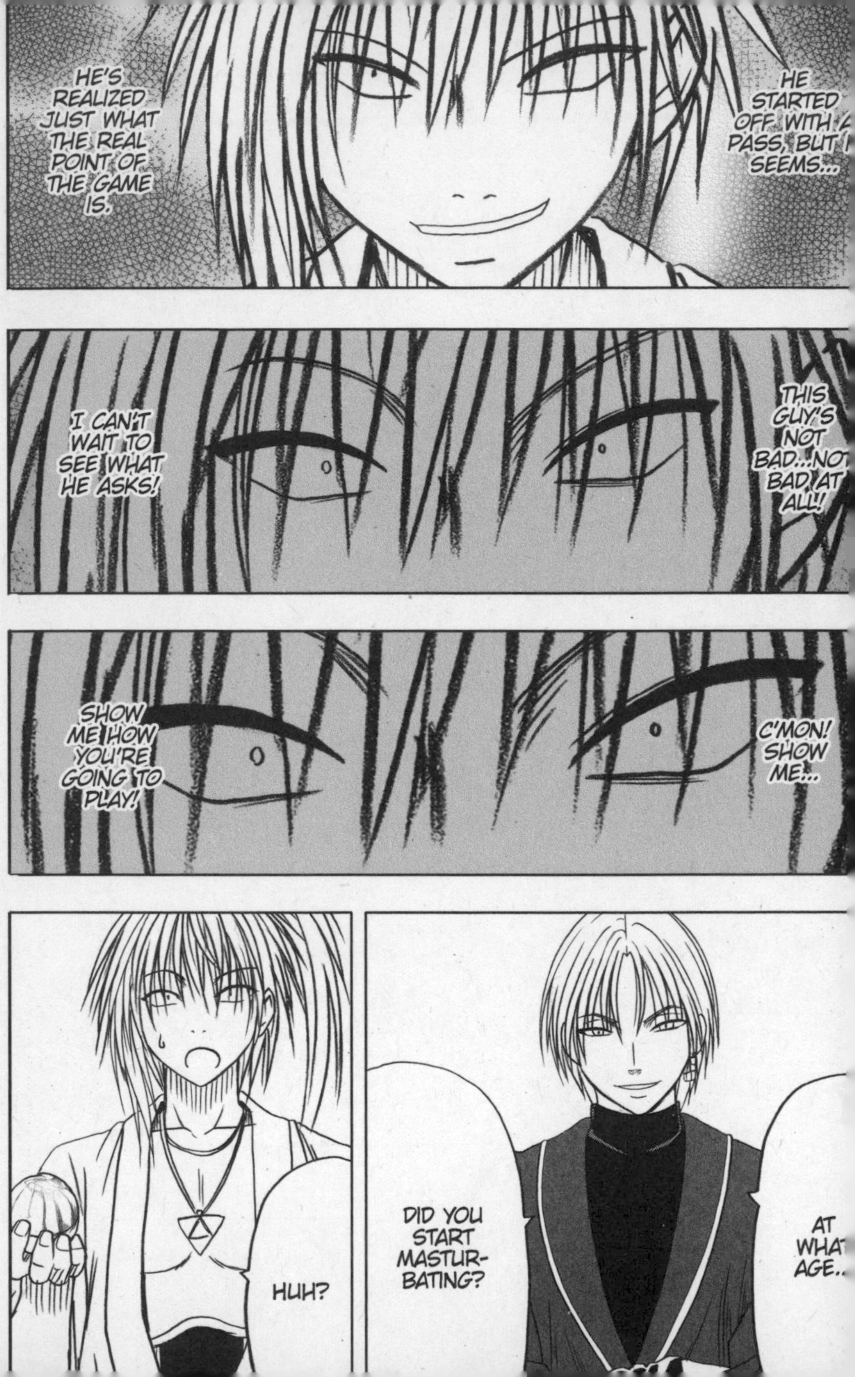
HE STARTED OFF WITH A PASS, BUT I SEEMS...
HE'S REALIZED JUST WHAT THE REAL POINT OF THE GAME IS.
THIS GUY'S NOT BAD...NOT BAD AT ALL!
I CAN'T WAIT TO SEE WHAT HE ASKS!
C'MON! SHOW ME...
SHOW ME HOW YOU'RE GOING TO PLAY!
AT WHAT AGE..
DID YOU START MASTUR-BATING?
HUH?

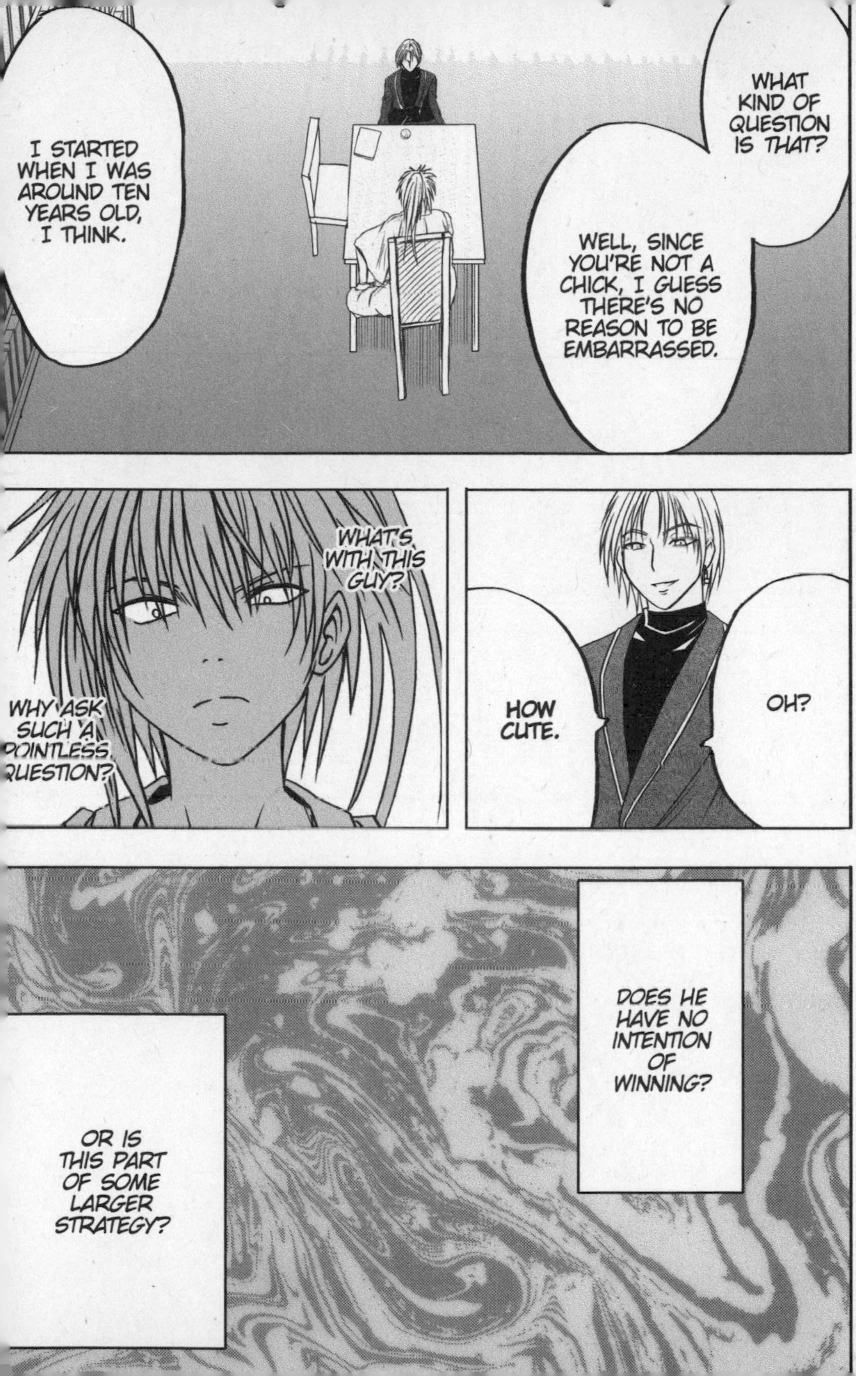
WHAT KIND OF QUESTION IS THAT?
WELL, SINCE YOU'RE NOT A CHICK, I GUESS THERE'S NO REASON TO BE EMBARRASSED.
I STARTED WHEN I WAS AROUND TEN YEARS OLD, I THINK.
OH?
HOW CUTE.
WHAT'S WITH THIS GUY?
WHY ASK SUCH A POINTLESS QUESTION?
DOES HE HAVE NO INTENTION OF WINNING?
OR IS THIS PART OF SOME LARGER STRATEGY?

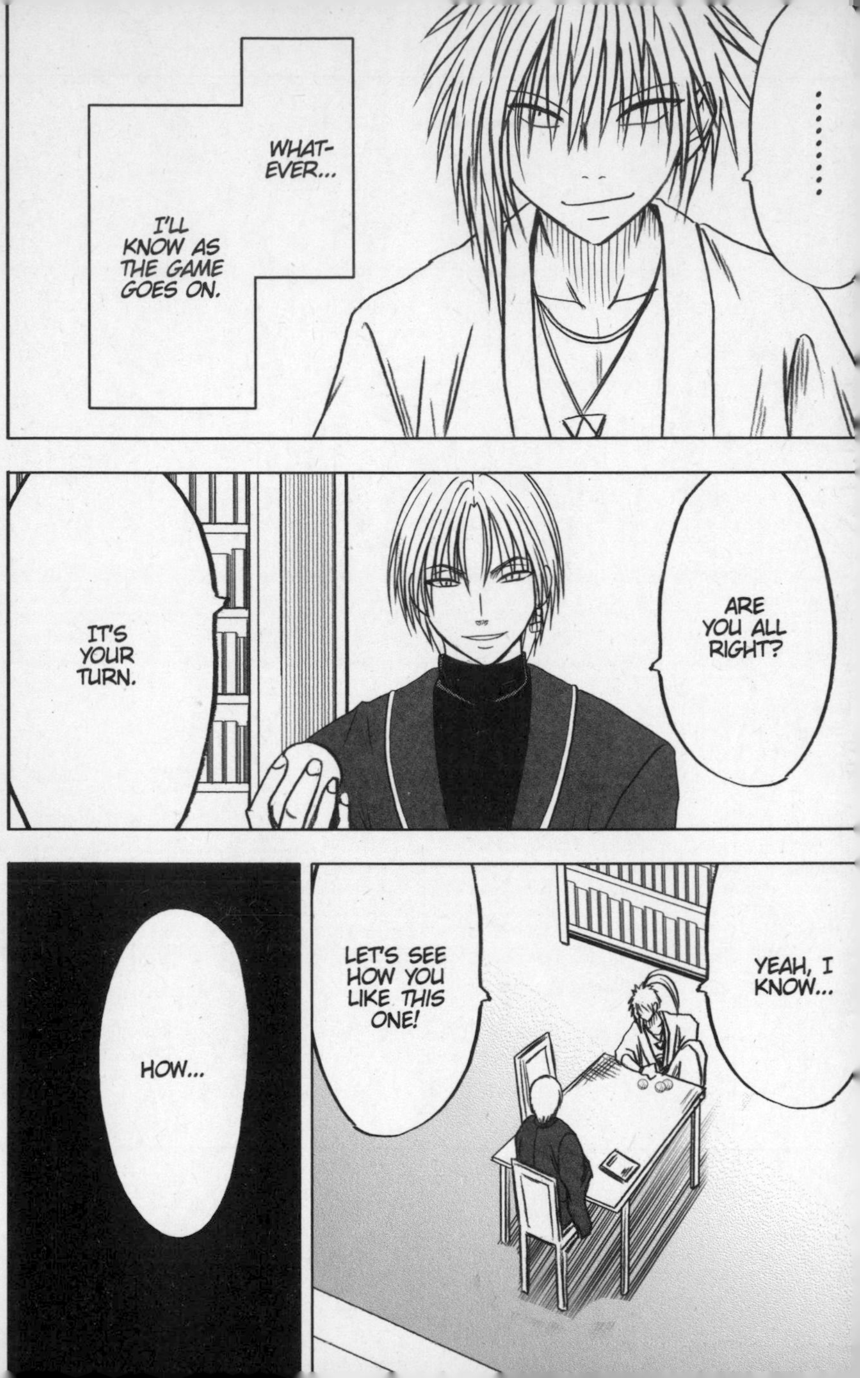
......
WHATEVER...
I'LL KNOW AS THE GAME GOES ON.
ARE YOU ALL RIGHT?
IT'S YOUR TURN.
YEAH, I KNOW...
LET'S SEE HOW YOU LIKE THIS ONE!
HOW...

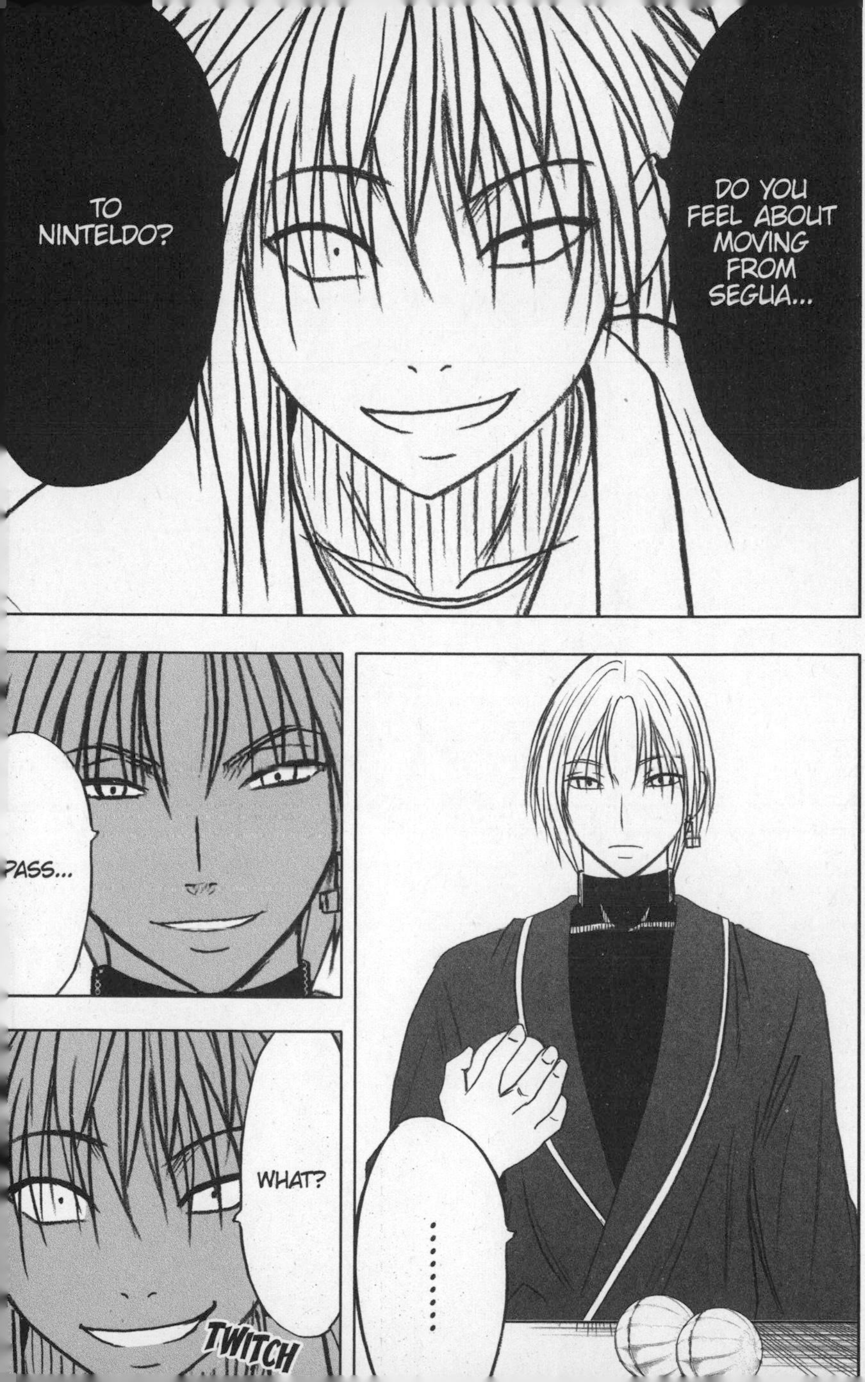
DO YOU FEEL ABOUT MOVING FROM SEGUA...
TO NINTELDO?
......
PASS...
WHAT?
TWITCH

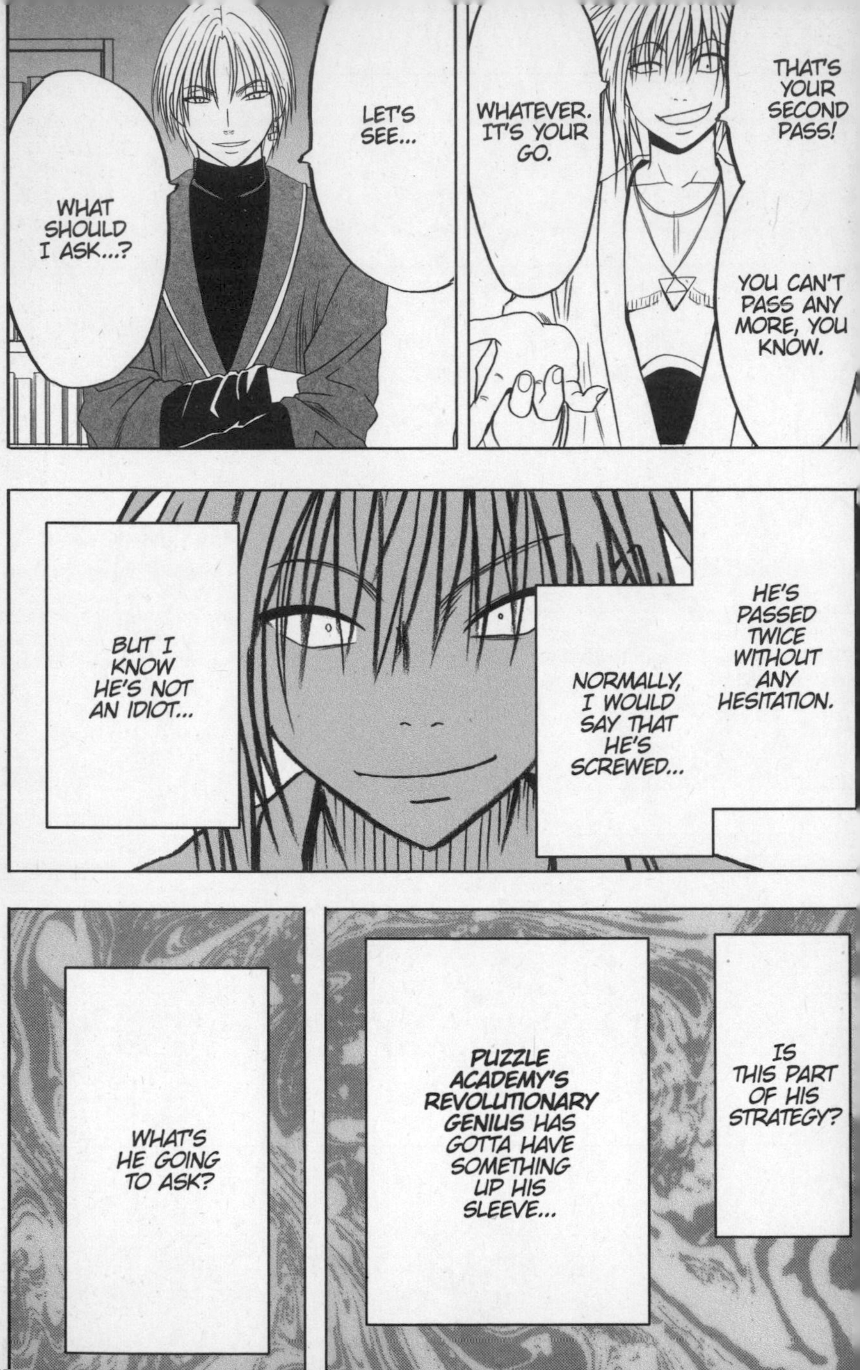
THAT'S YOUR SECOND PASS!
YOU CAN'T PASS ANY MORE, YOU KNOW.
WHATEVER. IT'S YOUR GO.
LET'S SEE...
WHAT SHOULD I ASK...?
HE'S PASSED TWICE WITHOUT ANY HESITATION.
NORMALLY, I WOULD SAY THAT HE'S SCREWED...
BUT I KNOW HE'S NOT AN IDIOT...
IS THIS PART OF HIS STRATEGY?
PUZZLE ACADEMY'S REVOLUTIONARY GENIUS HAS GOTTA HAVE SOMETHING UP HIS SLEEVE...
WHAT'S HE GOING TO ASK?

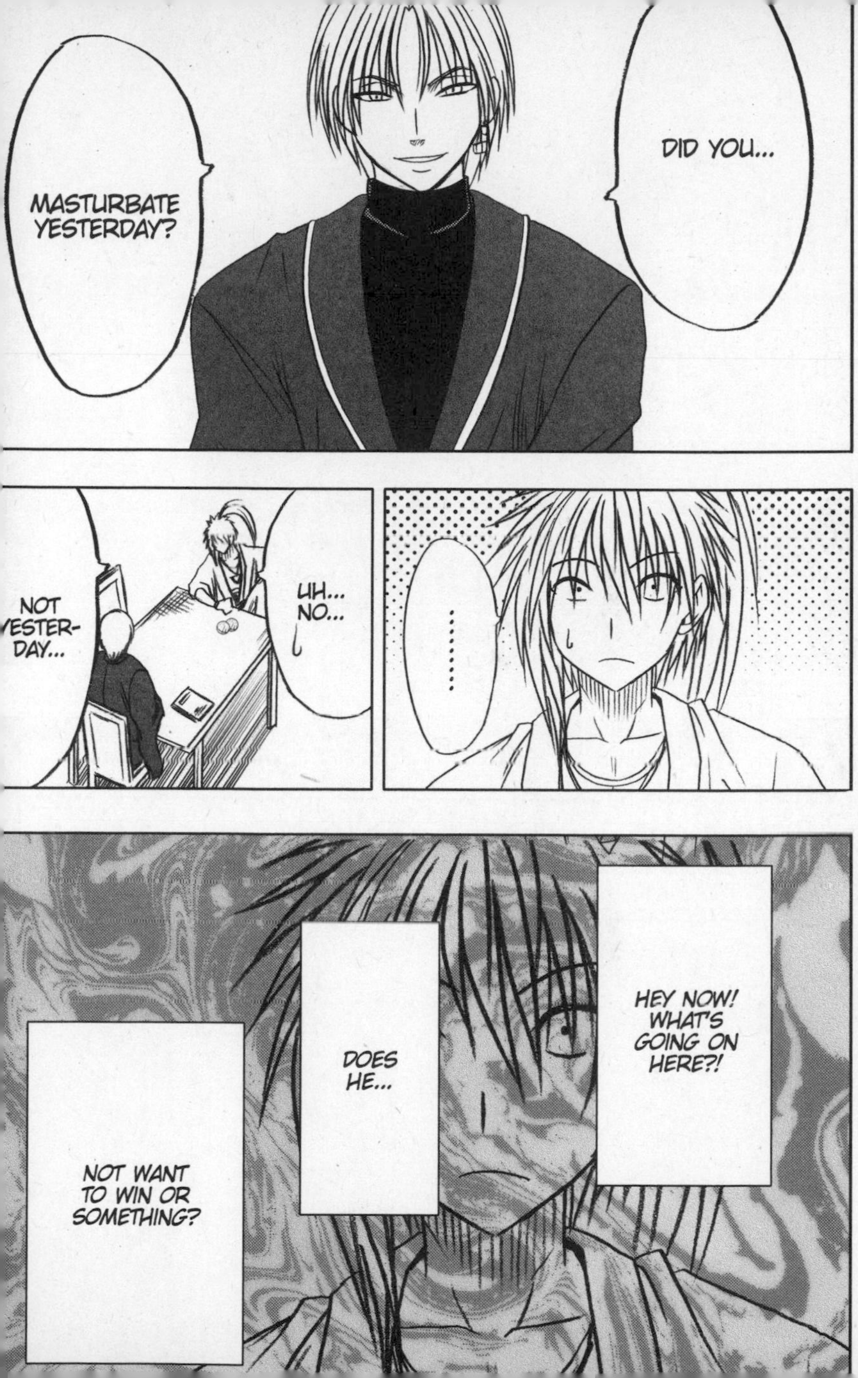
DID YOU...
MASTURBATE YESTERDAY?
......
UH... NO...
NOT YESTER-DAY...
HEY NOW! WHAT'S GOING ON HERE?!
DOES HE...
NOT WANT TO WIN OR SOMETHING?

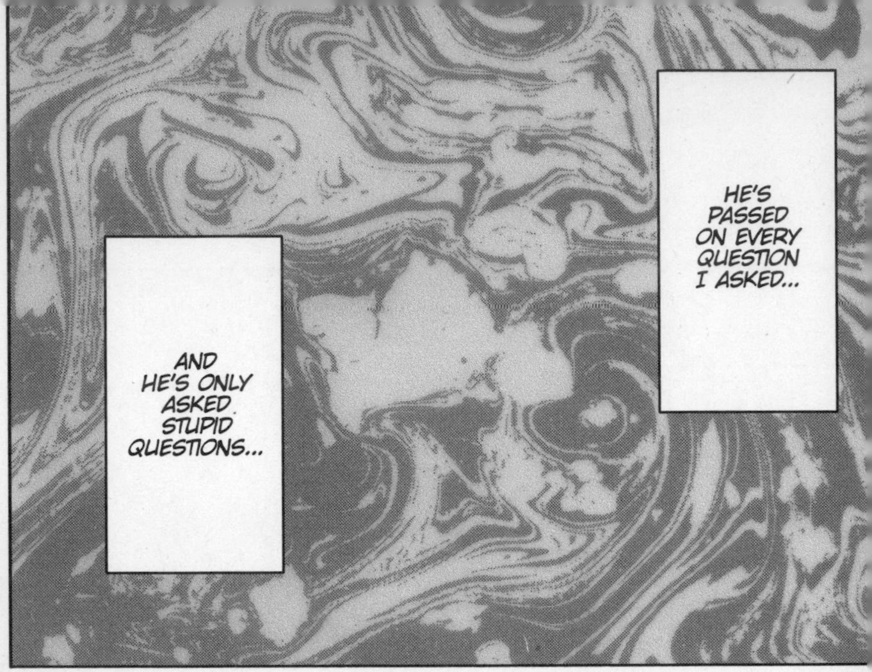
HE'S PASSED ON EVERY QUESTION I ASKED...
AND HE'S ONLY ASKED STUPID QUESTIONS...

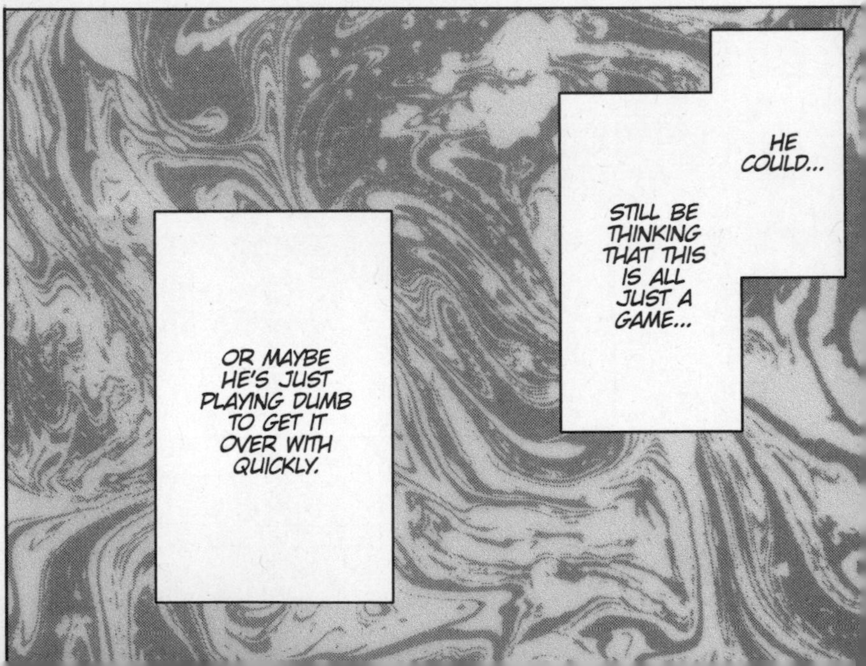
HE COULD...
STILL BE THINKING THAT THIS IS ALL JUST A GAME...
OR MAYBE HE'S JUST PLAYING DUMB TO GET IT OVER WITH QUICKLY.

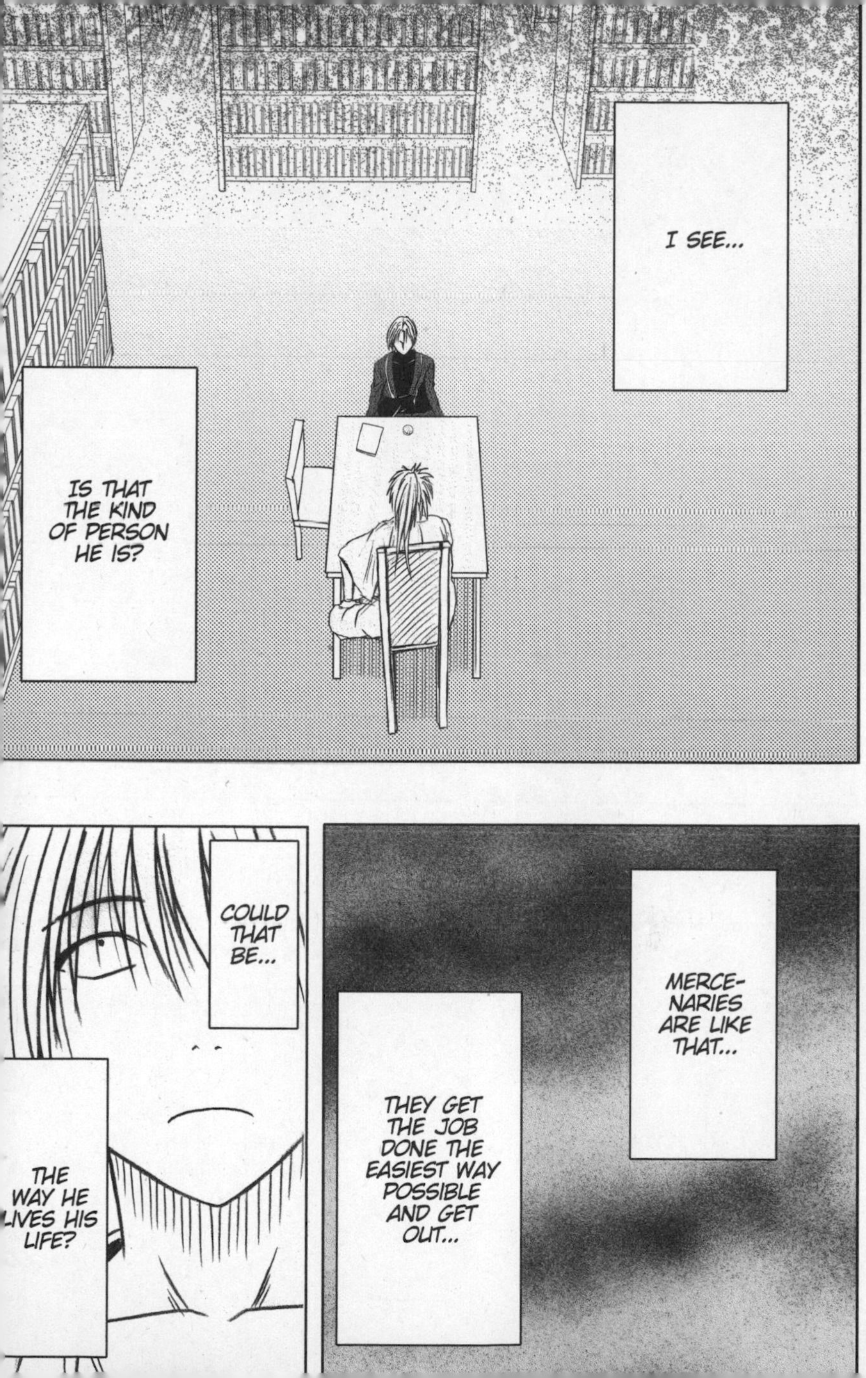
I SEE...
IS THAT THE KIND OF PERSON HE IS?
MERCE-NARIES ARE LIKE THAT...
THEY GET THE JOB DONE THE EASIEST WAY POSSIBLE AND GET OUT...
COULD THAT BE...
THE WAY HE LIVES HIS LIFE?

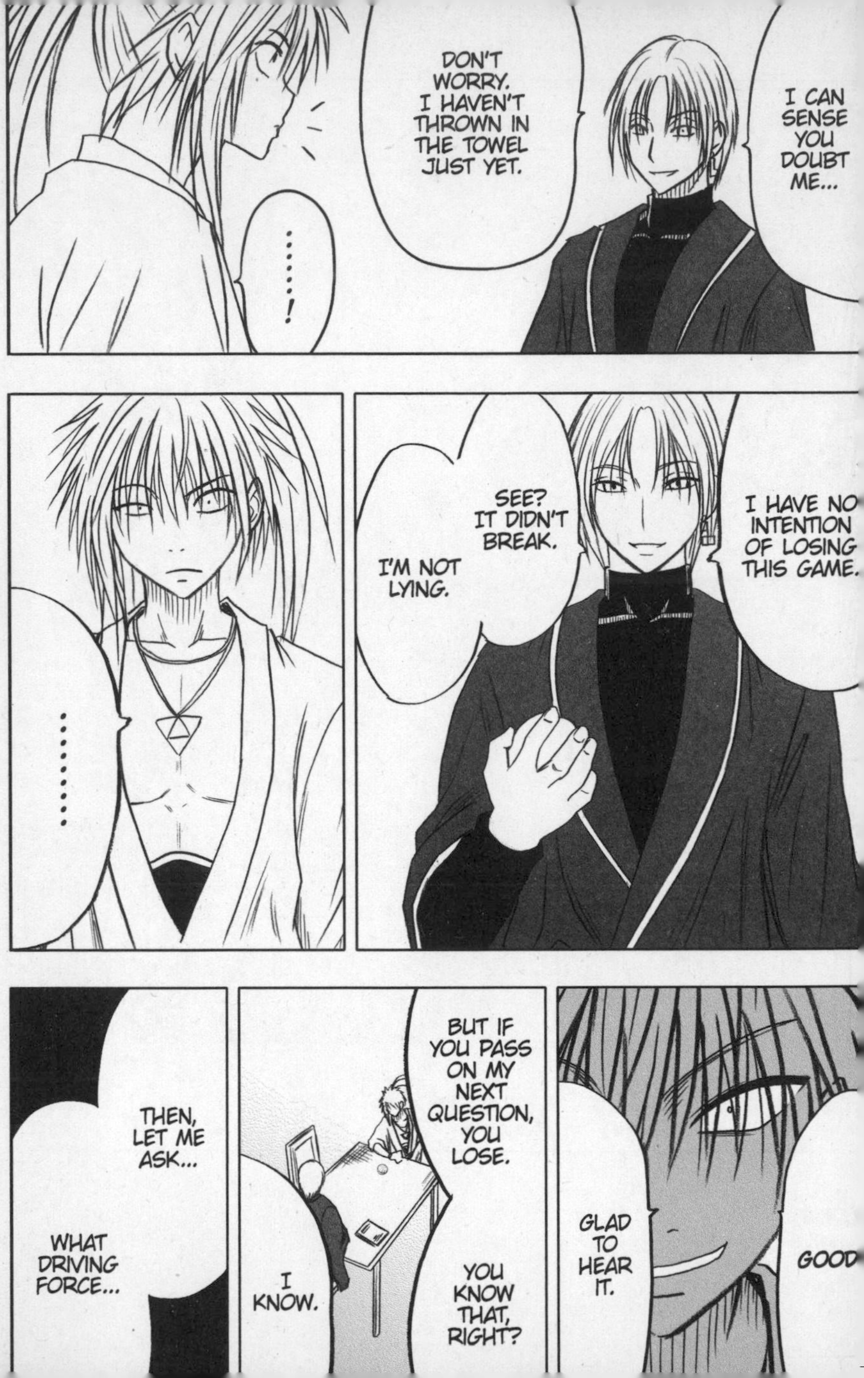
I CAN SENSE YOU DOUBT ME...
DON'T WORRY. I HAVEN'T THROWN IN THE TOWEL JUST YET.
......!
I HAVE NO INTENTION OF LOSING THIS GAME.
SEE? IT DIDN'T BREAK.
I'M NOT LYING.
....
GOOD
GLAD TO HEAR IT.
BUT IF YOU PASS ON MY NEXT QUESTION, YOU LOSE.
YOU KNOW THAT, RIGHT?
I KNOW.
THEN, LET ME ASK...
WHAT DRIVING FORCE...

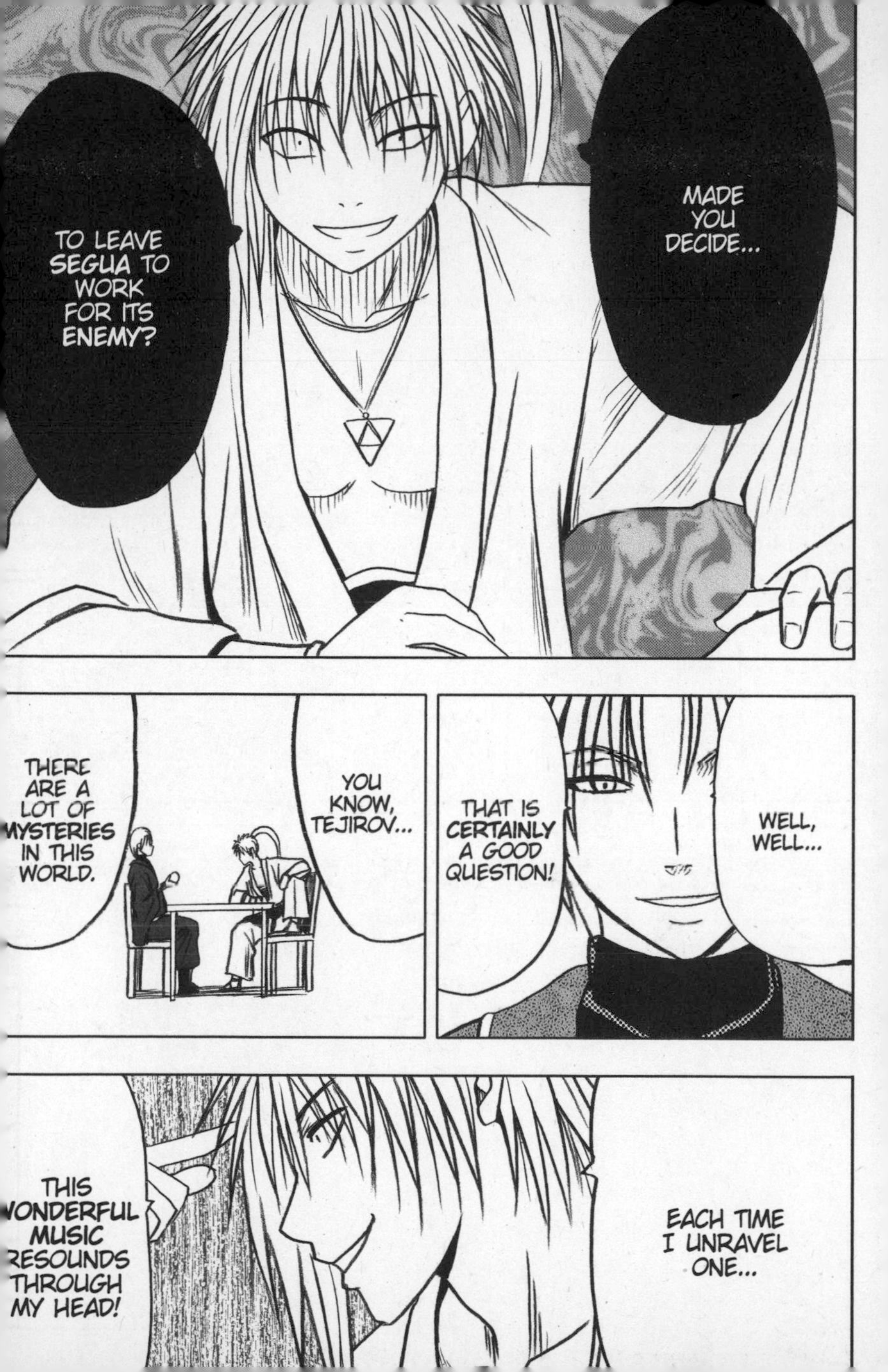
MADE YOU DECIDE...
TO LEAVE SEGUA TO WORK FOR ITS ENEMY?
WELL, WELL...
THAT IS CERTAINLY A GOOD QUESTION!
YOU KNOW, TEJIROV...
THERE ARE A LOT OF MYSTERIES IN THIS WORLD.
EACH TIME I UNRAVEL ONE...
THIS WONDERFUL MUSIC RESOUNDS THROUGH MY HEAD!

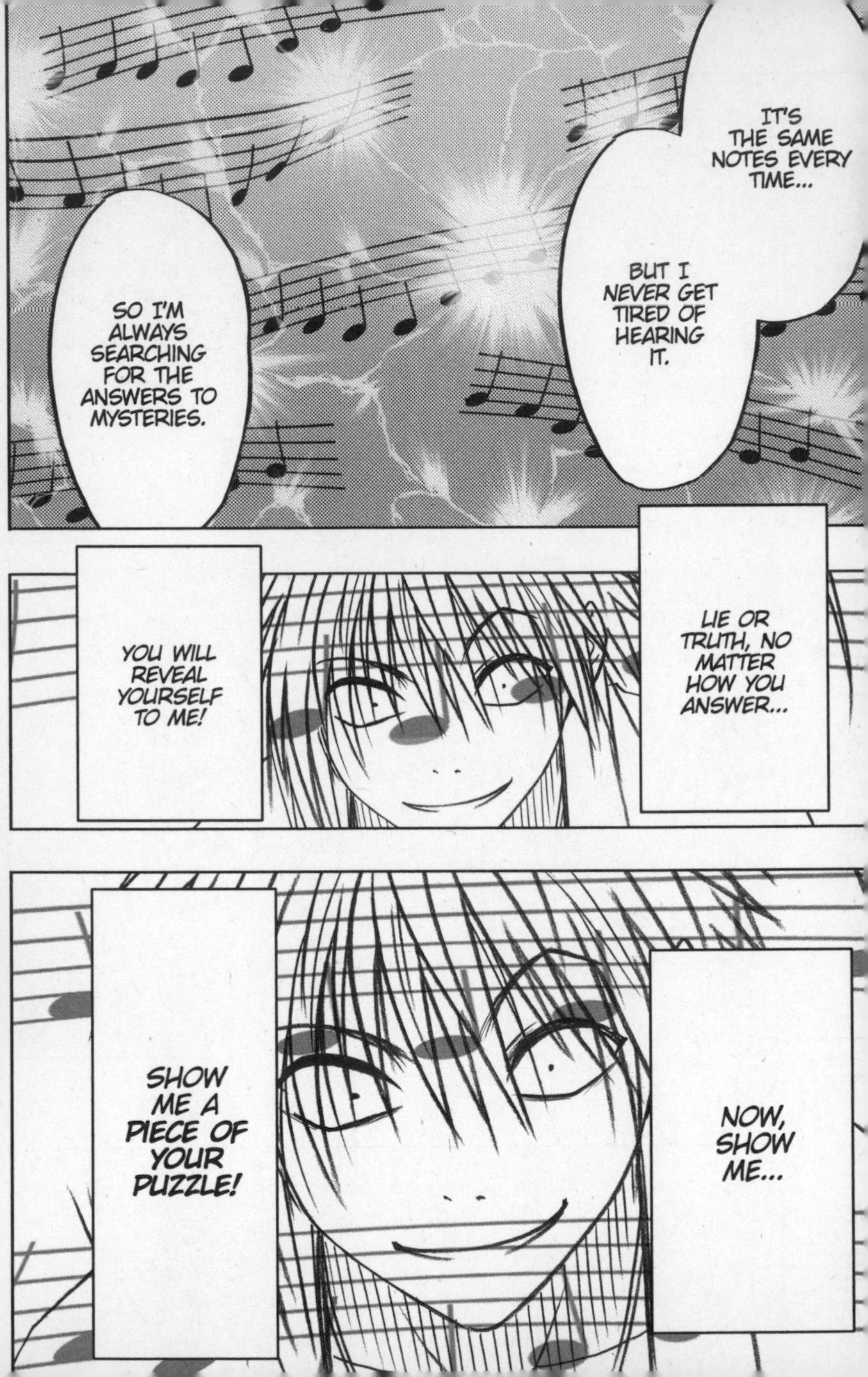
IT'S THE SAME NOTES EVERY TIME...
BUT I NEVER GET TIRED OF HEARING IT.
SO I'M ALWAYS SEARCHING FOR THE ANSWERS TO MYSTERIES.
LIE OR TRUTH, NO MATTER HOW YOU ANSWER...
YOU WILL REVEAL YOURSELF TO ME!
NOW, SHOW ME...
SHOW ME A PIECE OF YOUR PUZZLE!

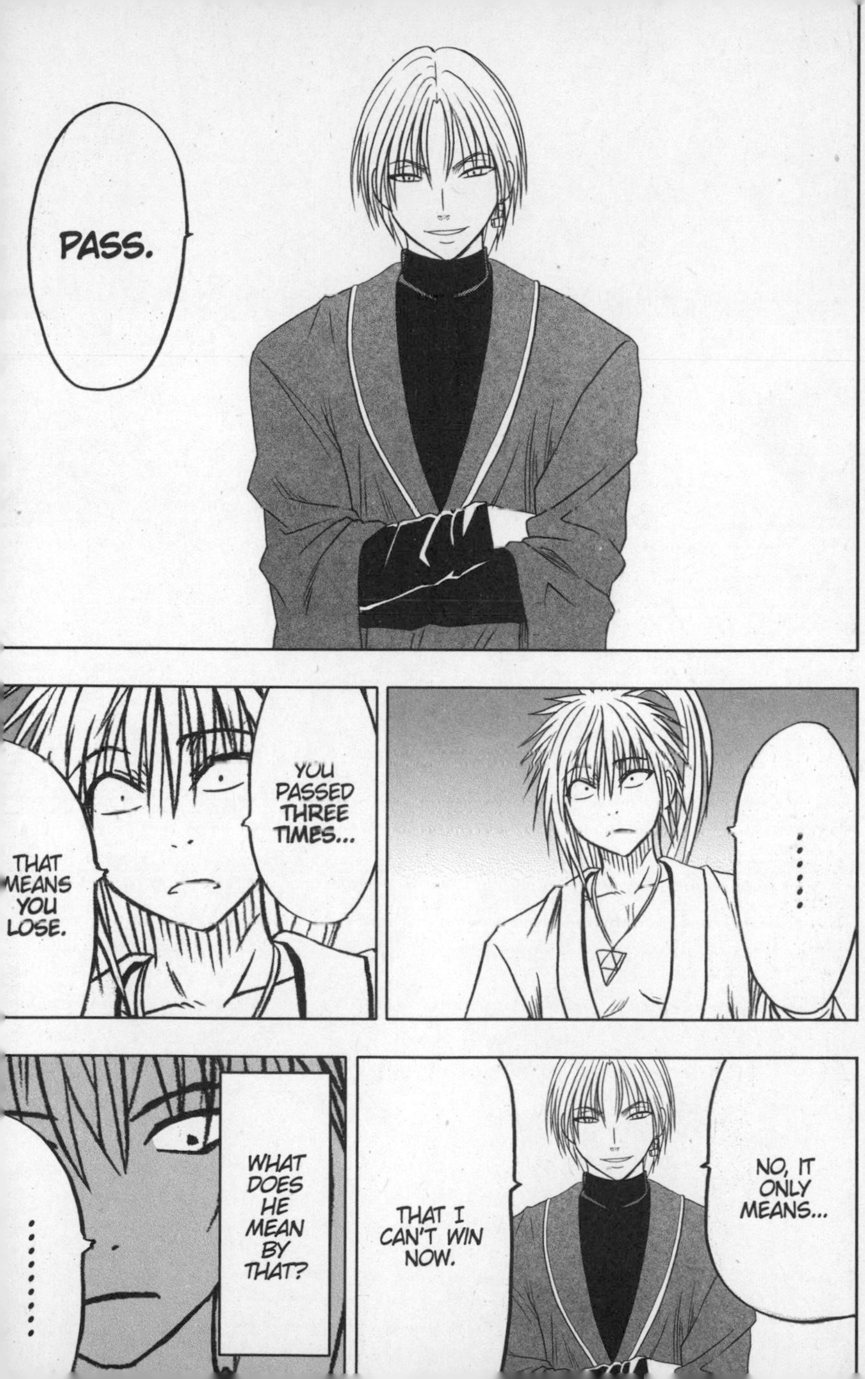
PASS.
......
YOU PASSED THREE TIMES...
THAT MEANS YOU LOSE.
NO, IT ONLY MEANS...
THAT I CAN'T WIN NOW.
WHAT DOES HE MEAN BY THAT?
....

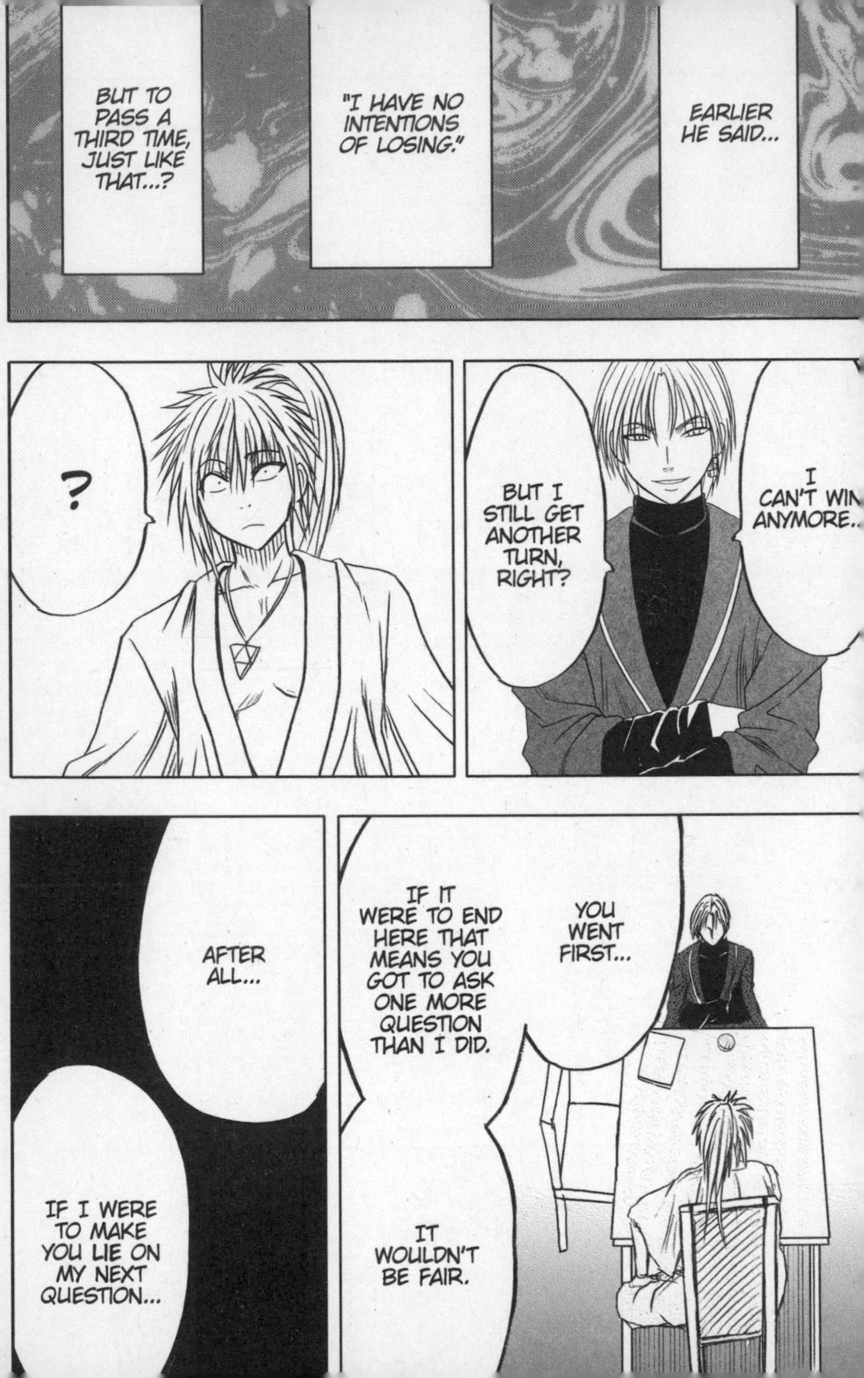
EARLIER HE SAID...
"I HAVE NO INTENTIONS OF LOSING."
BUT TO PASS A THIRD TIME, JUST LIKE THAT...?
I CAN'T WIN ANYMORE..
BUT I STILL GET ANOTHER TURN, RIGHT?
?
YOU WENT FIRST...
IF IT WERE TO END HERE THAT MEANS YOU GOT TO ASK ONE MORE QUESTION THAN I DID.
IT WOULDN'T BE FAIR.
AFTER ALL...
IF I WERE TO MAKE YOU LIE ON MY NEXT QUESTION...

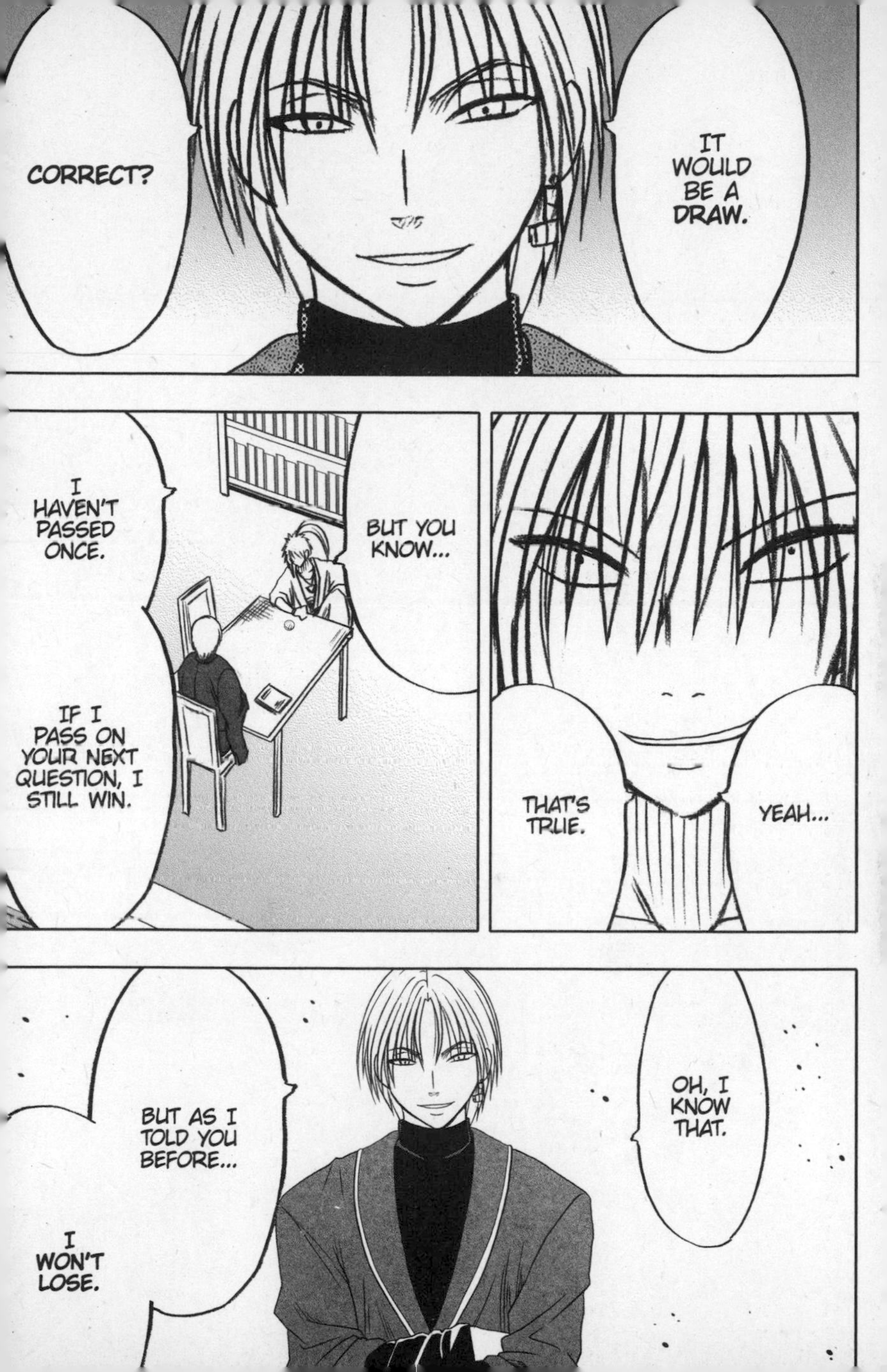
IT WOULD BE A DRAW.
CORRECT?
YEAH...
THAT'S TRUE.
BUT YOU KNOW...
I HAVEN'T PASSED ONCE.
IF I PASS ON YOUR NEXT QUESTION, I STILL WIN.
OH, I KNOW THAT.
BUT AS I TOLD YOU BEFORE...
I WON'T LOSE.

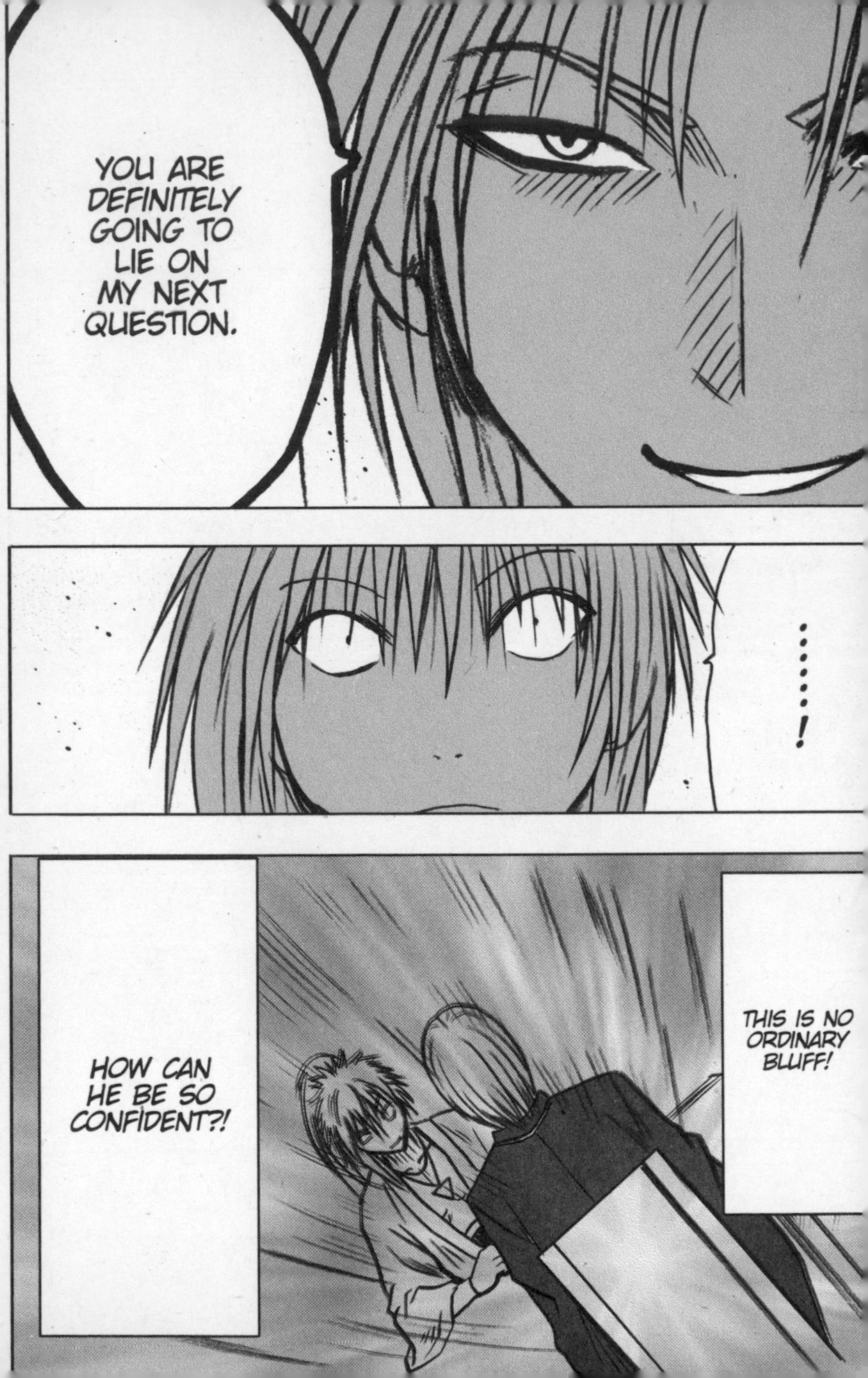
YOU ARE DEFINITELY GOING TO LIE ON MY NEXT QUESTION.
......!
THIS IS NO ORDINARY BLUFF!
HOW CAN HE BE SO CONFIDENT?!

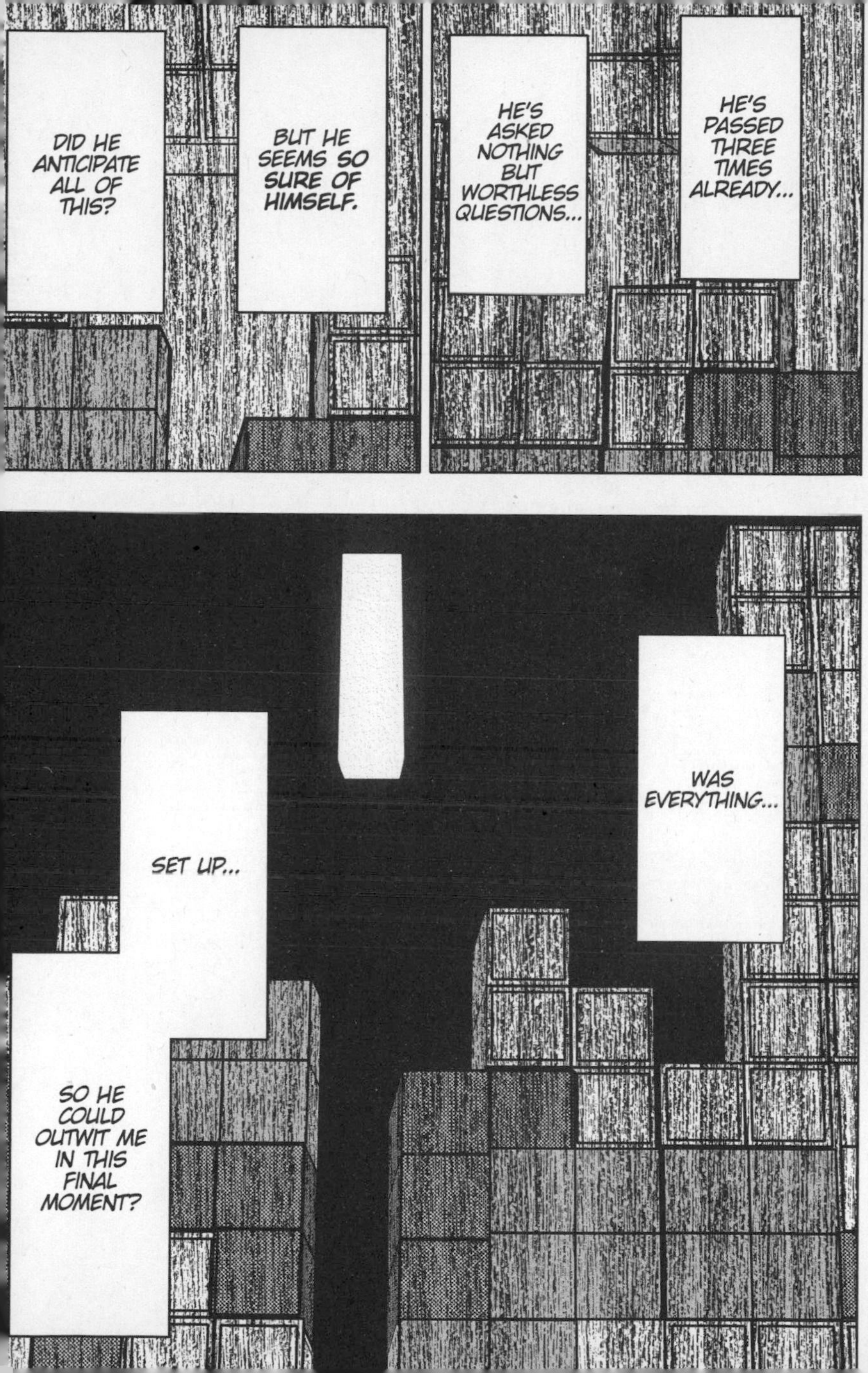
HE'S PASSED THREE TIMES ALREADY...
HE'S ASKED NOTHING BUT WORTHLESS QUESTIONS...
BUT HE SEEMS SO SURE OF HIMSELF.
DID HE ANTICIPATE ALL OF THIS?
WAS EVERYTHING...
SET UP...
SO HE COULD OUTWIT ME IN THIS FINAL MOMENT?

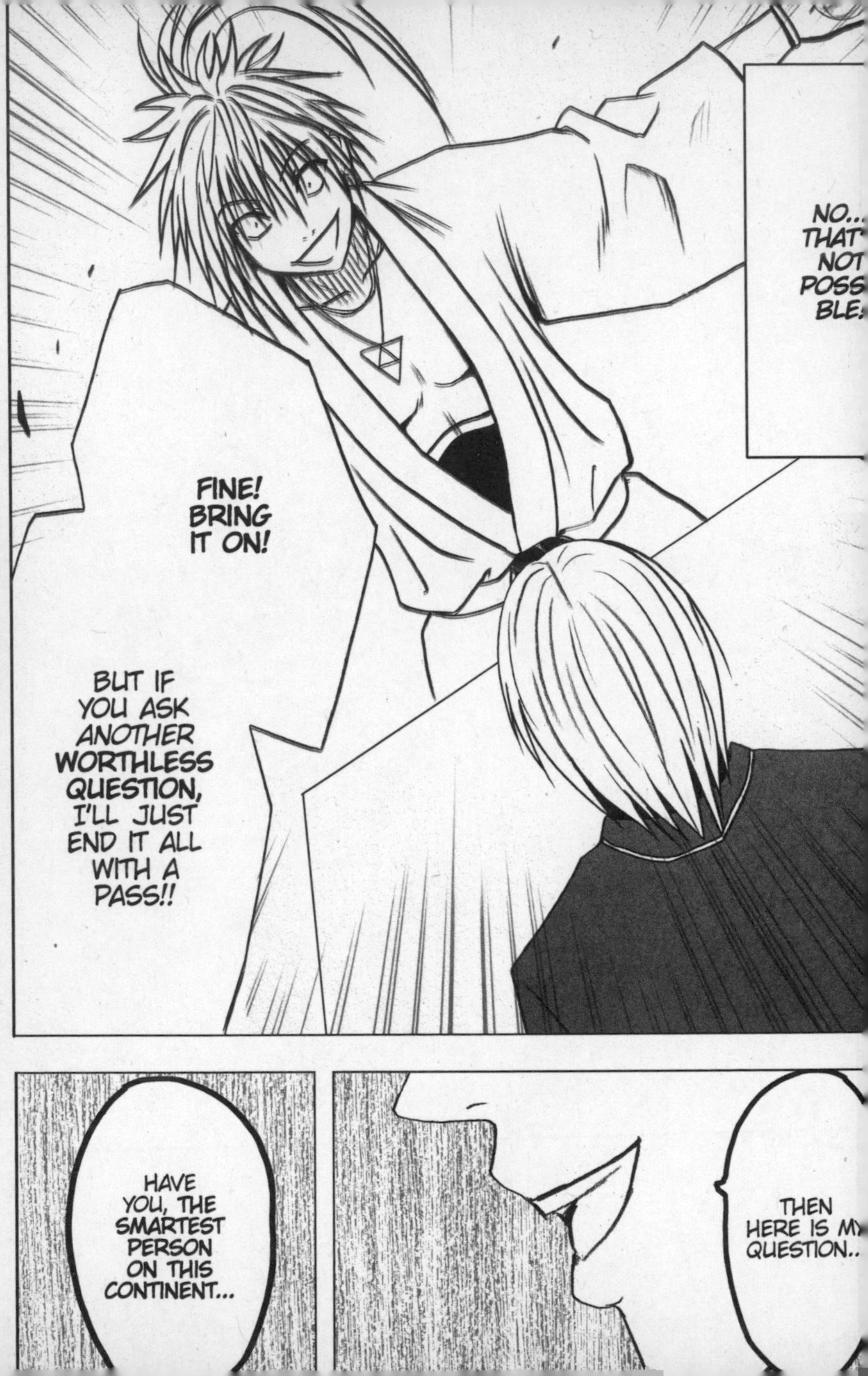
NO... THAT' NOT POSS BLE.
FINE! BRING IT ON!
BUT IF YOU ASK ANOTHER WORTHLESS QUESTION, I'LL JUST END IT ALL WITH A PASS!!
THEN HERE IS MY QUESTION...
HAVE YOU, THE SMARTEST PERSON ON THIS CONTINENT...

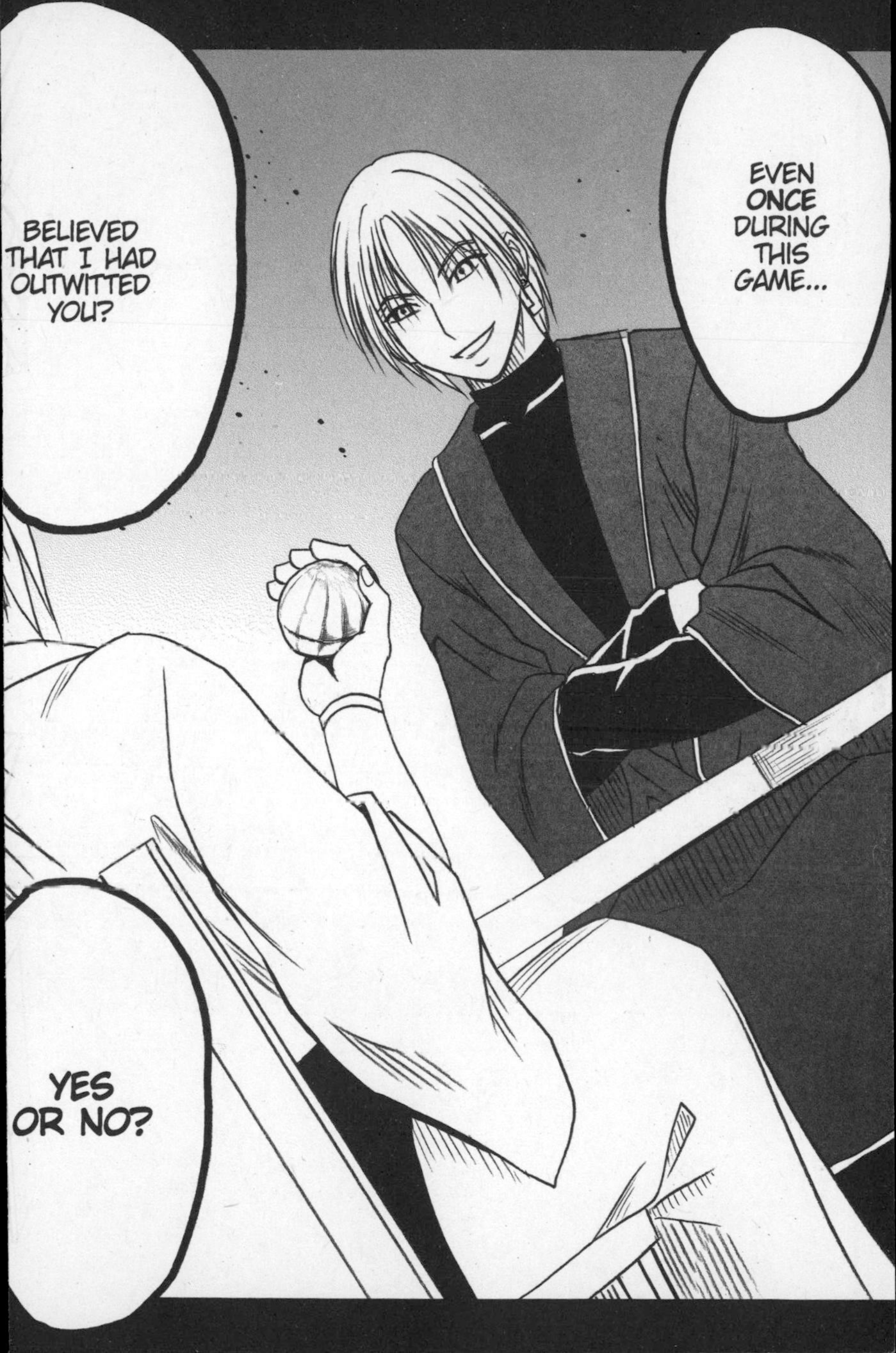
EVEN ONCE DURING THIS GAME...
BELIEVED THAT I HAD OUTWITTED YOU?
YES OR NO?

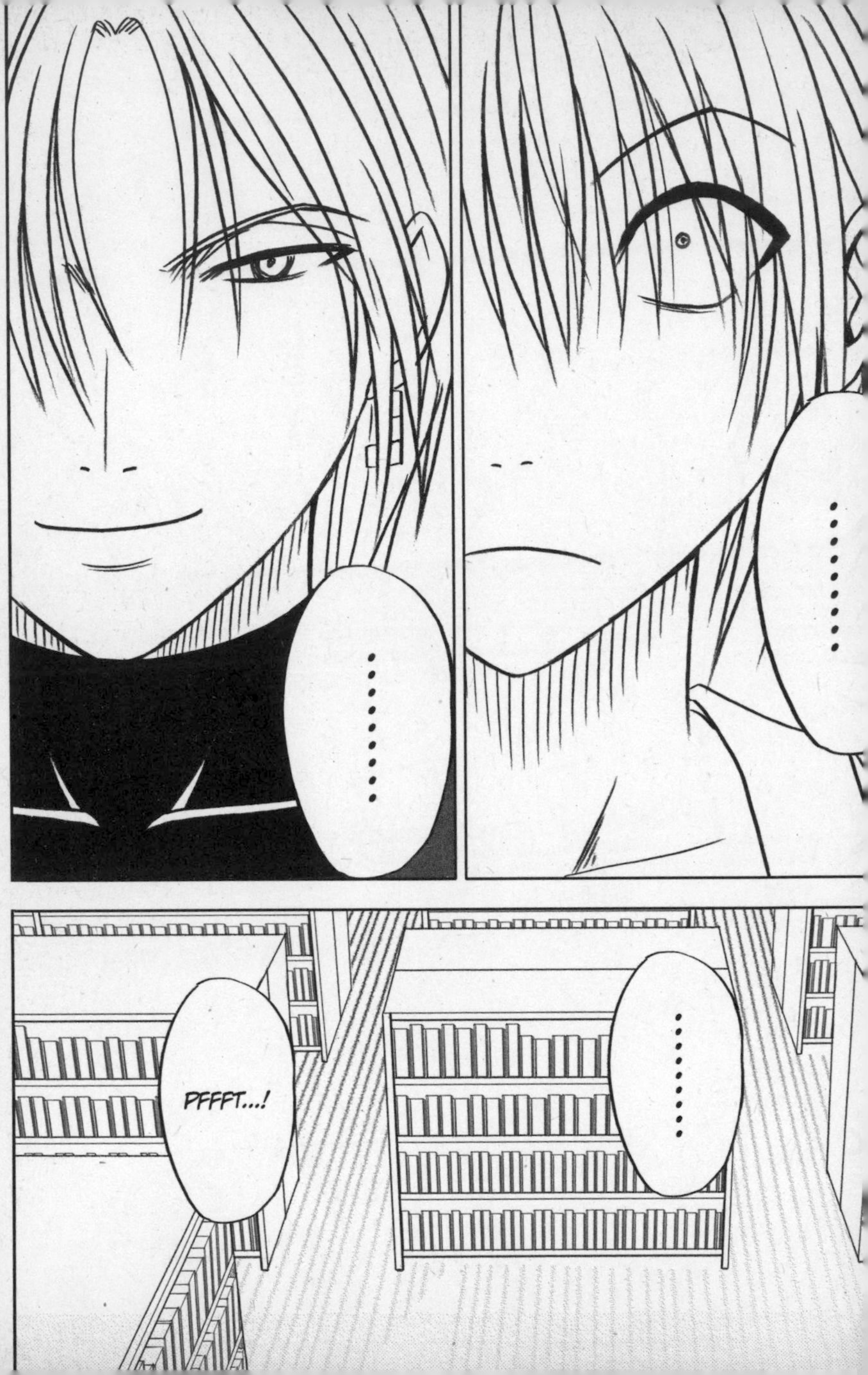

....
....
....
PFFFT...!

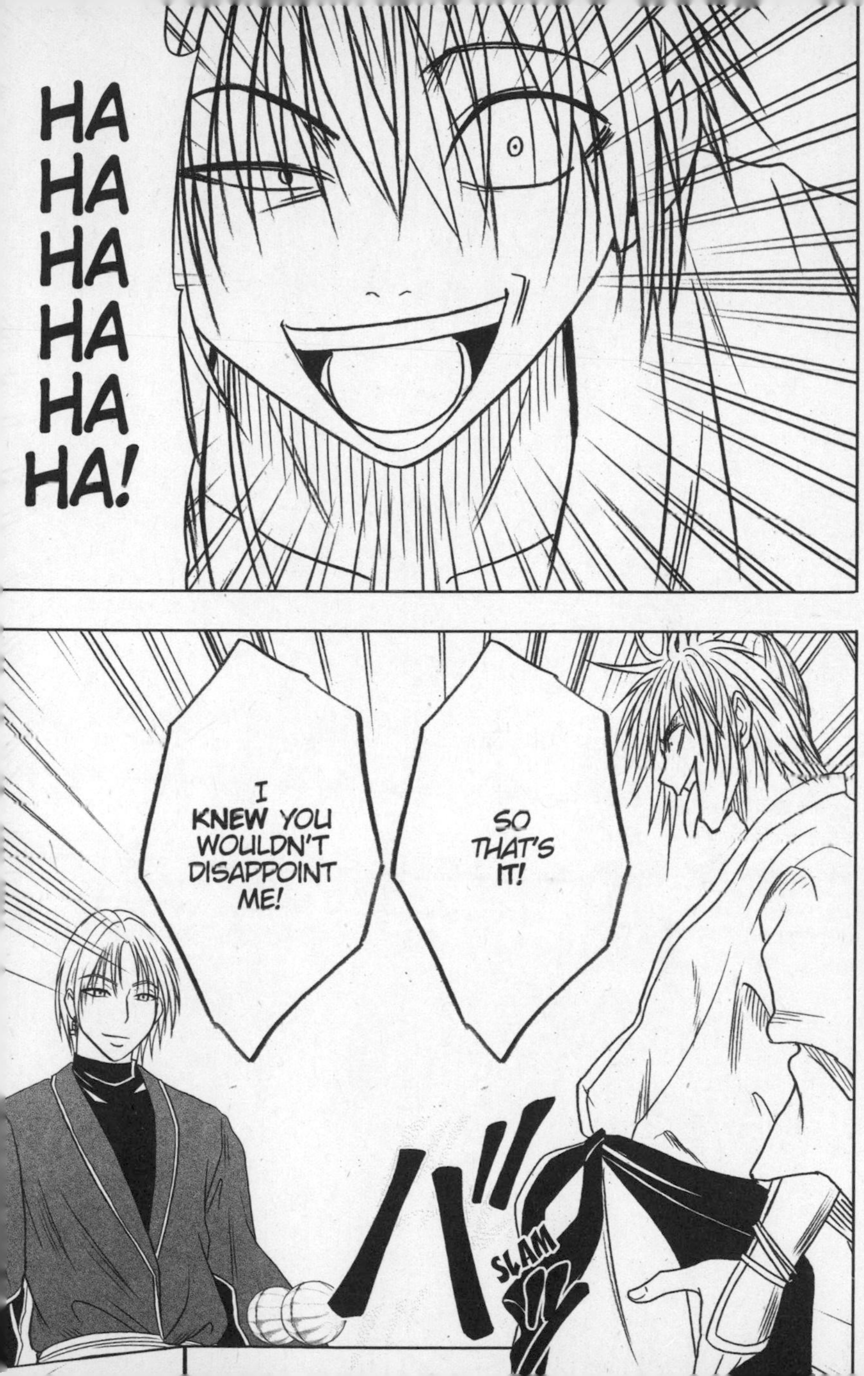
HA HA HA HA HA HA HA!
SO THAT'S IT!
I KNEW YOU WOULDN'T DISAPPOINT ME!
SLAM

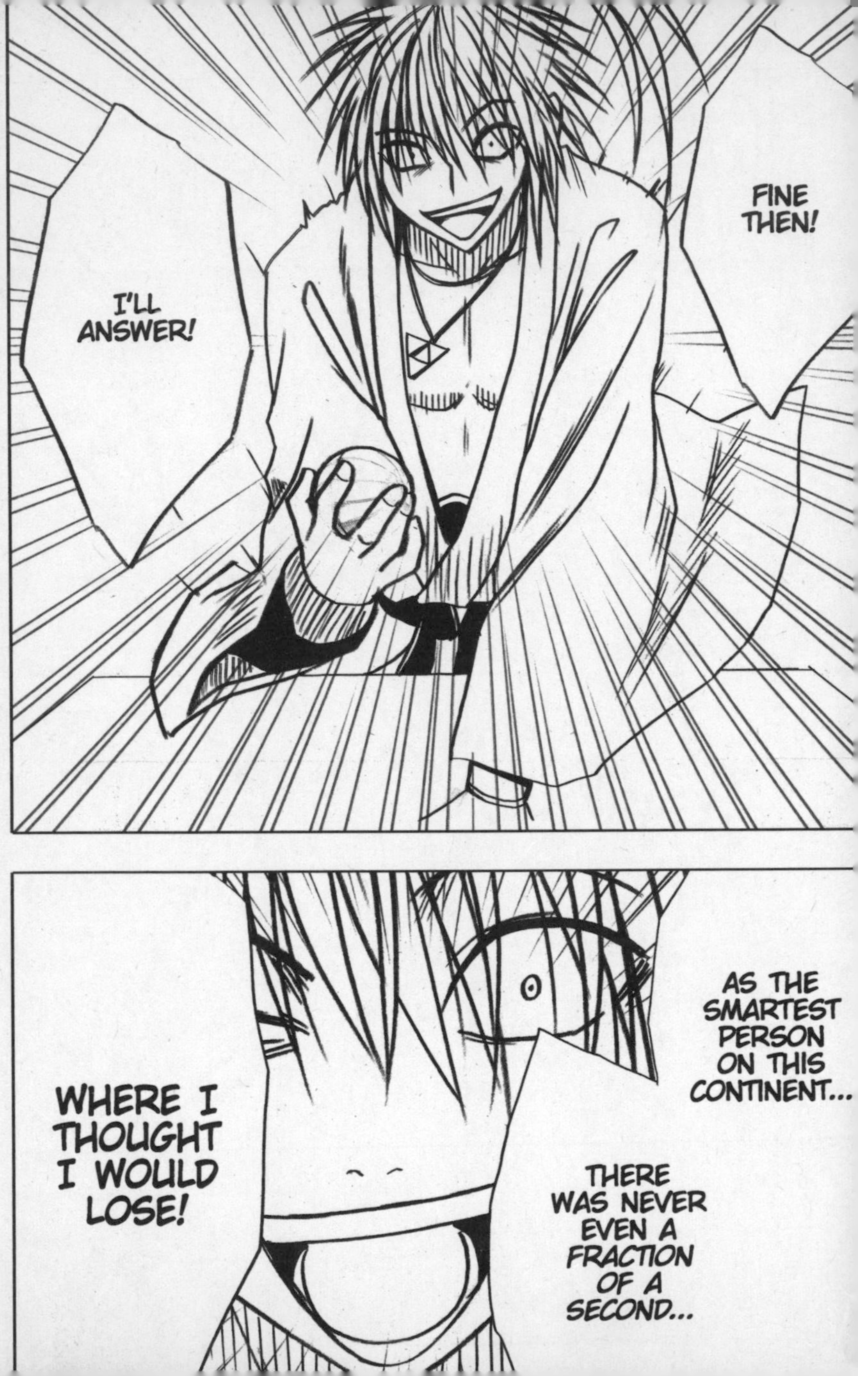
FINE THEN!
I'LL ANSWER!
AS THE SMARTEST PERSON ON THIS CONTINENT...
THERE WAS NEVER EVEN A FRACTION OF A SECOND...
WHERE I THOUGHT I WOULD LOSE!

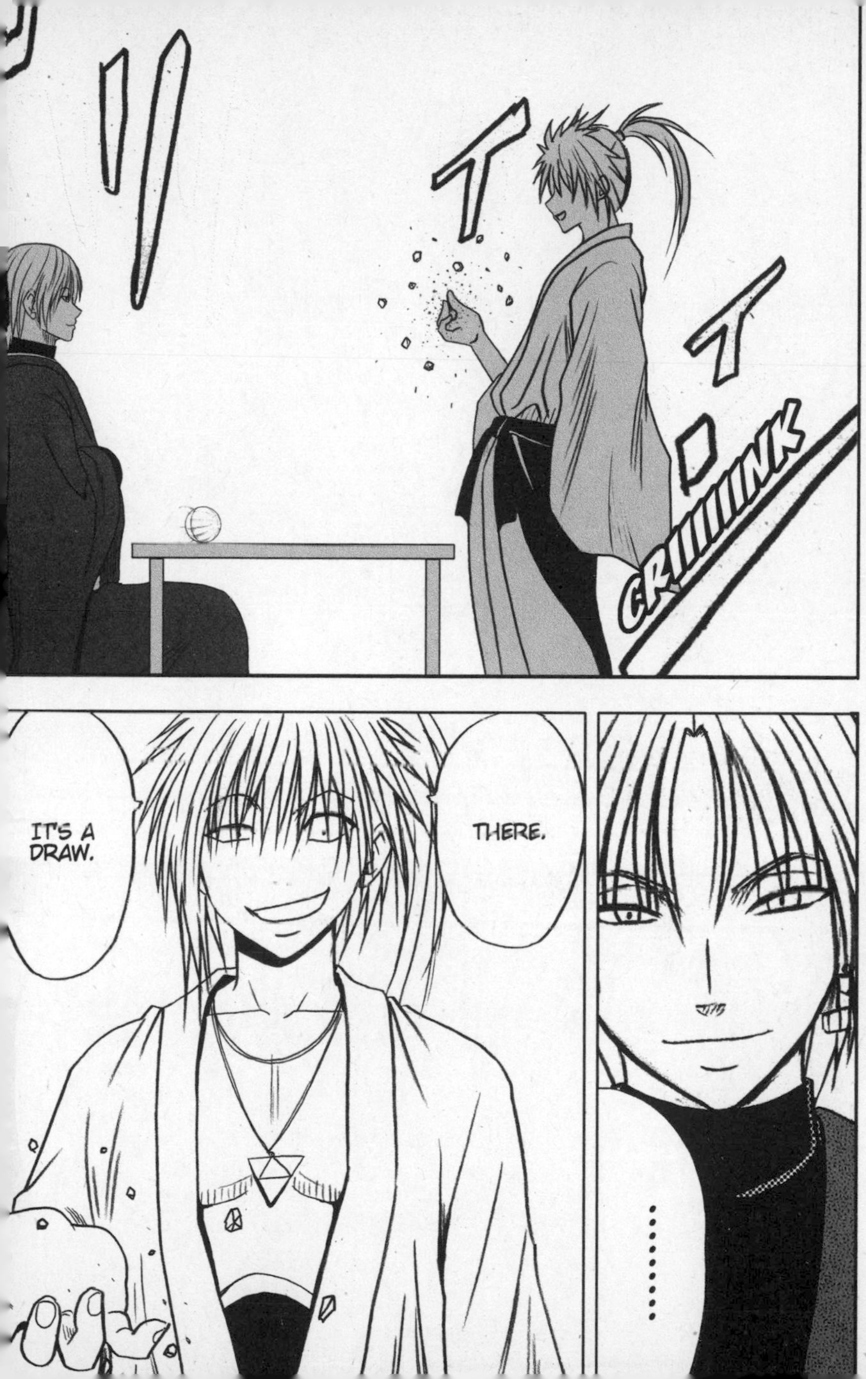
CRIIIIIINK
......
THERE.
IT'S A DRAW.

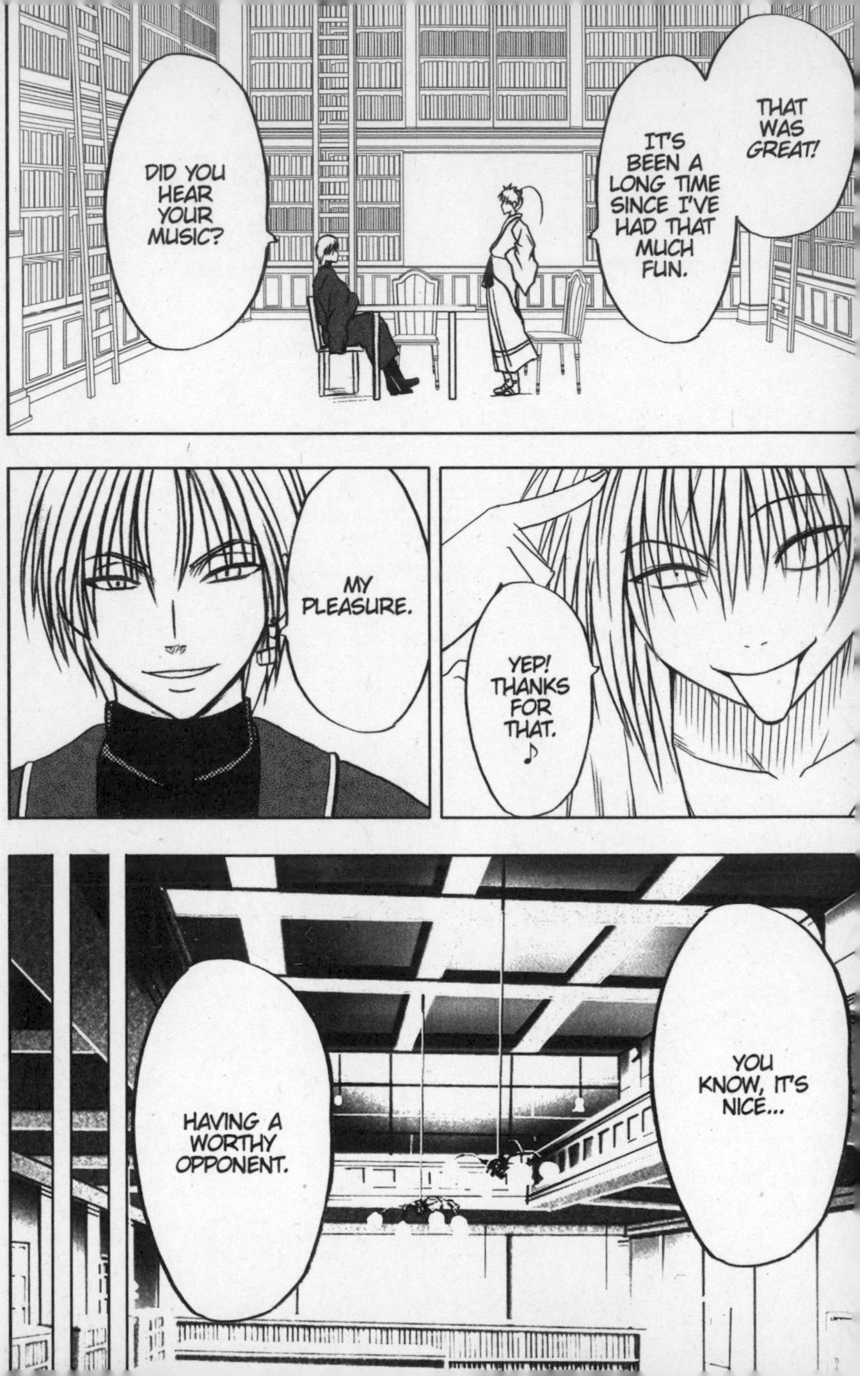
THAT WAS GREAT!
IT'S BEEN A LONG TIME SINCE I'VE HAD THAT MUCH FUN.
DID YOU HEAR YOUR MUSIC?
YEP! THANKS FOR THAT. ♪
MY PLEASURE.
YOU KNOW, IT'S NICE...
HAVING A WORTHY OPPONENT.

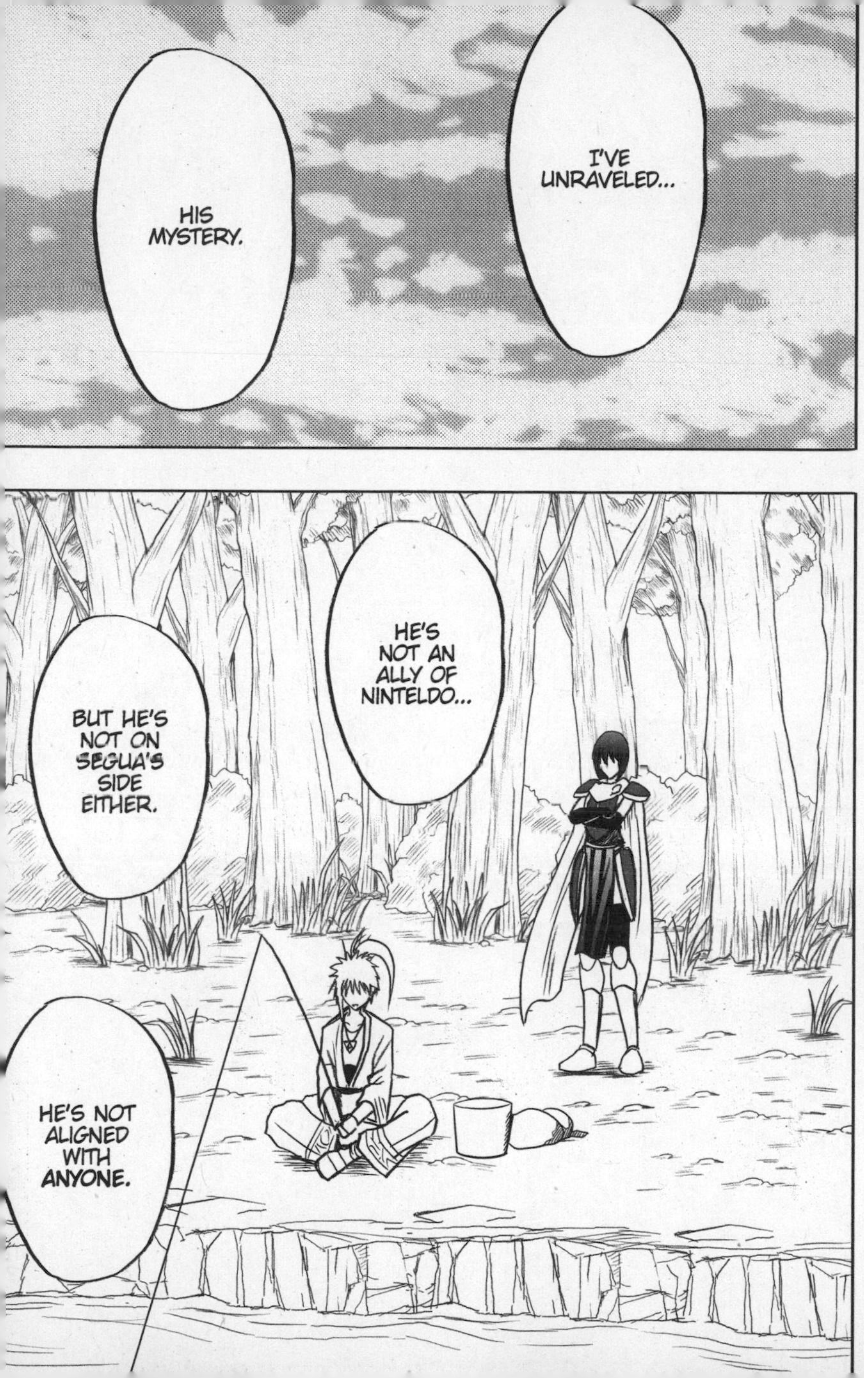
I'VE UNRAVELED...
HIS MYSTERY.
HE'S NOT AN ALLY OF NINTELDO...
BUT HE'S NOT ON SEGUA'S SIDE EITHER.
HE'S NOT ALIGNED WITH ANYONE.

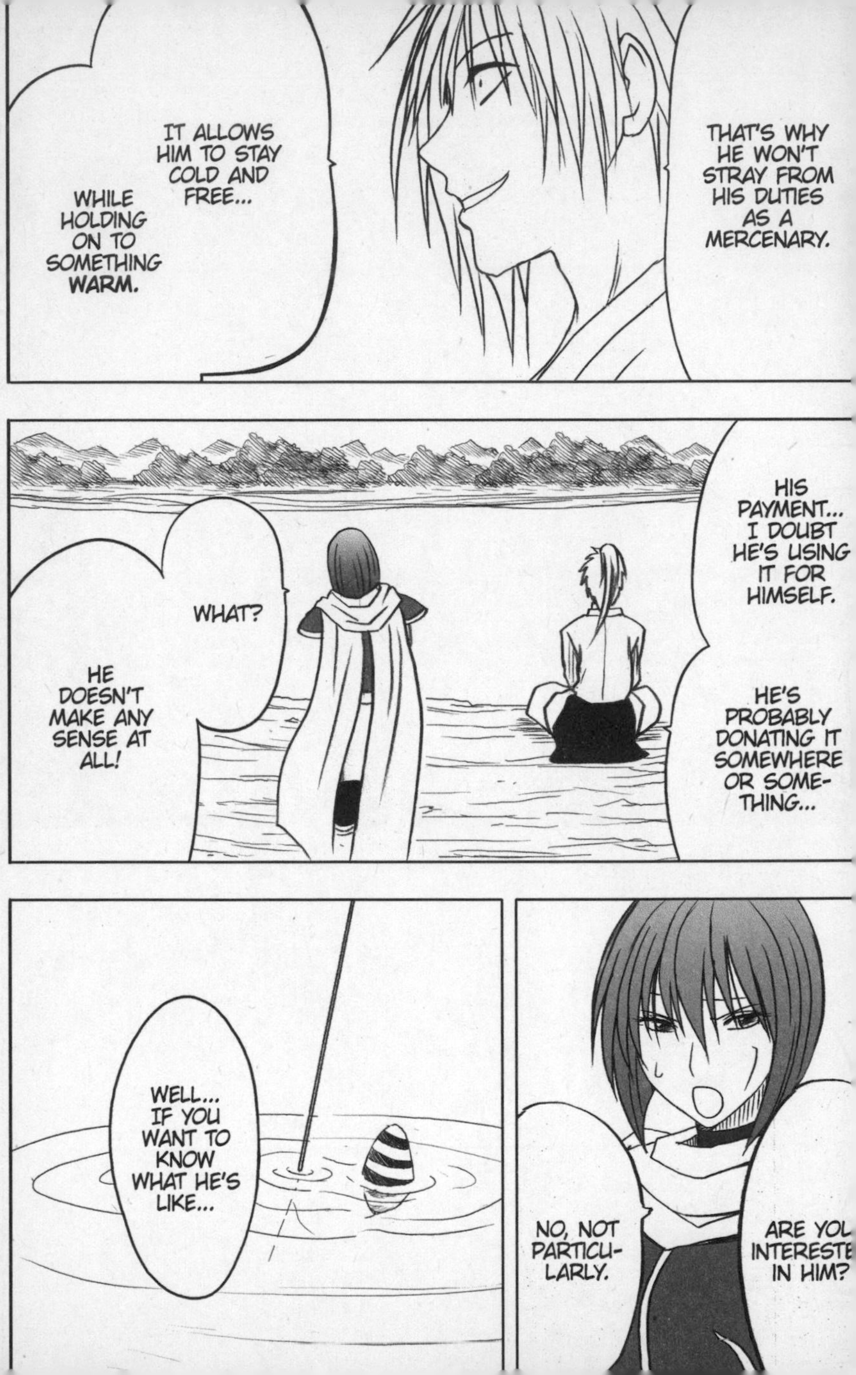
THAT'S WHY HE WON'T STRAY FROM HIS DUTIES AS A MERCENARY.
IT ALLOWS HIM TO STAY COLD AND FREE...
WHILE HOLDING ON TO SOMETHING WARM.
HIS PAYMENT... I DOUBT HE'S USING IT FOR HIMSELF.
HE'S PROBABLY DONATING IT SOMEWHERE OR SOME-THING...
WHAT?
HE DOESN'T MAKE ANY SENSE AT ALL!
ARE YO INTERESTE IN HIM?
NO, NOT PARTICU-LARLY.
WELL... IF YOU WANT TO KNOW WHAT HE'S LIKE...

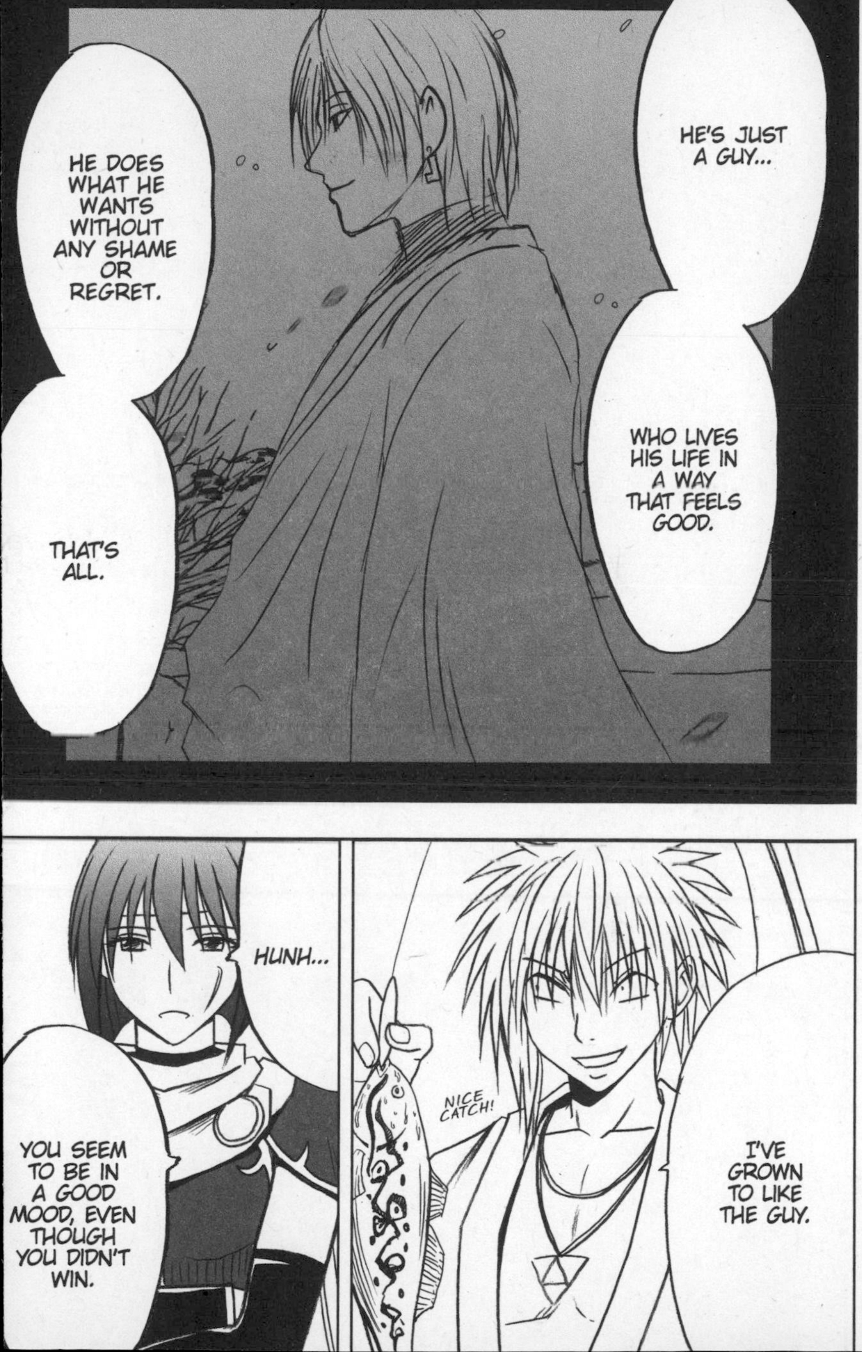
HE'S JUST A GUY...
WHO LIVES HIS LIFE IN A WAY THAT FEELS GOOD.
HE DOES WHAT HE WANTS WITHOUT ANY SHAME OR REGRET.
THAT'S ALL.
NICE CATCH!
I'VE GROWN TO LIKE THE GUY.
HUNH...
YOU SEEM TO BE IN A GOOD MOOD, EVEN THOUGH YOU DIDN'T WIN.

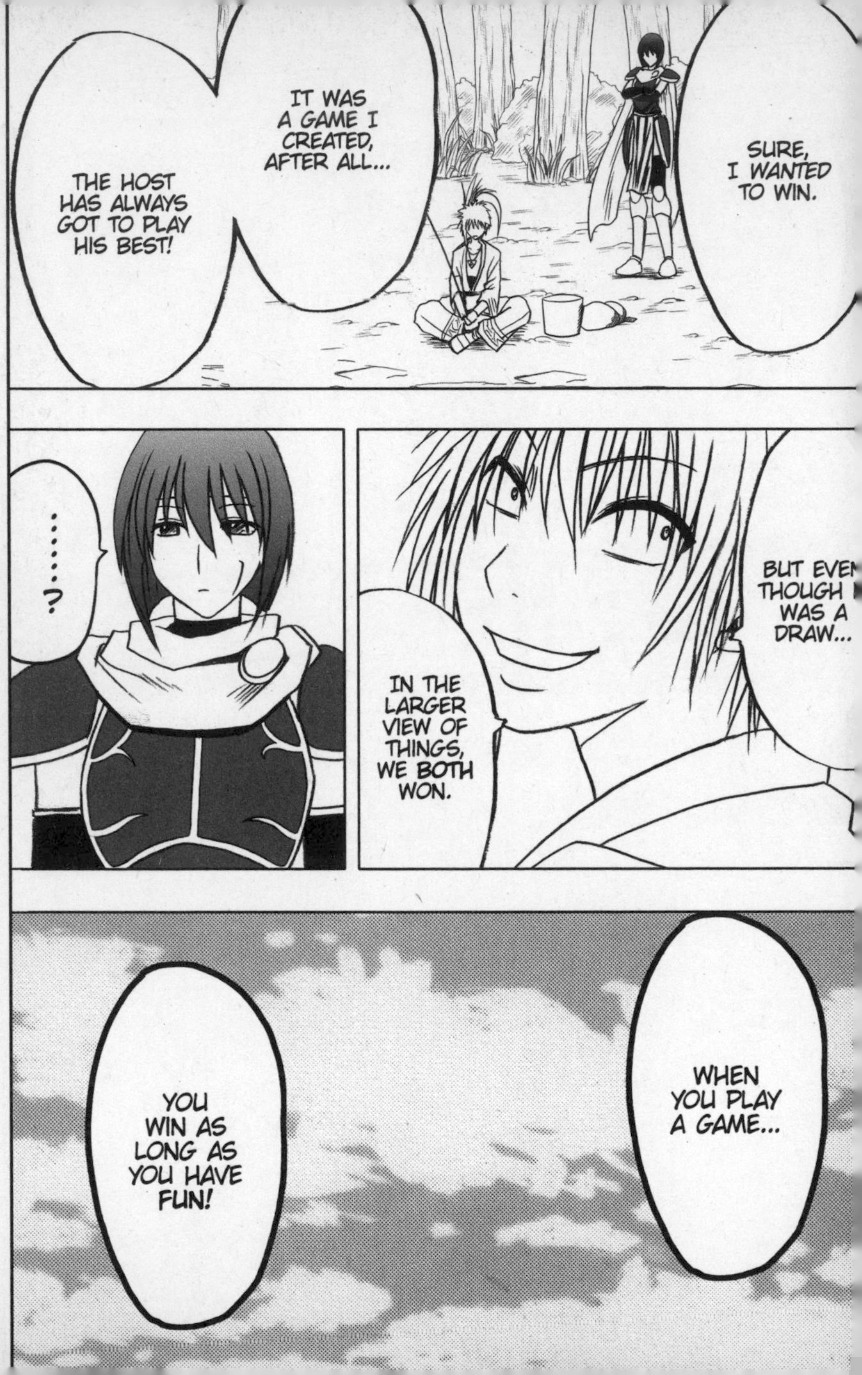
SURE, I WANTED TO WIN.
IT WAS A GAME I CREATED, AFTER ALL...
THE HOST HAS ALWAYS GOT TO PLAY HIS BEST!
BUT EVEN THOUGH WAS A DRAW...
IN THE LARGER VIEW OF THINGS, WE BOTH WON.
......?
WHEN YOU PLAY A GAME...
YOU WIN AS LONG AS YOU HAVE FUN!

Bonus Comic

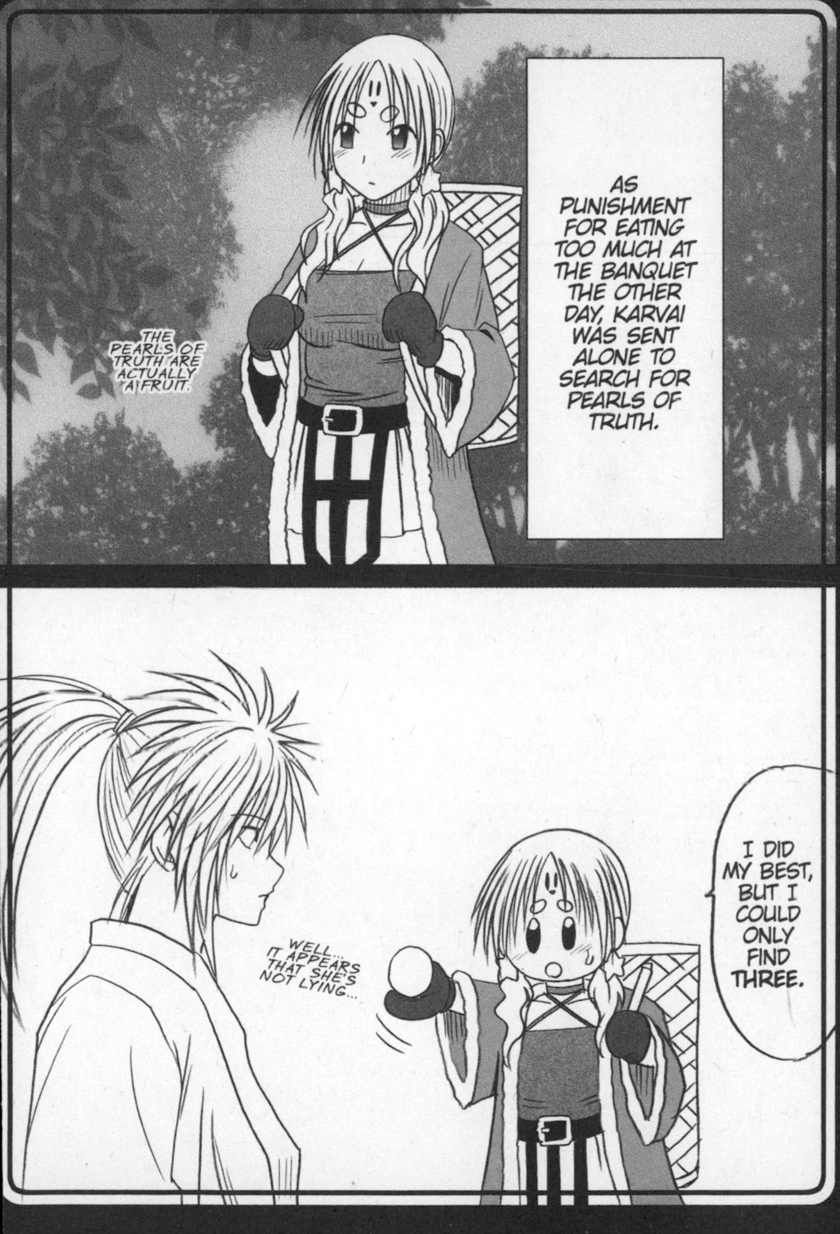
AS PUNISHMENT FOR EATING TOO MUCH AT THE BANQUET THE OTHER DAY, KARVAI WAS SENT ALONE TO SEARCH FOR PEARLS OF TRUTH.
THE PEARLS OF TRUTH ARE ACTUALLY A FRUIT.
I DID MY BEST, BUT I COULD ONLY FIND THREE.
WELL... IT APPEARS THAT SHE'S NOT LYING...

ON THE EDGE OF THE BLUE WORLD

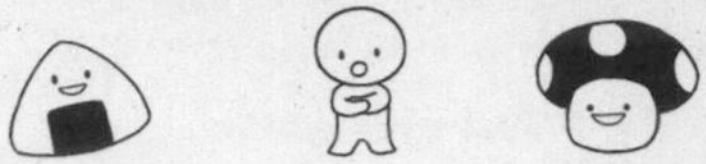
Dr. Onigiri
Mr. Why
Prof. Mushroom

Today's Topic

THE LEGEND OF ZELDA

Mr. Why: This time, we're going to discuss *The Legend of Zelda* from Nintendo.

Dr. Onigiri: Last time, we called *Zelda* "exciting" but the characters don't move really fast and the action part of the game isn't really all that great. Calling it "exciting" is a bit of a stretch, don't you think?

Prof. Mushroom: No way! While certainly the action isn't all that exciting, *The Legend of Zelda* presents the players with many puzzles that require them to push themselves. From that standpoint, it's very exciting.

Sometimes you'll come up against a boss with a really high defense, and you can't beat him on your first try. When you come back and use your items strategically, you get this sense of "Man, I'm really smart!" Then there's those mysterious chimes you hear every time you solve a puzzle. It really gives you a rush.

Mr. Why: Now that you mention it, is *Zelda* an action game? Or is it an RPG?

Prof Mushroom: That's a good question. You can use Heart Containers to increase your life, and the hero, Link, does grow in power and strength as you progress through the game, which is a basic component of RPGs. But you can also recover your lost health by finding small hearts or drinking potions or milk, and kill enemies that stand in your way, which are basic components of all action games. Since it has the components of both, it's called an Action RPG.

Mr. Why: Huh? You mean the hero's name isn't Zelda?

Prof. Mushroom: That's right. It's a common misconception. Zelda is the name of the princess. The hero of the story is Link.

Mr. Why: I see.

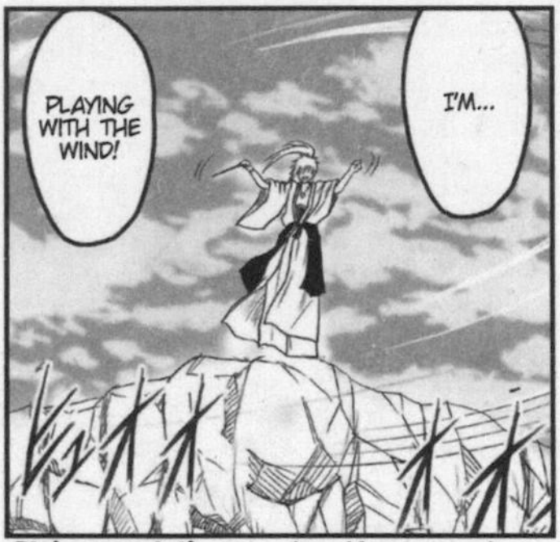
I'M...
PLAYING WITH THE WIND!

Shigeru Miyamoto, the creator of Zelda, would often play in the woods when he was a young boy.

Prof Mushroom: Yep! But that's not all. In *The Legend of Zelda: The Wind Waker,* they used polygons along with cel shading to give the art an anime look and feel to it. There were a lot of other new elements they added too.

Mr. Why: Why did they do that?

Dr. Onigiri: Adding new elements to older games can give them a fresh spin.

Prof Mushroom: Right.
For example, Nintendo added a challenge mode to *Tetris* so that you could play it with your friends. The result made *Tetris* even more fun, and more and more people began to enjoy the game.

Dr. Onigiri: It became a mega-hit, selling over 4 million copies. If Sega had done that...

Mr. Why: Another big win for Nintendo.

Prof. Mushroom: But we seem to be saying that if this game sold X million copies, it wins, but if this game didn't sell X million copies, it loses.

Mr. Why: Yeah...

Prof Mushroom: It certainly is one way to look at things, and copies sold is quite important to game makers... But it really has no importance for the players, does it? Rather than worrying about how many copies a game sells, we players just want to buy the game that's the most entertaining for us.

Mr. Why: So I guess the games that are the most interesting are the winners.

To Be Continued...

Prof Mushroom: Another important feature of the *Zelda* series are the numerous mini-games that aren't related to the main story. For example, in the 2002 release of *The Legend of Zelda: The Wind Waker* for the Gamecube, you could use the wind waker to control the wind, have boat races, and travel to various islands to take on side quests. The little detours were a ton of fun!

Then there was *The Legend of Zelda: Twilight Princess,* which launched in 2006 on Gamecube and the Wii. There were spots in the game where you could immerse yourself in catching ordon catfish, one after another. It was a nice break from the difficult dungeons. Because it challenges your mind and your reflexes, the *Zelda* series has a popularity that compares even to the *Mario* series.

Mr. Why: It must be an awesome game.

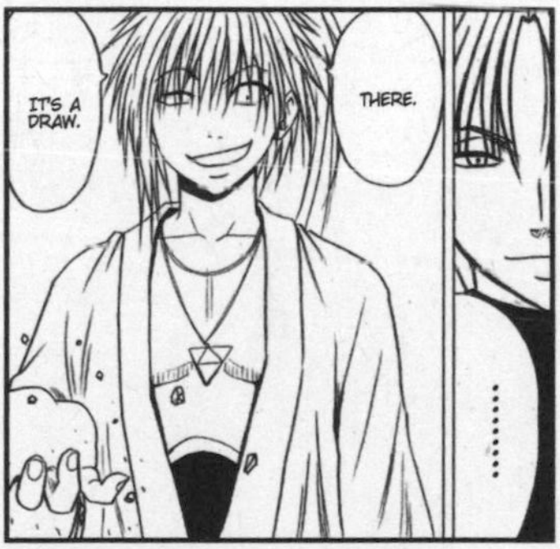
THERE.
IT'S A DRAW.
....

The battle for the title of "Smartest Person on the Continent" ended in a draw, but both parties enjoyed themselves and there were no hard feelings.

Bonus Comic

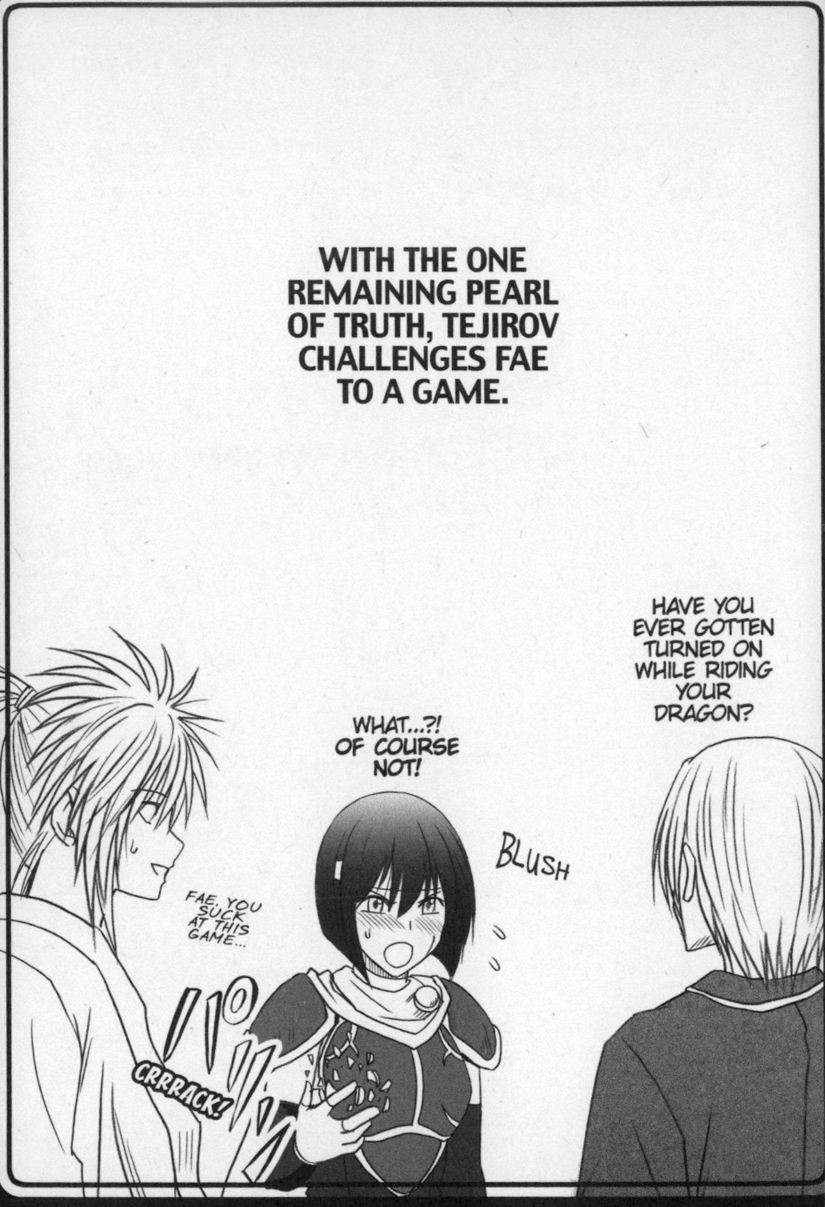
WITH THE ONE REMAINING PEARL OF TRUTH, TEJIROV CHALLENGES FAE TO A GAME.
HAVE YOU EVER GOTTEN TURNED ON WHILE RIDING YOUR DRAGON?
WHAT...?! OF COURSE NOT!
BLUSH
FAE, YOU SUCK AT THIS GAME...
CRRRACK!

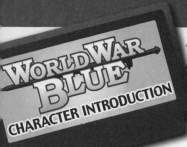

WORLD WAR BLUE
CHARACTER INTRODUCTION

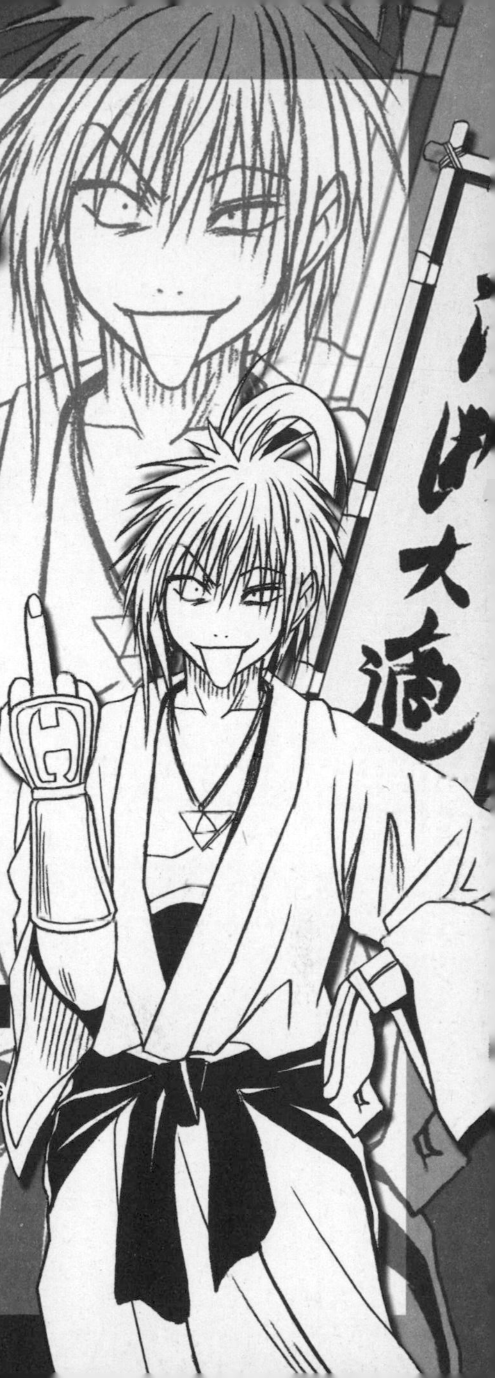

The Unraveler of Mysteries
ZELIG

Hails from Ninteldo

The commander of Ninteldo's six generals, it is said that he possesses the greatest mind on the entire continent of Consume.

He loves solving riddles so much it's earned him the title "The Unraveler of Mysteries."

Like Flame Emperor Marcus, he studied battle tactics under Master Shigen.

He fights using a variety of different tools and items. Bombs and the boomerang are his specialty.

He's left-handed.

Author Comment

In part 1, Gear was the main hero, but in part 2 and beyond, the story will center on a variety of characters so it won't necessarily follow Gear all the time.

Zelig will be one of the "new" main characters.

His clothes have changed quite a bit from his appearance in the webcomic.

Side Story

WORLD WAR BLUE

SHIITAKE
MUSHROOMS

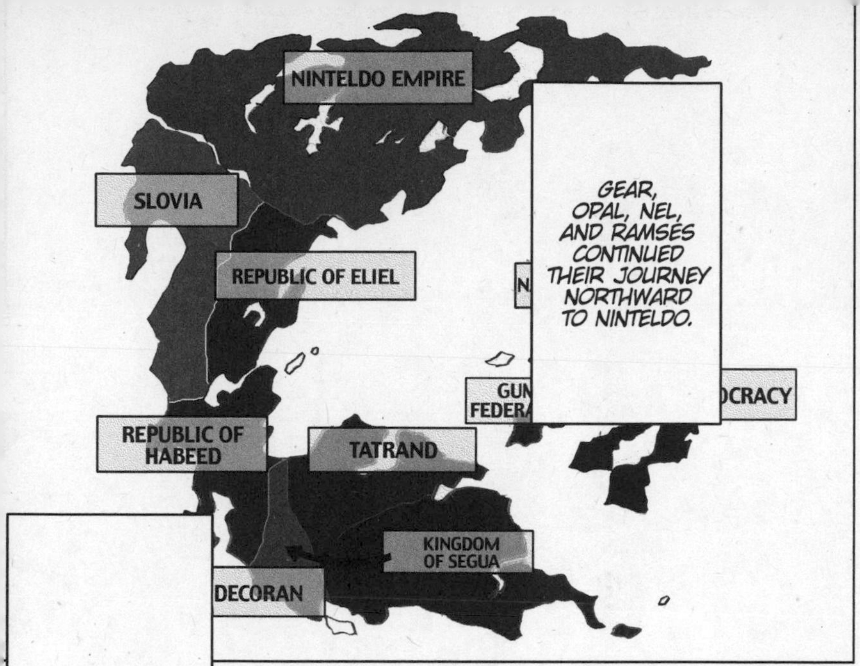
GEAR, OPAL, NEL, AND RAMSES CONTINUED THEIR JOURNEY NORTHWARD TO NINTELDO.
NINTELDO EMPIRE
SLOVIA
REPUBLIC OF ELIEL
REPUBLIC OF HABEED
TATRAND
KINGDOM OF SEGUA
DECORAN

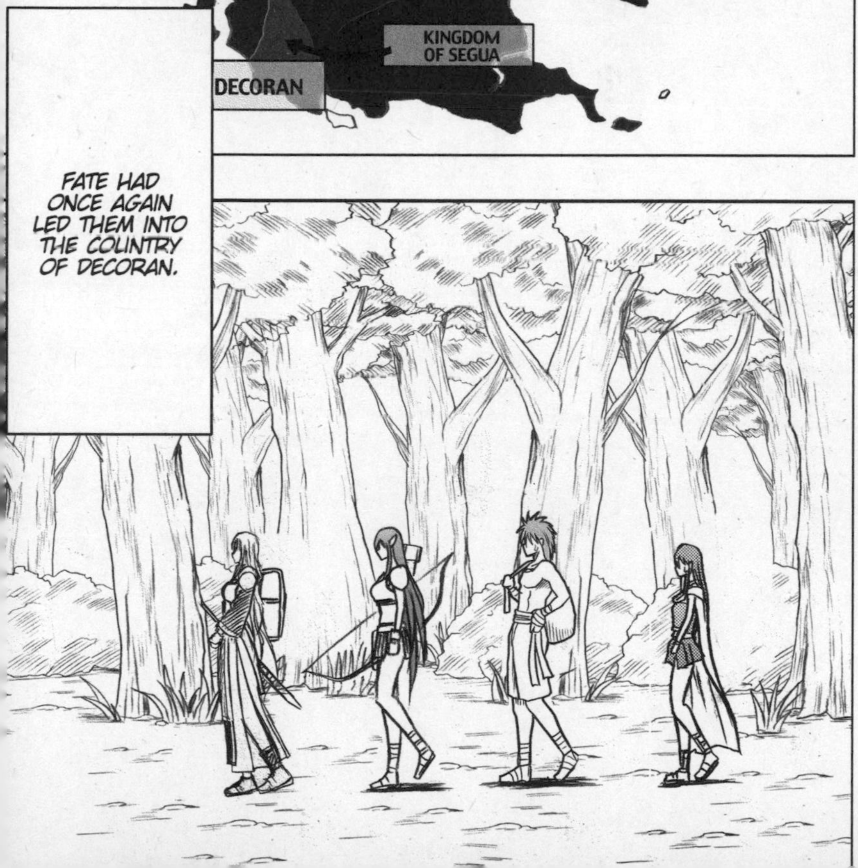
FATE HAD ONCE AGAIN LED THEM INTO THE COUNTRY OF DECORAN.

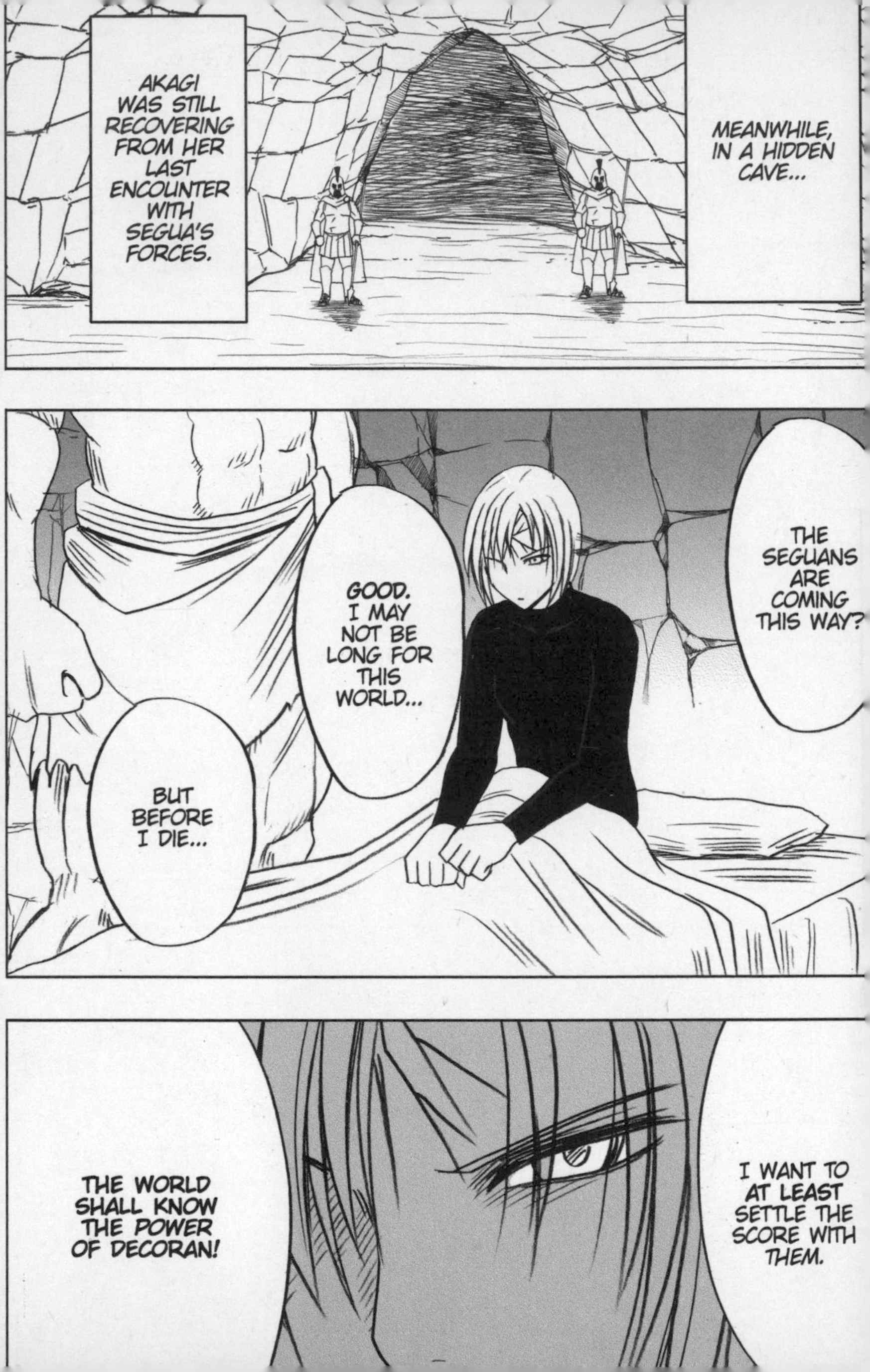
MEANWHILE, IN A HIDDEN CAVE...
AKAGI WAS STILL RECOVERING FROM HER LAST ENCOUNTER WITH SEGUA'S FORCES.
THE SEGUANS ARE COMING THIS WAY?
GOOD. I MAY NOT BE LONG FOR THIS WORLD...
BUT BEFORE I DIE...
I WANT TO AT LEAST SETTLE THE SCORE WITH THEM.
THE WORLD SHALL KNOW THE POWER OF DECORAN!

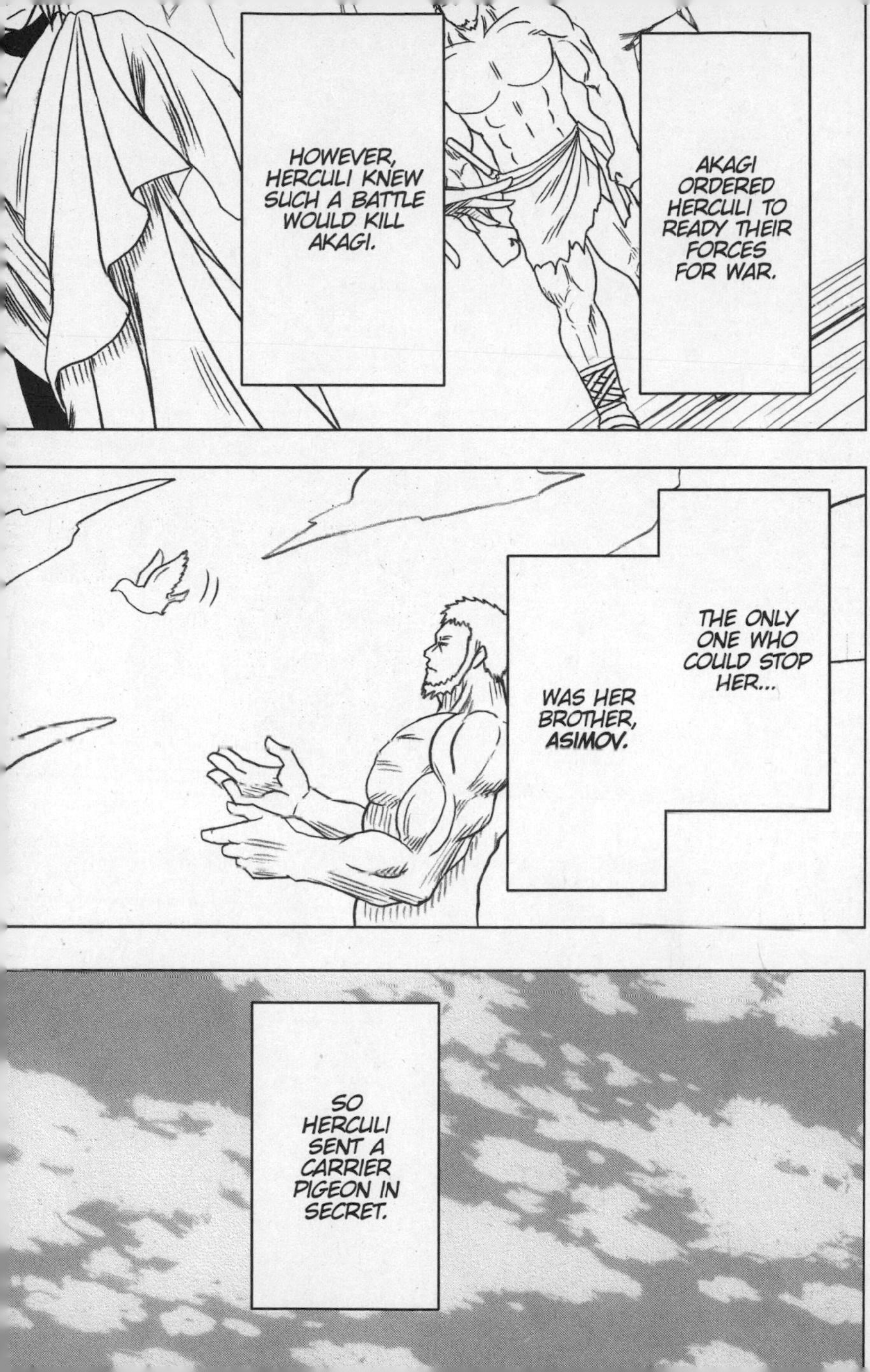
AKAGI ORDERED HERCULI TO READY THEIR FORCES FOR WAR.
HOWEVER, HERCULI KNEW SUCH A BATTLE WOULD KILL AKAGI.
THE ONLY ONE WHO COULD STOP HER...
WAS HER BROTHER, ASIMOV.
SO HERCULI SENT A CARRIER PIGEON IN SECRET.

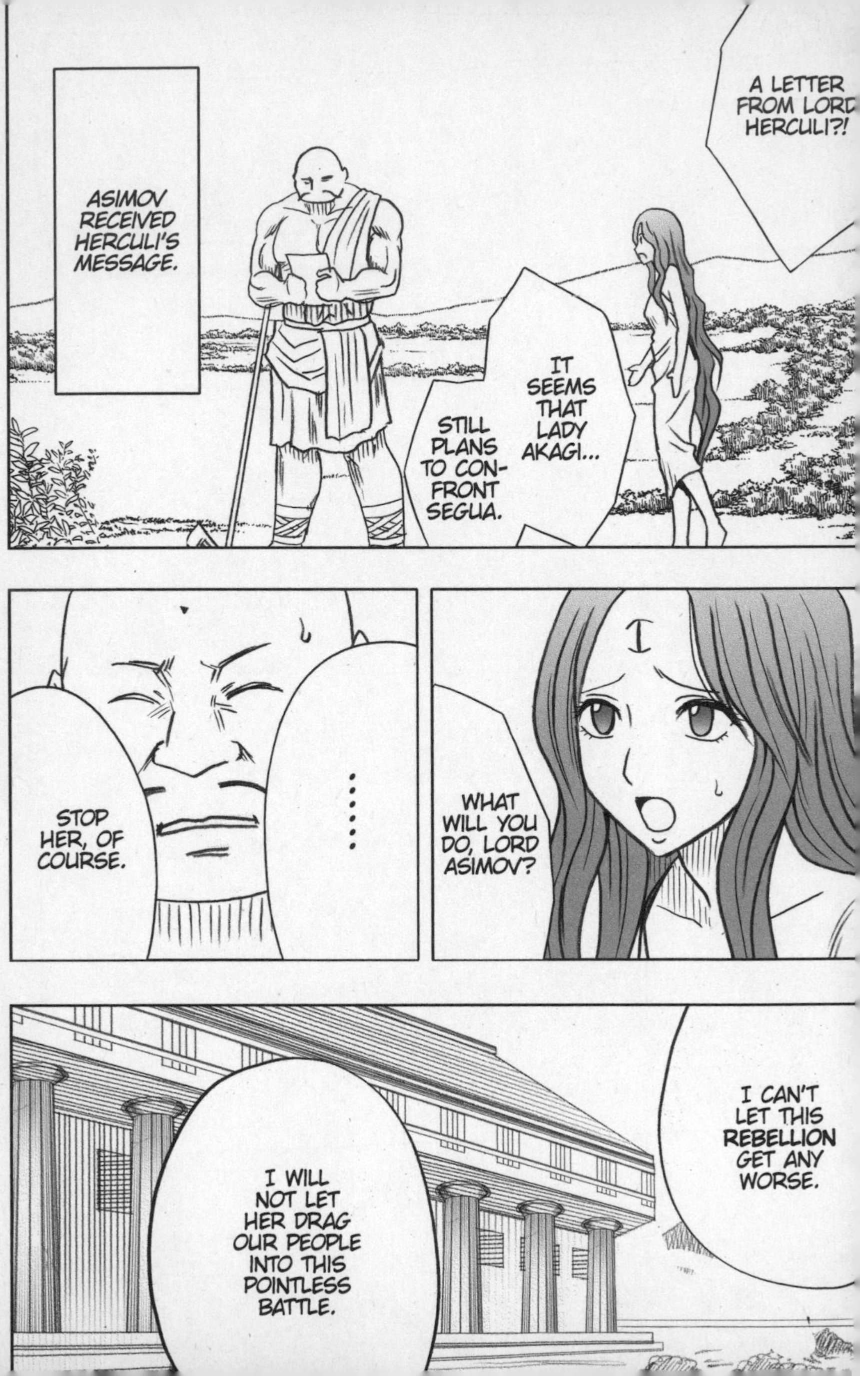
A LETTER FROM LORD HERCULI?!
ASIMOV RECEIVED HERCULI'S MESSAGE.
IT SEEMS THAT LADY AKAGI...
STILL PLANS TO CON-FRONT SEGUA.
WHAT WILL YOU DO, LORD ASIMOV?
......
STOP HER, OF COURSE.
I CAN'T LET THIS REBELLION GET ANY WORSE.
I WILL NOT LET HER DRAG OUR PEOPLE INTO THIS POINTLESS BATTLE.

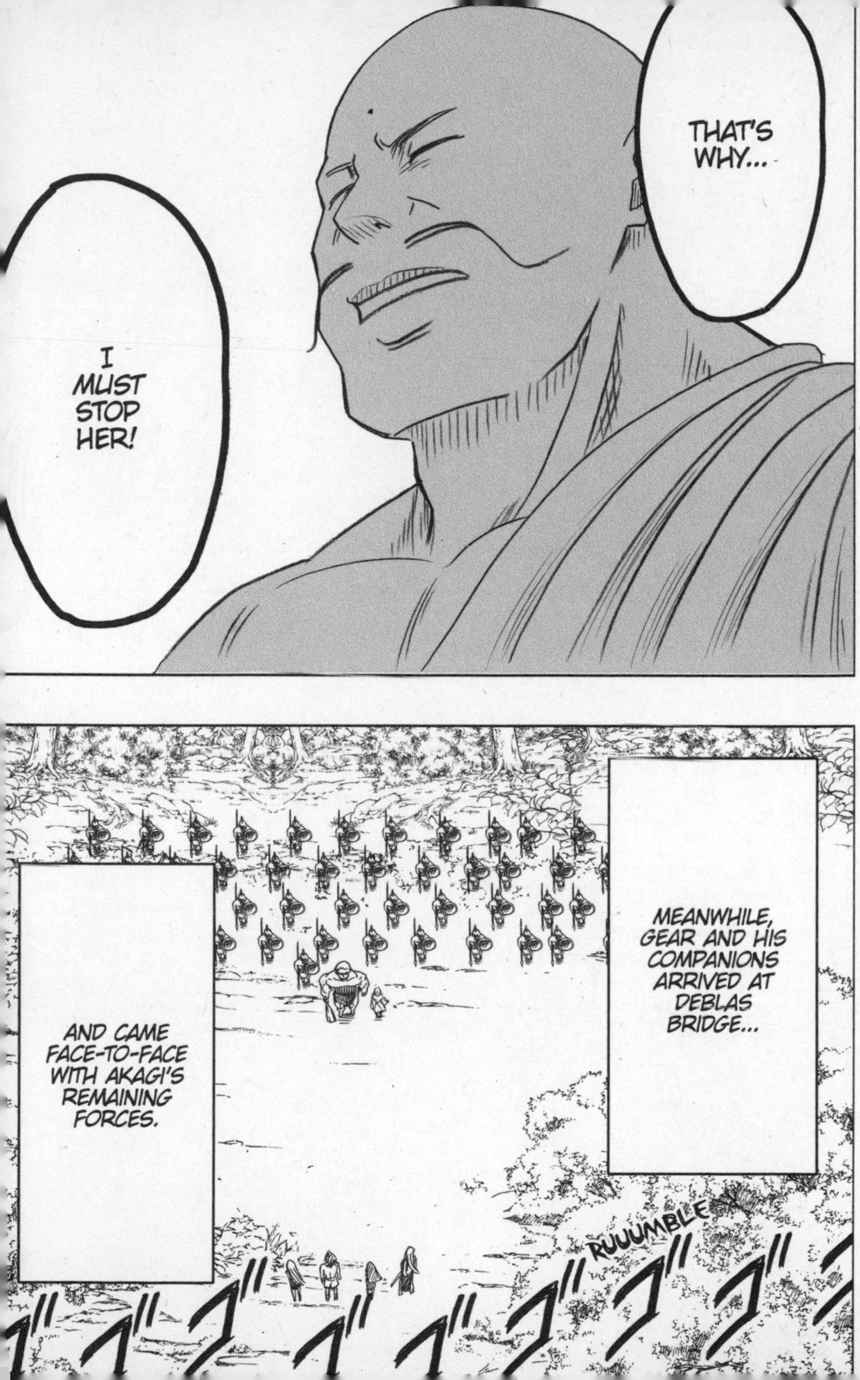
THAT'S WHY...
I MUST STOP HER!
MEANWHILE, GEAR AND HIS COMPANIONS ARRIVED AT DEBLAS BRIDGE...
AND CAME FACE-TO-FACE WITH AKAGI'S REMAINING FORCES.
RUUUMBLE

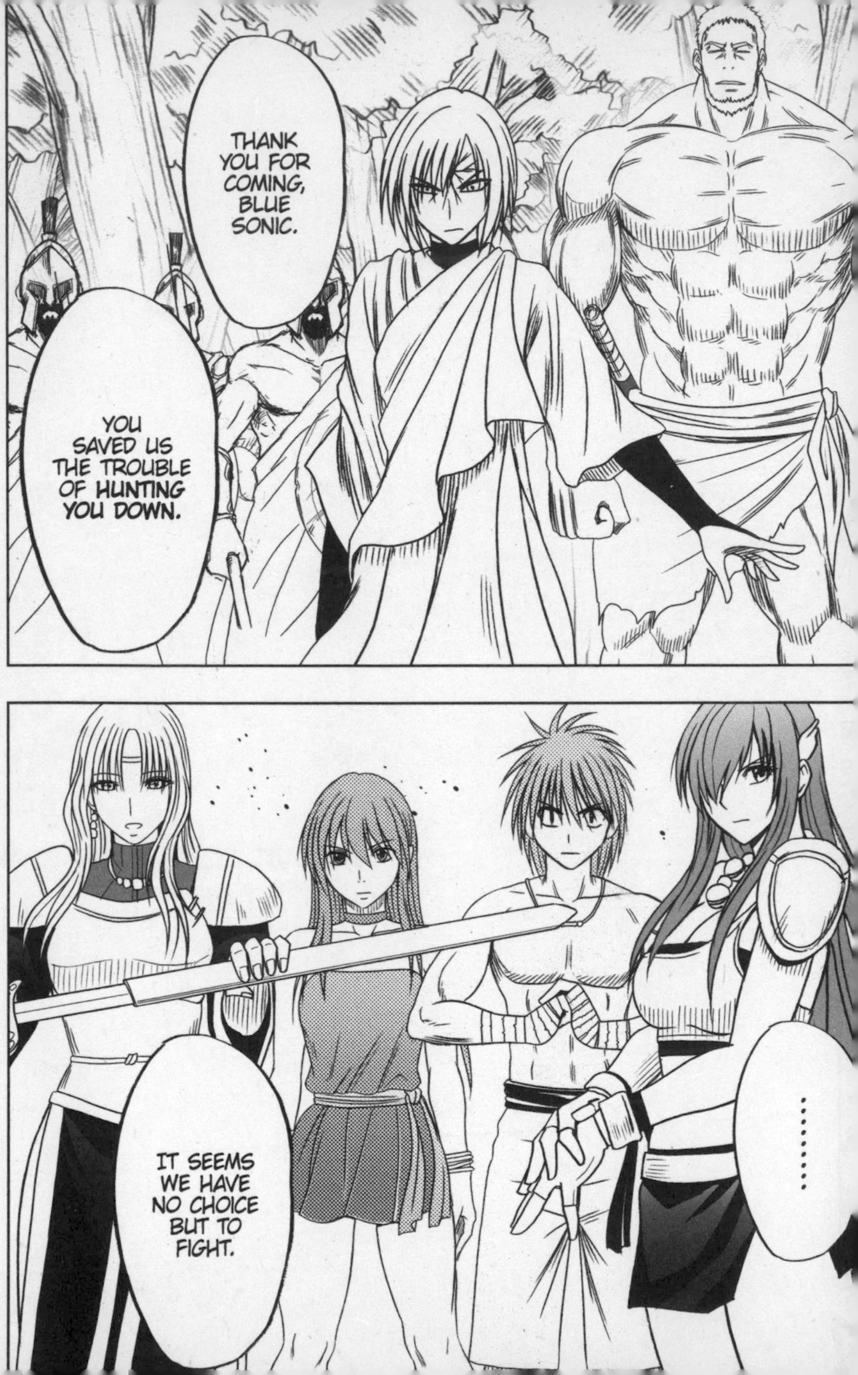
THANK YOU FOR COMING, BLUE SONIC.
YOU SAVED US THE TROUBLE OF HUNTING YOU DOWN.
....
IT SEEMS WE HAVE NO CHOICE BUT TO FIGHT.

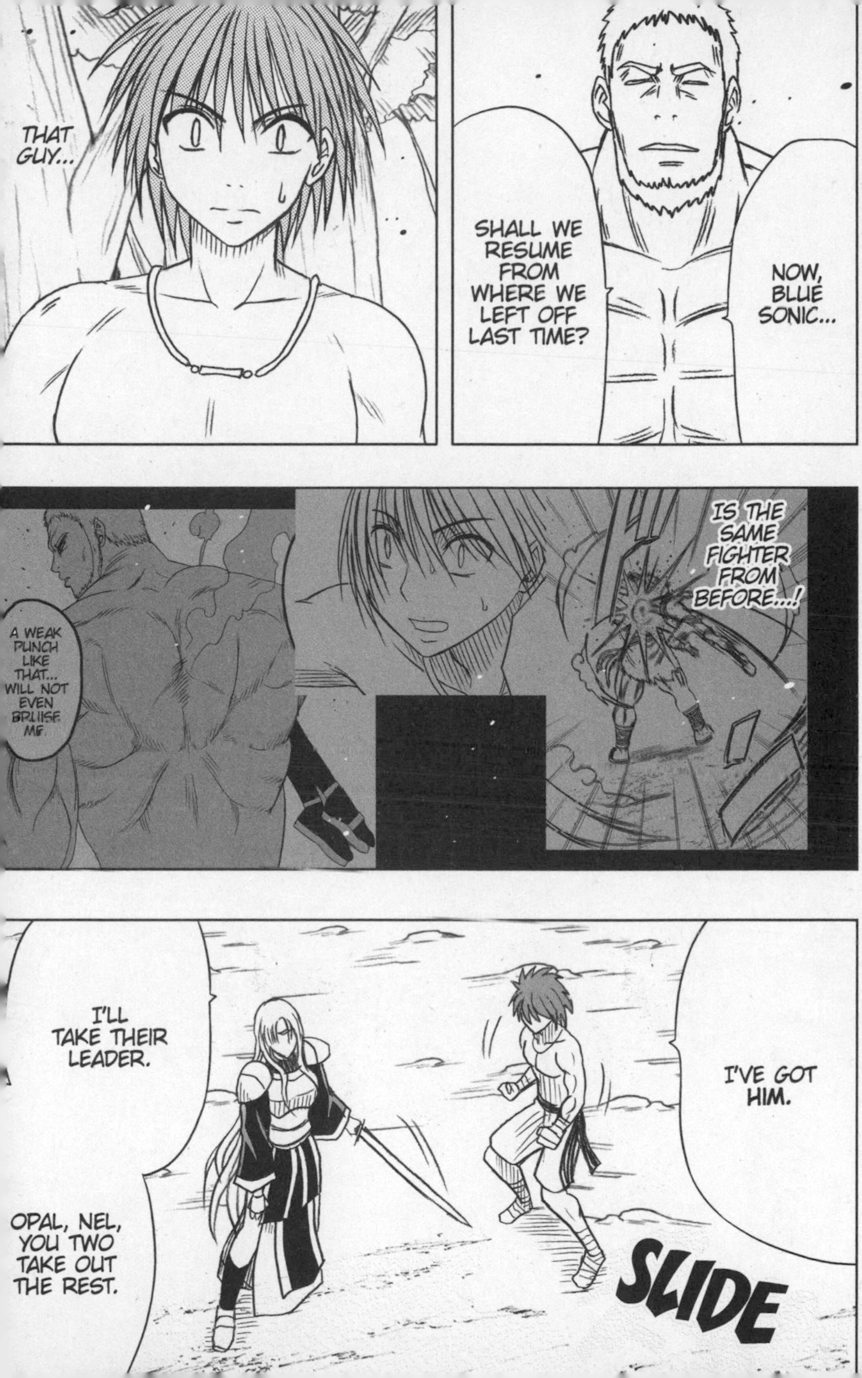
NOW, BLUE SONIC...
SHALL WE RESUME FROM WHERE WE LEFT OFF LAST TIME?
THAT GUY...
IS THE SAME FIGHTER FROM BEFORE...!
A WEAK PUNCH LIKE THAT... WILL NOT EVEN BRUISE ME.
I'VE GOT HIM.
I'LL TAKE THEIR LEADER.
SLIDE
OPAL, NEL, YOU TWO TAKE OUT THE REST.

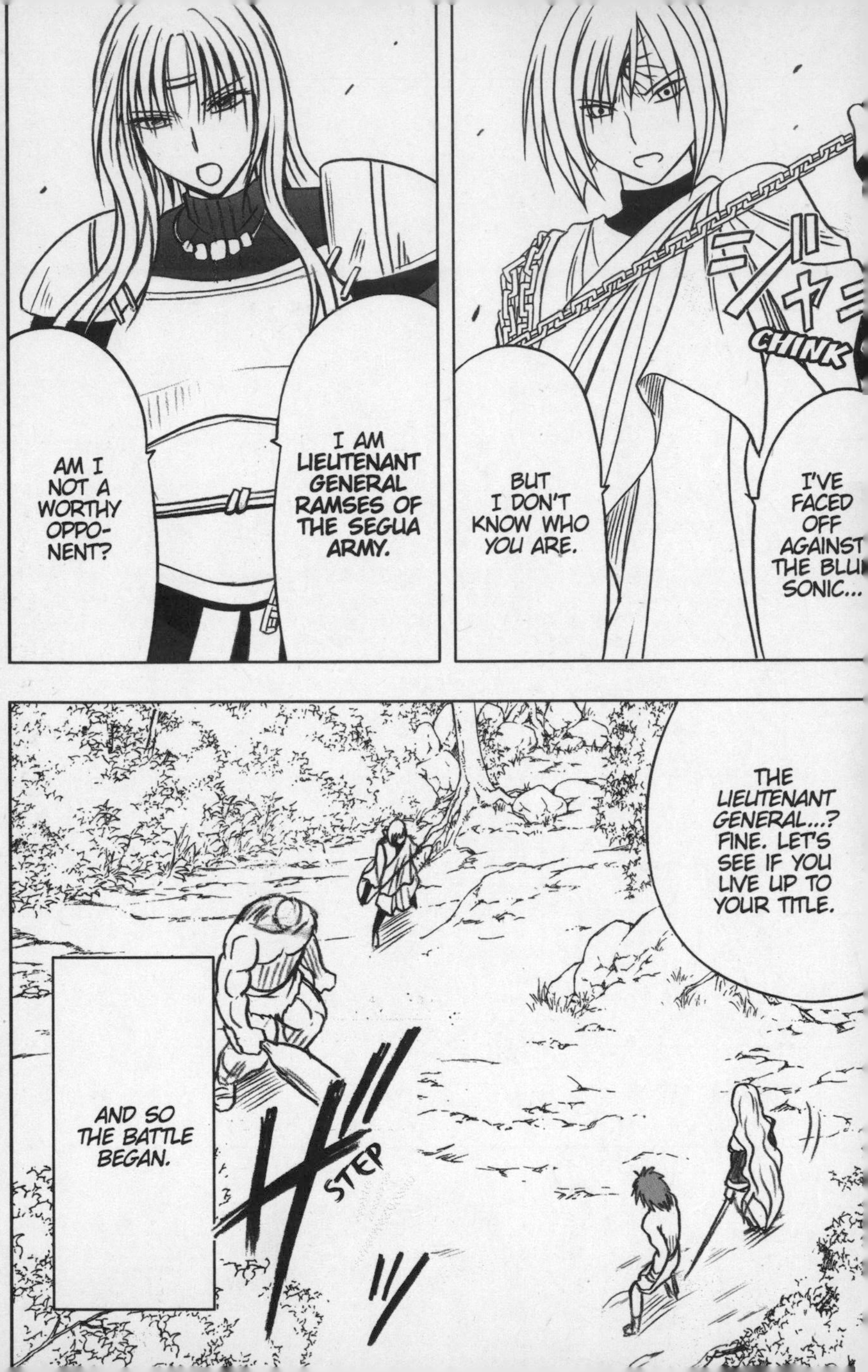
I'VE FACED OFF AGAINST THE BLU SONIC...
BUT I DON'T KNOW WHO YOU ARE.
CHINK
I AM LIEUTENANT GENERAL RAMSES OF THE SEGUA ARMY.
AM I NOT A WORTHY OPPO-NENT?
THE LIEUTENANT GENERAL...? FINE. LET'S SEE IF YOU LIVE UP TO YOUR TITLE.
STEP
AND SO THE BATTLE BEGAN.

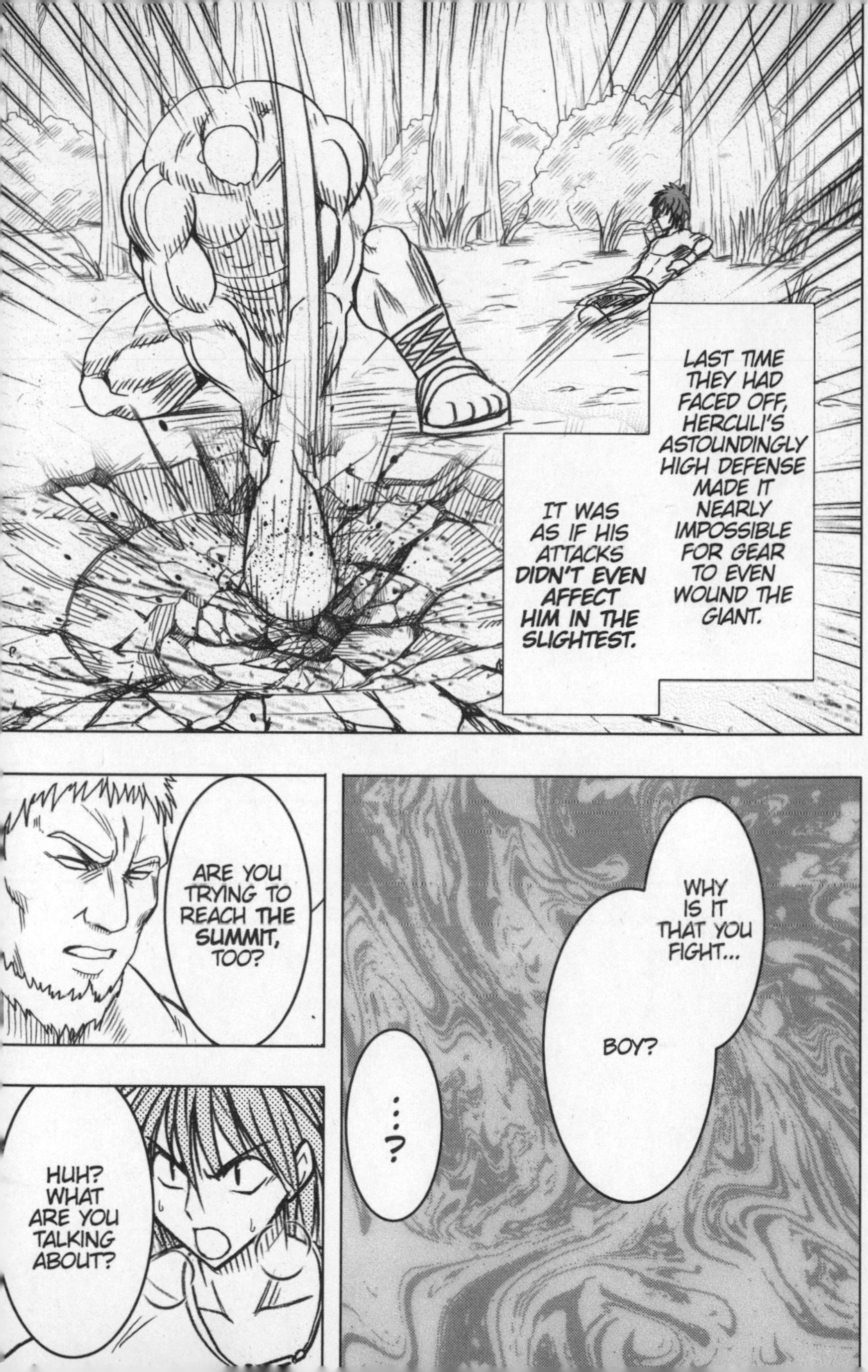
LAST TIME THEY HAD FACED OFF, HERCULI'S ASTOUNDINGLY HIGH DEFENSE MADE IT NEARLY IMPOSSIBLE FOR GEAR TO EVEN WOUND THE GIANT.
IT WAS AS IF HIS ATTACKS DIDN'T EVEN AFFECT HIM IN THE SLIGHTEST.
WHY IS IT THAT YOU FIGHT... BOY?
...?
ARE YOU TRYING TO REACH THE SUMMIT, TOO?
HUH? WHAT ARE YOU TALKING ABOUT?

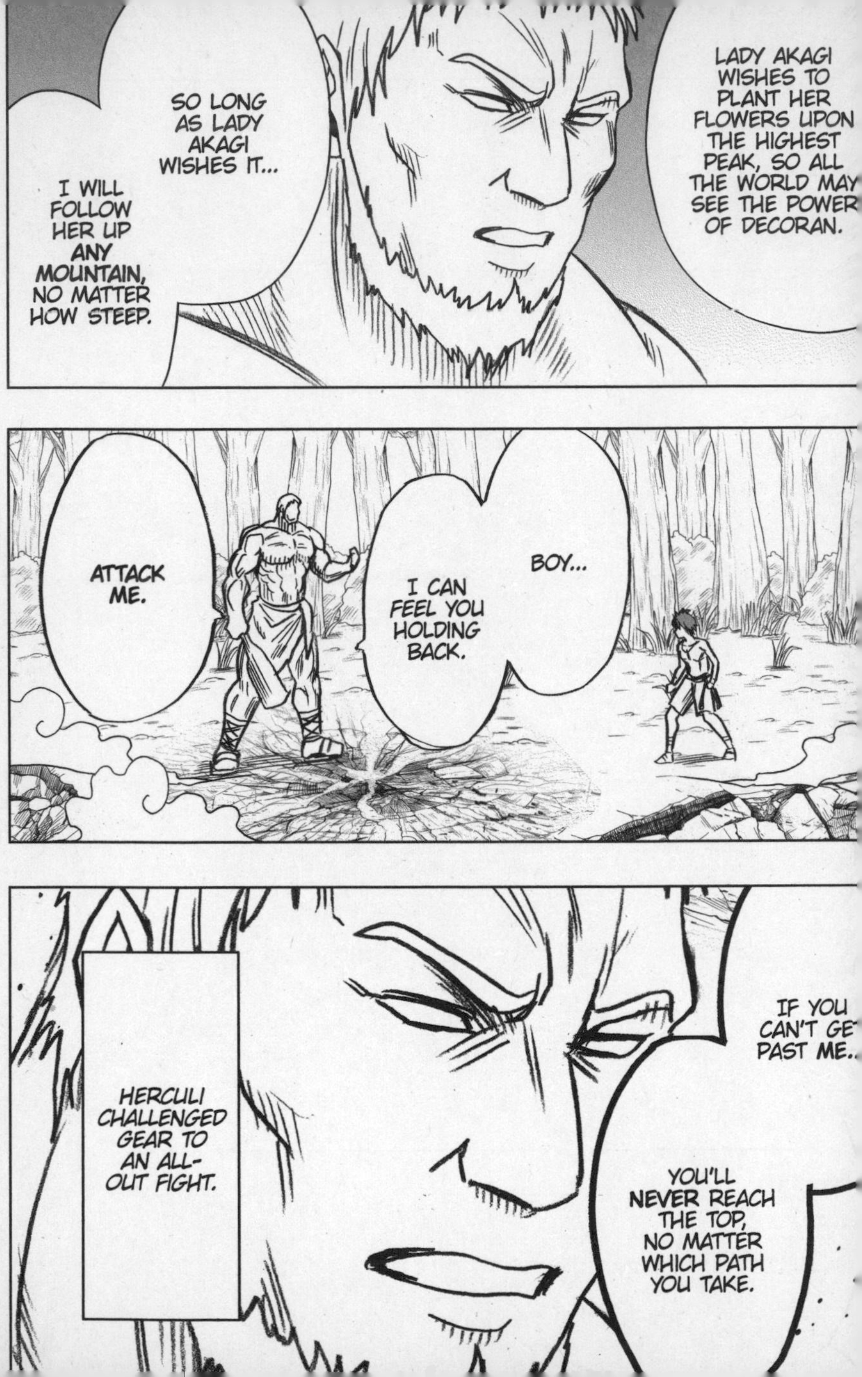
LADY AKAGI WISHES TO PLANT HER FLOWERS UPON THE HIGHEST PEAK, SO ALL THE WORLD MAY SEE THE POWER OF DECORAN.
SO LONG AS LADY AKAGI WISHES IT...
I WILL FOLLOW HER UP ANY MOUNTAIN, NO MATTER HOW STEEP.
BOY...
I CAN FEEL YOU HOLDING BACK.
ATTACK ME.
IF YOU CAN'T GE PAST ME..
YOU'LL NEVER REACH THE TOP, NO MATTER WHICH PATH YOU TAKE.
HERCULI CHALLENGED GEAR TO AN ALL-OUT FIGHT.

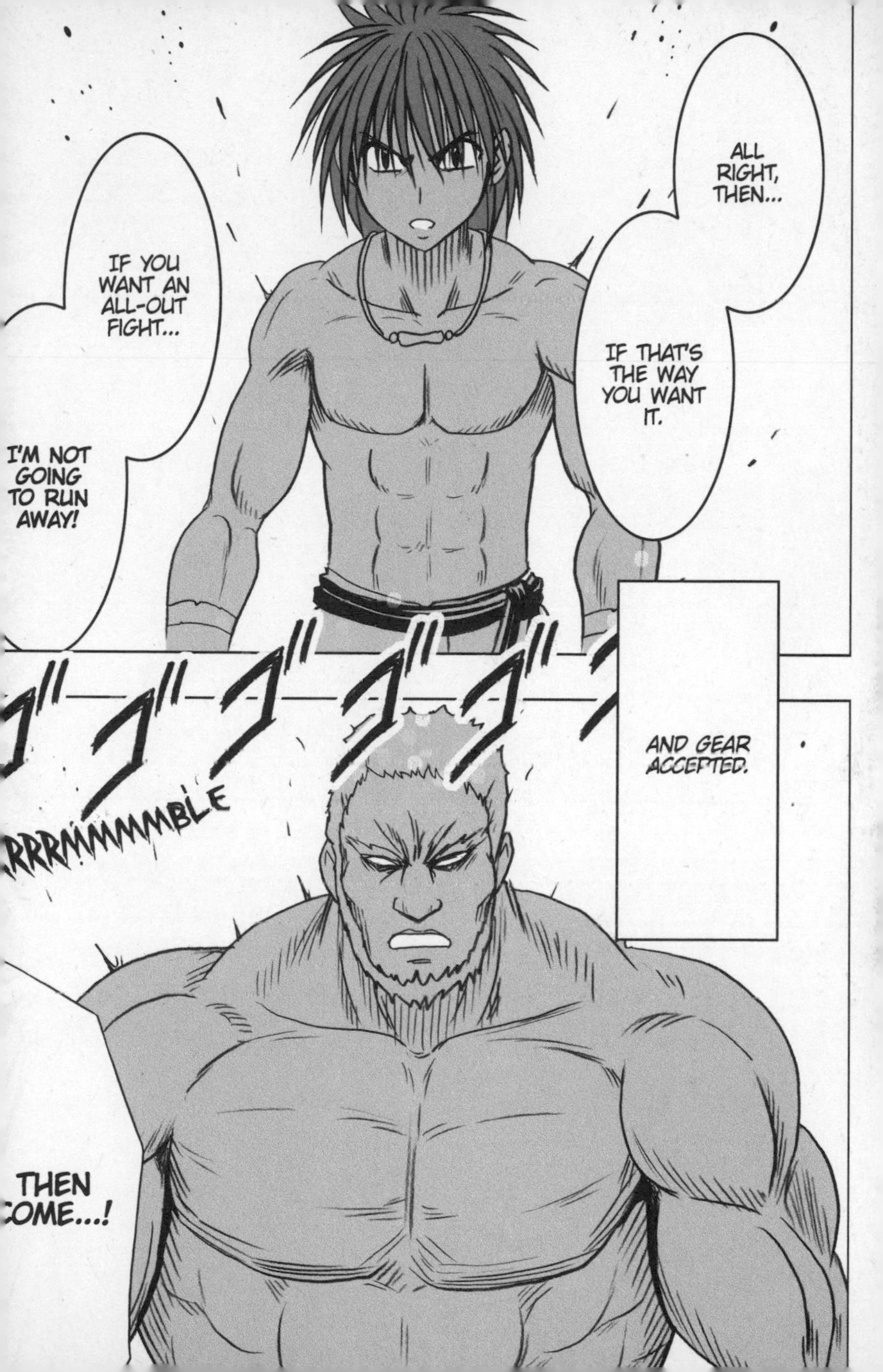
ALL RIGHT, THEN...
IF THAT'S THE WAY YOU WANT IT.
IF YOU WANT AN ALL-OUT FIGHT...
I'M NOT GOING TO RUN AWAY!
AND GEAR ACCEPTED.
RRRMMMMMBLE
THEN COME...!

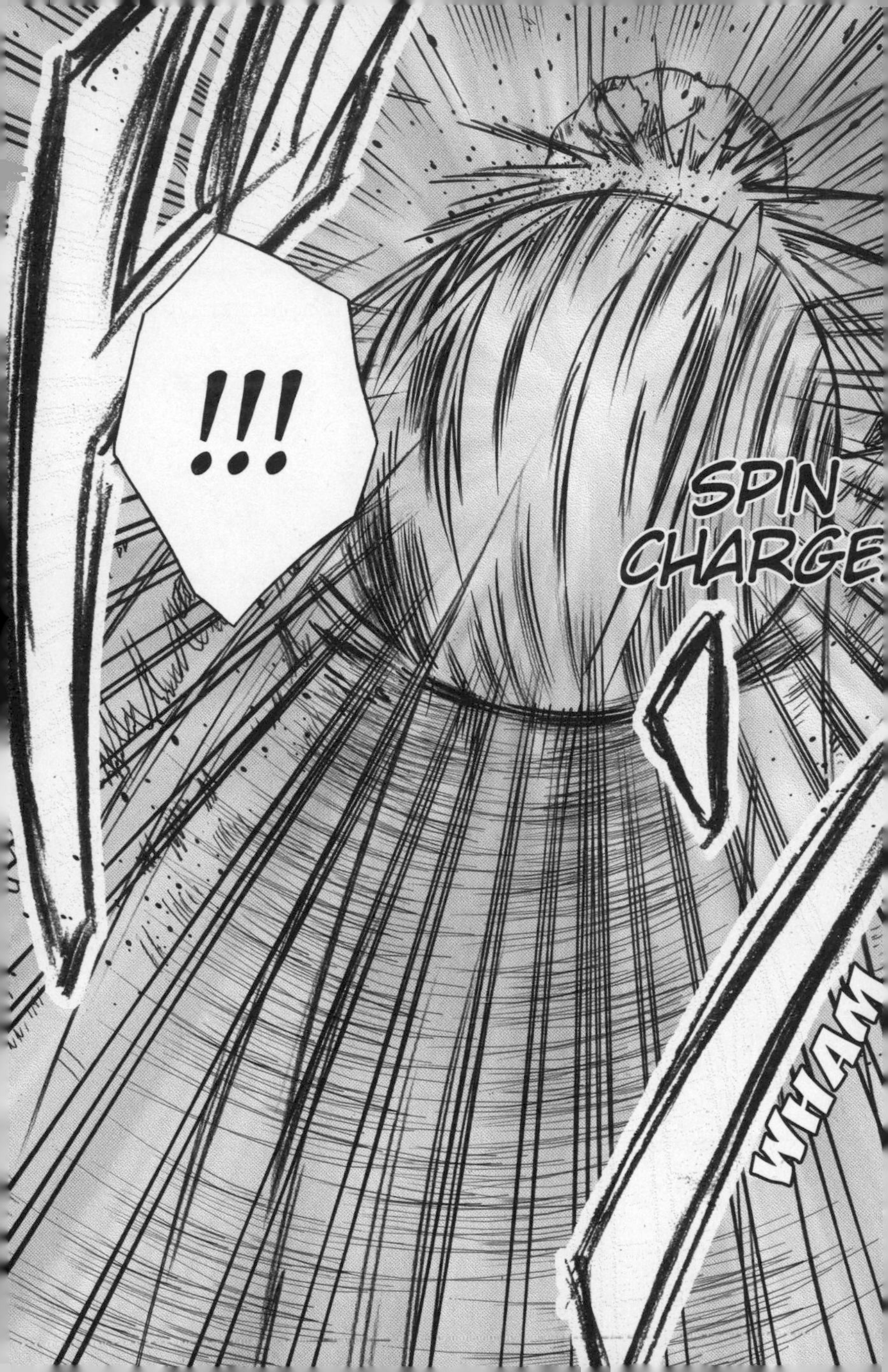
SPIN CHARGE
WHAM
!!!

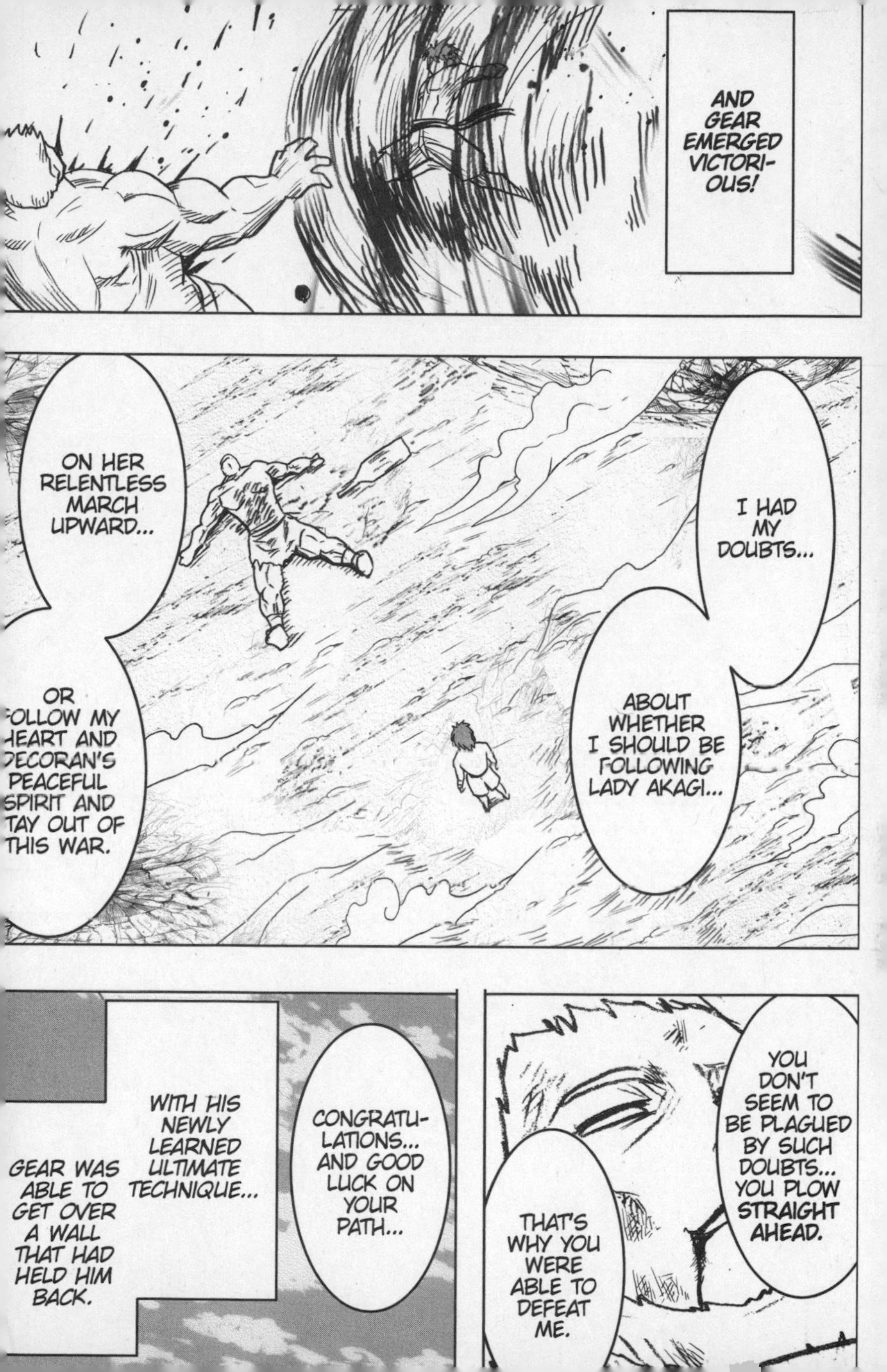
AND GEAR EMERGED VICTORIOUS!
I HAD MY DOUBTS...
ABOUT WHETHER I SHOULD BE FOLLOWING LADY AKAGI...
ON HER RELENTLESS MARCH UPWARD...
OR FOLLOW MY HEART AND DECORAN'S PEACEFUL SPIRIT AND STAY OUT OF THIS WAR.
YOU DON'T SEEM TO BE PLAGUED BY SUCH DOUBTS... YOU PLOW STRAIGHT AHEAD.
THAT'S WHY YOU WERE ABLE TO DEFEAT ME.
CONGRATULATIONS... AND GOOD LUCK ON YOUR PATH...
WITH HIS NEWLY LEARNED ULTIMATE TECHNIQUE...
GEAR WAS ABLE TO GET OVER A WALL THAT HAD HELD HIM BACK.

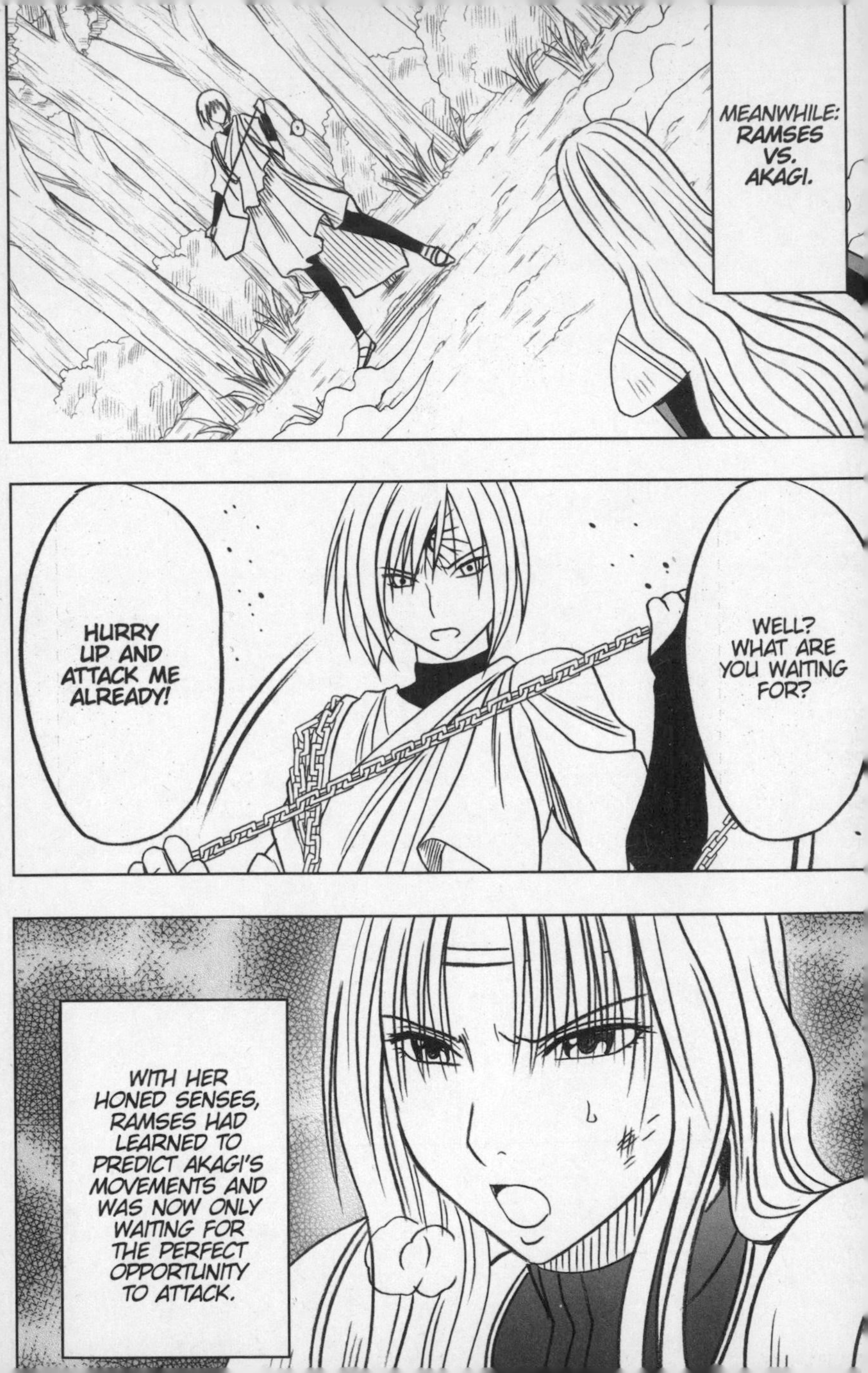
MEANWHILE: RAMSES VS. AKAGI.
WELL? WHAT ARE YOU WAITING FOR?
HURRY UP AND ATTACK ME ALREADY!
WITH HER HONED SENSES, RAMSES HAD LEARNED TO PREDICT AKAGI'S MOVEMENTS AND WAS NOW ONLY WAITING FOR THE PERFECT OPPORTUNITY TO ATTACK.

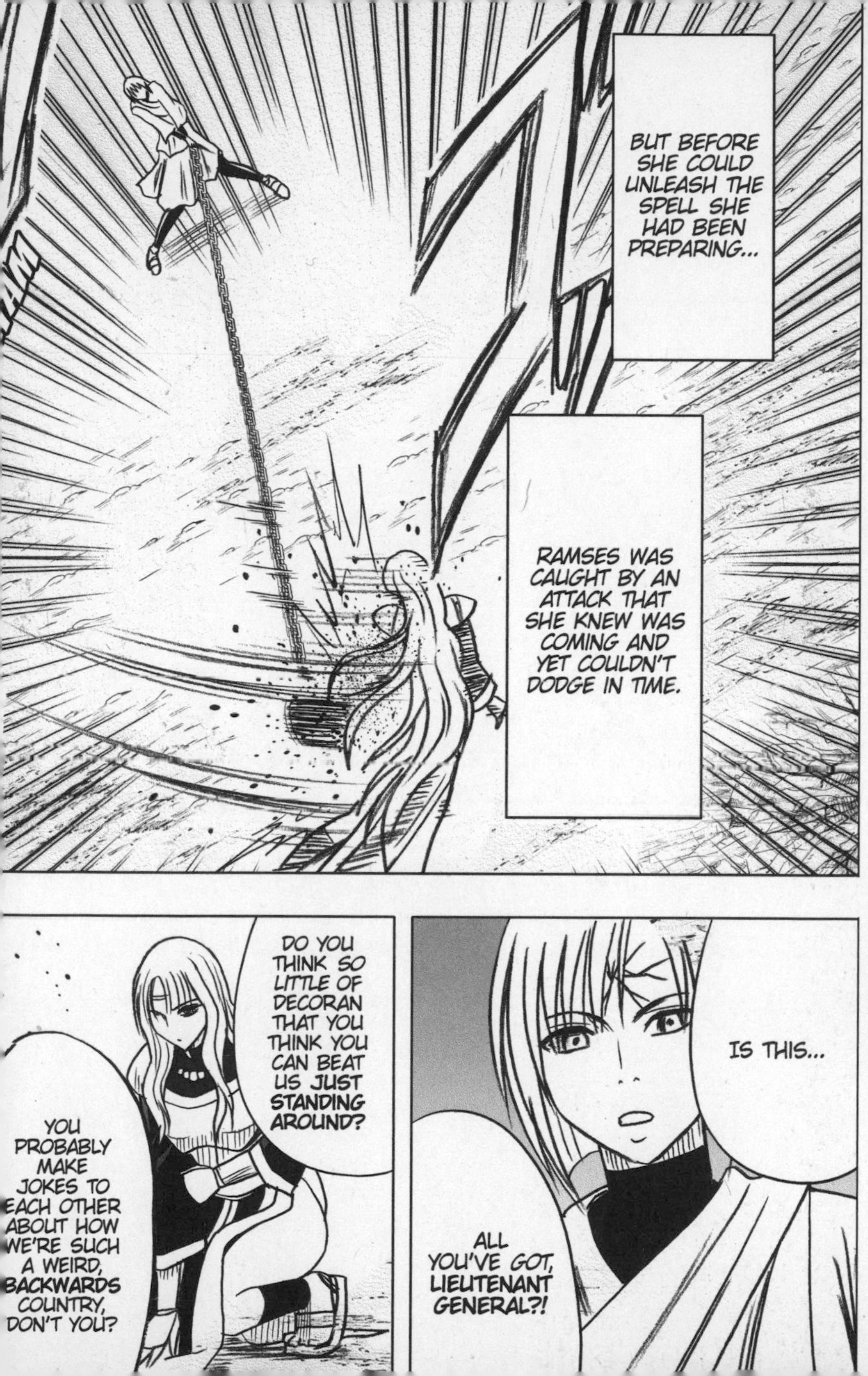
BUT BEFORE SHE COULD UNLEASH THE SPELL SHE HAD BEEN PREPARING...
RAMSES WAS CAUGHT BY AN ATTACK THAT SHE KNEW WAS COMING AND YET COULDN'T DODGE IN TIME.
IS THIS...
ALL YOU'VE GOT, LIEUTENANT GENERAL?!
DO YOU THINK SO LITTLE OF DECORAN THAT YOU THINK YOU CAN BEAT US JUST STANDING AROUND?
YOU PROBABLY MAKE JOKES TO EACH OTHER ABOUT HOW WE'RE SUCH A WEIRD, BACKWARDS COUNTRY, DON'T YOU?

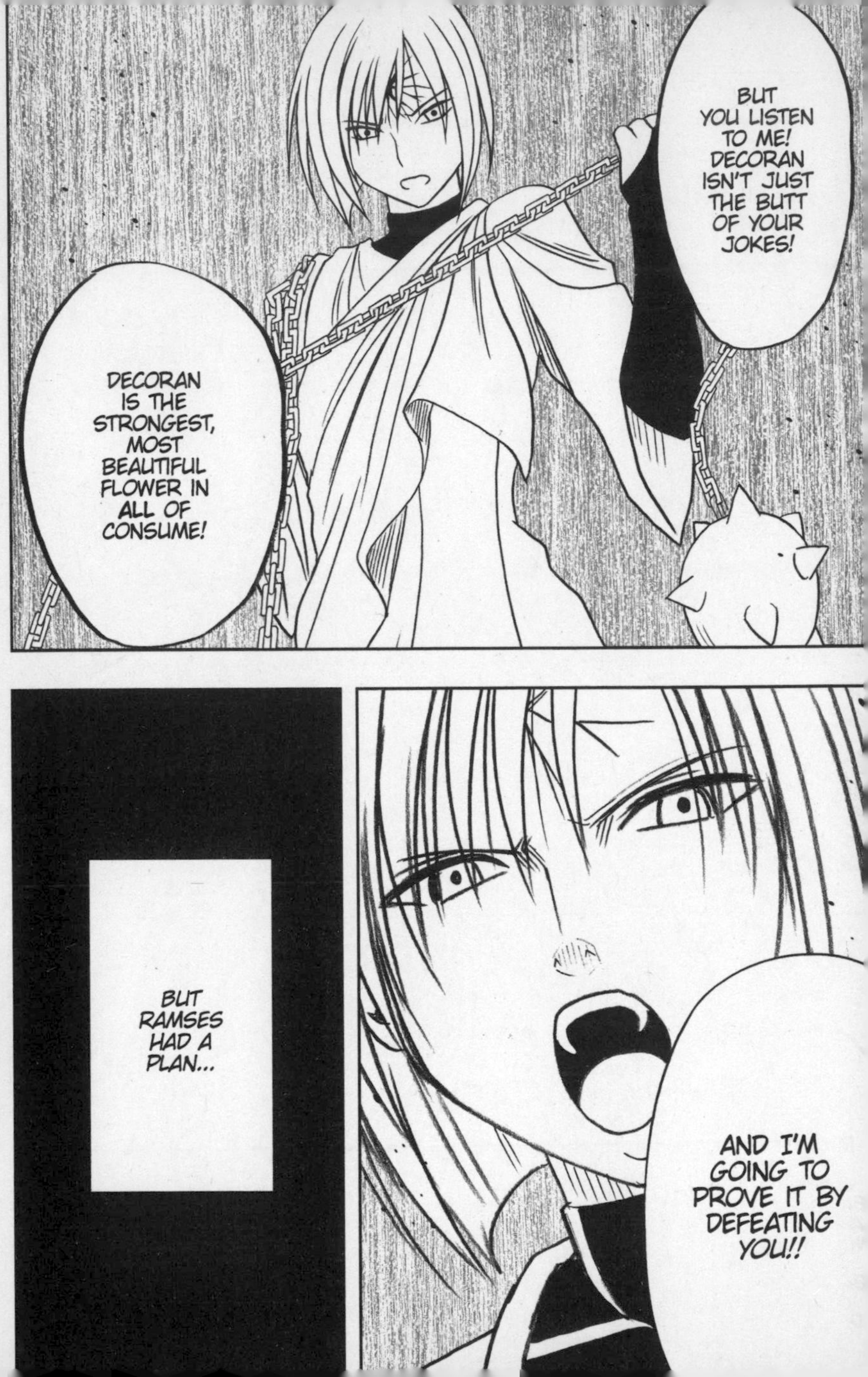
BUT YOU LISTEN TO ME! DECORAN ISN'T JUST THE BUTT OF YOUR JOKES!
DECORAN IS THE STRONGEST, MOST BEAUTIFUL FLOWER IN ALL OF CONSUME!
AND I'M GOING TO PROVE IT BY DEFEATING YOU!!
BUT RAMSES HAD A PLAN...

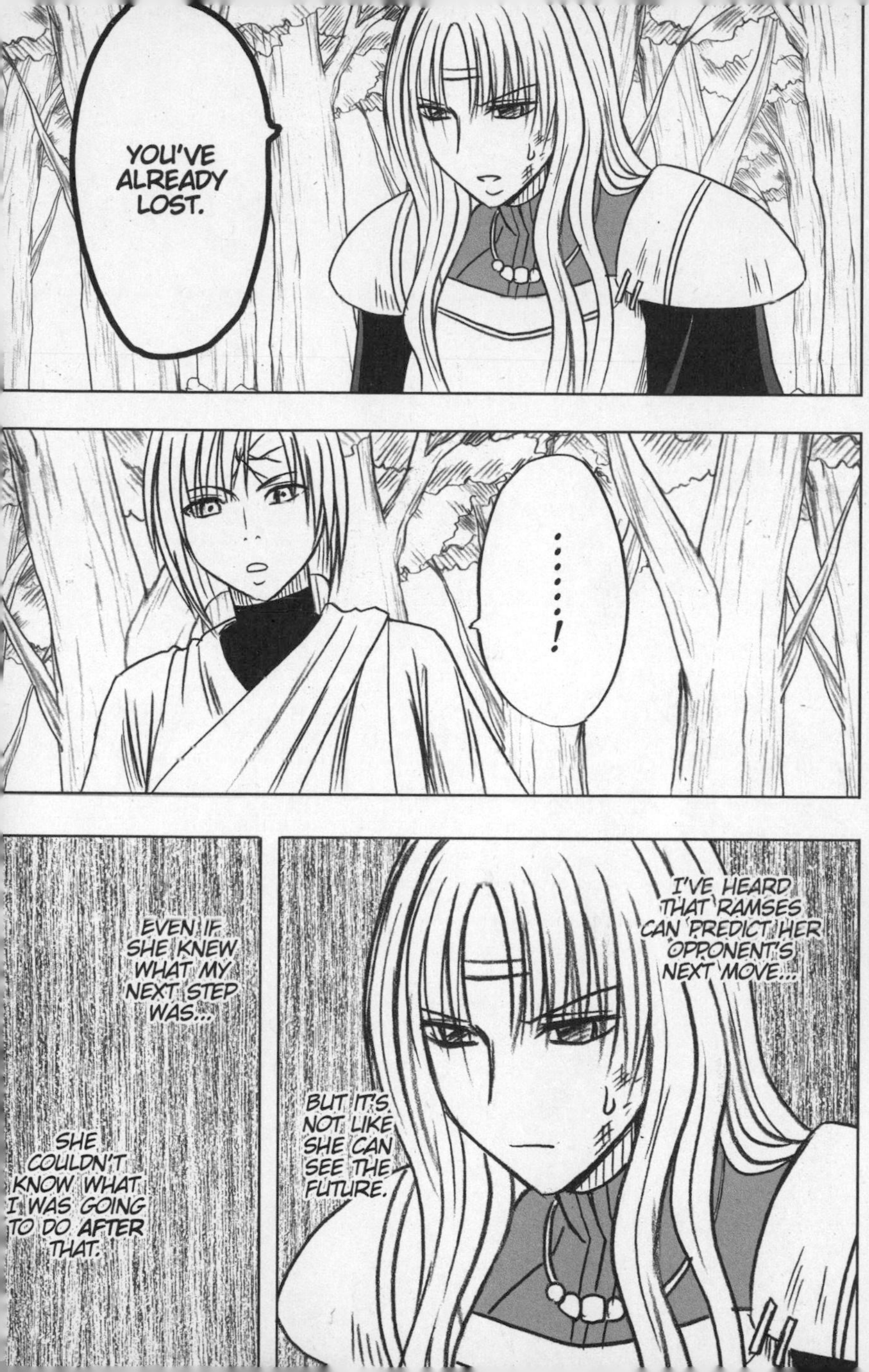
YOU'VE ALREADY LOST.
......!
I'VE HEARD THAT RAMSES CAN PREDICT HER OPPONENT'S NEXT MOVE...
BUT IT'S NOT LIKE SHE CAN SEE THE FUTURE.
EVEN IF SHE KNEW WHAT MY NEXT STEP WAS...
SHE COULDN'T KNOW WHAT I WAS GOING TO DO AFTER THAT.

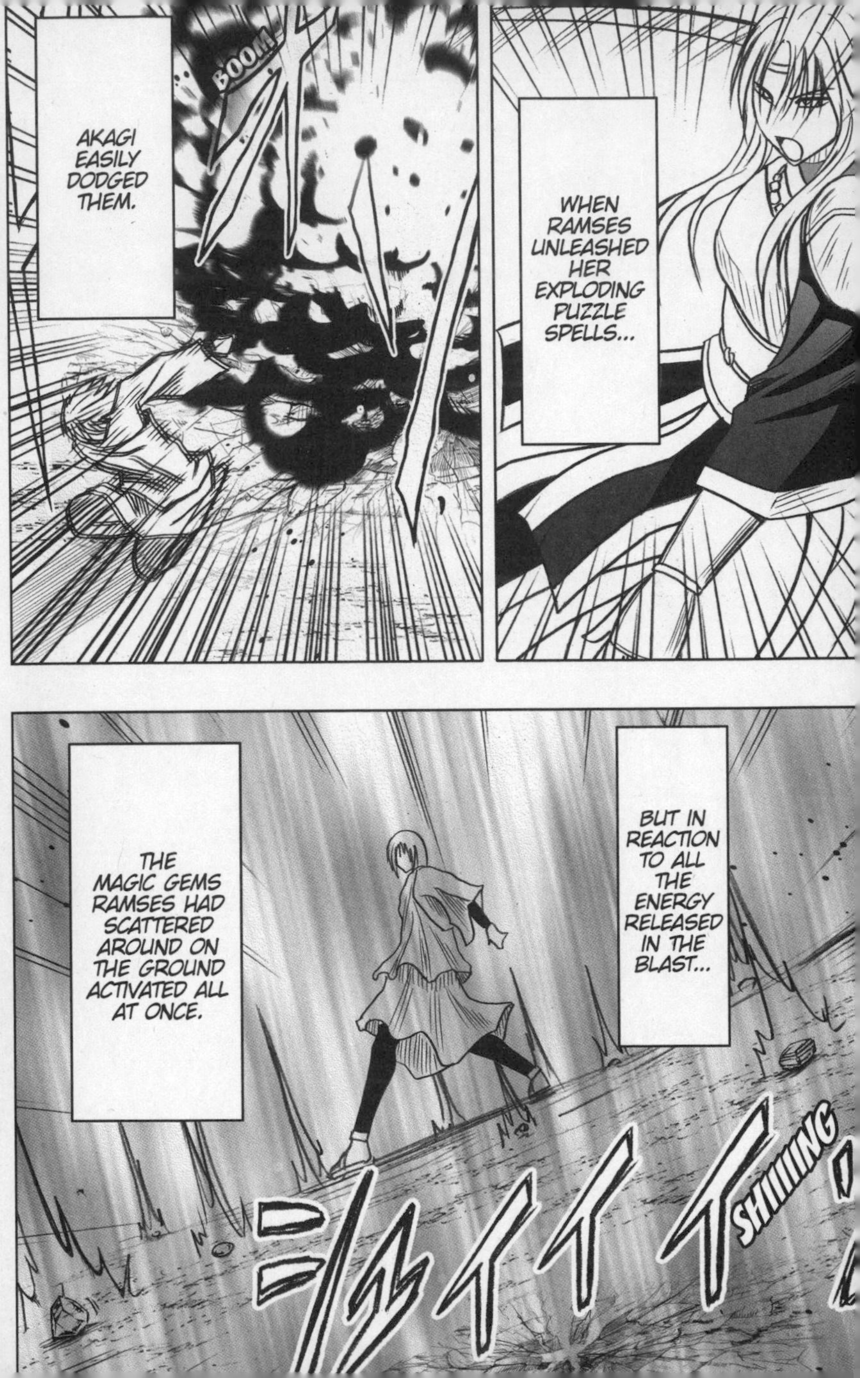
WHEN RAMSES UNLEASHED HER EXPLODING PUZZLE SPELLS...
BOOM
AKAGI EASILY DODGED THEM.
BUT IN REACTION TO ALL THE ENERGY RELEASED IN THE BLAST...
THE MAGIC GEMS RAMSES HAD SCATTERED AROUND ON THE GROUND ACTIVATED ALL AT ONCE.
SHIIIING

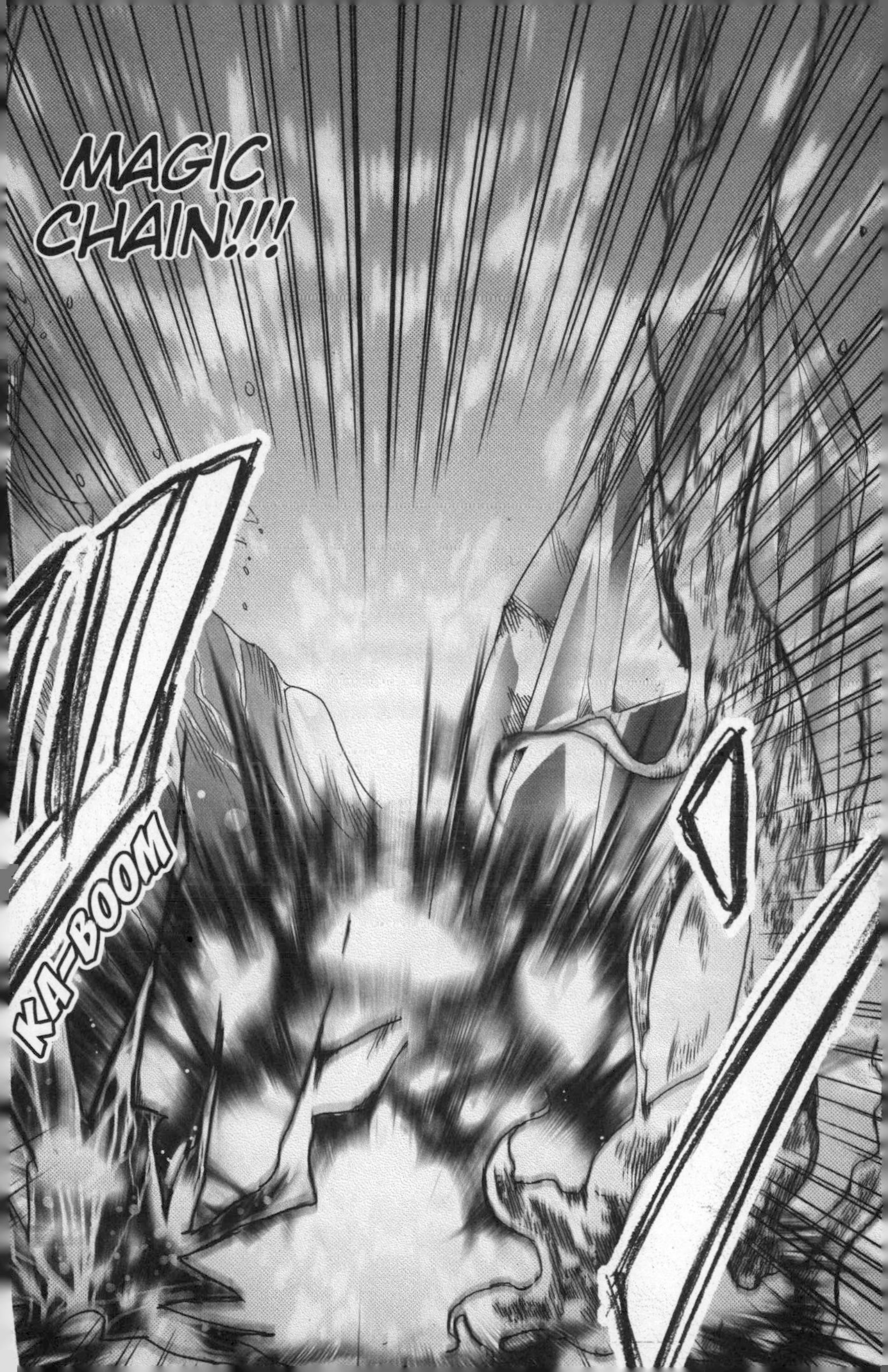
MAGIC CHAIN!!!
KA-BOOM

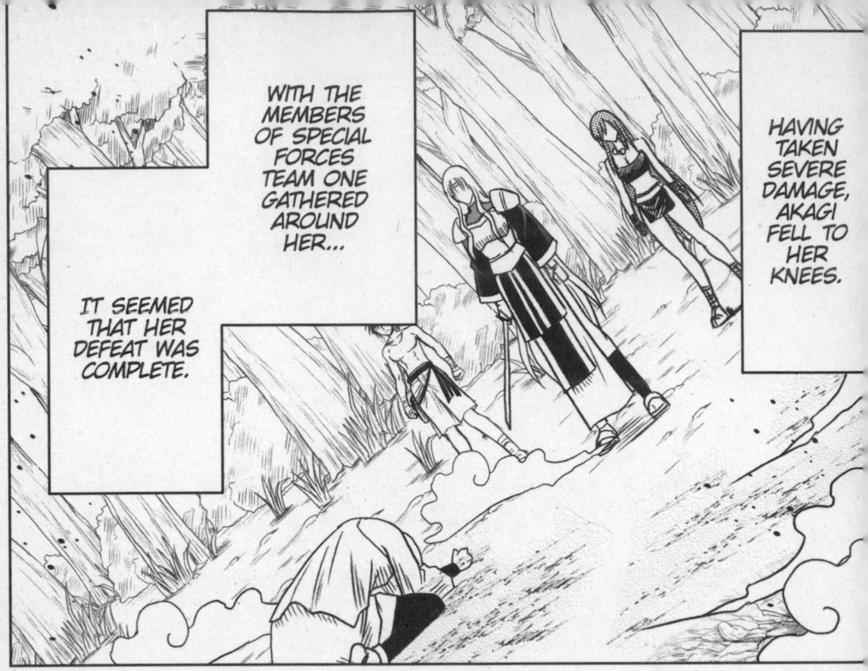
HAVING TAKEN SEVERE DAMAGE, AKAGI FELL TO HER KNEES.
WITH THE MEMBERS OF SPECIAL FORCES TEAM ONE GATHERED AROUND HER...
IT SEEMED THAT HER DEFEAT WAS COMPLETE.
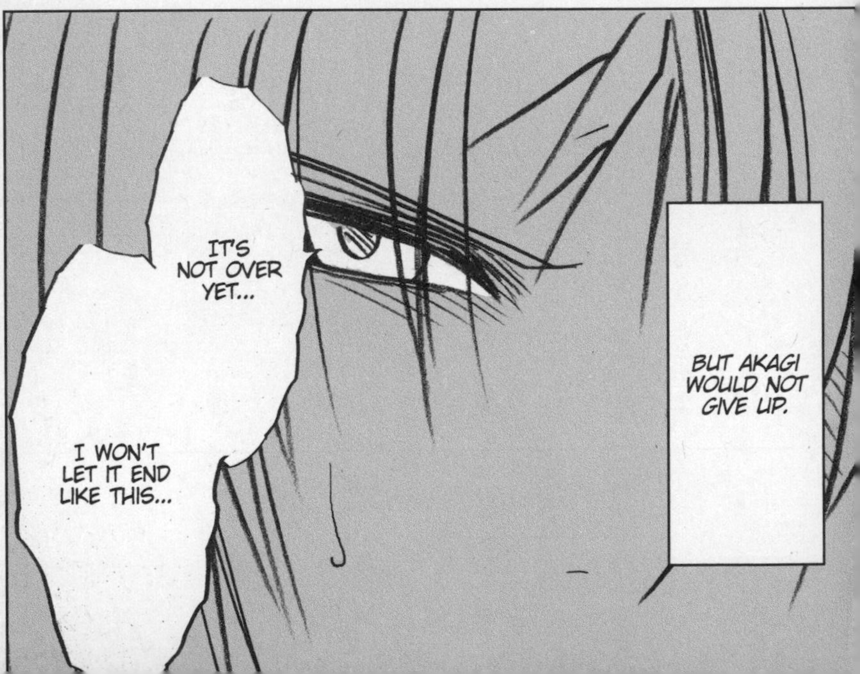
BUT AKAGI WOULD NOT GIVE UP.
IT'S NOT OVER YET...
I WON'T LET IT END LIKE THIS...

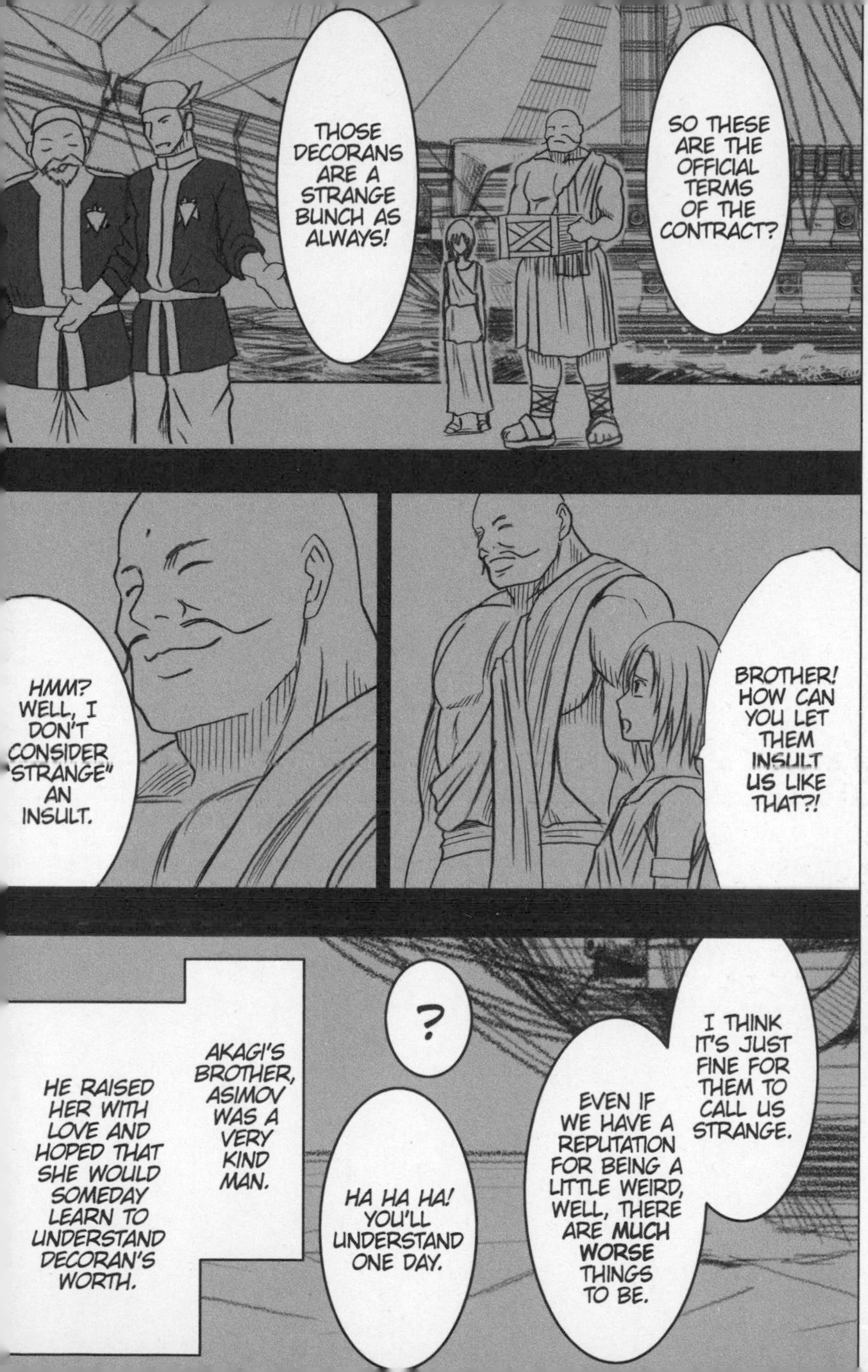
SO THESE ARE THE OFFICIAL TERMS OF THE CONTRACT?
THOSE DECORANS ARE A STRANGE BUNCH AS ALWAYS!
BROTHER! HOW CAN YOU LET THEM INSULT US LIKE THAT?!
HMM? WELL, I DON'T CONSIDER "STRANGE" AN INSULT.
I THINK IT'S JUST FINE FOR THEM TO CALL US STRANGE.
EVEN IF WE HAVE A REPUTATION FOR BEING A LITTLE WEIRD, WELL, THERE ARE MUCH WORSE THINGS TO BE.
?
HA HA HA! YOU'LL UNDERSTAND ONE DAY.
AKAGI'S BROTHER, ASIMOV WAS A VERY KIND MAN.
HE RAISED HER WITH LOVE AND HOPED THAT SHE WOULD SOMEDAY LEARN TO UNDERSTAND DECORAN'S WORTH.

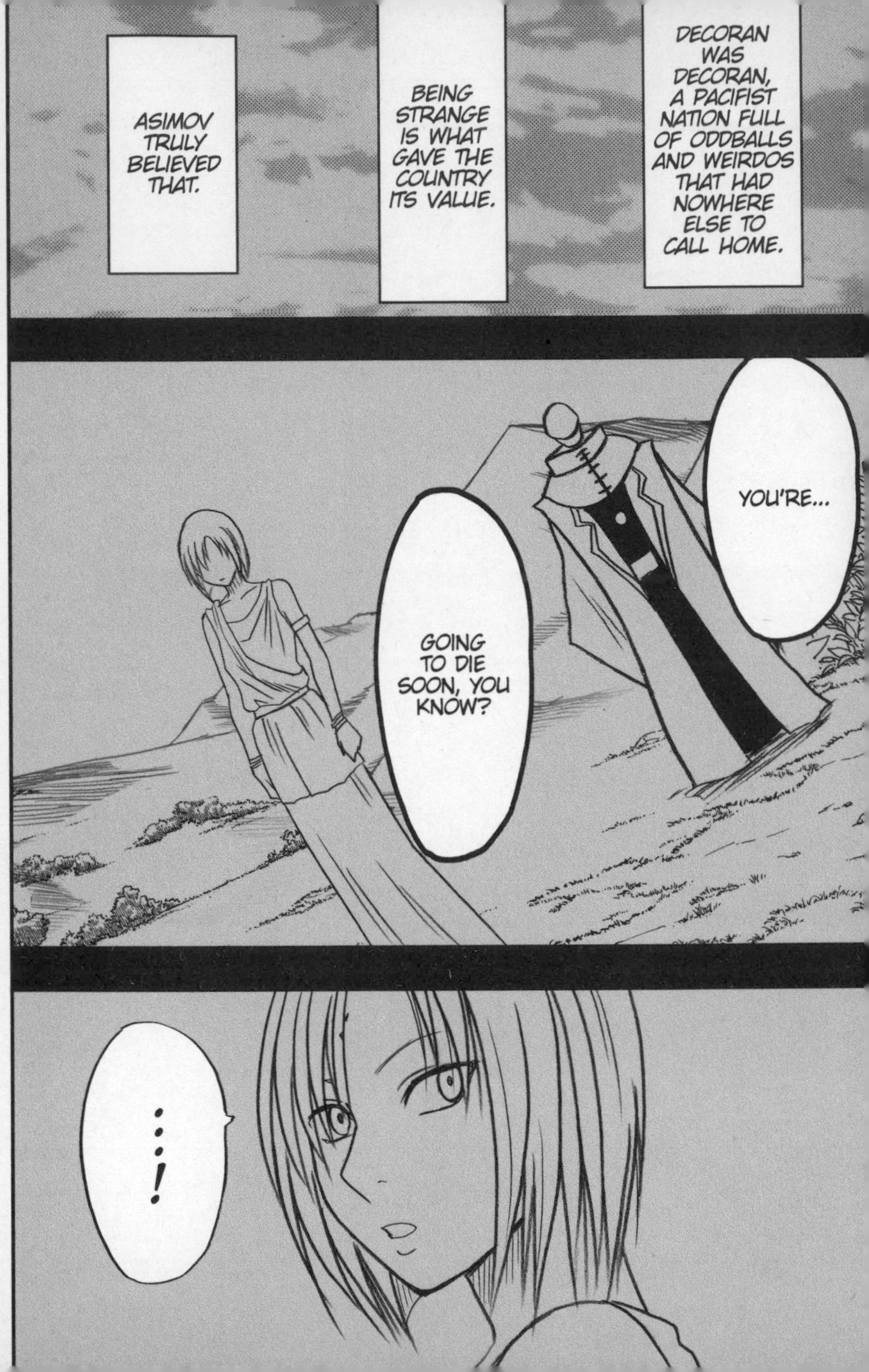
DECORAN WAS DECORAN, A PACIFIST NATION FULL OF ODDBALLS AND WEIRDOS THAT HAD NOWHERE ELSE TO CALL HOME.
BEING STRANGE IS WHAT GAVE THE COUNTRY ITS VALUE.
ASIMOV TRULY BELIEVED THAT.
YOU'RE...
GOING TO DIE SOON, YOU KNOW?
...!

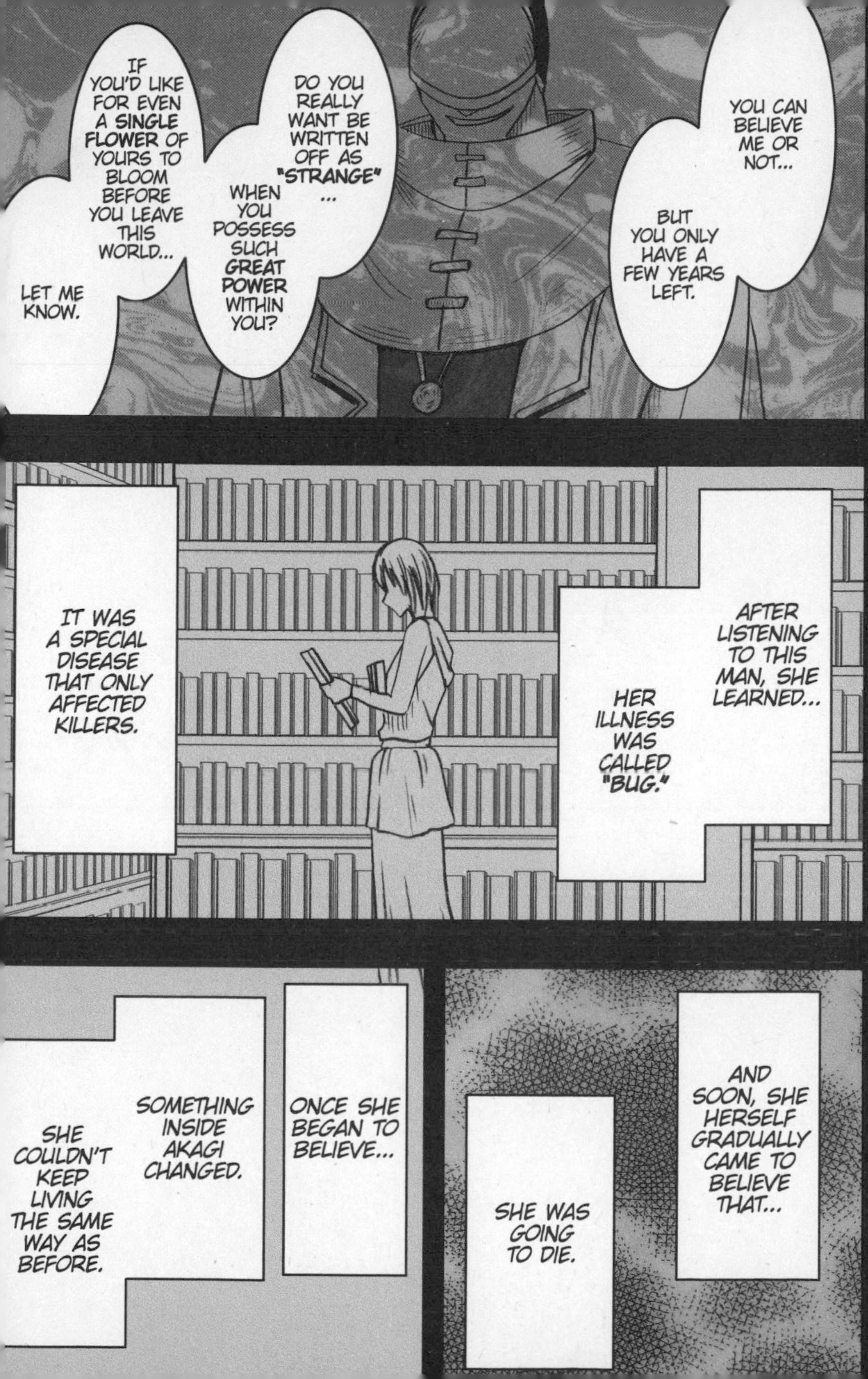
YOU CAN BELIEVE ME OR NOT...
BUT YOU ONLY HAVE A FEW YEARS LEFT.
DO YOU REALLY WANT BE WRITTEN OFF AS "STRANGE"...
WHEN YOU POSSESS SUCH GREAT POWER WITHIN YOU?
IF YOU'D LIKE FOR EVEN A SINGLE FLOWER OF YOURS TO BLOOM BEFORE YOU LEAVE THIS WORLD...
LET ME KNOW.
AFTER LISTENING TO THIS MAN, SHE LEARNED...
HER ILLNESS WAS CALLED "BUG."
IT WAS A SPECIAL DISEASE THAT ONLY AFFECTED KILLERS.
AND SOON, SHE HERSELF GRADUALLY CAME TO BELIEVE THAT...
SHE WAS GOING TO DIE.
ONCE SHE BEGAN TO BELIEVE...
SOMETHING INSIDE AKAGI CHANGED.
SHE COULDN'T KEEP LIVING THE SAME WAY AS BEFORE.

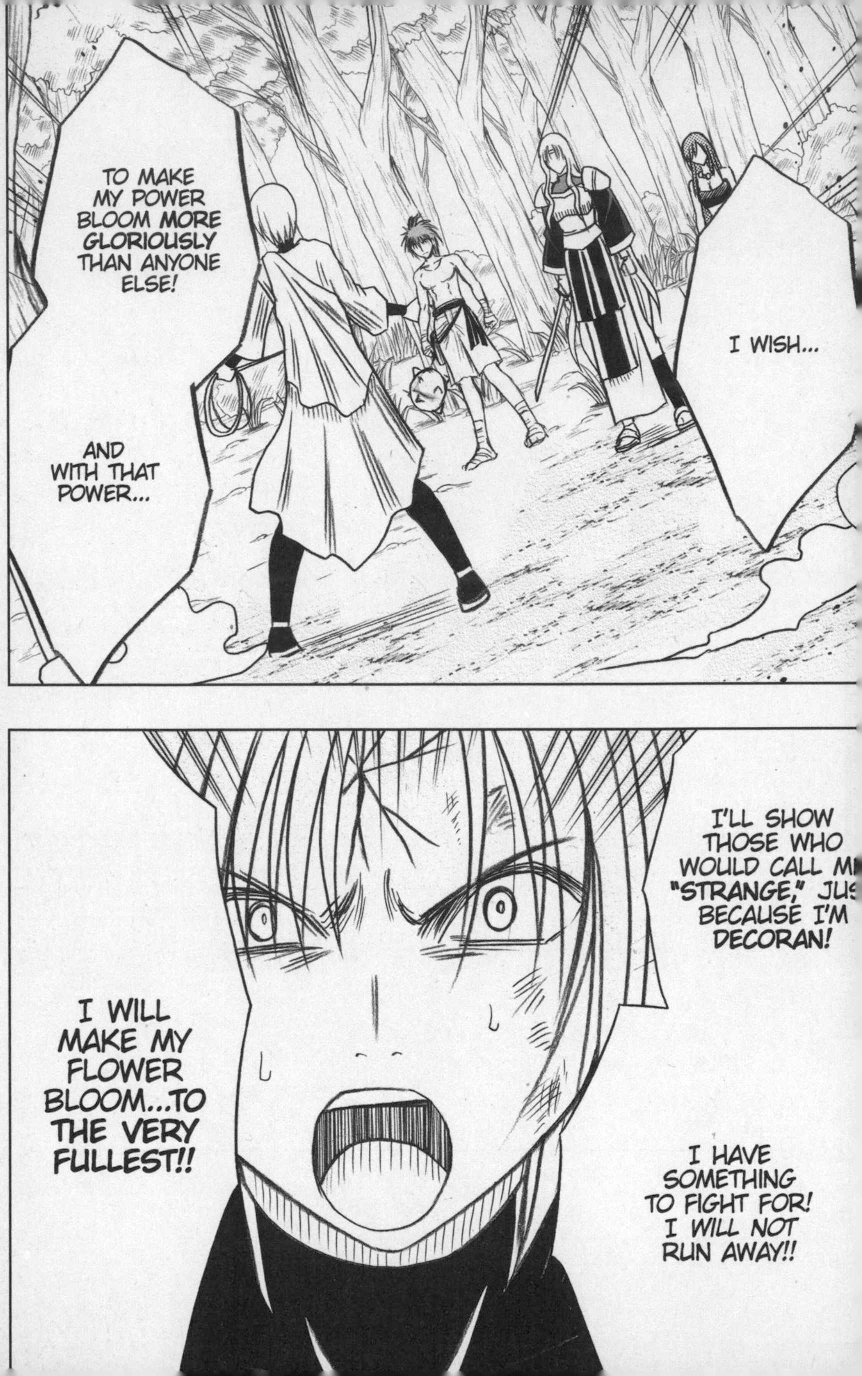
I WISH...
TO MAKE MY POWER BLOOM MORE GLORIOUSLY THAN ANYONE ELSE!
AND WITH THAT POWER...
I'LL SHOW THOSE WHO WOULD CALL M "STRANGE," JUS BECAUSE I'M DECORAN!
I HAVE SOMETHING TO FIGHT FOR! I WILL NOT RUN AWAY!!
I WILL MAKE MY FLOWER BLOOM...TO THE VERY FULLEST!!

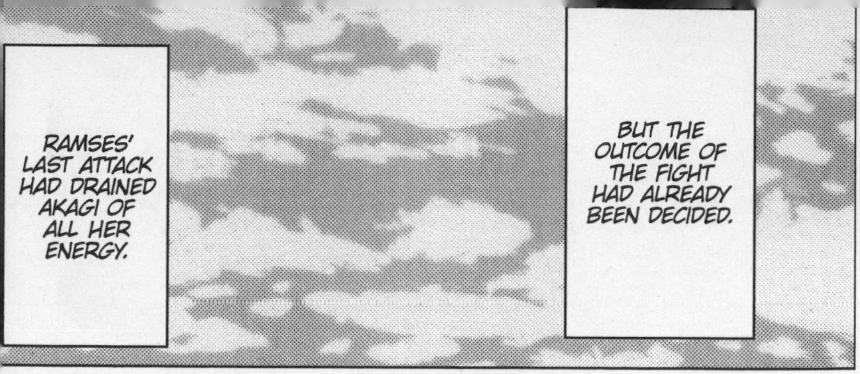
BUT THE OUTCOME OF THE FIGHT HAD ALREADY BEEN DECIDED.
RAMSES' LAST ATTACK HAD DRAINED AKAGI OF ALL HER ENERGY.
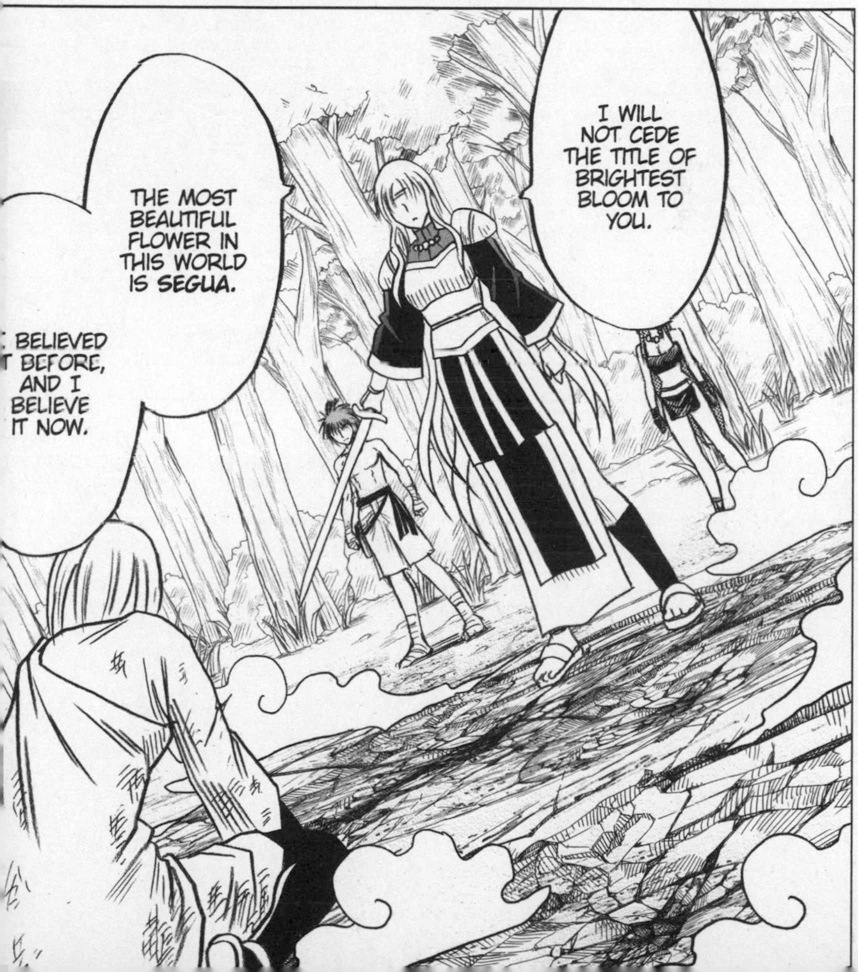
I WILL NOT CEDE THE TITLE OF BRIGHTEST BLOOM TO YOU.
THE MOST BEAUTIFUL FLOWER IN THIS WORLD IS SEGUA.
BELIEVED T BEFORE, AND I BELIEVE IT NOW.

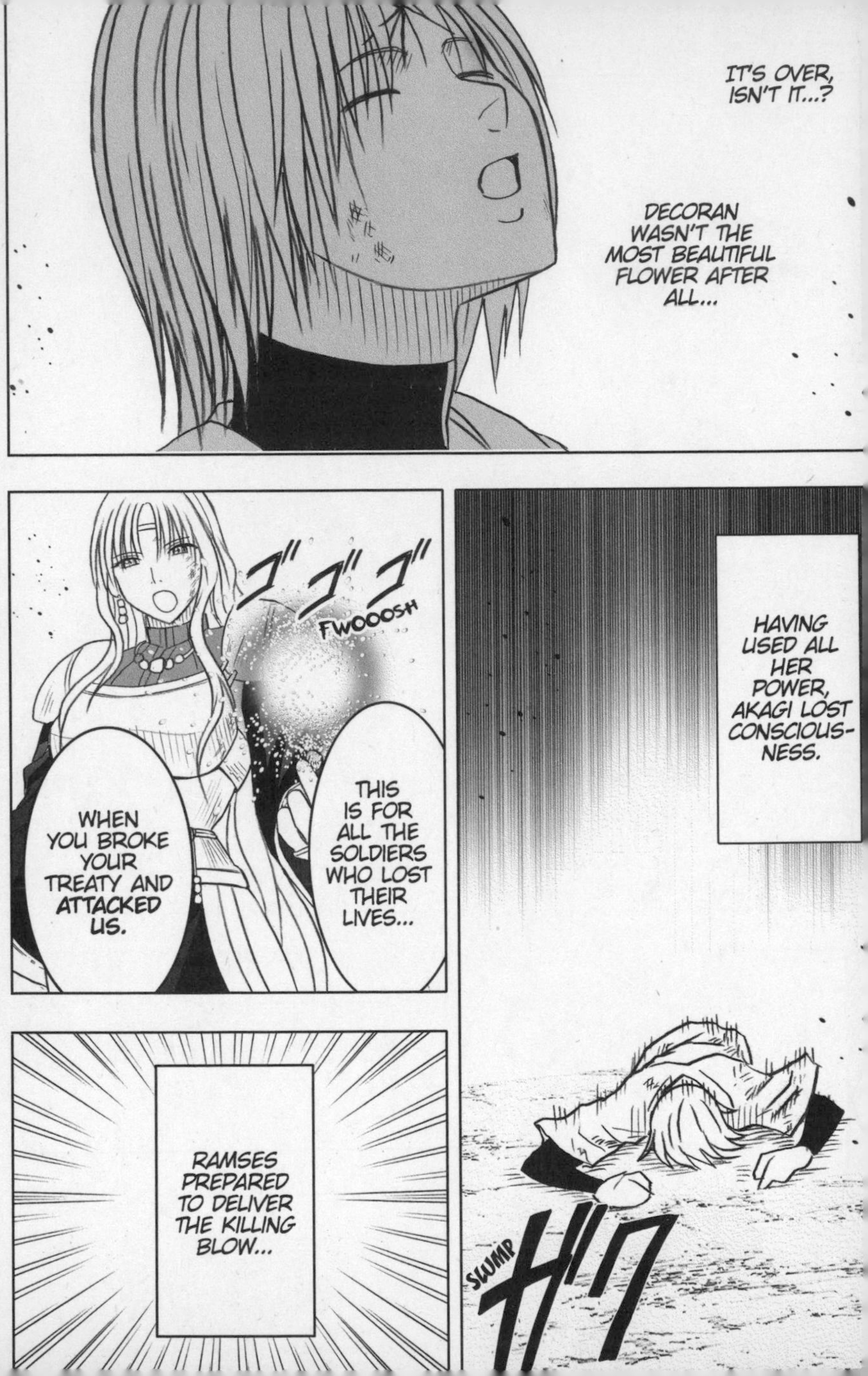
IT'S OVER, ISN'T IT...?
DECORAN WASN'T THE MOST BEAUTIFUL FLOWER AFTER ALL...
HAVING USED ALL HER POWER, AKAGI LOST CONSCIOUS-NESS.
ガク
SWUMP
ゴゴゴ
FWOOOSH
THIS IS FOR ALL THE SOLDIERS WHO LOST THEIR LIVES...
WHEN YOU BROKE YOUR TREATY AND ATTACKED US.
RAMSES PREPARED TO DELIVER THE KILLING BLOW...

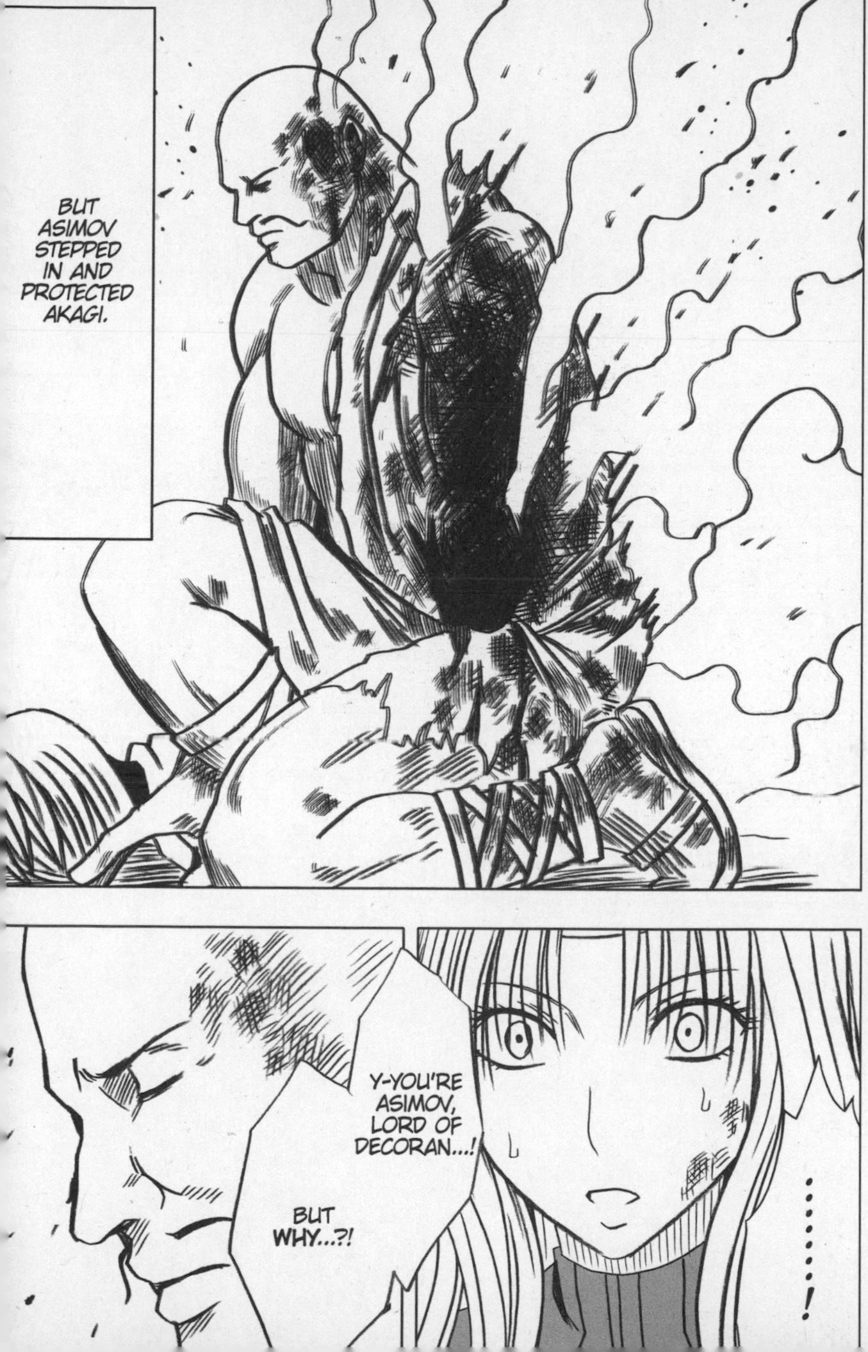
BUT ASIMOV STEPPED IN AND PROTECTED AKAGI.
Y-YOU'RE ASIMOV, LORD OF DECORAN...!
BUT WHY...?!
......!

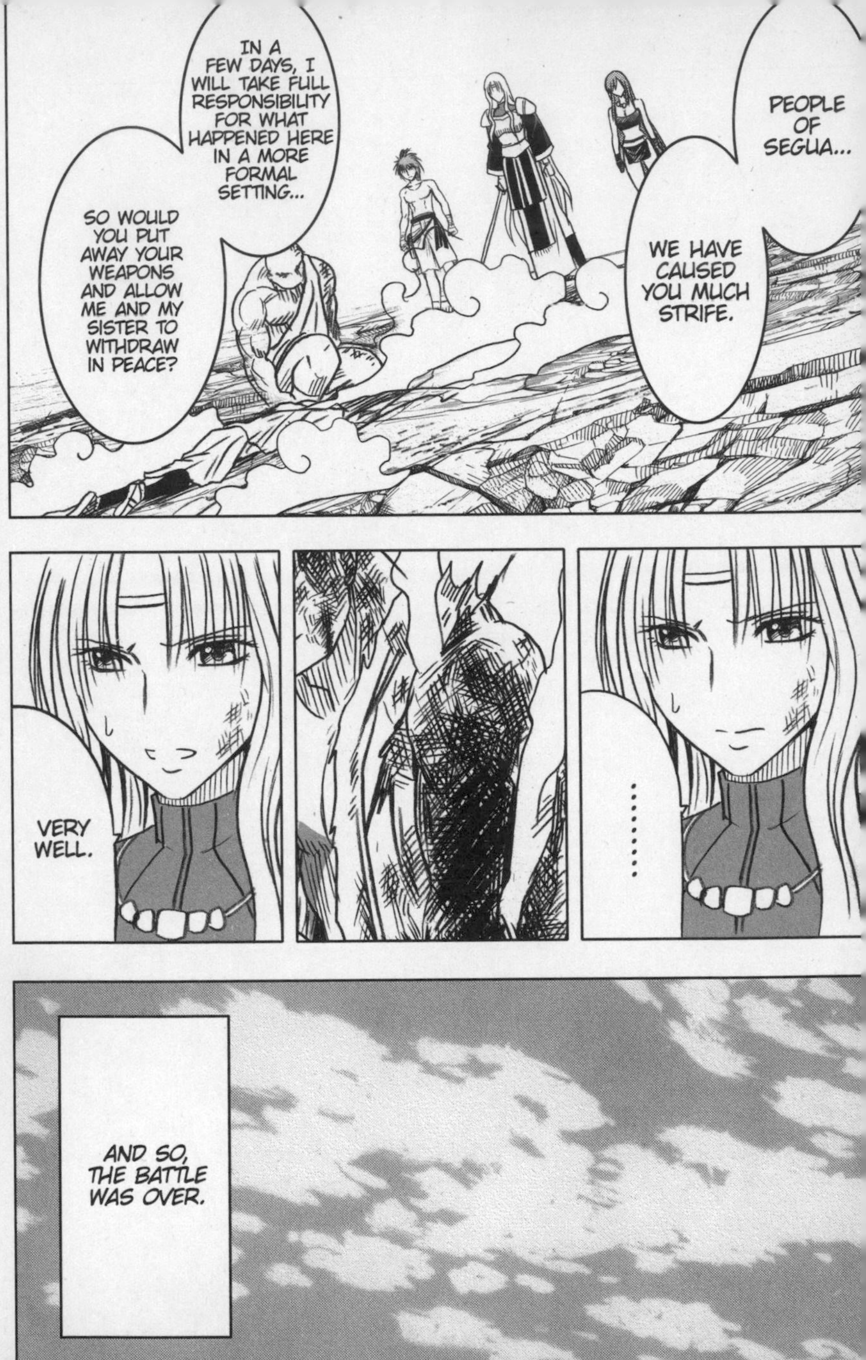

PEOPLE OF SEGUA...
WE HAVE CAUSED YOU MUCH STRIFE.
IN A FEW DAYS, I WILL TAKE FULL RESPONSIBILITY FOR WHAT HAPPENED HERE IN A MORE FORMAL SETTING...
SO WOULD YOU PUT AWAY YOUR WEAPONS AND ALLOW ME AND MY SISTER TO WITHDRAW IN PEACE?
....
VERY WELL.
AND SO, THE BATTLE WAS OVER.

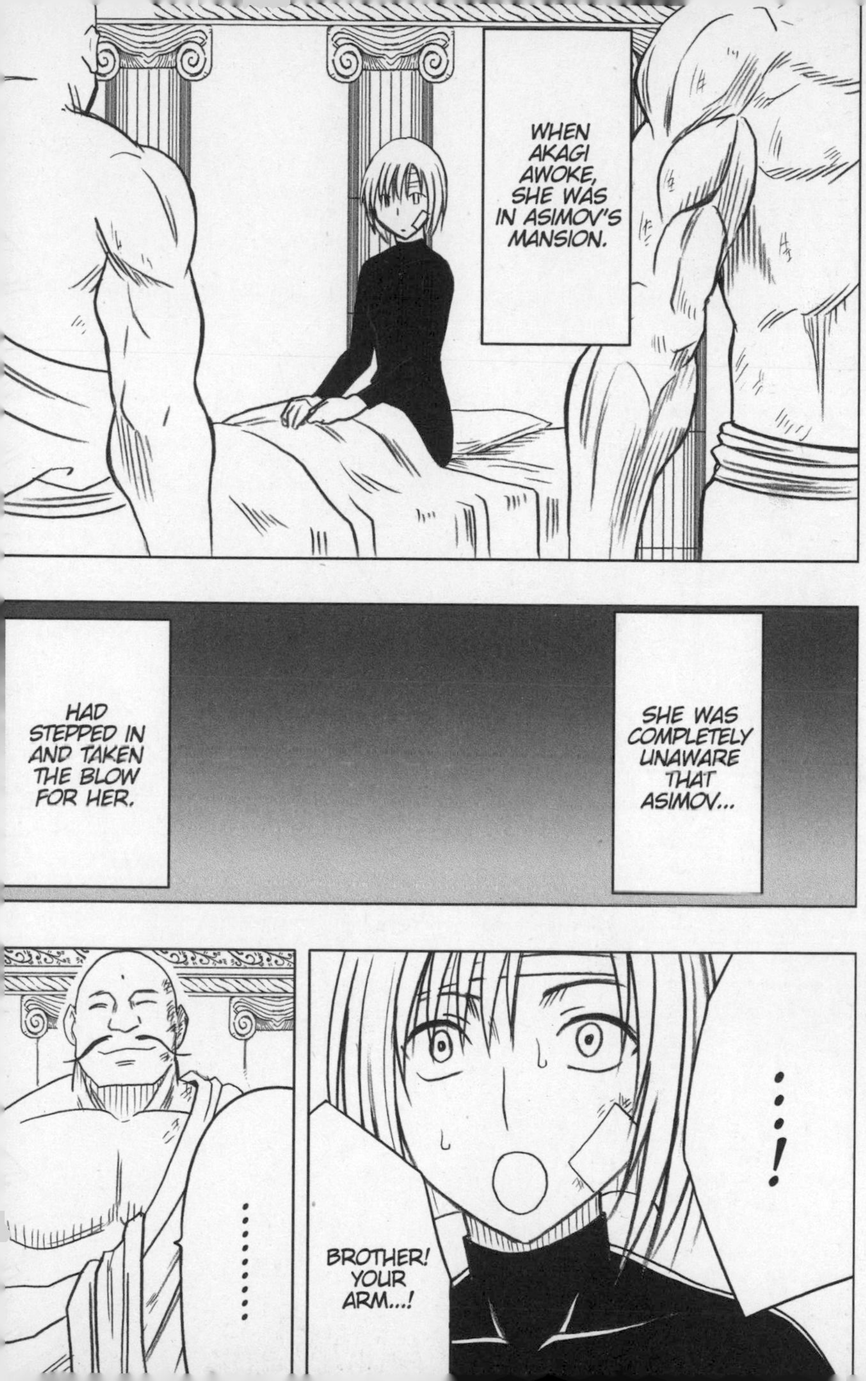
WHEN AKAGI AWOKE, SHE WAS IN ASIMOV'S MANSION.
SHE WAS COMPLETELY UNAWARE THAT ASIMOV...
HAD STEPPED IN AND TAKEN THE BLOW FOR HER.
...!
BROTHER! YOUR ARM...!
....

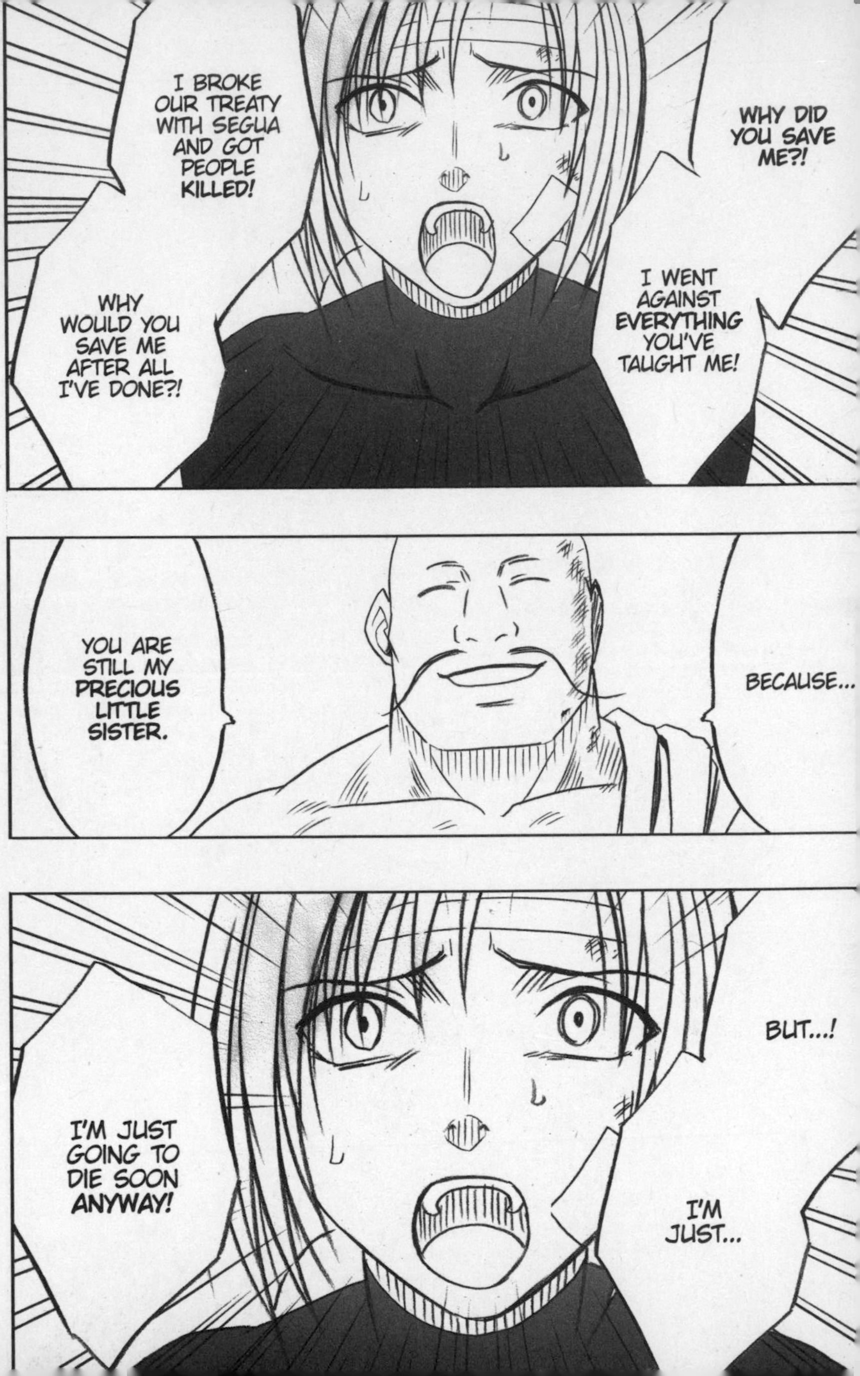
WHY DID YOU SAVE ME?!
I BROKE OUR TREATY WITH SEGUA AND GOT PEOPLE KILLED!
I WENT AGAINST EVERYTHING YOU'VE TAUGHT ME!
WHY WOULD YOU SAVE ME AFTER ALL I'VE DONE?!
BECAUSE...
YOU ARE STILL MY PRECIOUS LITTLE SISTER.
BUT...!
I'M JUST...
I'M JUST GOING TO DIE SOON ANYWAY!

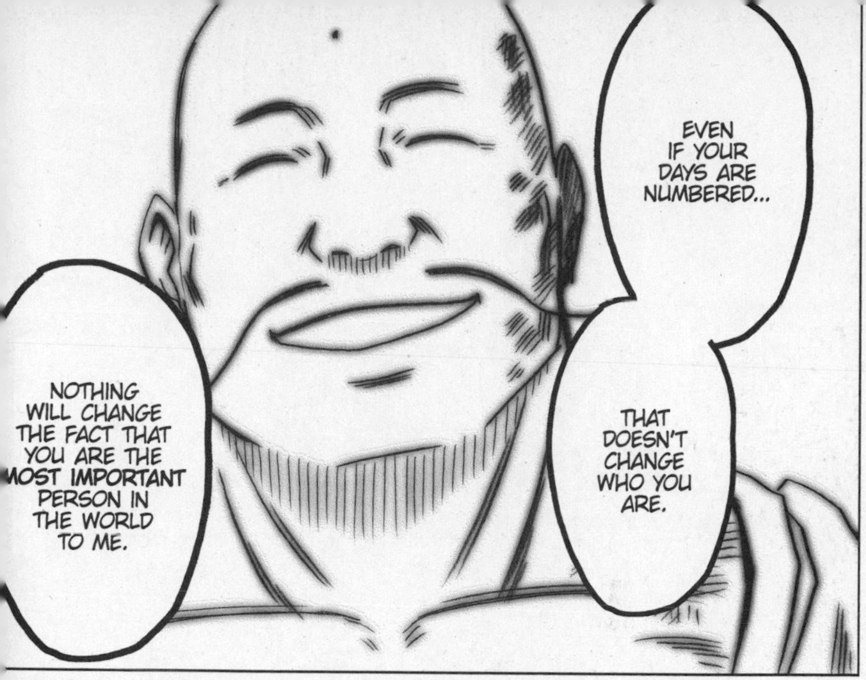
EVEN IF YOUR DAYS ARE NUMBERED...
THAT DOESN'T CHANGE WHO YOU ARE.
NOTHING WILL CHANGE THE FACT THAT YOU ARE THE MOST IMPORTANT PERSON IN THE WORLD TO ME.

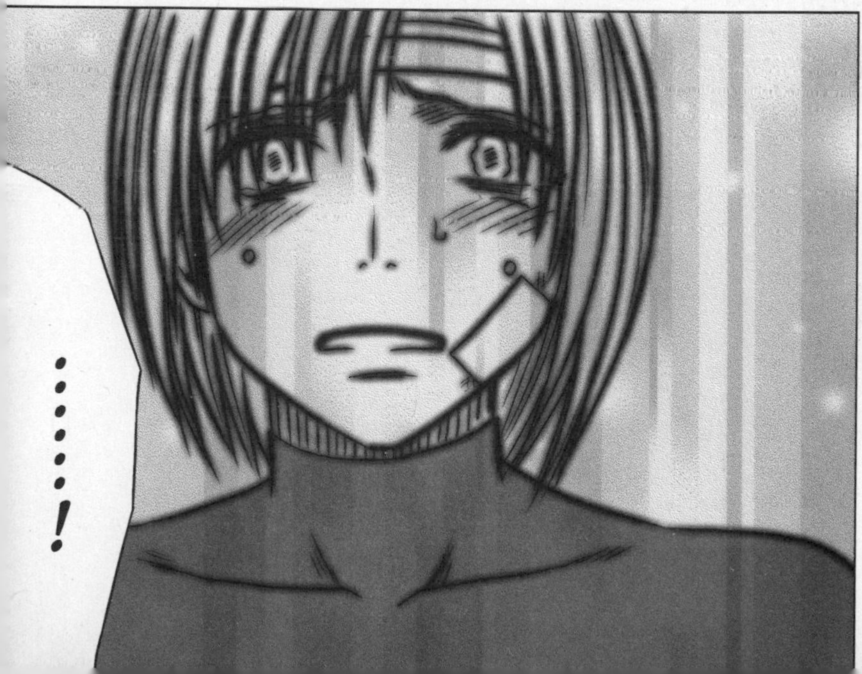
......!

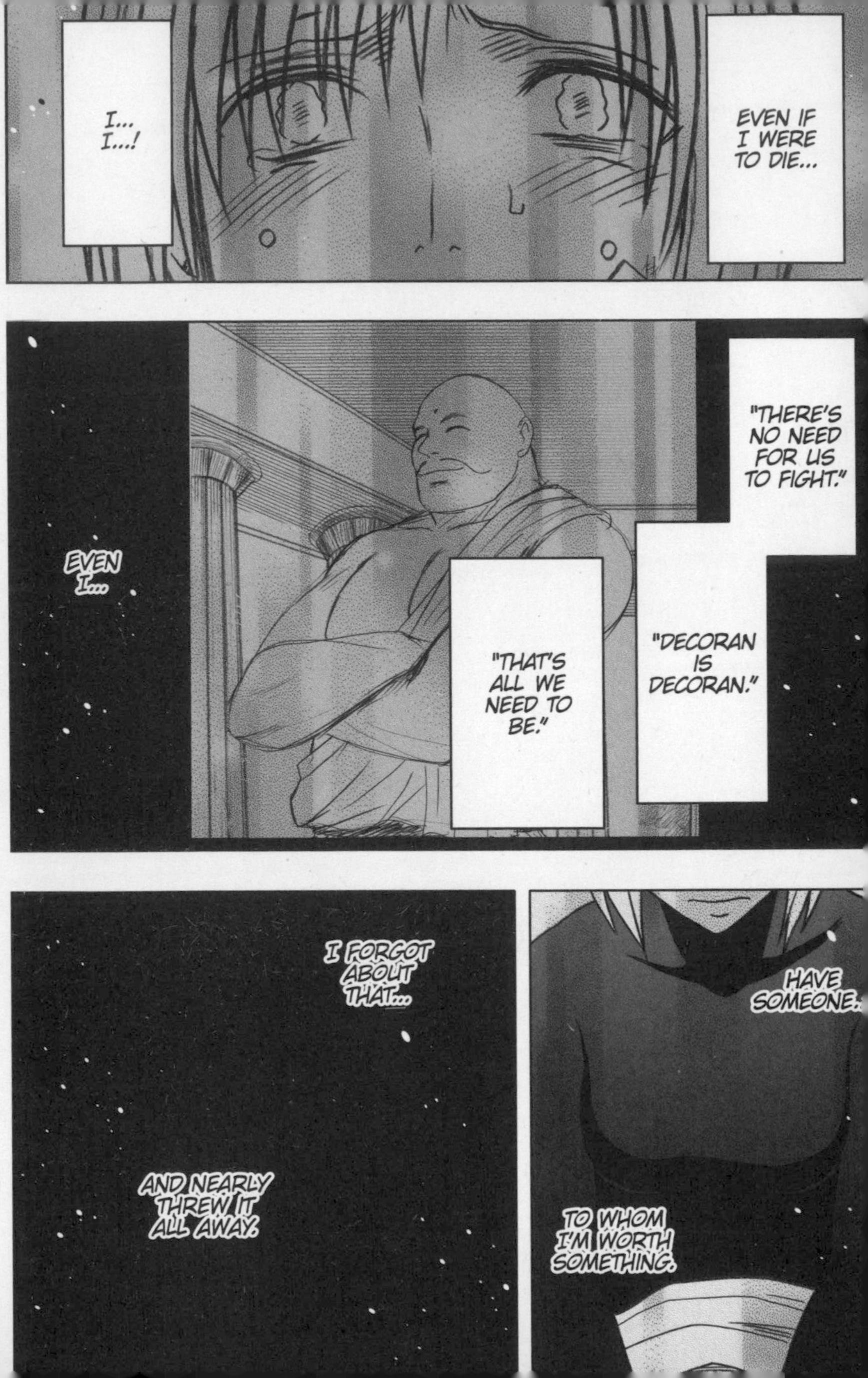
EVEN IF I WERE TO DIE...
I... I...!
"THERE'S NO NEED FOR US TO FIGHT."
"DECORAN IS DECORAN."
"THAT'S ALL WE NEED TO BE."
EVEN I...
HAVE SOMEONE.
TO WHOM I'M WORTH SOMETHING.
I FORGOT ABOUT THAT...
AND NEARLY THREW IT ALL AWAY.

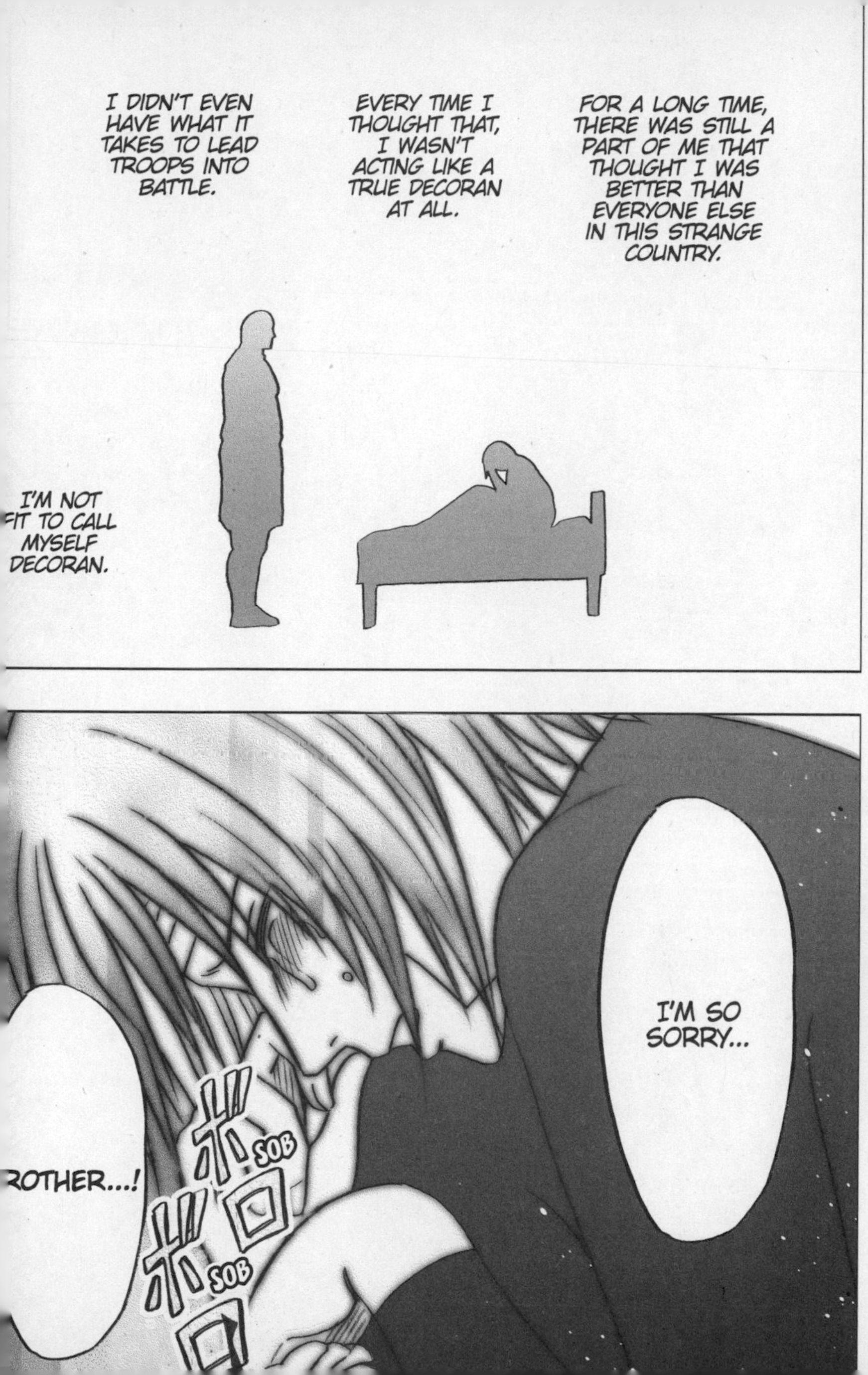
FOR A LONG TIME, THERE WAS STILL A PART OF ME THAT THOUGHT I WAS BETTER THAN EVERYONE ELSE IN THIS STRANGE COUNTRY.
EVERY TIME I THOUGHT THAT, I WASN'T ACTING LIKE A TRUE DECORAN AT ALL.
I DIDN'T EVEN HAVE WHAT IT TAKES TO LEAD TROOPS INTO BATTLE.
I'M NOT FIT TO CALL MYSELF DECORAN.
I'M SO SORRY...
ROTHER...!
SOB
SOB

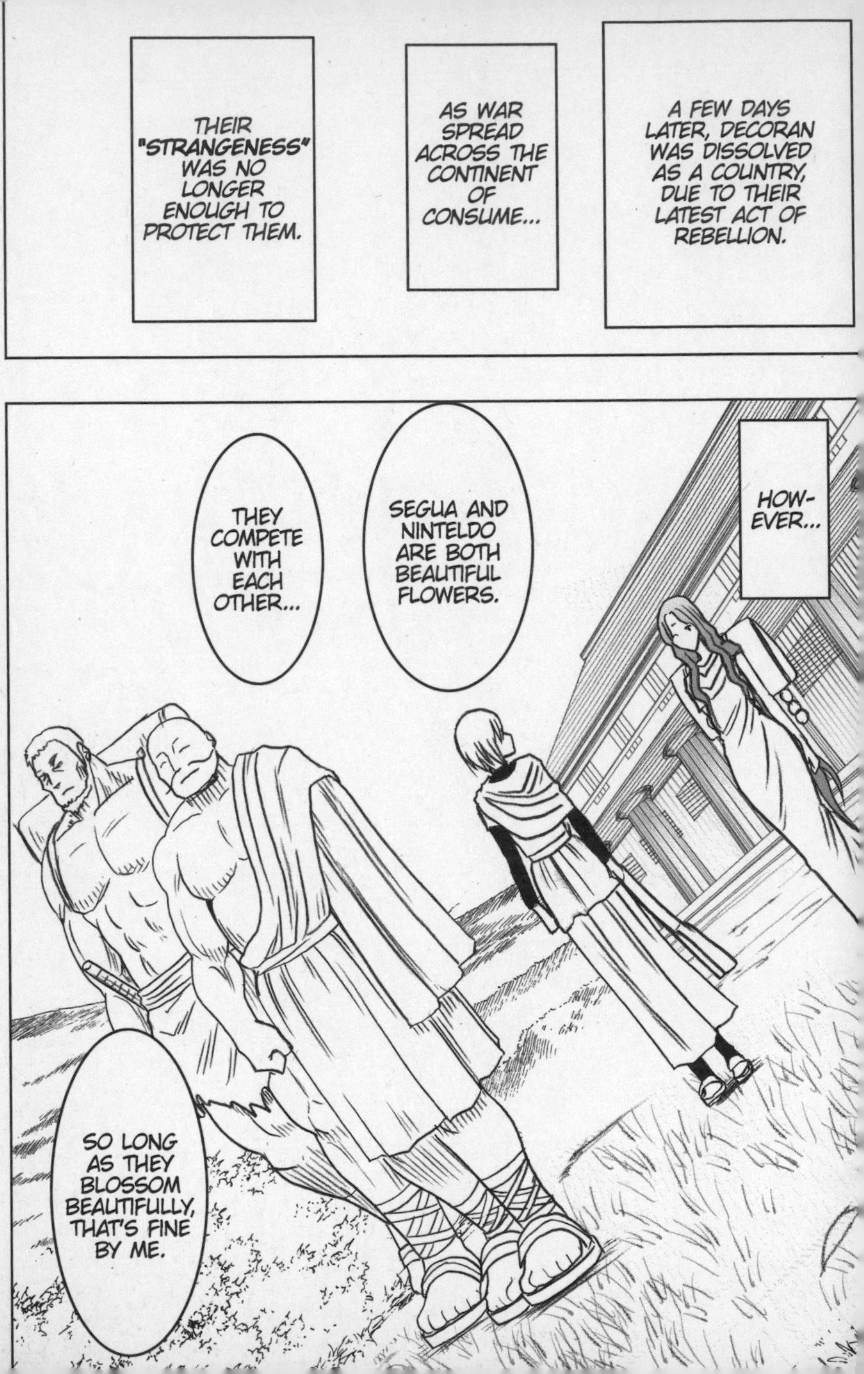
A FEW DAYS LATER, DECORAN WAS DISSOLVED AS A COUNTRY, DUE TO THEIR LATEST ACT OF REBELLION.
AS WAR SPREAD ACROSS THE CONTINENT OF CONSUME...
THEIR "STRANGENESS" WAS NO LONGER ENOUGH TO PROTECT THEM.
HOW-EVER...
SEGUA AND NINTELDO ARE BOTH BEAUTIFUL FLOWERS.
THEY COMPETE WITH EACH OTHER...
SO LONG AS THEY BLOSSOM BEAUTIFULLY, THAT'S FINE BY ME.

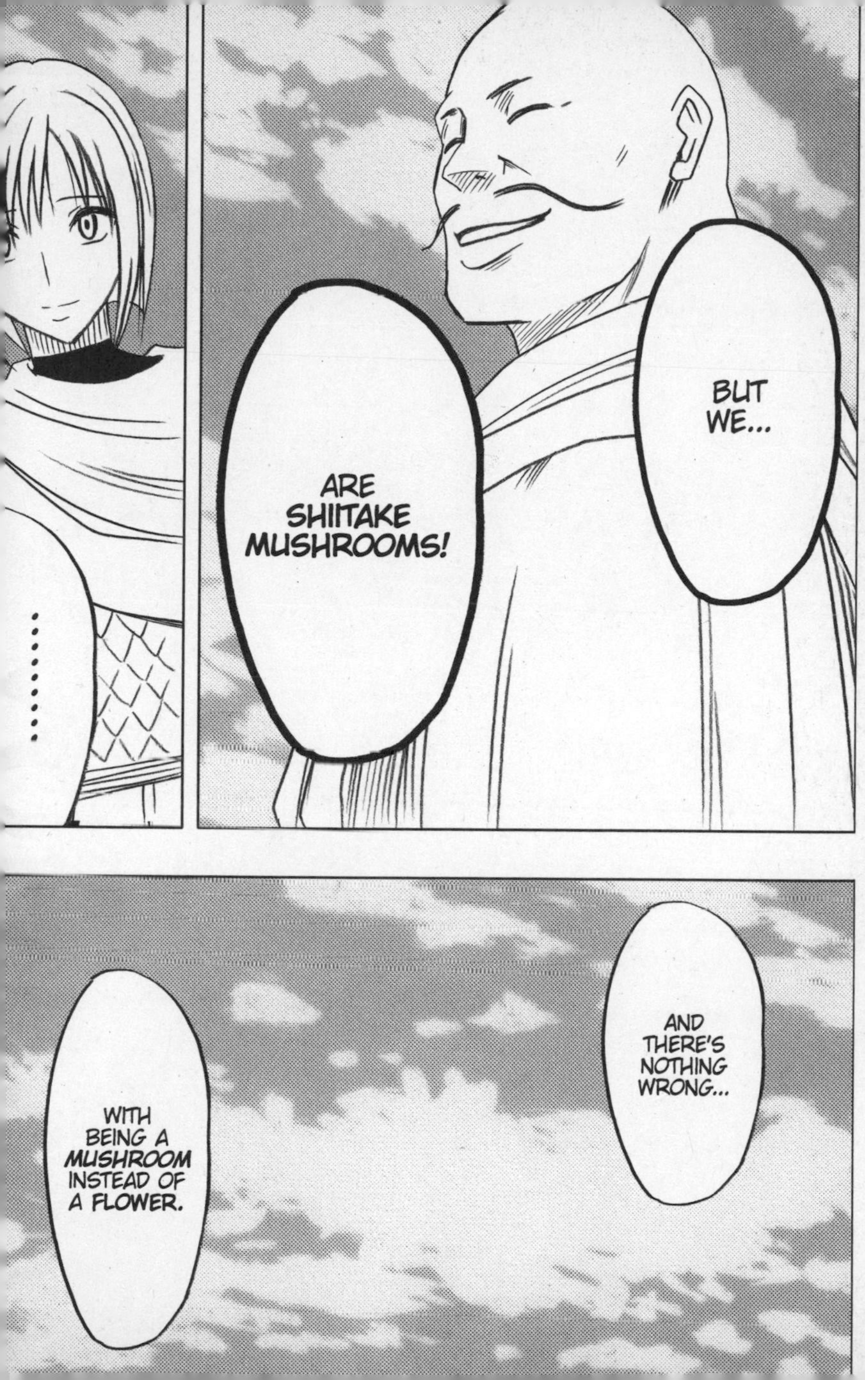
BUT WE...
ARE SHIITAKE MUSHROOMS!
......
AND THERE'S NOTHING WRONG...
WITH BEING A *MUSHROOM* INSTEAD OF A FLOWER.

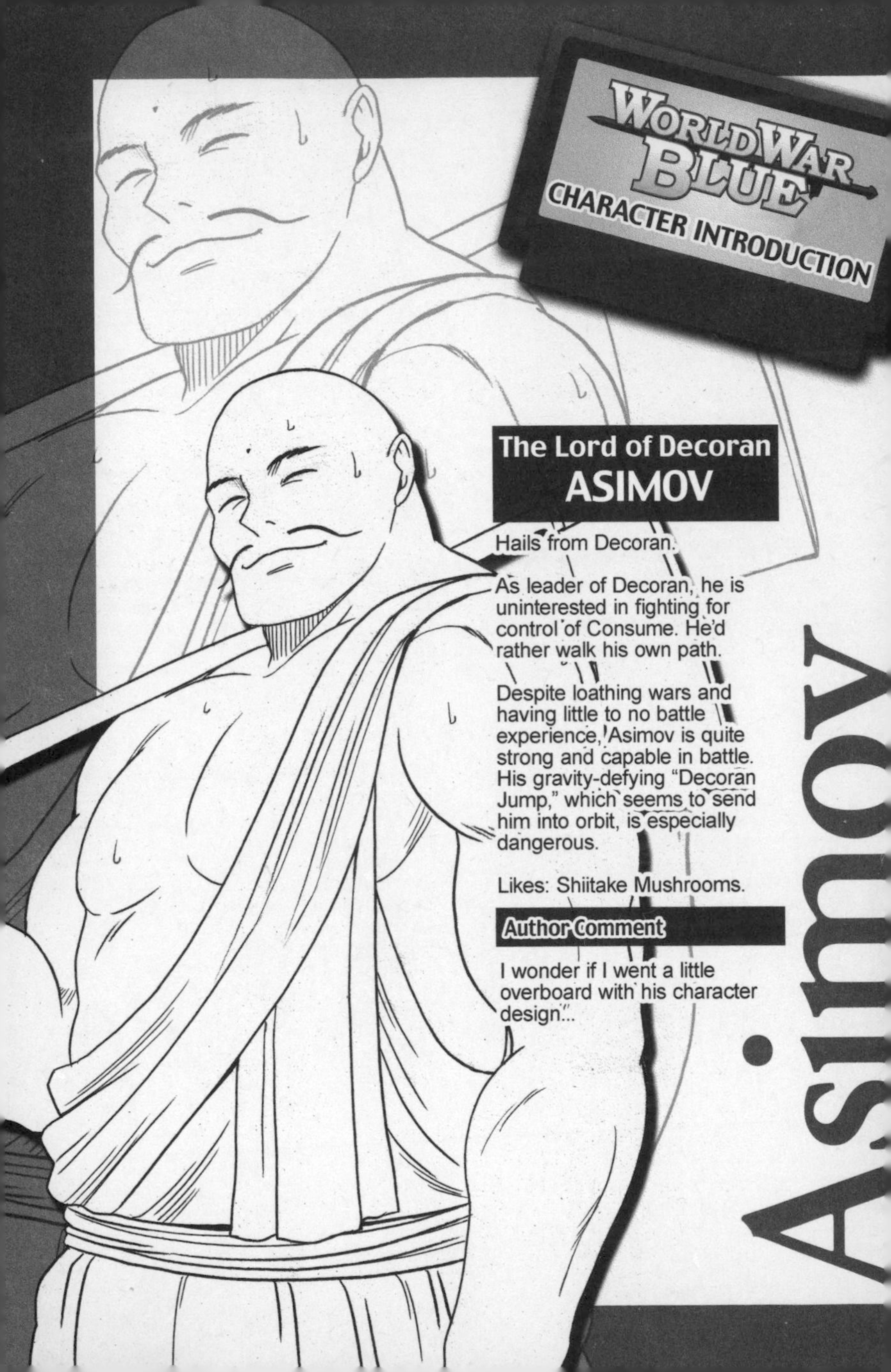
WORLD WAR BLUE
CHARACTER INTRODUCTION
Asimov

The Lord of Decoran
ASIMOV

Hails from Decoran.

As leader of Decoran, he is uninterested in fighting for control of Consume. He'd rather walk his own path.

Despite loathing wars and having little to no battle experience, Asimov is quite strong and capable in battle. His gravity-defying "Decoran Jump," which seems to send him into orbit, is especially dangerous.

Likes: Shiitake Mushrooms.

Author Comment

I wonder if I went a little overboard with his character design...

Perusing Video Game History

ON THE EDGE OF THE BLUE WORLD

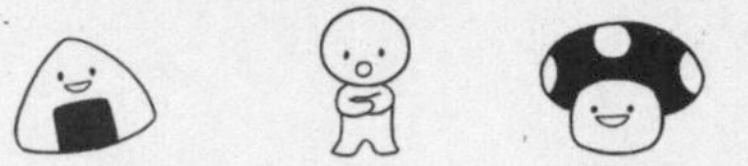
Dr. Onigiri
Mr. Why
Prof. Mushroom

Today's Topic

DATA EAST #3

Mr. Why: Mr. Why: All right, this time we're returning to the topic of Data East, who just love shiitake!

Prof. Mushroom: We talk about Data East too much in this corner.

Dr. Onigiri: Well, they were just that good.

Mr. Why: But they're also not around any more...

Dr. Onigiri: They sold shiitake mushrooms as a side business and made a lot of strange games, such as *Karnov*, where the protagonist was a half naked bald guy. They also made a game where you could not move backwards, *Chelnov (Atomic Runner)*, and the *Glory of Heracles* with its immortal hero. Unfortunately they went bankrupt in 2003.

Prof. Mushroom: Plus, there was that one character, World, from *Magical Drop (AKA: Chain Reaction)*, who wore that skimpy outfit and had a third eye on her forehead. She was kinda cute, and really popular too.

Dr. Onigiri: By the way, in the fighting game *Fighter's History: Mizuguchi Kiki Ippatsu!!*, Karnov and Chelnov both appeared as fighters you could play. The game was released in Japan for the Super Famicom in 1995.

Prof. Mushroom: So, while Data East may no longer be with us, some of its series have been continued by other companies. You can play them as digital downloads to this day.

Dr. Onigiri: They made a lot of entertaining games, in part due to how strange they often were.

To Be Continued...

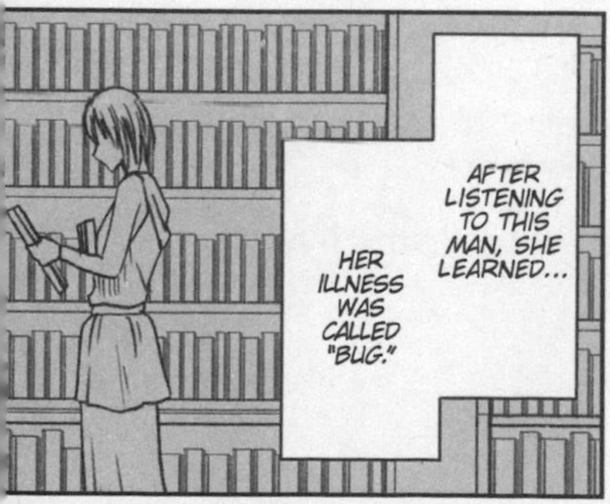
AFTER LISTENING TO THIS MAN, SHE LEARNED...
HER ILLNESS WAS CALLED "BUG."

...n inconvenient programming error is ...alled a "bug." Sometimes they can be ...o severe that it kills the whole game.

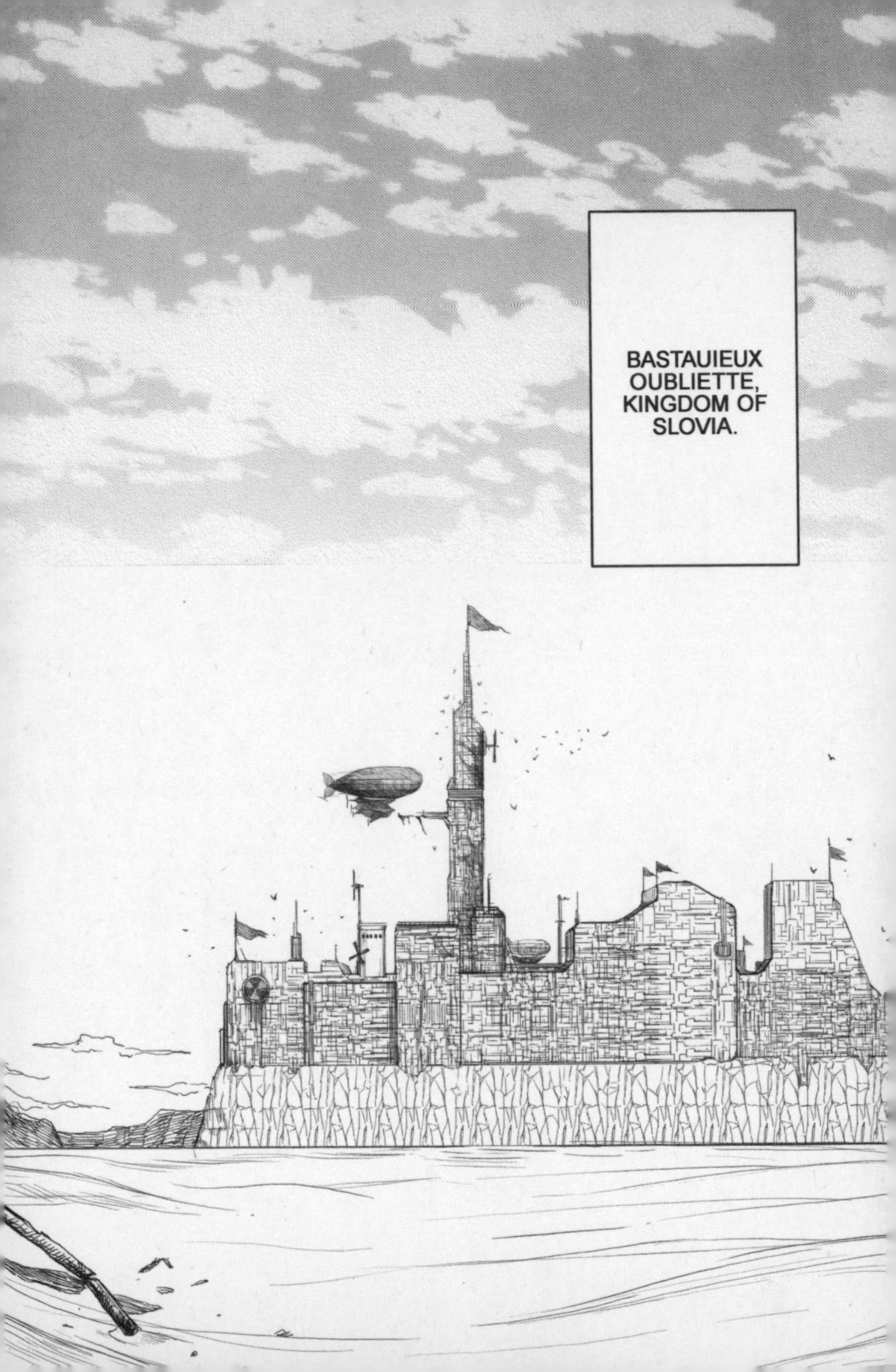
BASTAUIEUX OUBLIETTE, KINGDOM OF SLOVIA.

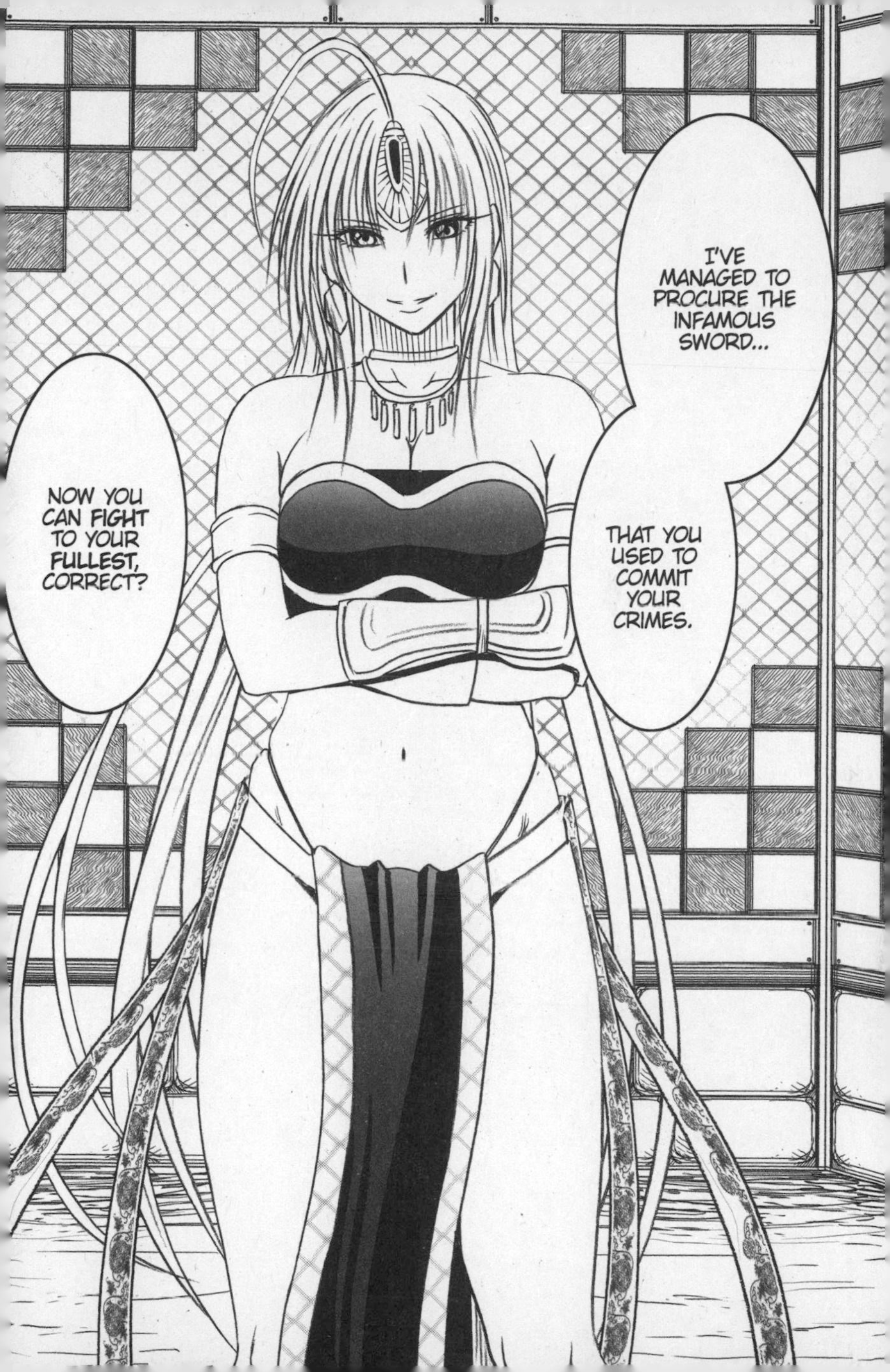
I'VE MANAGED TO PROCURE THE INFAMOUS SWORD...
THAT YOU USED TO COMMIT YOUR CRIMES.
NOW YOU CAN FIGHT TO YOUR FULLEST, CORRECT?

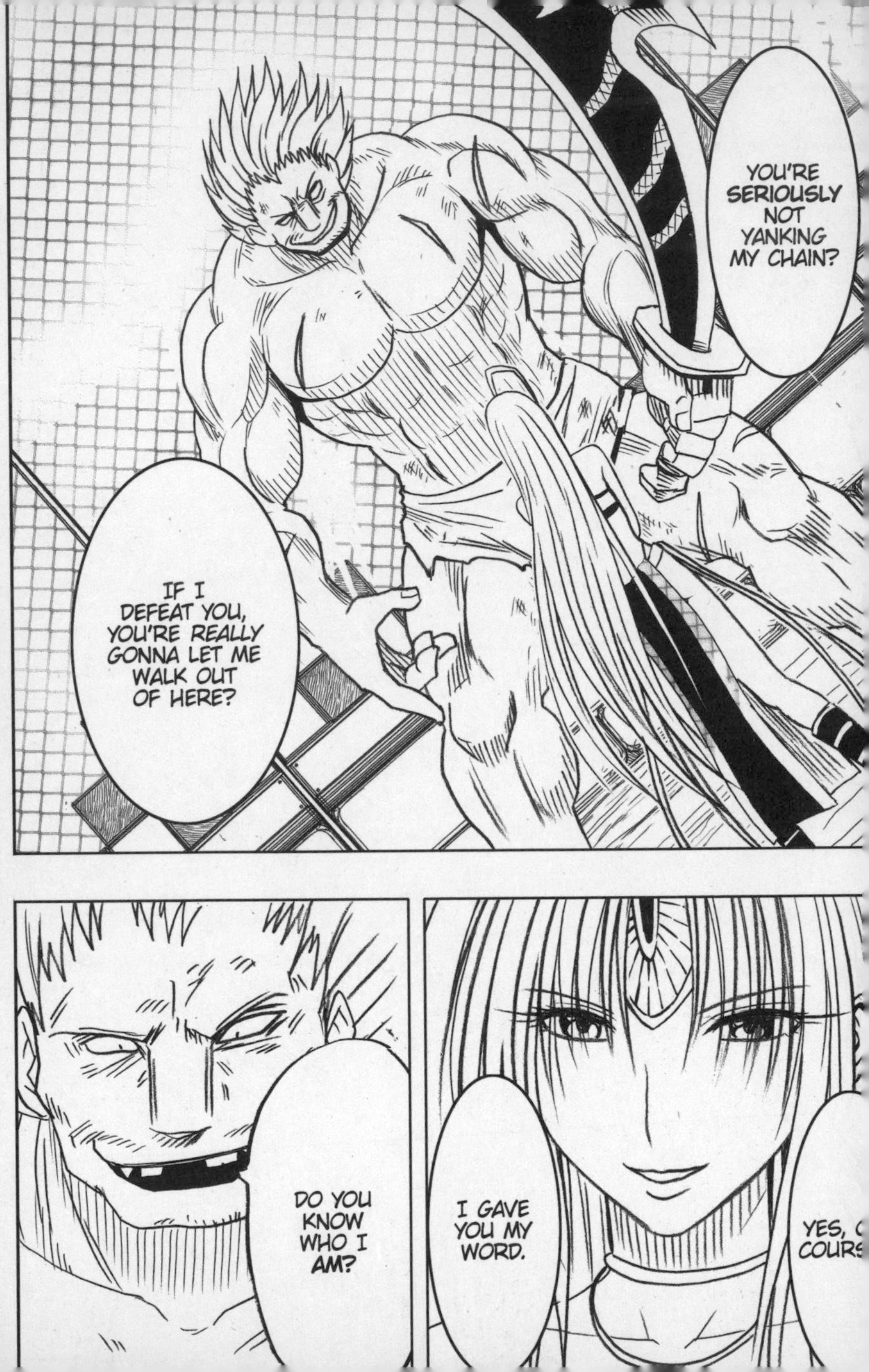
YOU'RE SERIOUSLY NOT YANKING MY CHAIN?
IF I DEFEAT YOU, YOU'RE REALLY GONNA LET ME WALK OUT OF HERE?
YES, C COURS
I GAVE YOU MY WORD.
DO YOU KNOW WHO I AM?

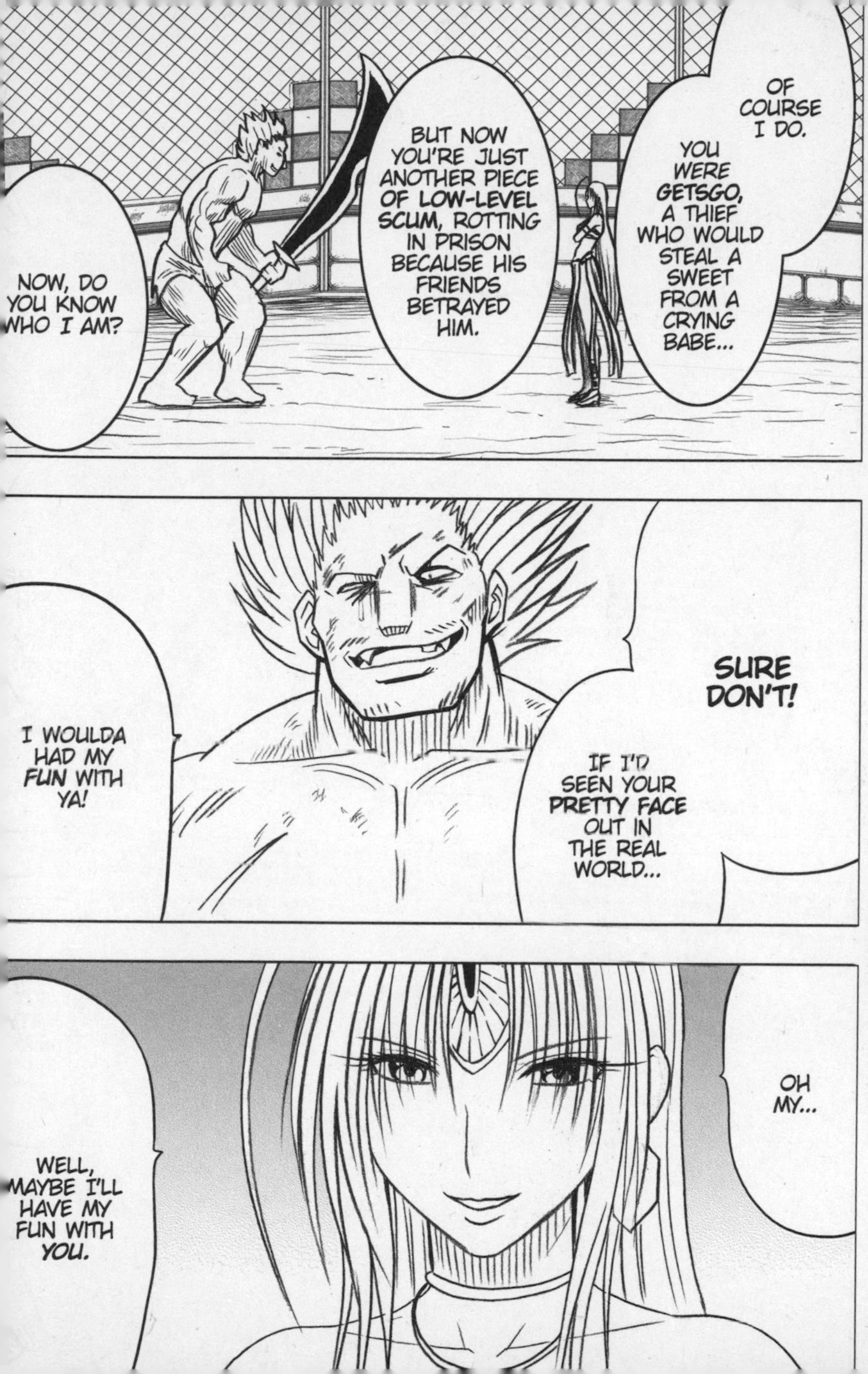
OF COURSE I DO.
YOU WERE GETSGO, A THIEF WHO WOULD STEAL A SWEET FROM A CRYING BABE...
BUT NOW YOU'RE JUST ANOTHER PIECE OF LOW-LEVEL SCUM, ROTTING IN PRISON BECAUSE HIS FRIENDS BETRAYED HIM.
NOW, DO YOU KNOW WHO I AM?
SURE DON'T!
IF I'D SEEN YOUR PRETTY FACE OUT IN THE REAL WORLD...
I WOULDA HAD MY FUN WITH YA!
OH MY...
WELL, MAYBE I'LL HAVE MY FUN WITH YOU.

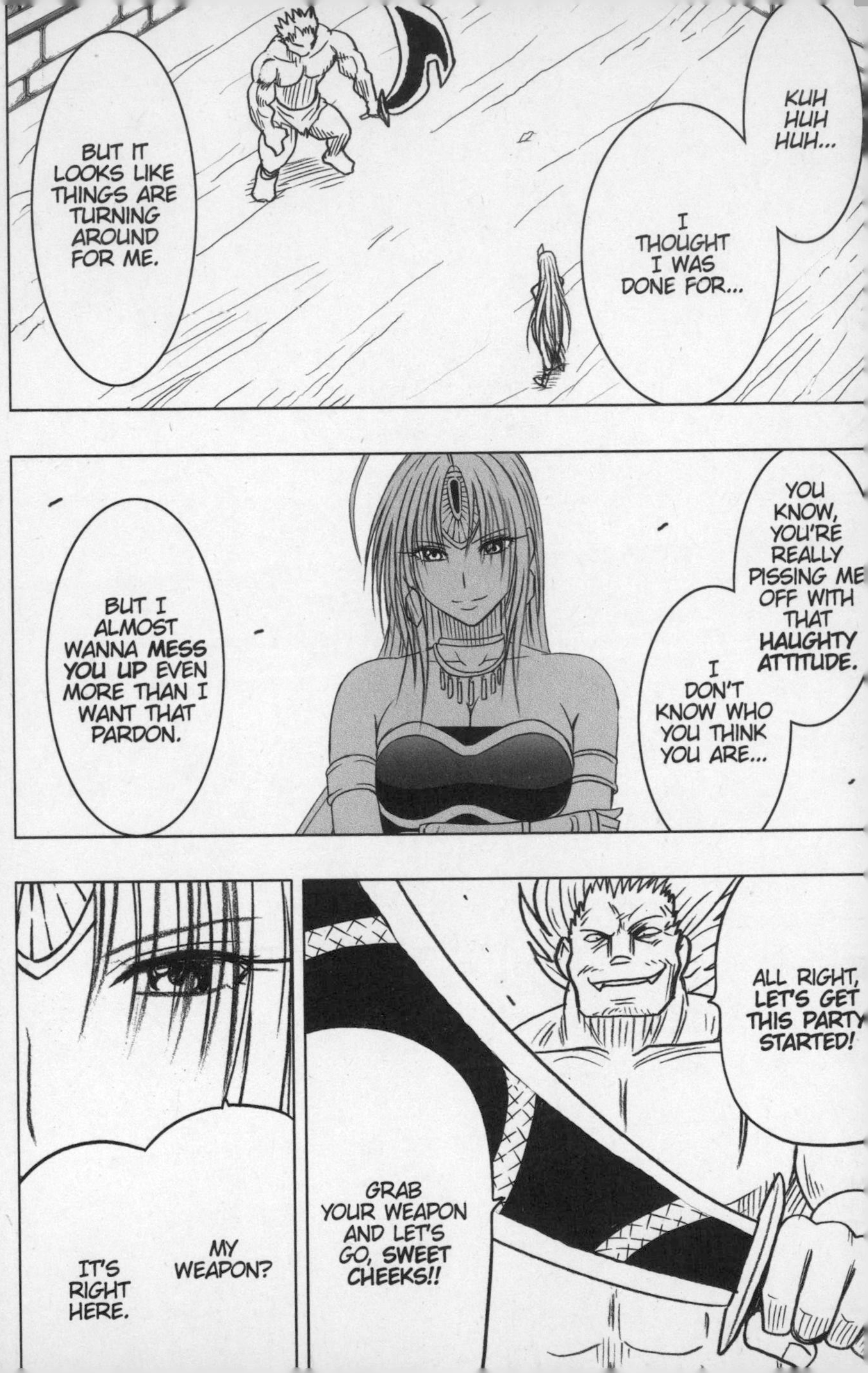
KUH HUH HUH...
I THOUGHT I WAS DONE FOR...
BUT IT LOOKS LIKE THINGS ARE TURNING AROUND FOR ME.
YOU KNOW, YOU'RE REALLY PISSING ME OFF WITH THAT HAUGHTY ATTITUDE.
I DON'T KNOW WHO YOU THINK YOU ARE...
BUT I ALMOST WANNA MESS YOU UP EVEN MORE THAN I WANT THAT PARDON.
ALL RIGHT, LET'S GET THIS PARTY STARTED!
GRAB YOUR WEAPON AND LET'S GO, SWEET CHEEKS!!
MY WEAPON?
IT'S RIGHT HERE.

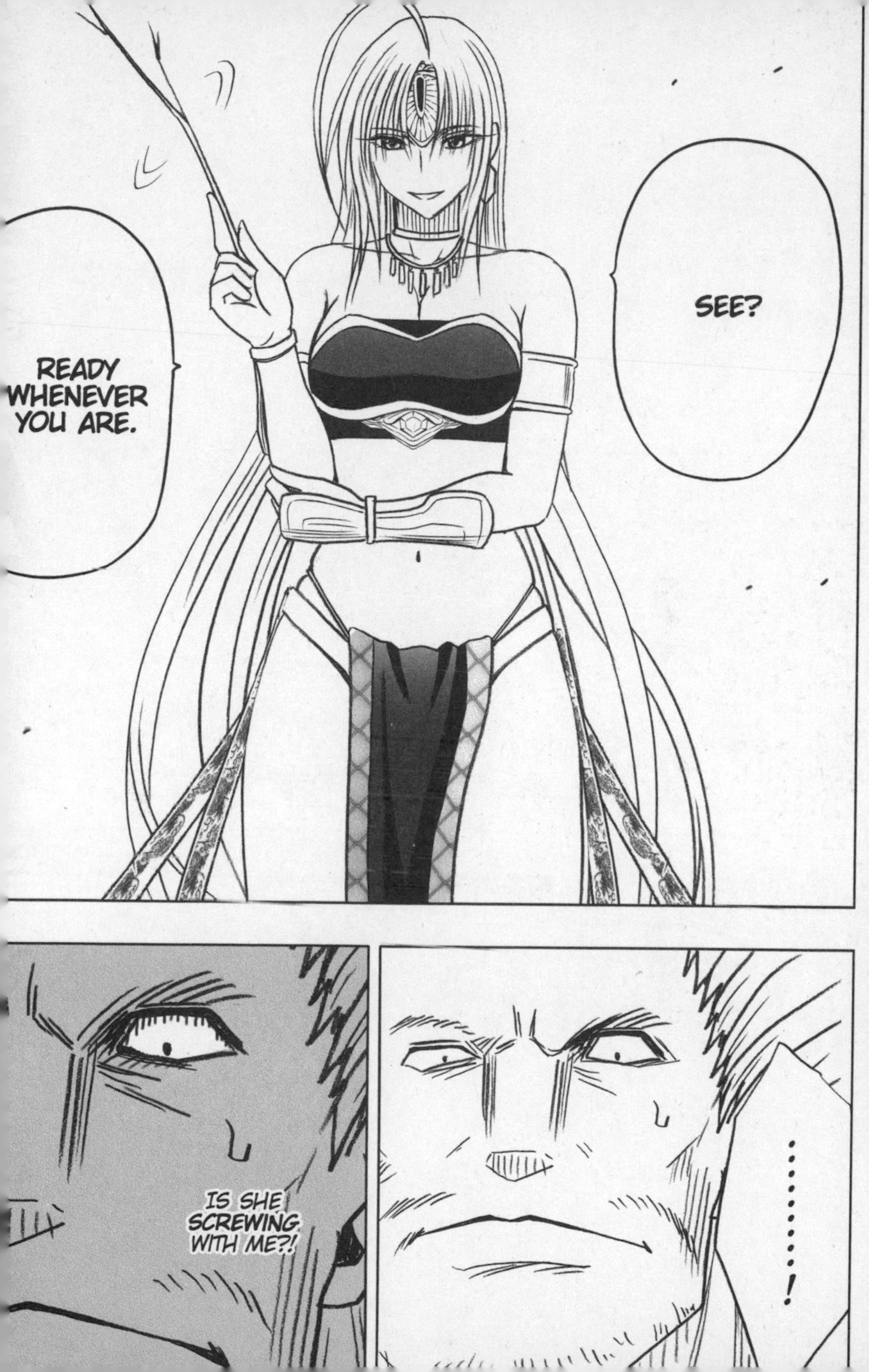
SEE?
READY WHENEVER YOU ARE.
......!
IS SHE SCREWING WITH ME?!

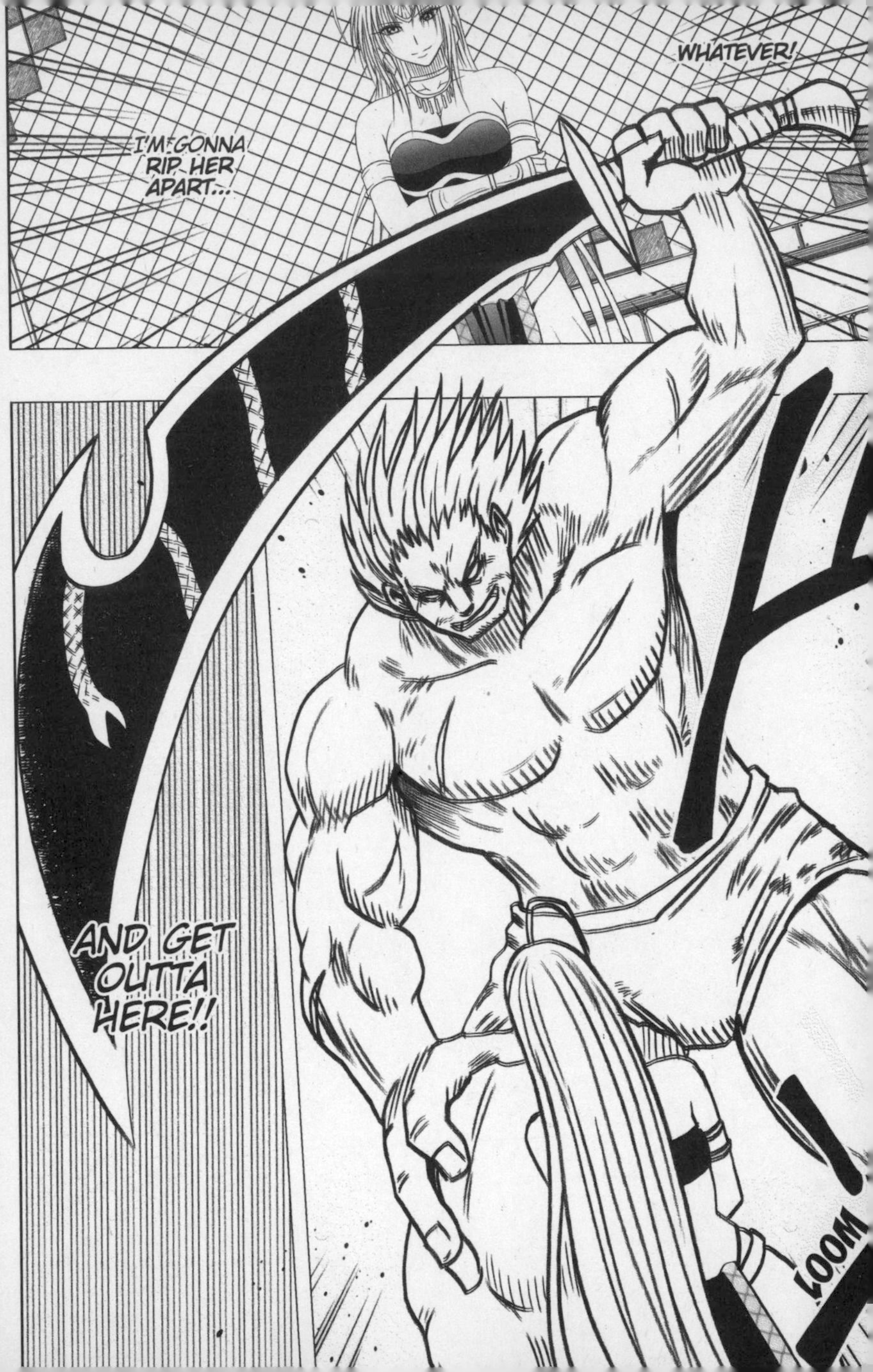
WHATEVER!
I'M GONNA RIP HER APART...
AND GET OUTTA HERE!!
FOOM

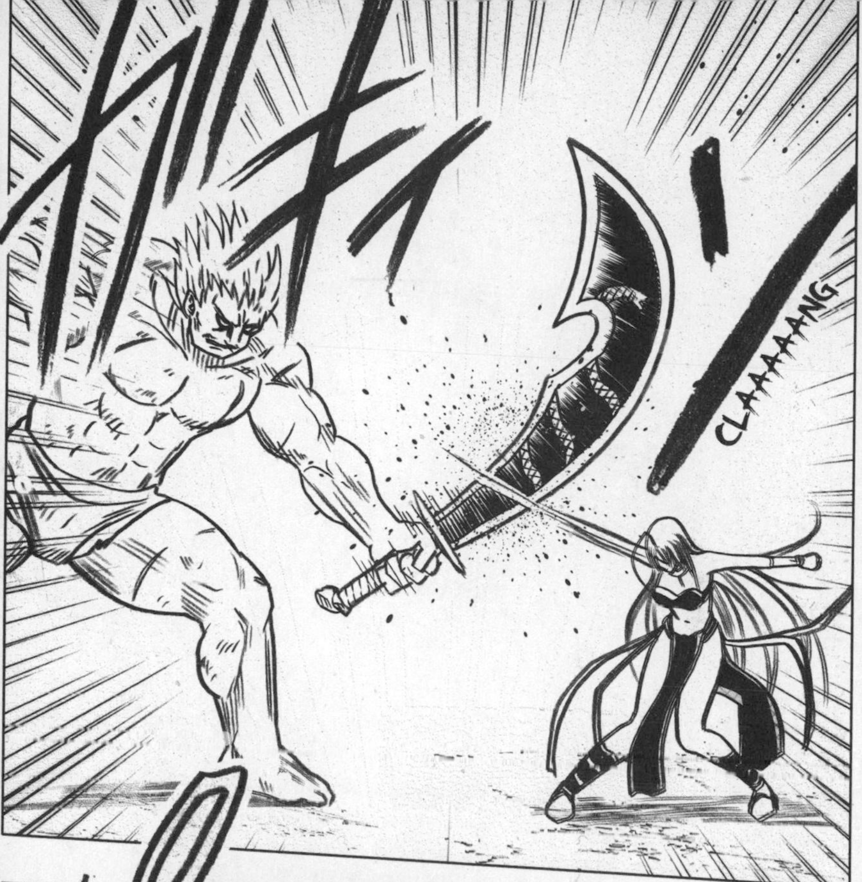
CLAAAAAANG
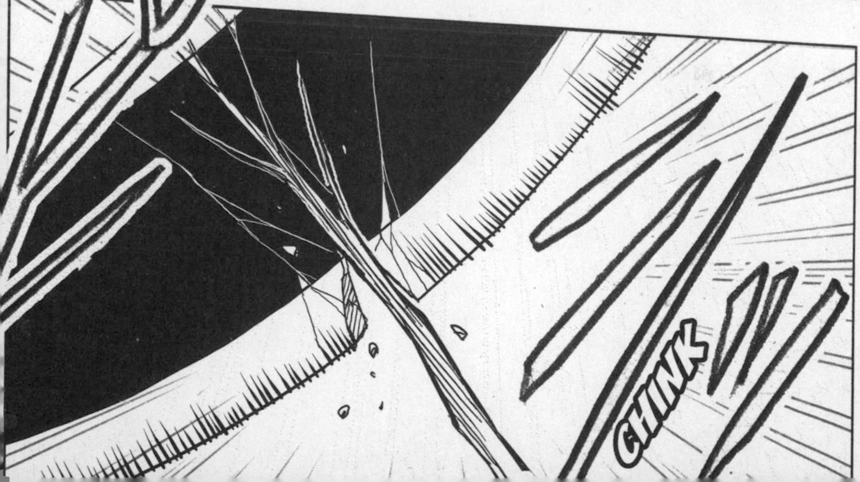
CHINK

WHAT...?

THAT'S NOT POSSIBLE!

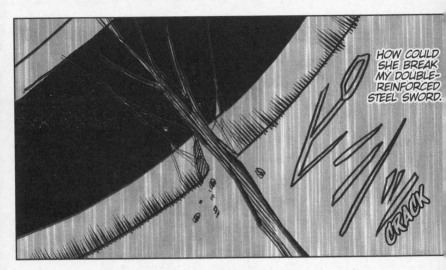

HOW COULD SHE BREAK MY DOUBLE-REINFORCED STEEL SWORD.

CRACK

WITH JUST A STUPID LITTLE STICK?!

Part 2

CHAPTER 19

ROLE-PLAYING

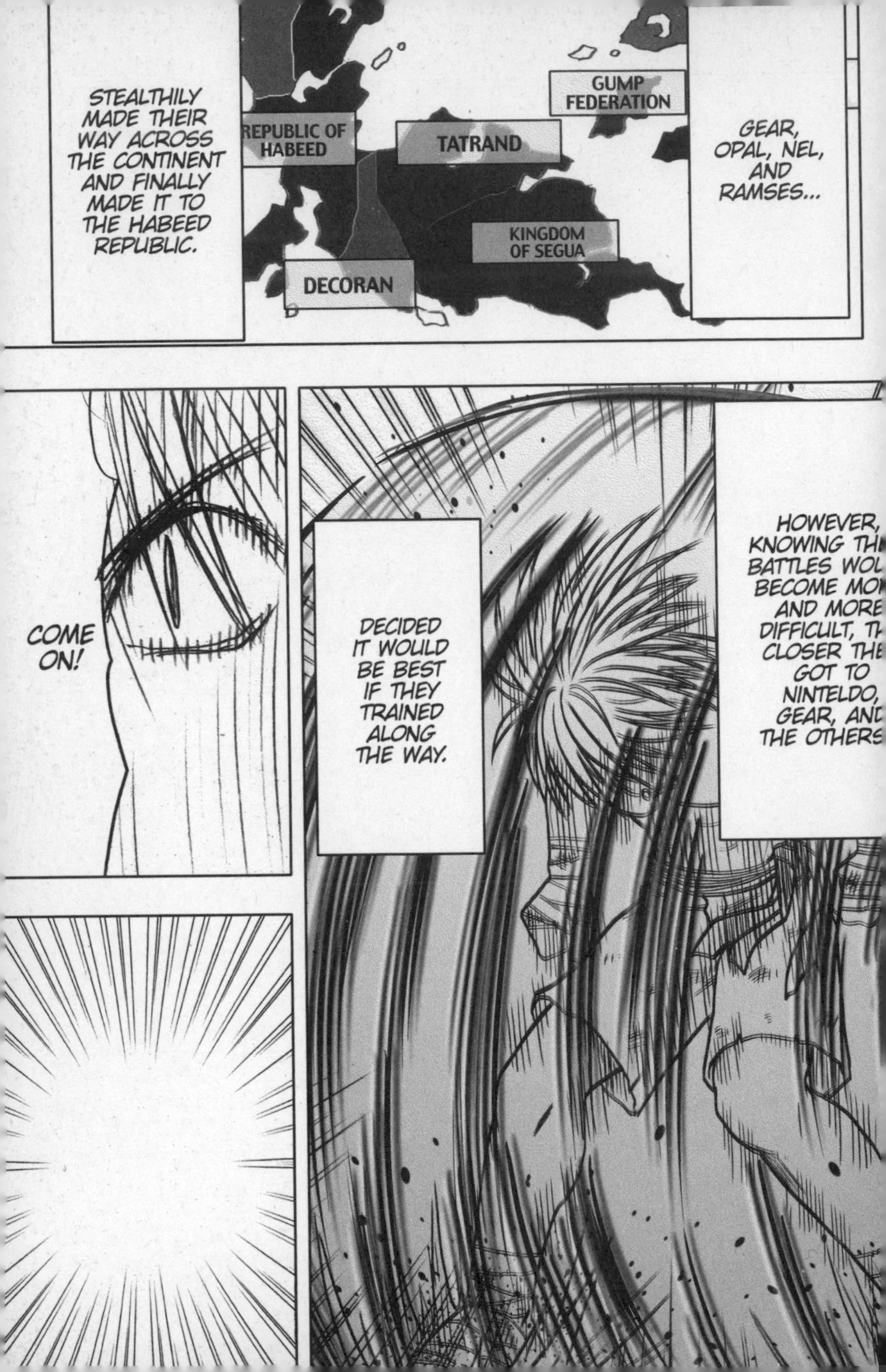
GEAR, OPAL, NEL, AND RAMSES...
GUMP FEDERATION
TATRAND
REPUBLIC OF HABEED
KINGDOM OF SEGUA
DECORAN
STEALTHILY MADE THEIR WAY ACROSS THE CONTINENT AND FINALLY MADE IT TO THE HABEED REPUBLIC.
HOWEVER, KNOWING TH BATTLES WOL BECOME MO AND MORE DIFFICULT, TH CLOSER THE GOT TO NINTELDO, GEAR, AND THE OTHERS
DECIDED IT WOULD BE BEST IF THEY TRAINED ALONG THE WAY.
COME ON!

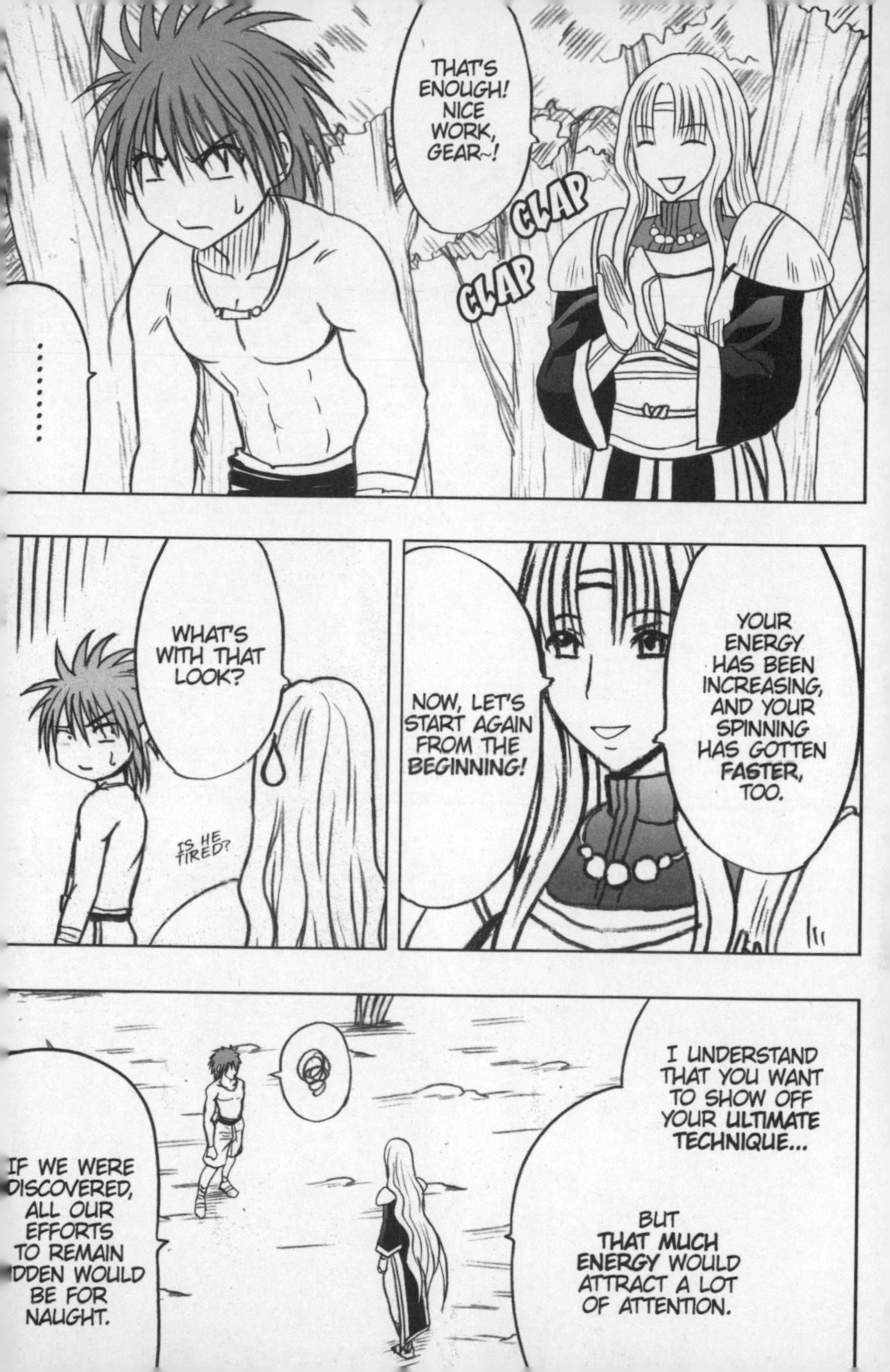
THAT'S ENOUGH! NICE WORK, GEAR~!
CLAP
CLAP
......
YOUR ENERGY HAS BEEN INCREASING, AND YOUR SPINNING HAS GOTTEN FASTER, TOO.
NOW, LET'S START AGAIN FROM THE BEGINNING!
WHAT'S WITH THAT LOOK?
IS HE TIRED?
I UNDERSTAND THAT YOU WANT TO SHOW OFF YOUR ULTIMATE TECHNIQUE...
BUT THAT MUCH ENERGY WOULD ATTRACT A LOT OF ATTENTION.
IF WE WERE DISCOVERED, ALL OUR EFFORTS TO REMAIN IDDEN WOULD BE FOR NAUGHT.

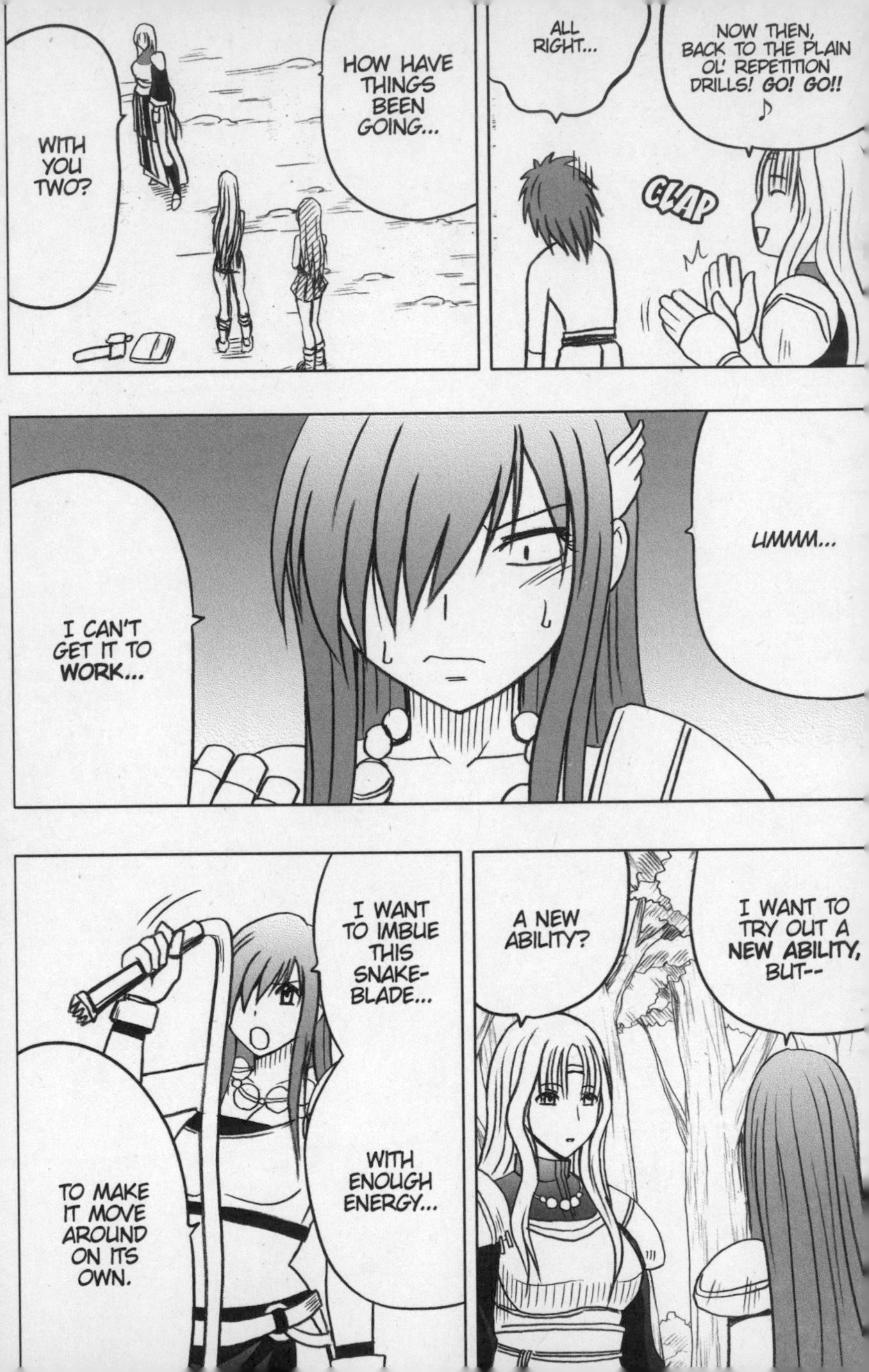
NOW THEN, BACK TO THE PLAIN OL' REPETITION DRILLS! GO! GO!! ♪
ALL RIGHT...
CLAP
HOW HAVE THINGS BEEN GOING...
WITH YOU TWO?
UMMM...
I CAN'T GET IT TO WORK...
I WANT TO TRY OUT A NEW ABILITY, BUT--
A NEW ABILITY?
I WANT TO IMBUE THIS SNAKE-BLADE...
WITH ENOUGH ENERGY...
TO MAKE IT MOVE AROUND ON ITS OWN.

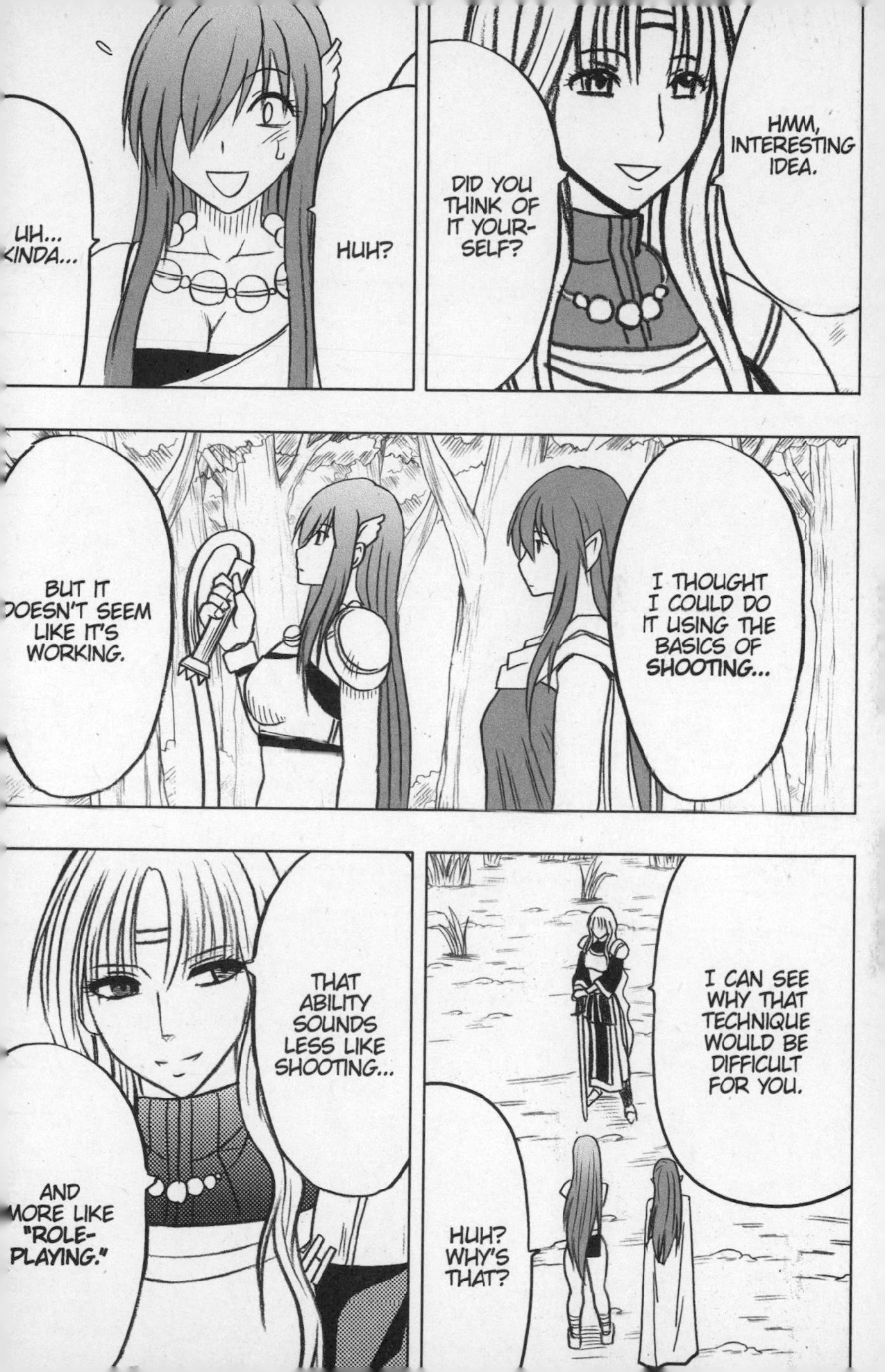
HMM, INTERESTING IDEA.
DID YOU THINK OF IT YOURSELF?
HUH?
UH... KINDA...
I THOUGHT I COULD DO IT USING THE BASICS OF SHOOTING...
BUT IT DOESN'T SEEM LIKE IT'S WORKING.
I CAN SEE WHY THAT TECHNIQUE WOULD BE DIFFICULT FOR YOU.
HUH? WHY'S THAT?
THAT ABILITY SOUNDS LESS LIKE SHOOTING...
AND MORE LIKE "ROLE-PLAYING."

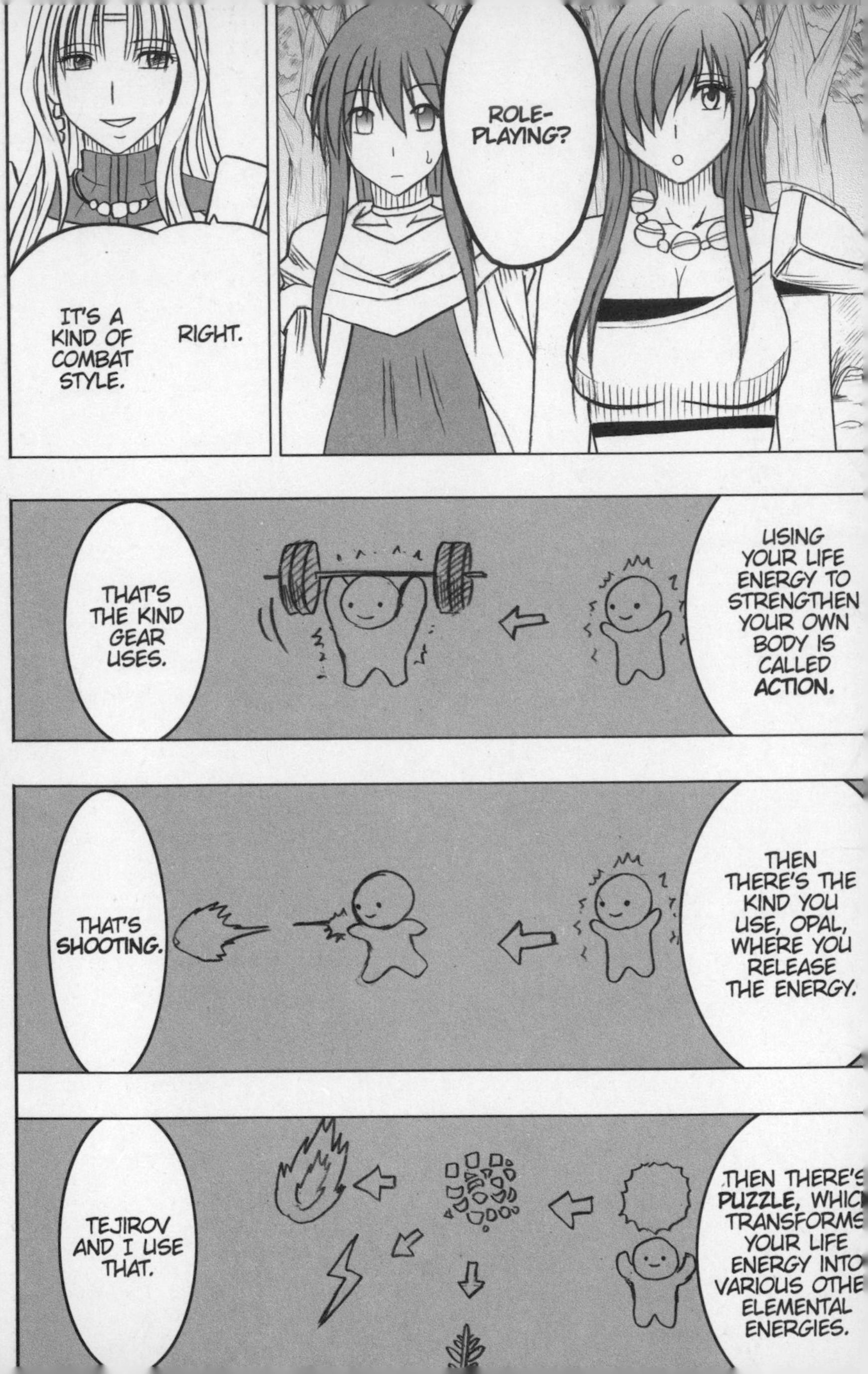
ROLE-PLAYING?
RIGHT.
IT'S A KIND OF COMBAT STYLE.
USING YOUR LIFE ENERGY TO STRENGTHEN YOUR OWN BODY IS CALLED ACTION.
THAT'S THE KIND GEAR USES.
THEN THERE'S THE KIND YOU USE, OPAL, WHERE YOU RELEASE THE ENERGY.
THAT'S SHOOTING.
THEN THERE'S PUZZLE, WHIC TRANSFORMS YOUR LIFE ENERGY INTO VARIOUS OTHE ELEMENTAL ENERGIES.
TEJIROV AND I USE THAT.

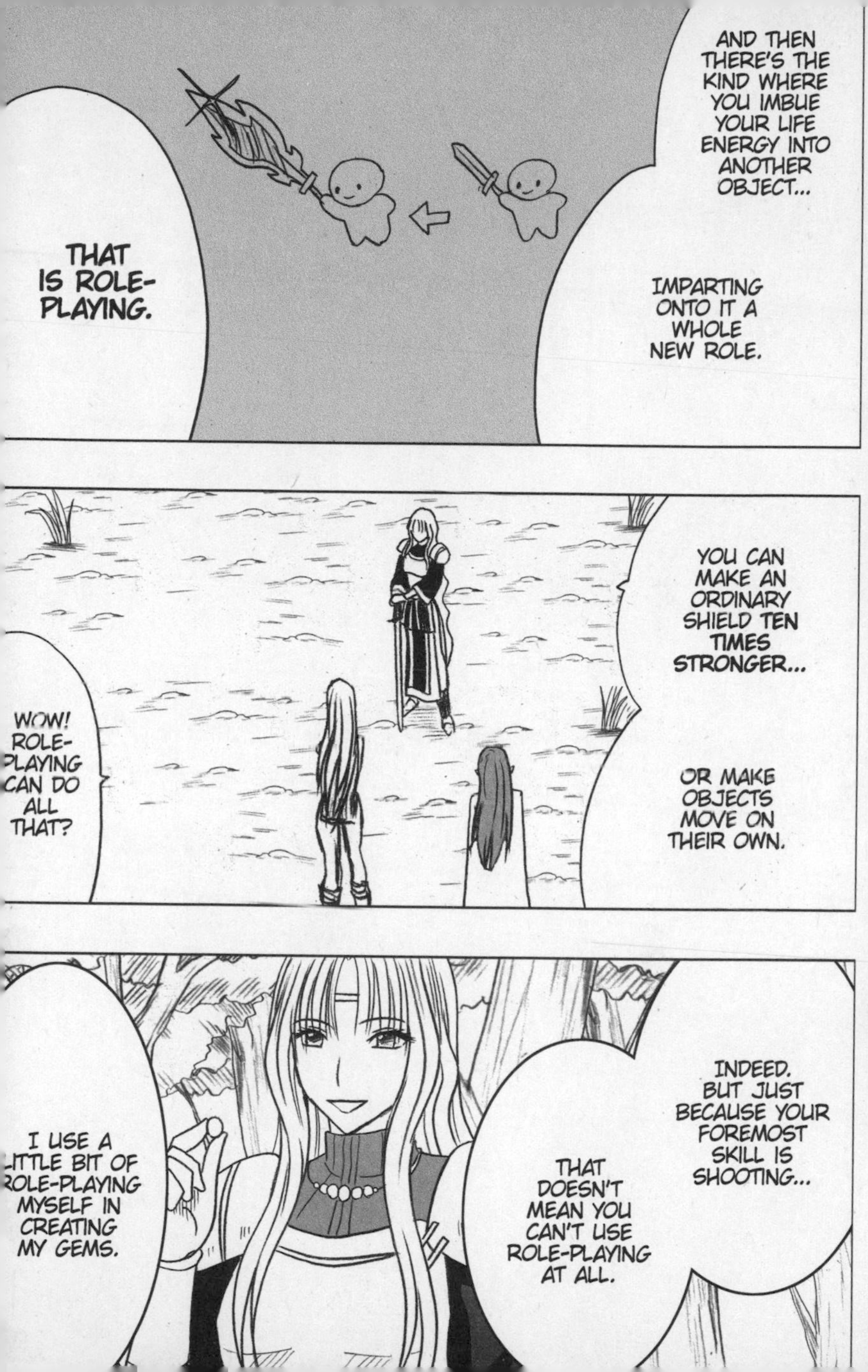
AND THEN THERE'S THE KIND WHERE YOU IMBUE YOUR LIFE ENERGY INTO ANOTHER OBJECT...
IMPARTING ONTO IT A WHOLE NEW ROLE.
THAT IS ROLE-PLAYING.
YOU CAN MAKE AN ORDINARY SHIELD TEN TIMES STRONGER...
OR MAKE OBJECTS MOVE ON THEIR OWN.
WOW! ROLE-PLAYING CAN DO ALL THAT?
INDEED. BUT JUST BECAUSE YOUR FOREMOST SKILL IS SHOOTING...
THAT DOESN'T MEAN YOU CAN'T USE ROLE-PLAYING AT ALL.
I USE A LITTLE BIT OF ROLE-PLAYING MYSELF IN CREATING MY GEMS.

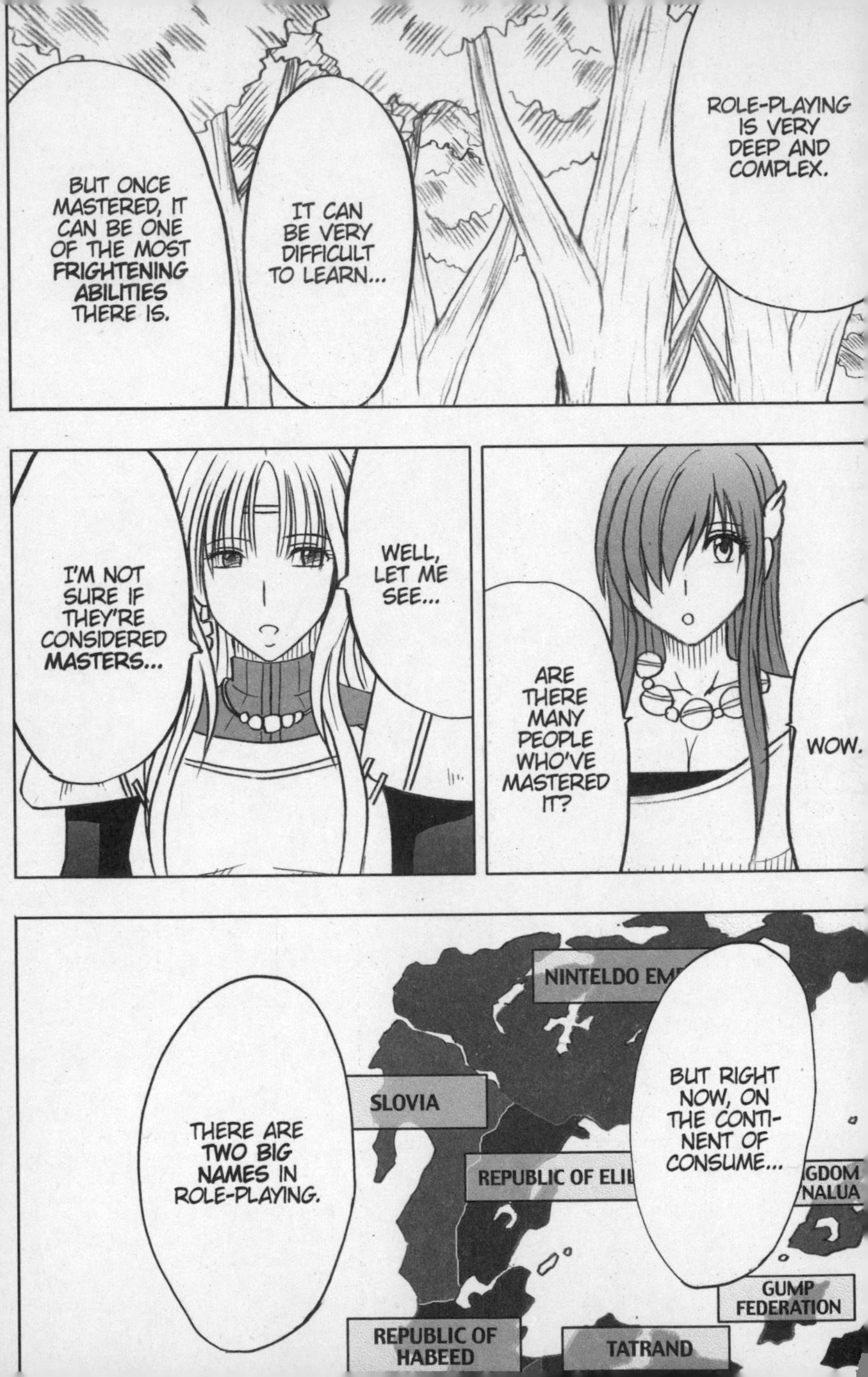
ROLE-PLAYING IS VERY DEEP AND COMPLEX.
IT CAN BE VERY DIFFICULT TO LEARN...
BUT ONCE MASTERED, IT CAN BE ONE OF THE MOST FRIGHTENING ABILITIES THERE IS.
WOW.
ARE THERE MANY PEOPLE WHO'VE MASTERED IT?
WELL, LET ME SEE...
I'M NOT SURE IF THEY'RE CONSIDERED MASTERS...
BUT RIGHT NOW, ON THE CONTINENT OF CONSUME...
THERE ARE TWO BIG NAMES IN ROLE-PLAYING.
SLOVIA
GUMP FEDERATION
TATRAND
REPUBLIC OF HABEED

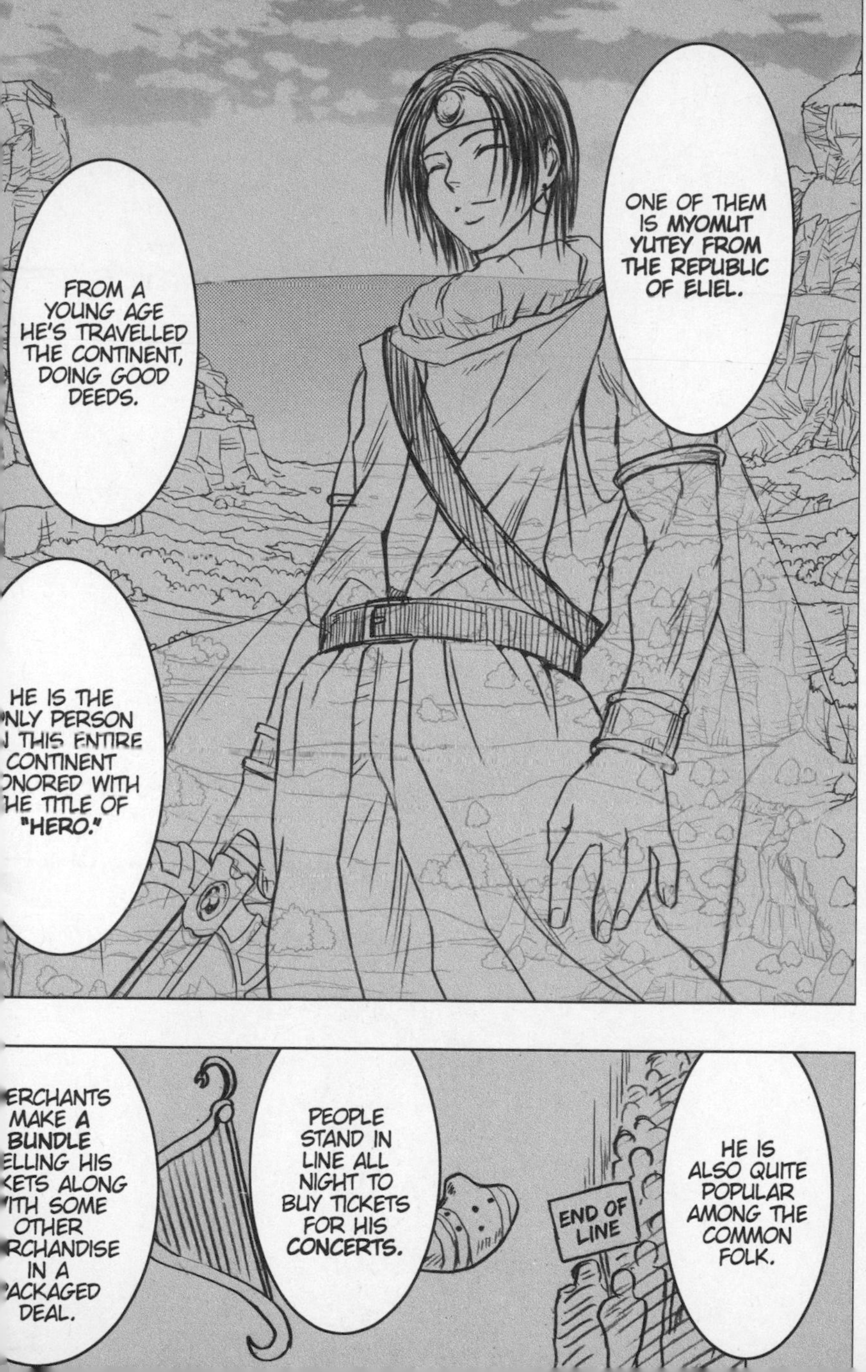
ONE OF THEM IS MYOMUT YUTEY FROM THE REPUBLIC OF ELIEL.
FROM A YOUNG AGE HE'S TRAVELLED THE CONTINENT, DOING GOOD DEEDS.
HE IS THE NLY PERSON N THIS ENTIRE CONTINENT ONORED WITH HE TITLE OF "HERO."
HE IS ALSO QUITE POPULAR AMONG THE COMMON FOLK.
END OF LINE
PEOPLE STAND IN LINE ALL NIGHT TO BUY TICKETS FOR HIS CONCERTS.
ERCHANTS MAKE A BUNDLE ELLING HIS KETS ALONG ITH SOME OTHER RCHANDISE IN A ACKAGED DEAL.

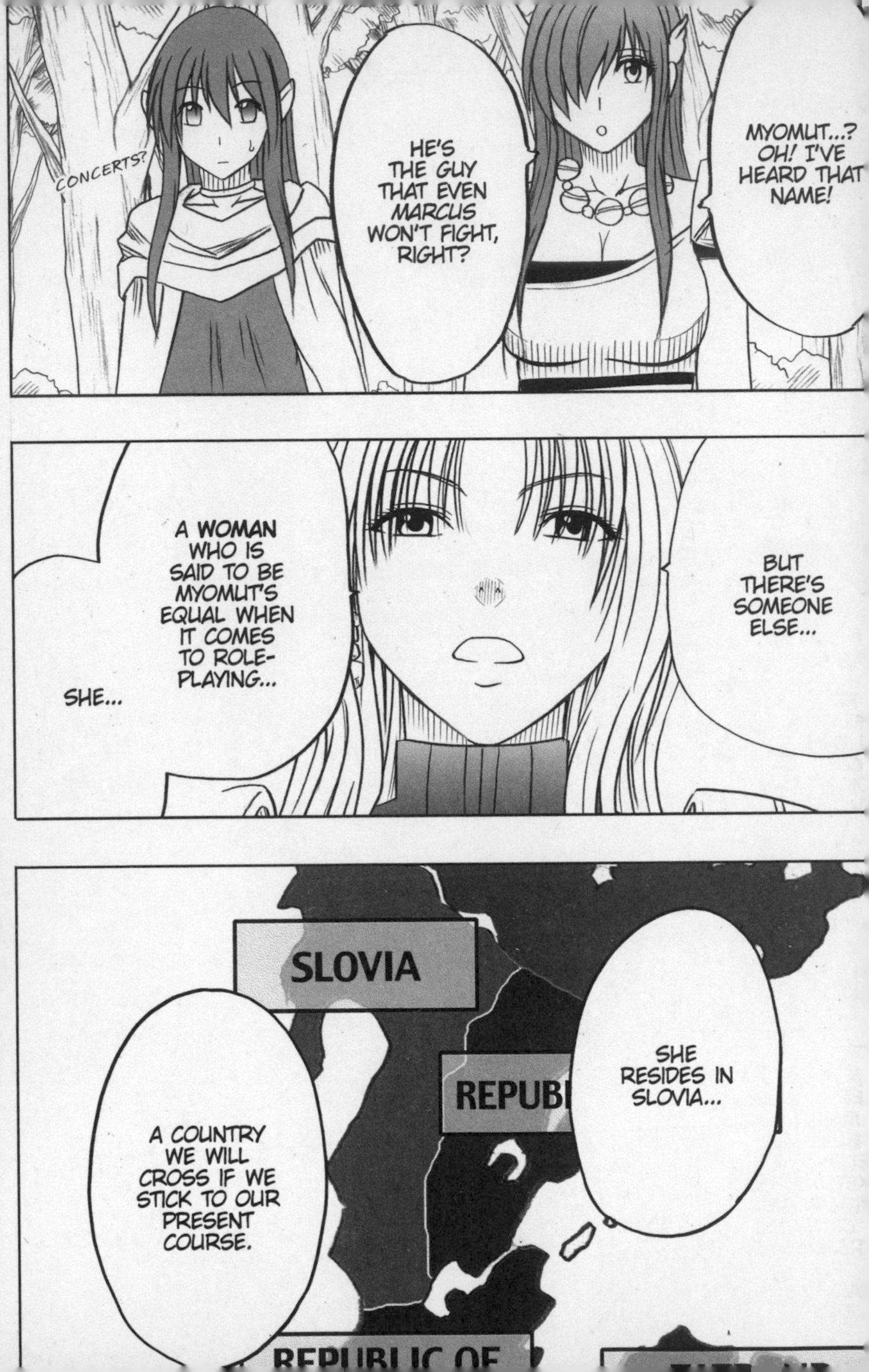
MYOMUT...? OH! I'VE HEARD THAT NAME!
HE'S THE GUY THAT EVEN MARCUS WON'T FIGHT, RIGHT?
CONCERTS?
BUT THERE'S SOMEONE ELSE...
A WOMAN WHO IS SAID TO BE MYOMUT'S EQUAL WHEN IT COMES TO ROLE-PLAYING...
SHE...
SLOVIA
SHE RESIDES IN SLOVIA...
A COUNTRY WE WILL CROSS IF WE STICK TO OUR PRESENT COURSE.

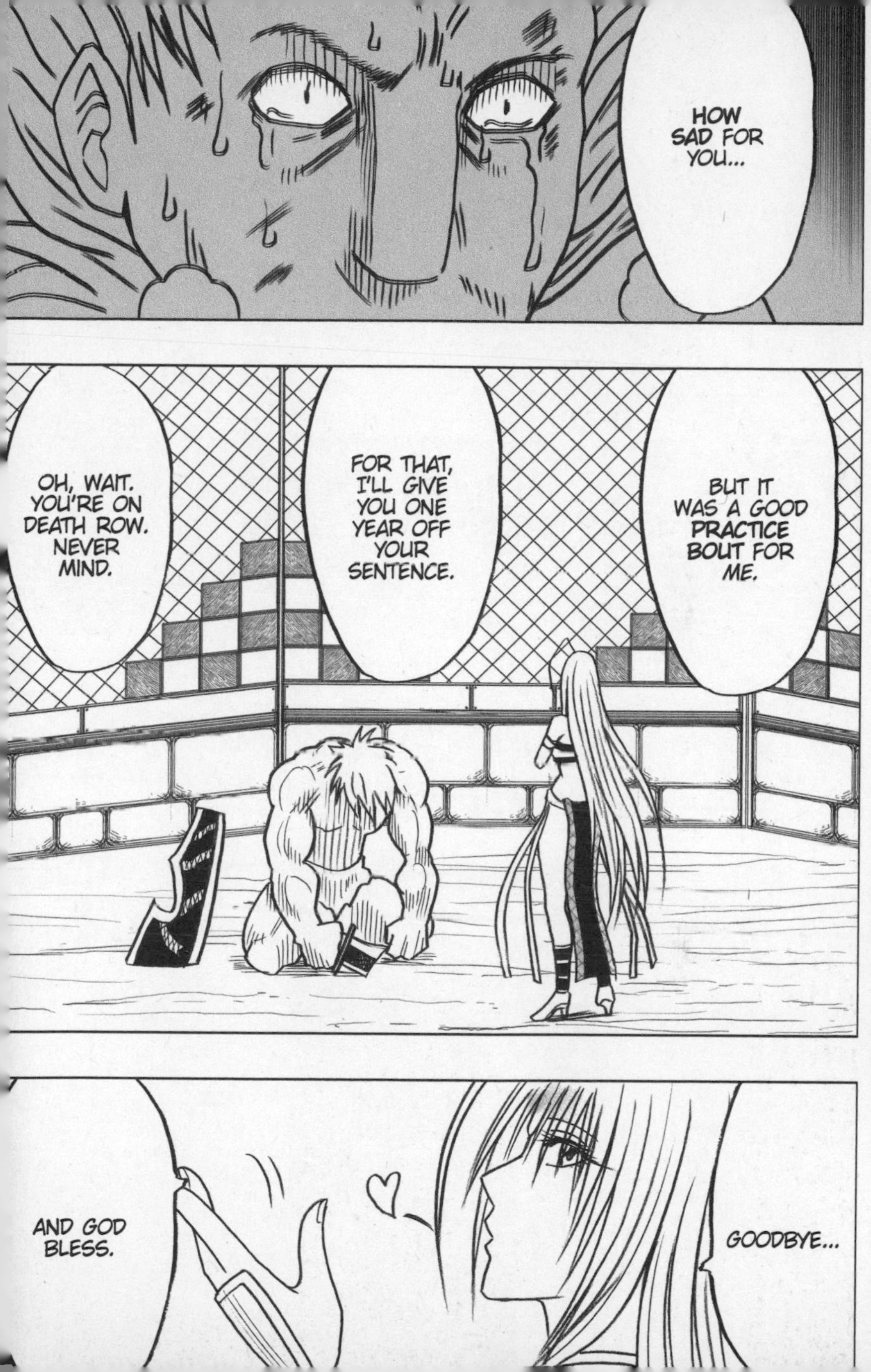
HOW SAD FOR YOU...
BUT IT WAS A GOOD PRACTICE BOUT FOR ME.
FOR THAT, I'LL GIVE YOU ONE YEAR OFF YOUR SENTENCE.
OH, WAIT. YOU'RE ON DEATH ROW. NEVER MIND.
GOODBYE...
AND GOD BLESS.

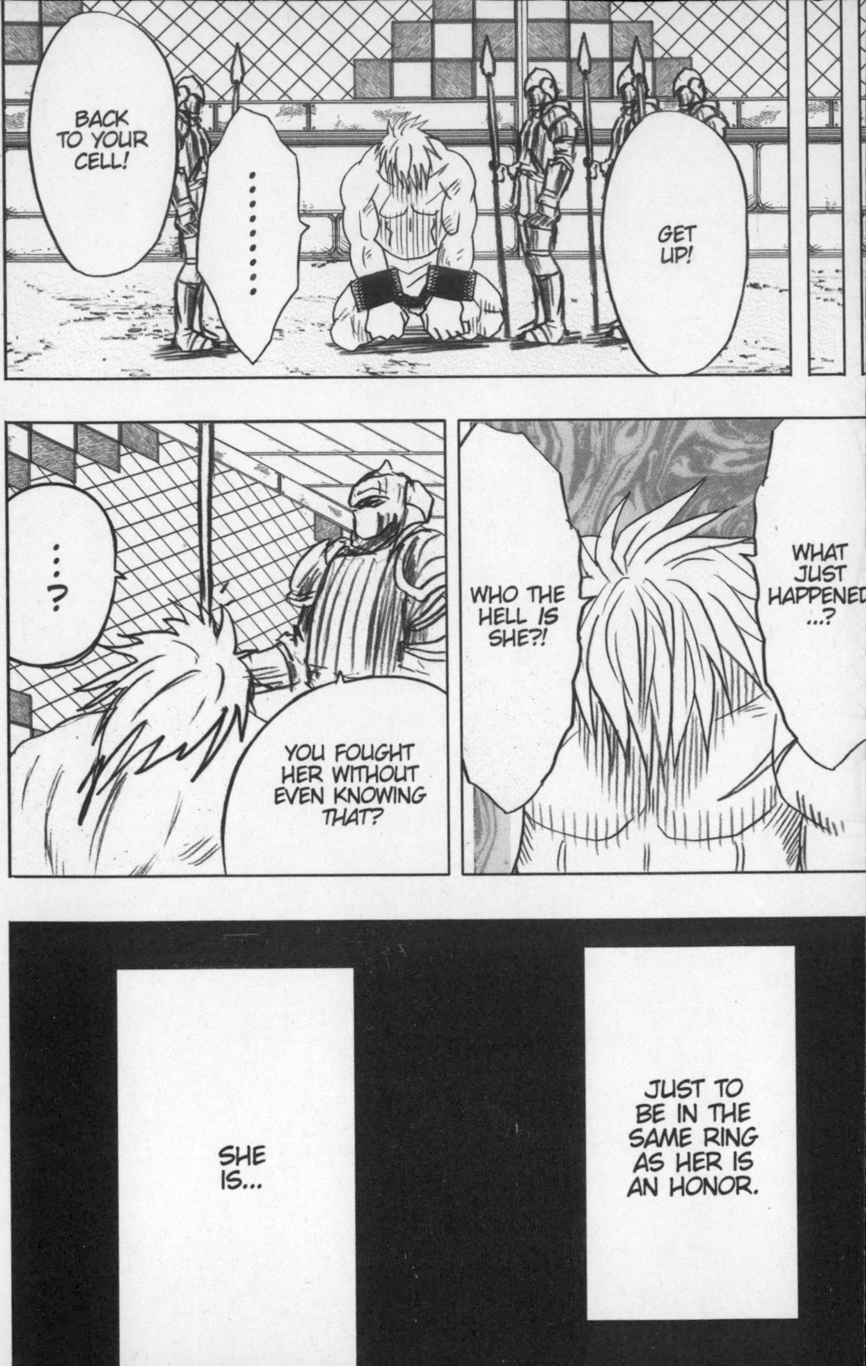
GET UP!
BACK TO YOUR CELL!
....
WHAT JUST HAPPENED ...?
WHO THE HELL IS SHE?!
...?
YOU FOUGHT HER WITHOUT EVEN KNOWING THAT?
JUST TO BE IN THE SAME RING AS HER IS AN HONOR.
SHE IS...

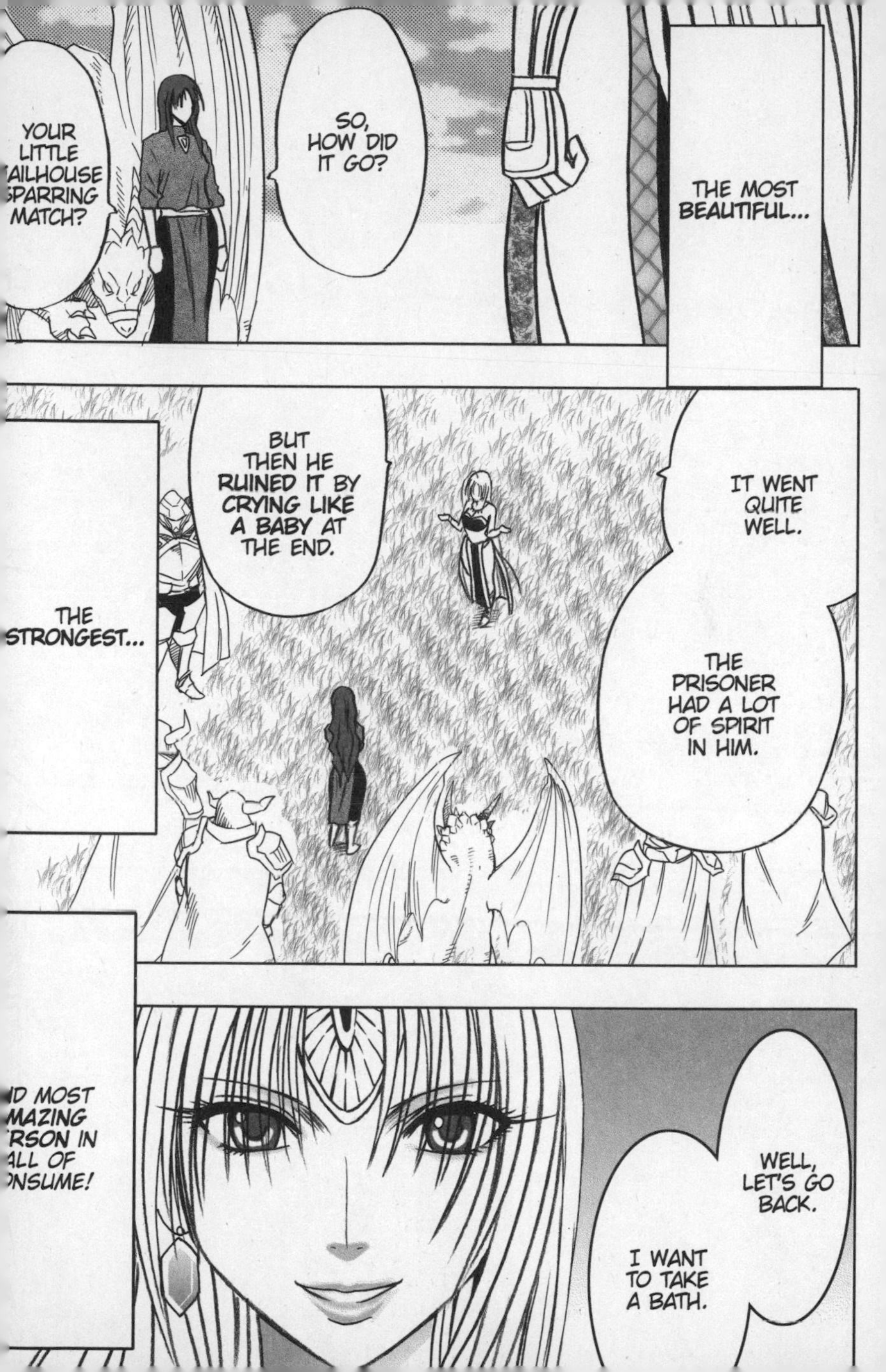
THE MOST BEAUTIFUL...
SO, HOW DID IT GO?
YOUR LITTLE AILHOUSE SPARRING MATCH?
IT WENT QUITE WELL.
THE PRISONER HAD A LOT OF SPIRIT IN HIM.
BUT THEN HE RUINED IT BY CRYING LIKE A BABY AT THE END.
THE STRONGEST...
WELL, LET'S GO BACK.
I WANT TO TAKE A BATH.
ID MOST MAZING RSON IN ALL OF NSUME!

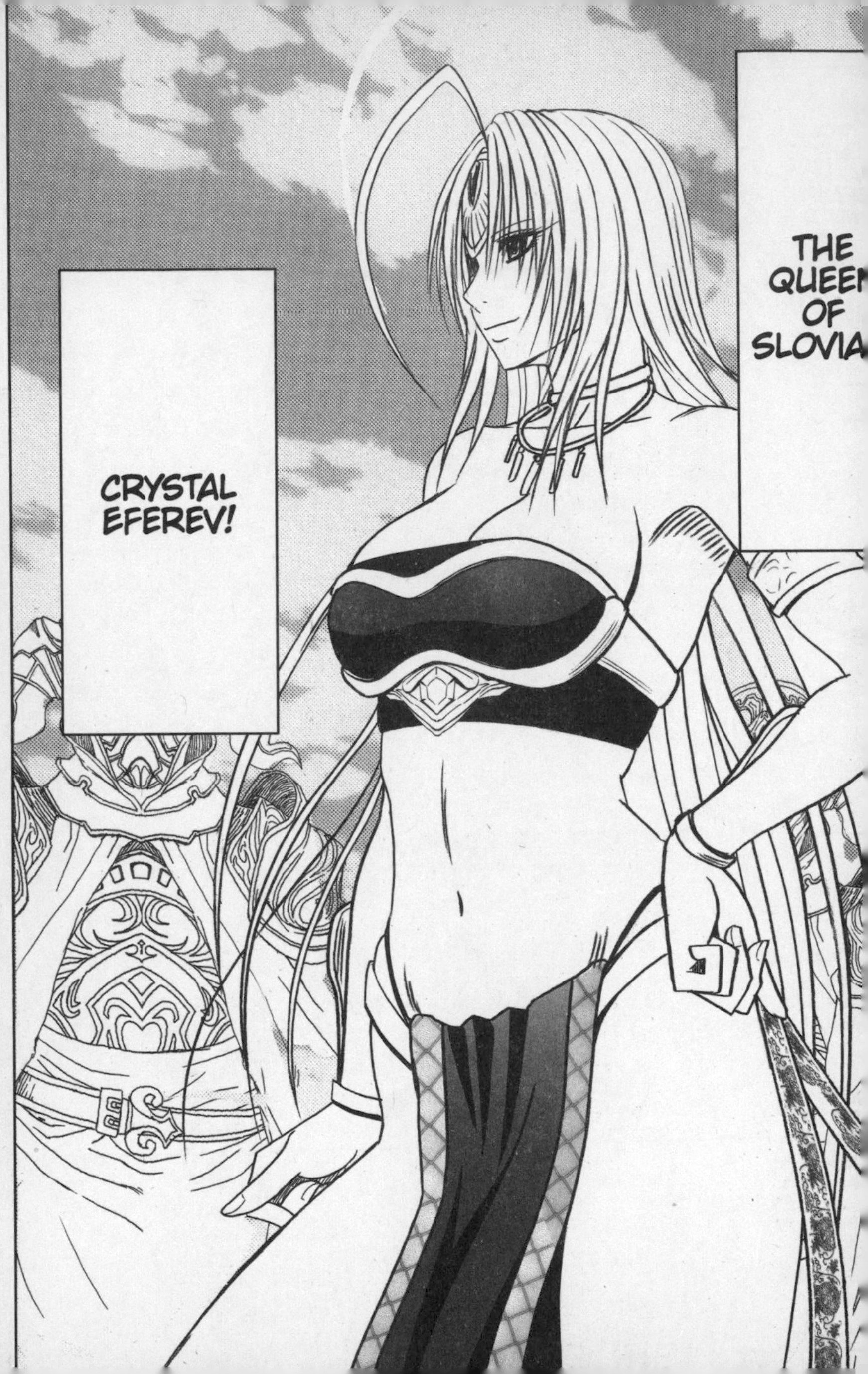
THE QUEEN OF SLOVIA
CRYSTAL EFEREV!

WORLD WAR BLUE

CHARACTER INTRODUCTION

Crystal

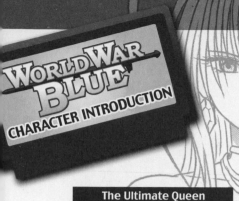

The Ultimate Queen
CRYSTAL

Hails from Slovia.

She takes great pride in her battle skills, her appearance and her unrelenting pursuit of quality. She is far too proud to allow anyone else to take her spot as Number 1.

For some reason or another, she has named Myomut her rival, though he does not reciprocate the feeling.

She is far more chatty than one might expect of her.

Author Comment

I haven't really drawn her as much as I'd like, but she is one of my favorite characters.

Her character design took considerable time to come up with.

In the webcomic, the width of her hips fluctuated a bit! In the first volume, there wasn't much to them, but they increased in volume 4.

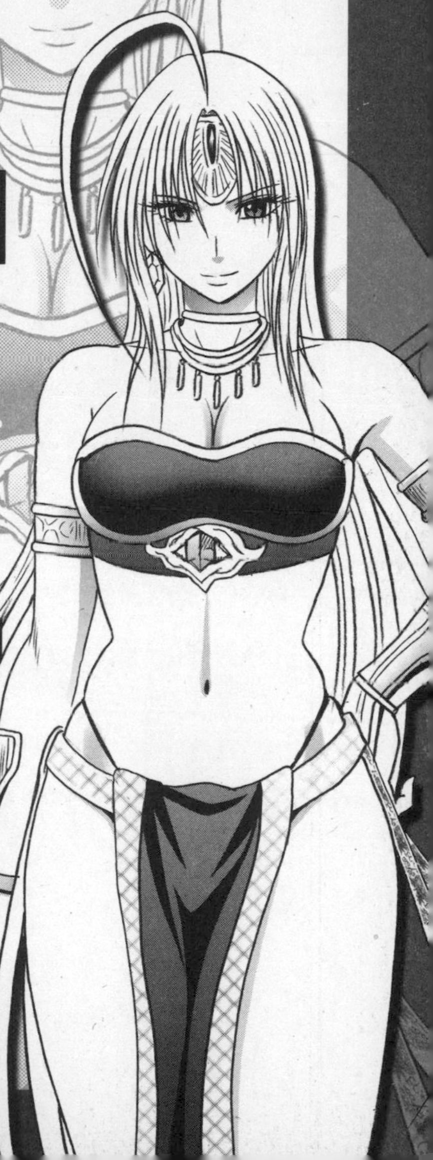

Bonus Comic

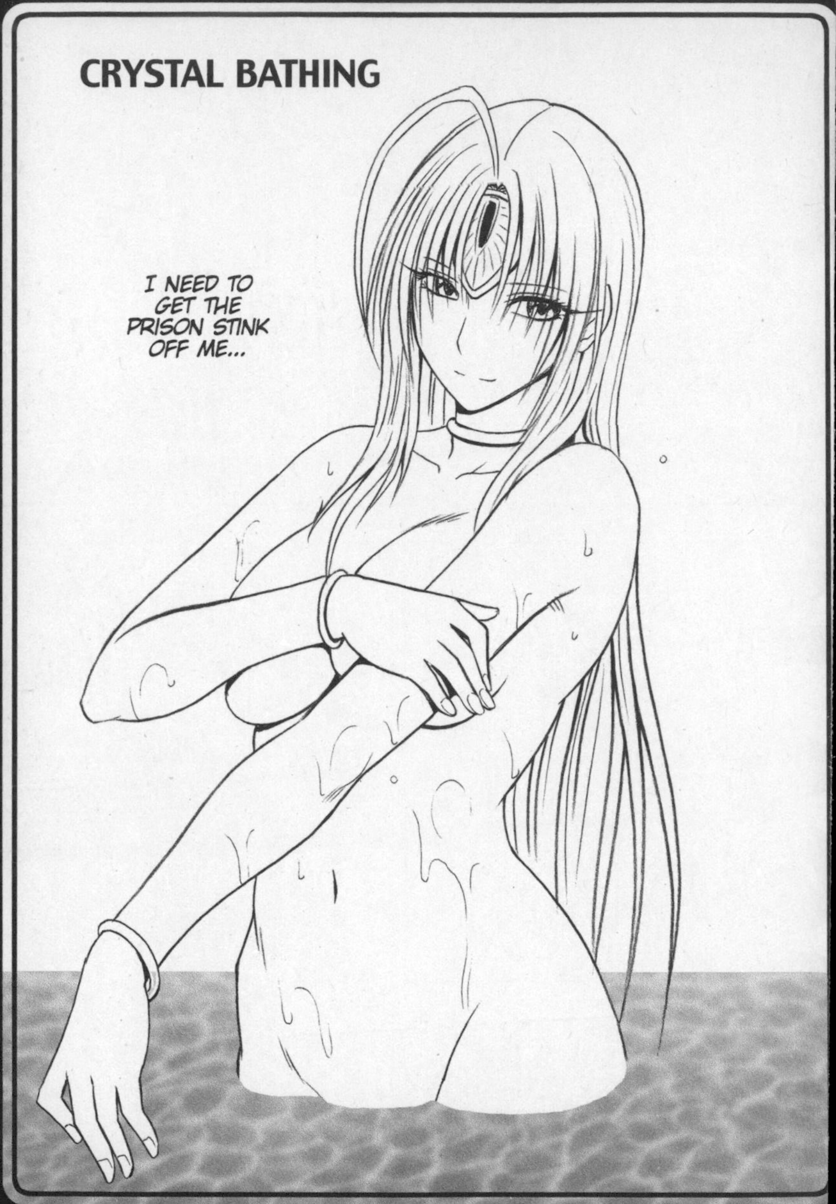
CRYSTAL BATHING
I NEED TO GET THE PRISON STINK OFF ME...

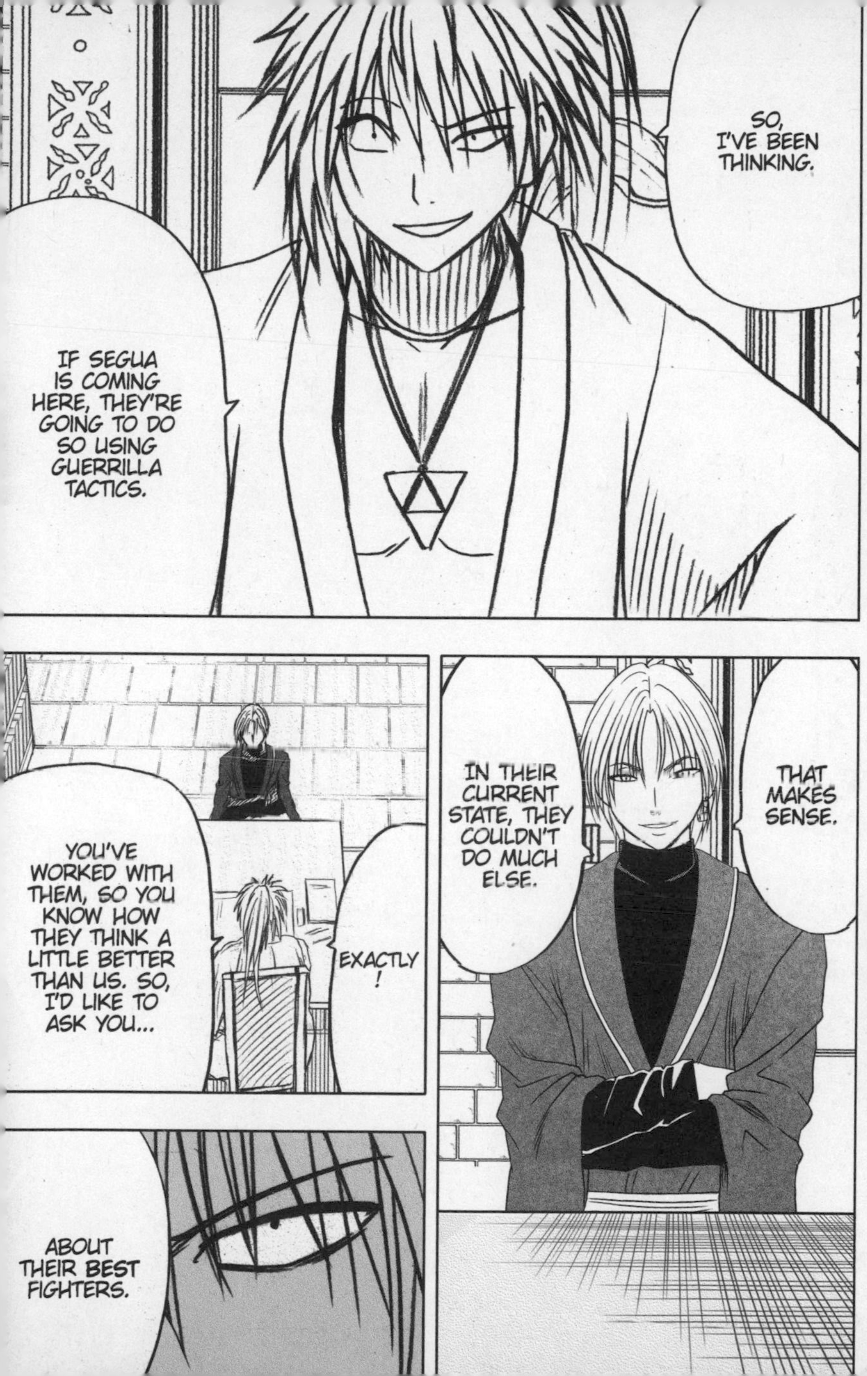
SO, I'VE BEEN THINKING.
IF SEGUA IS COMING HERE, THEY'RE GOING TO DO SO USING GUERRILLA TACTICS.
THAT MAKES SENSE.
IN THEIR CURRENT STATE, THEY COULDN'T DO MUCH ELSE.
EXACTLY!
YOU'VE WORKED WITH THEM, SO YOU KNOW HOW THEY THINK A LITTLE BETTER THAN US. SO, I'D LIKE TO ASK YOU...
ABOUT THEIR BEST FIGHTERS.

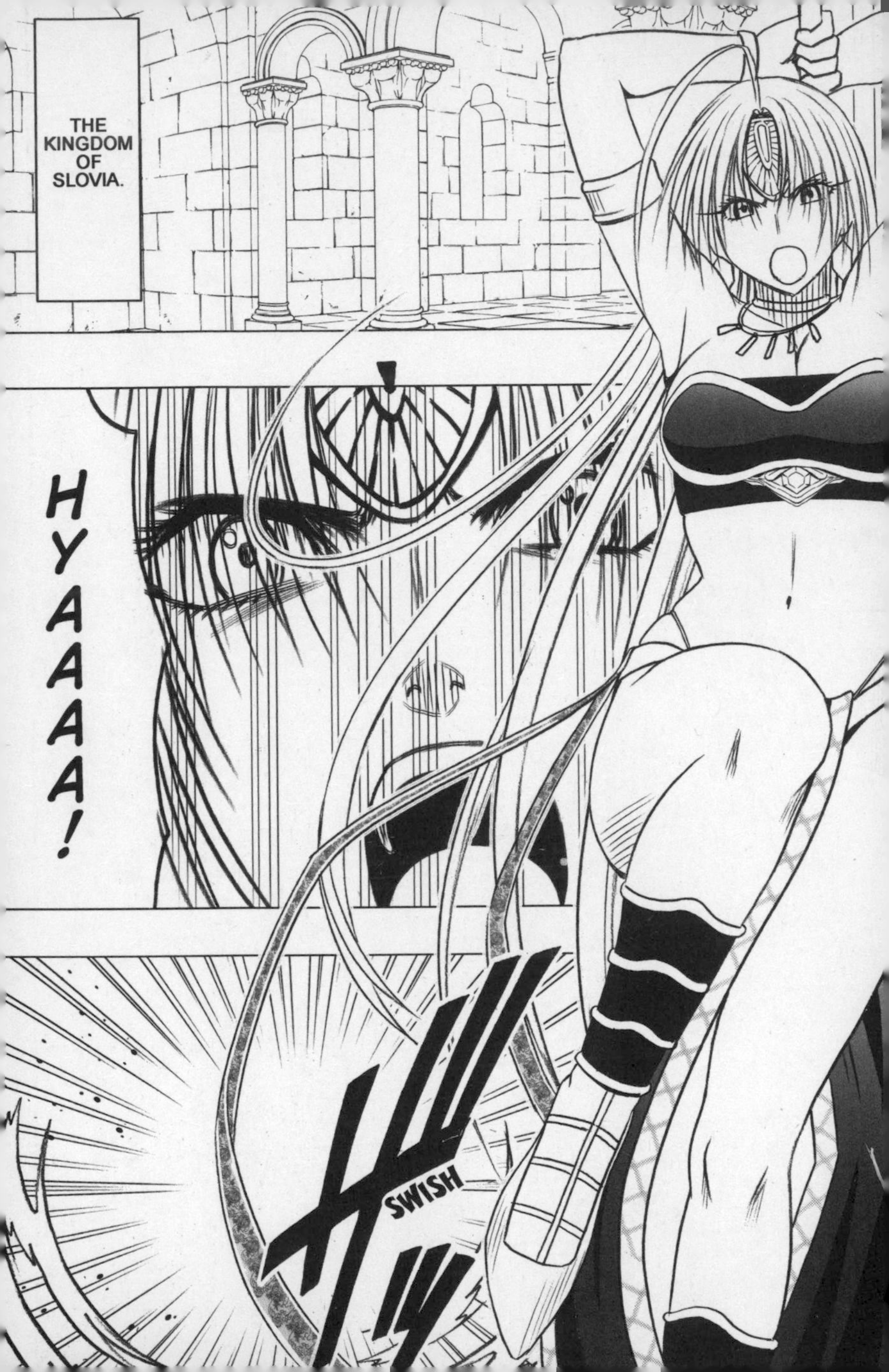
THE KINGDOM OF SLOVIA.
HYAAAAA!
SWISH

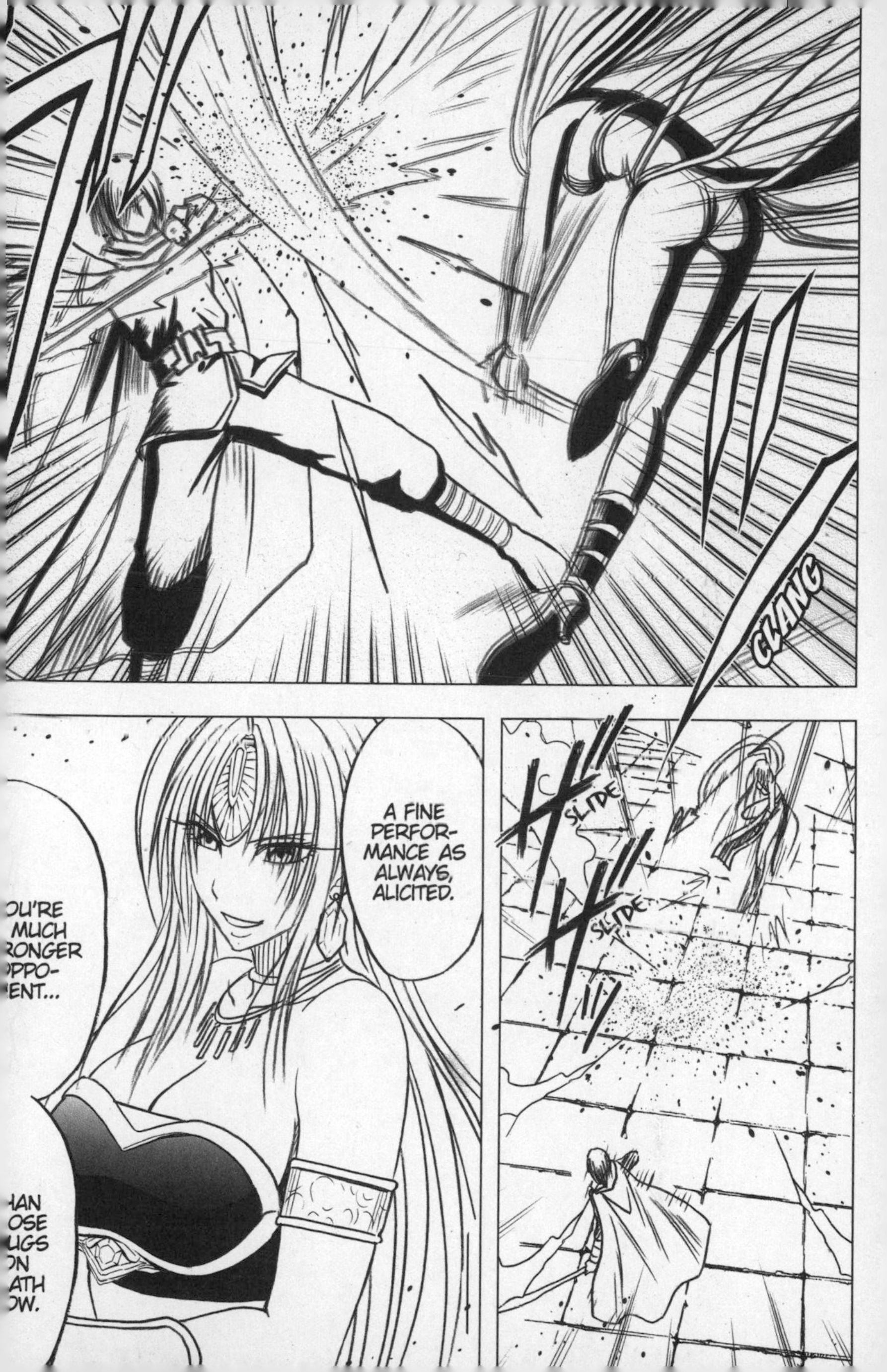
CLANG
SLIDE
SLIDE
A FINE PERFOR-MANCE AS ALWAYS, ALICITED.
OU'RE MUCH RONGER PPO- ENT...
HAN OSE UGS ON ATH OW.

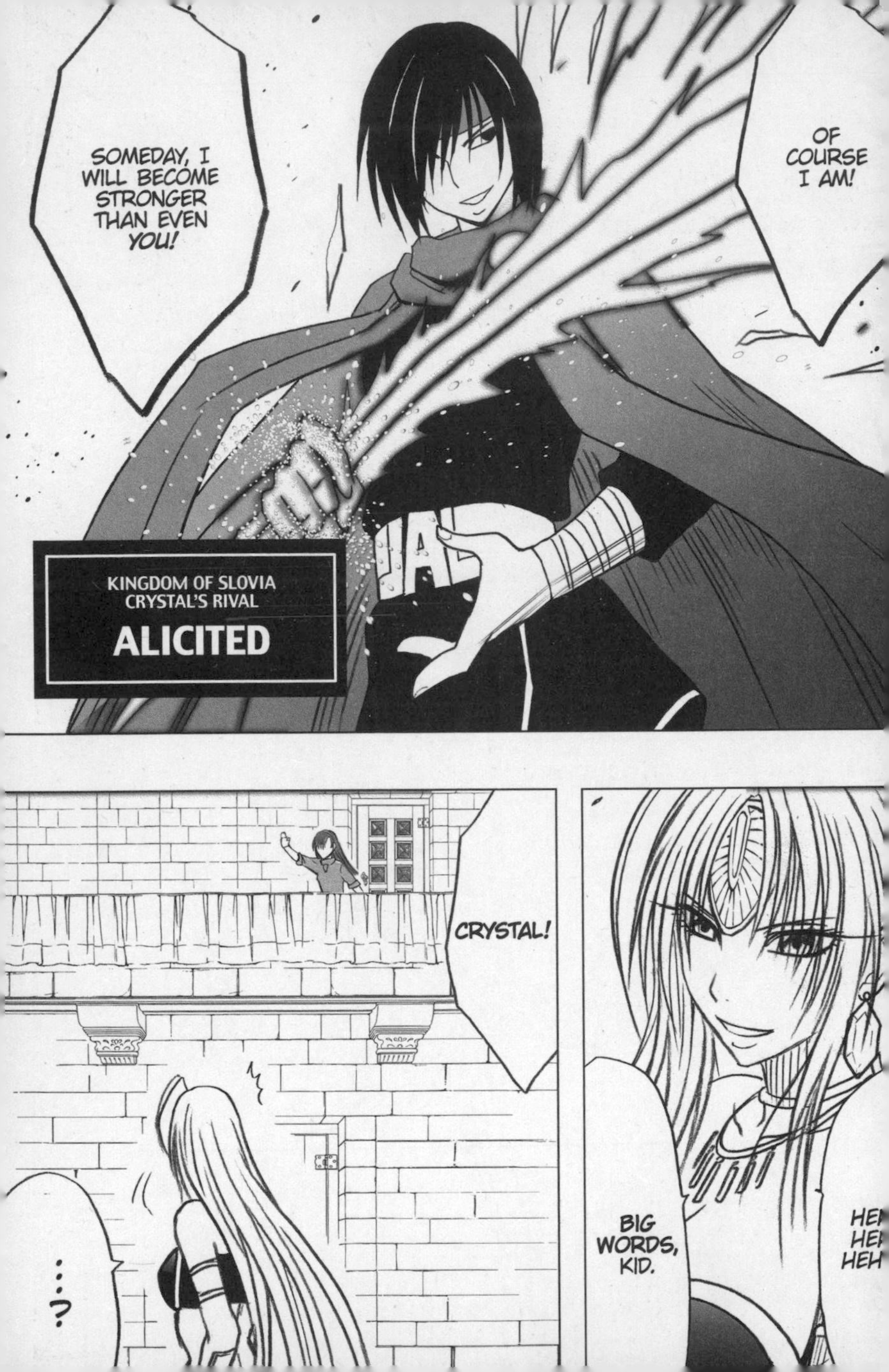
OF COURSE I AM!
SOMEDAY, I WILL BECOME STRONGER THAN EVEN YOU!
KINGDOM OF SLOVIA CRYSTAL'S RIVAL
ALICITED
HEH HEH HEH
BIG WORDS, KID.
CRYSTAL!
...?

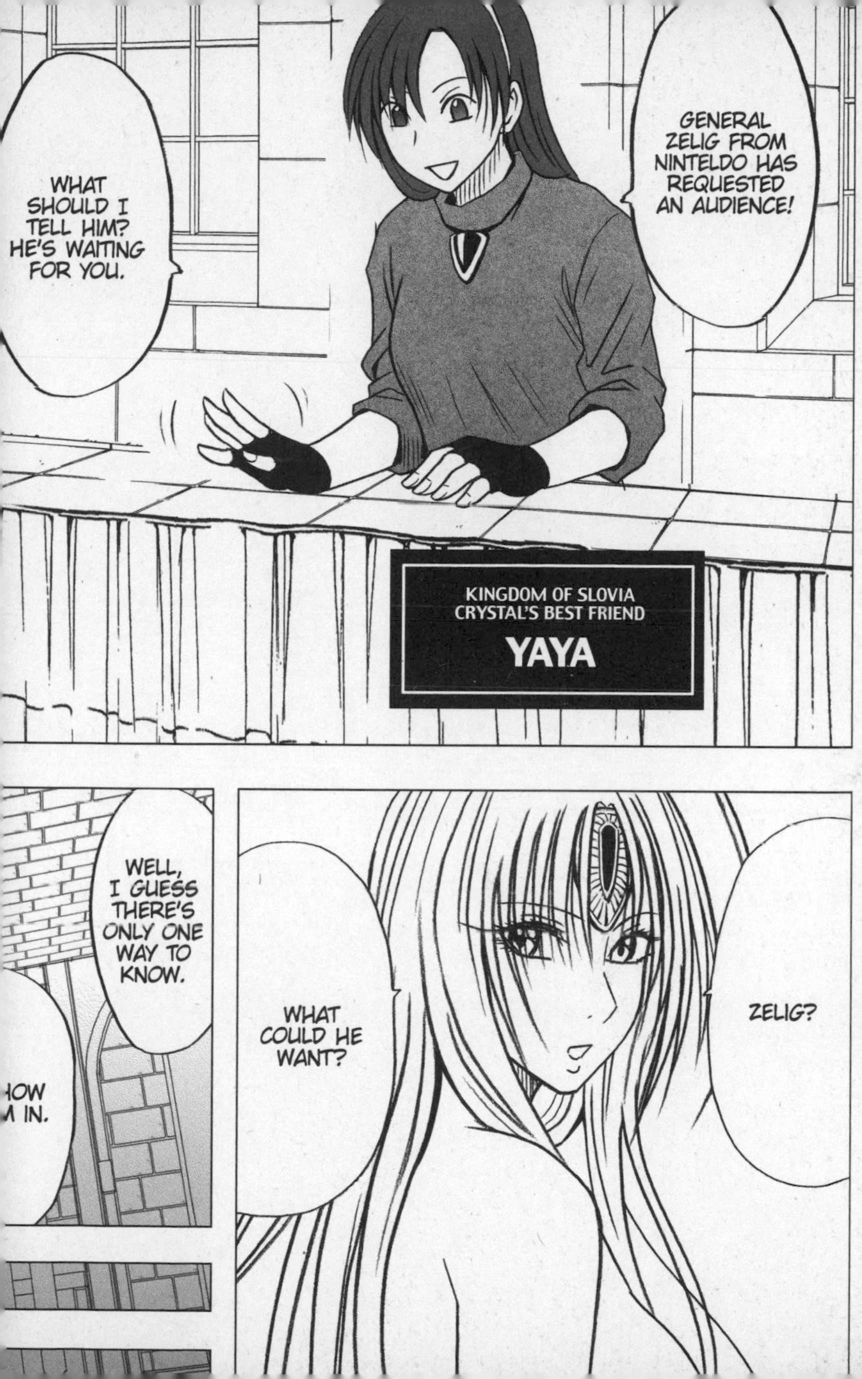
GENERAL ZELIG FROM NINTELDO HAS REQUESTED AN AUDIENCE!
WHAT SHOULD I TELL HIM? HE'S WAITING FOR YOU.
KINGDOM OF SLOVIA CRYSTAL'S BEST FRIEND
YAYA
ZELIG?
WHAT COULD HE WANT?
WELL, I GUESS THERE'S ONLY ONE WAY TO KNOW.
HOW M IN.

HOISTING LIGHT AND DARKNESS

DISC 1

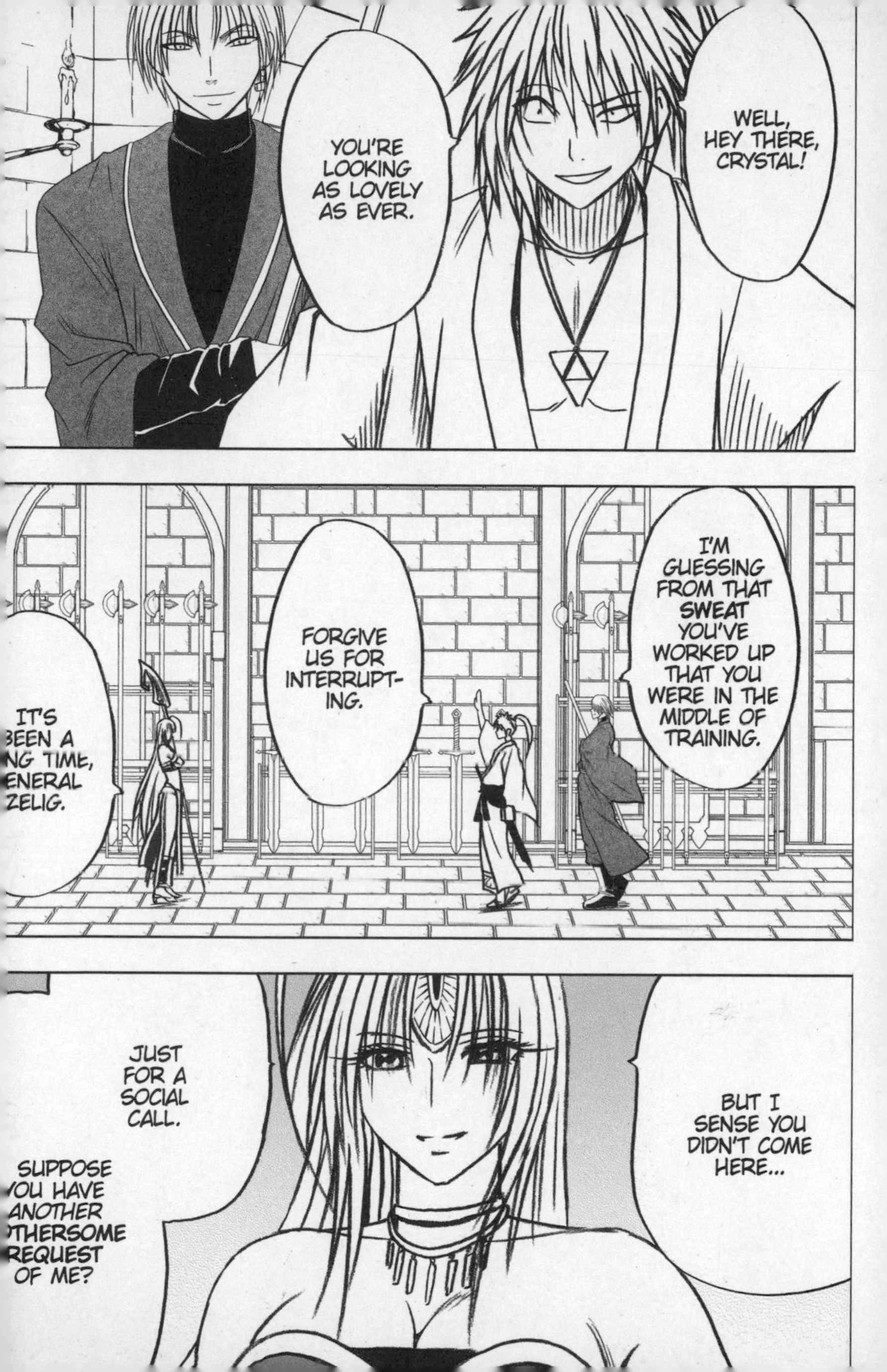
WELL, HEY THERE, CRYSTAL!
YOU'RE LOOKING AS LOVELY AS EVER.
I'M GUESSING FROM THAT SWEAT YOU'VE WORKED UP THAT YOU WERE IN THE MIDDLE OF TRAINING.
FORGIVE US FOR INTERRUPT-ING.
IT'S BEEN A NG TIME, ENERAL ZELIG.
BUT I SENSE YOU DIDN'T COME HERE...
JUST FOR A SOCIAL CALL.
SUPPOSE OU HAVE NOTHER OTHERSOME REQUEST OF ME?

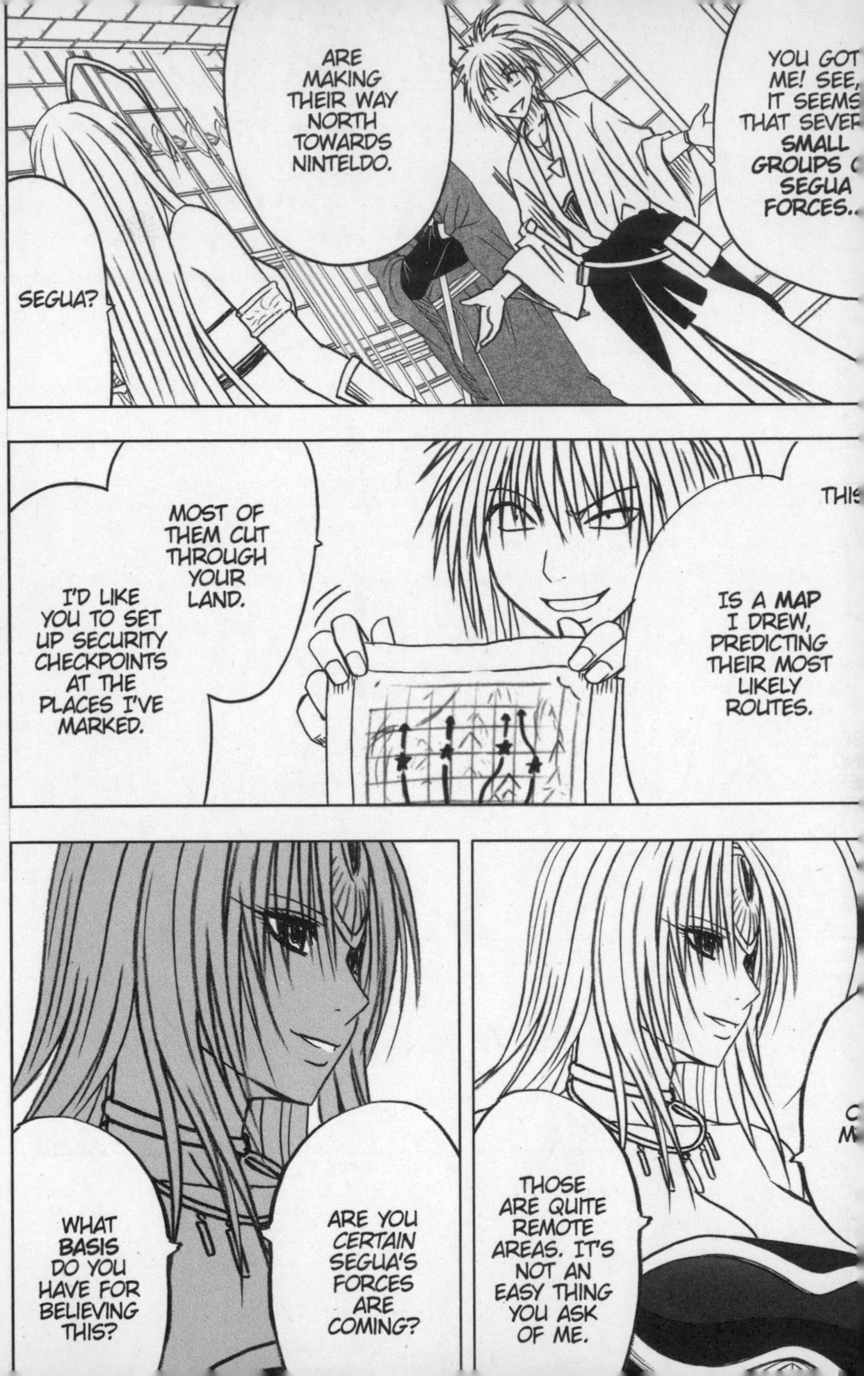

YOU GOT ME! SEE, IT SEEMS THAT SEVER SMALL GROUPS SEGUA FORCES...
ARE MAKING THEIR WAY NORTH TOWARDS NINTELDO.
SEGUA?
THIS
IS A MAP I DREW, PREDICTING THEIR MOST LIKELY ROUTES.
MOST OF THEM CUT THROUGH YOUR LAND.
I'D LIKE YOU TO SET UP SECURITY CHECKPOINTS AT THE PLACES I'VE MARKED.
THOSE ARE QUITE REMOTE AREAS. IT'S NOT AN EASY THING YOU ASK OF ME.
ARE YOU CERTAIN SEGUA'S FORCES ARE COMING?
WHAT BASIS DO YOU HAVE FOR BELIEVING THIS?

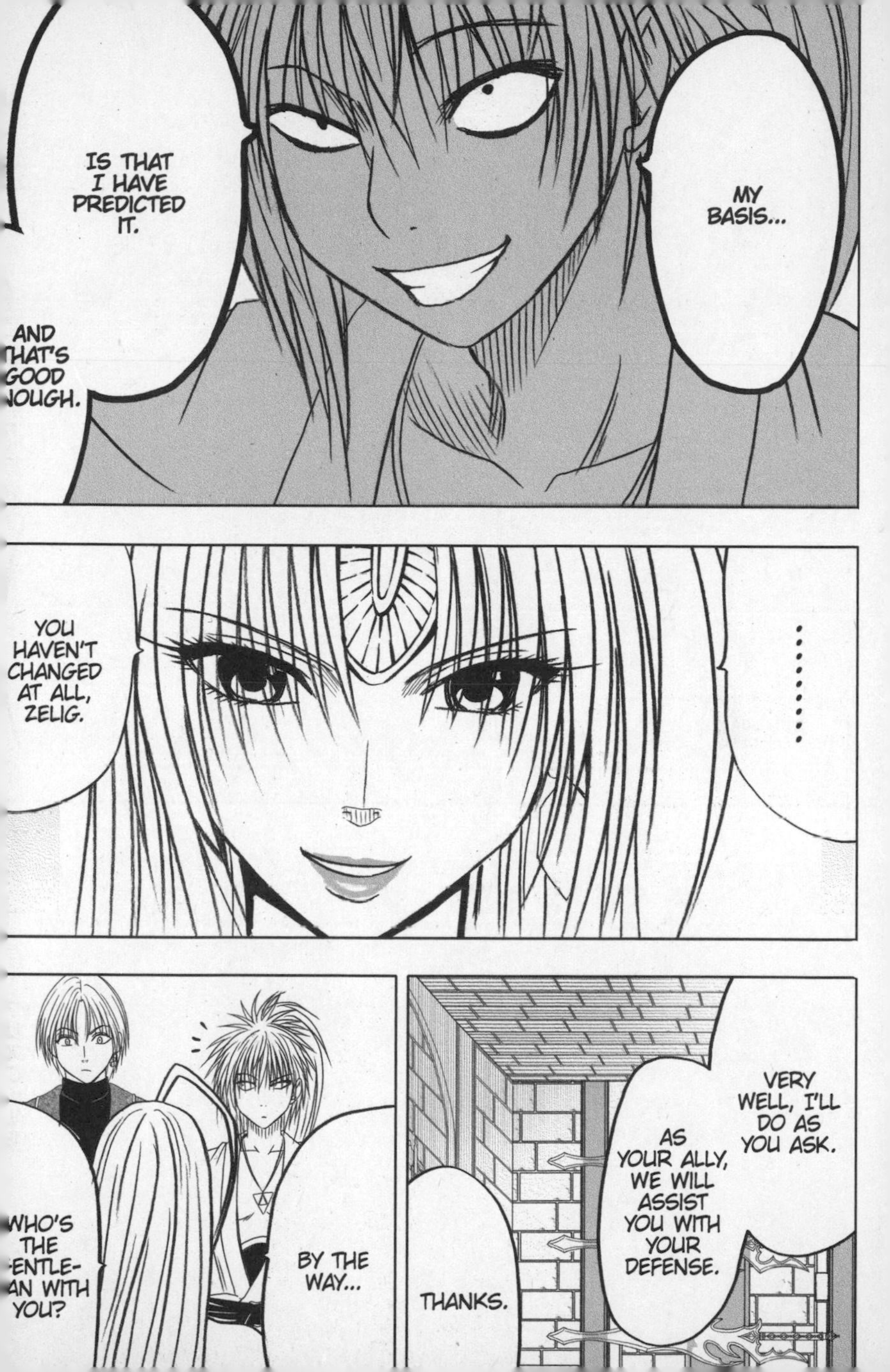
MY BASIS...
IS THAT I HAVE PREDICTED IT.
AND THAT'S GOOD NOUGH.
......
YOU HAVEN'T CHANGED AT ALL, ZELIG.
VERY WELL, I'LL DO AS YOU ASK.
AS YOUR ALLY, WE WILL ASSIST YOU WITH YOUR DEFENSE.
THANKS.
BY THE WAY...
WHO'S THE ENTLE- AN WITH YOU?

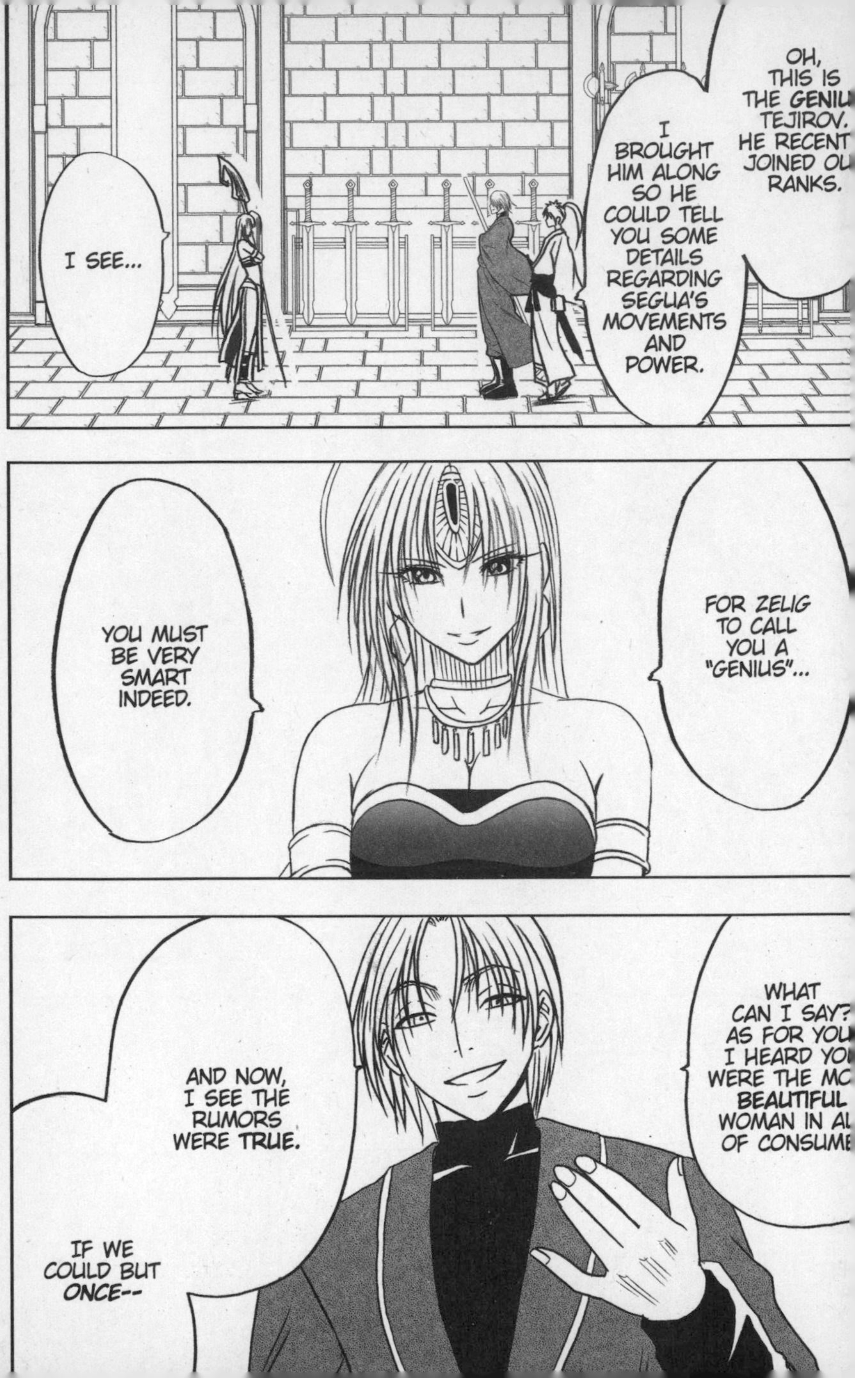
OH, THIS IS THE GENIU TEJIROV. HE RECENT JOINED OU RANKS.
I BROUGHT HIM ALONG SO HE COULD TELL YOU SOME DETAILS REGARDING SEGUA'S MOVEMENTS AND POWER.
I SEE...
FOR ZELIG TO CALL YOU A "GENIUS"...
YOU MUST BE VERY SMART INDEED.
WHAT CAN I SAY? AS FOR YOU I HEARD YO WERE THE MO BEAUTIFUL WOMAN IN AL OF CONSUME
AND NOW, I SEE THE RUMORS WERE TRUE.
IF WE COULD BUT ONCE--

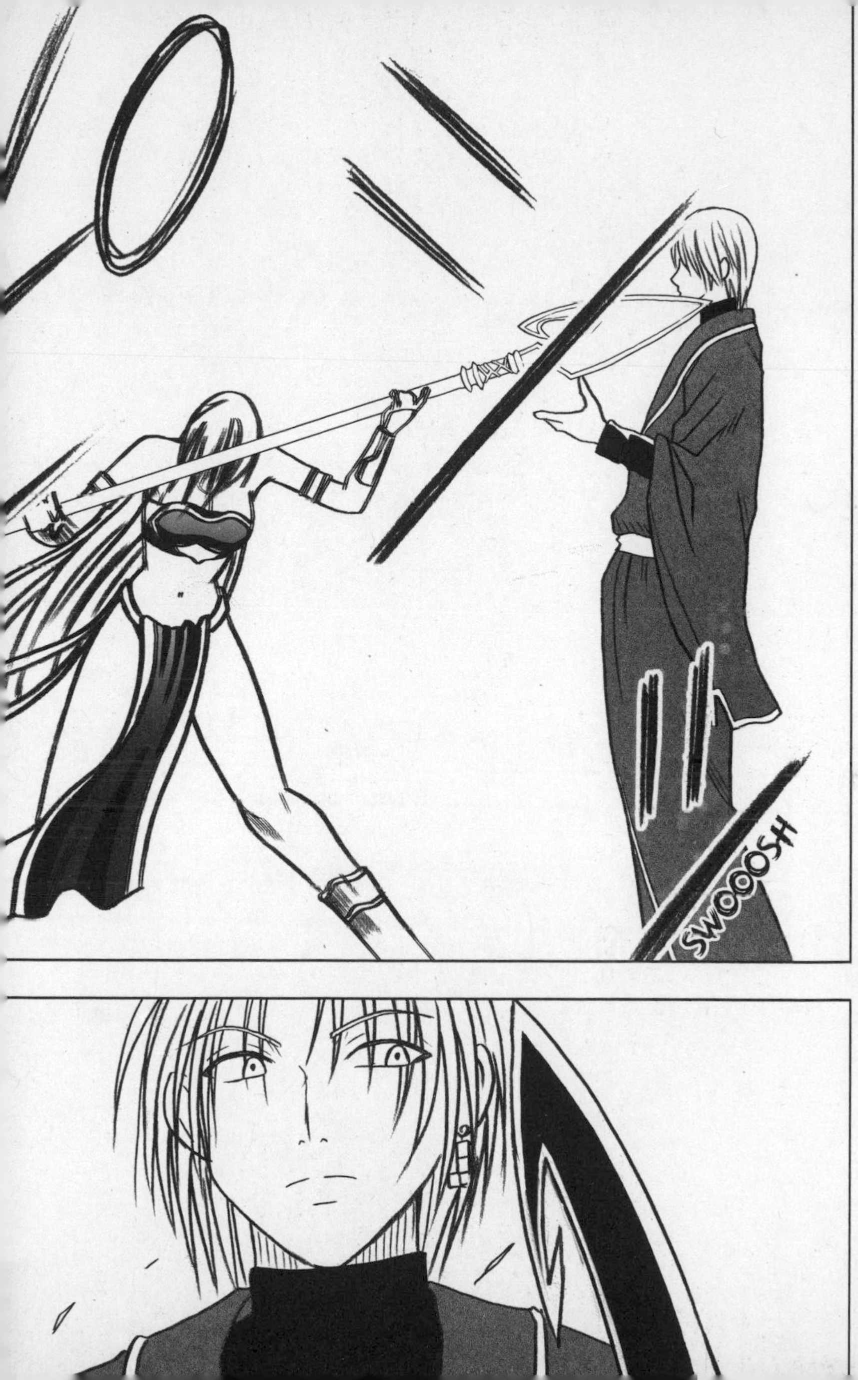
SWOOOSH

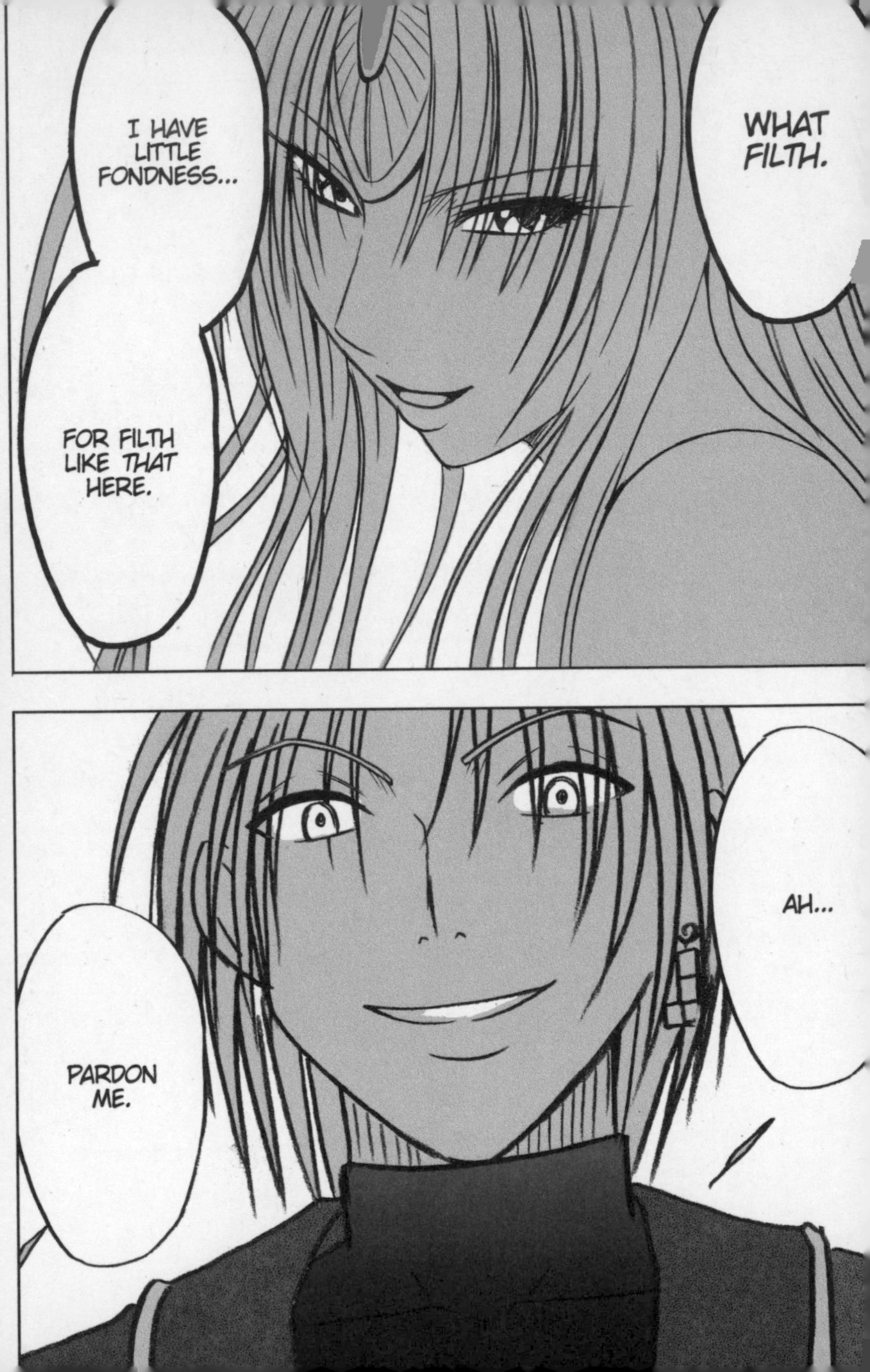
WHAT FILTH.
I HAVE LITTLE FONDNESS...
FOR FILTH LIKE THAT HERE.
AH...
PARDON ME.

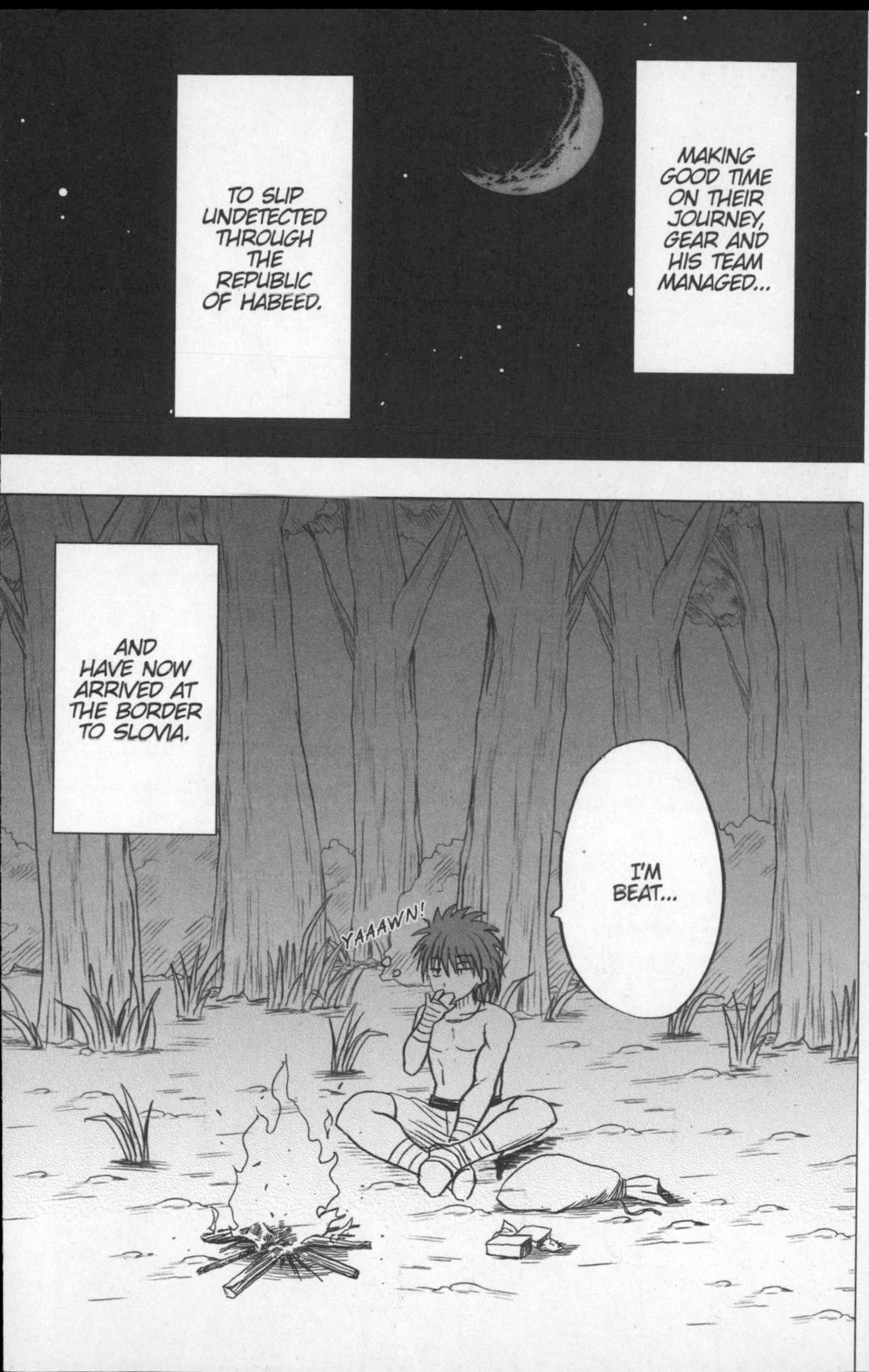
MAKING GOOD TIME ON THEIR JOURNEY, GEAR AND HIS TEAM MANAGED...
TO SLIP UNDETECTED THROUGH THE REPUBLIC OF HABEED.
AND HAVE NOW ARRIVED AT THE BORDER TO SLOVIA.
YAAAWN!
I'M BEAT...

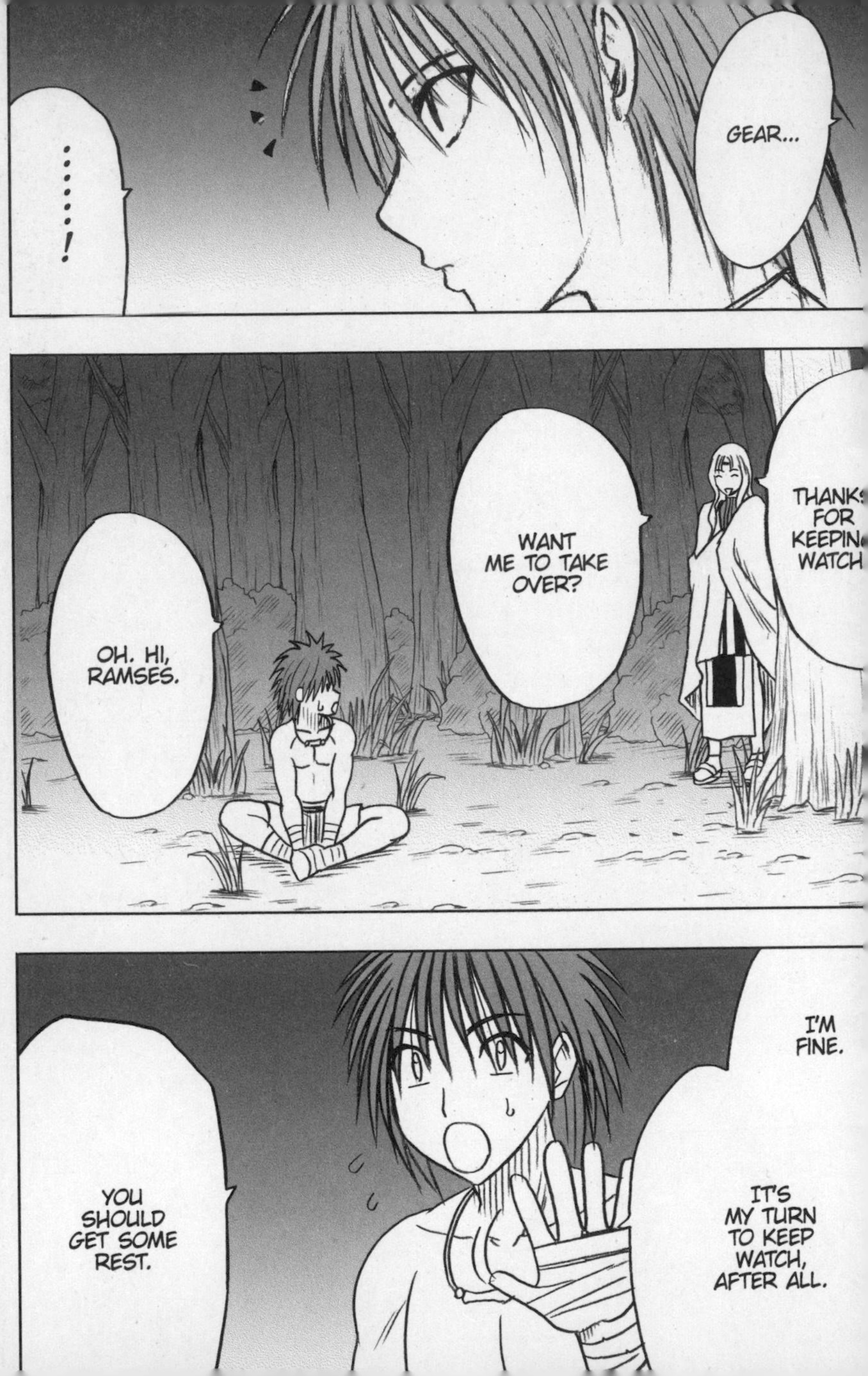
GEAR...
......!
THANKS FOR KEEPIN WATCH
WANT ME TO TAKE OVER?
OH. HI, RAMSES.
I'M FINE.
IT'S MY TURN TO KEEP WATCH, AFTER ALL.
YOU SHOULD GET SOME REST.

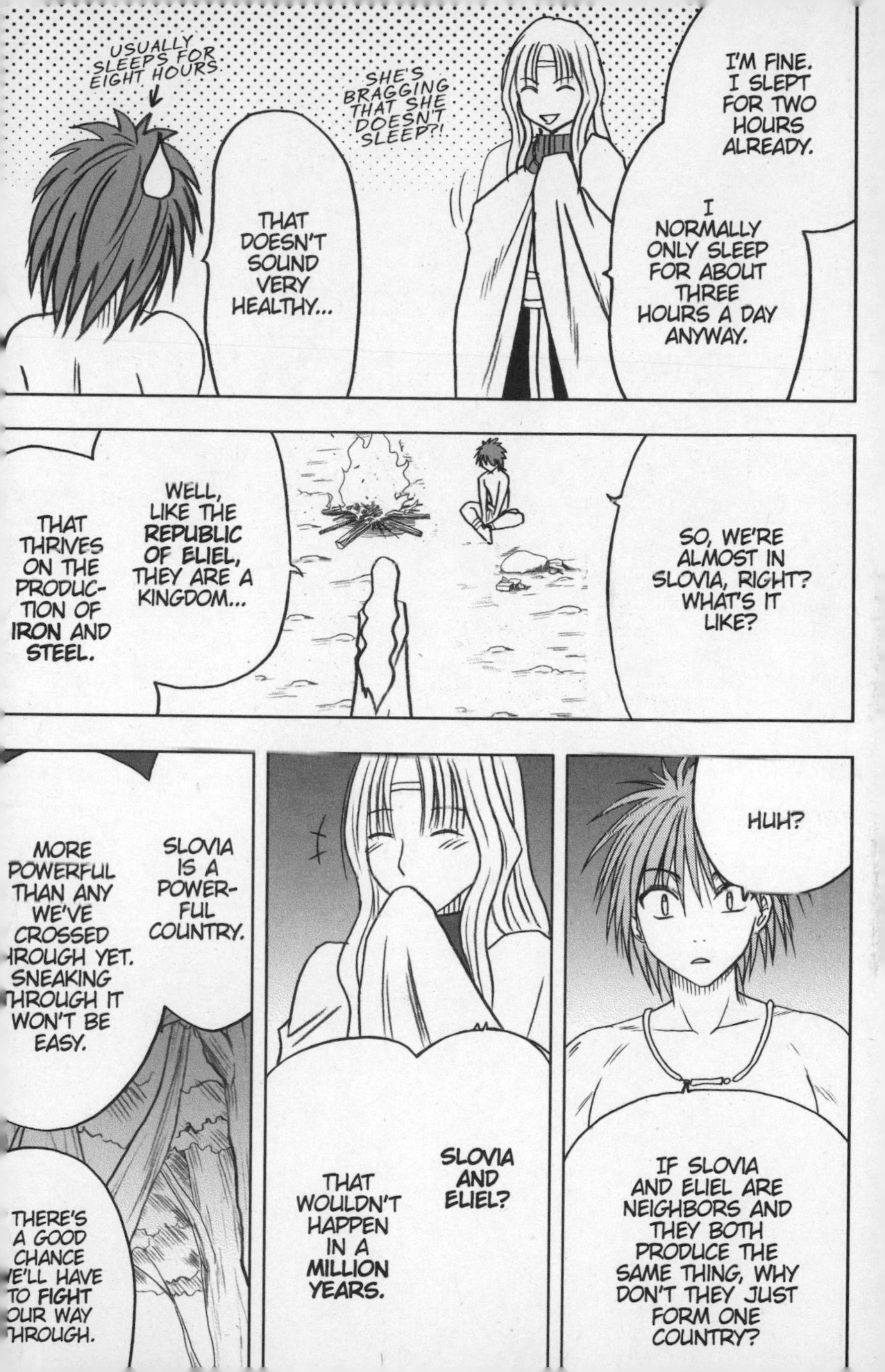
I'M FINE. I SLEPT FOR TWO HOURS ALREADY.
I NORMALLY ONLY SLEEP FOR ABOUT THREE HOURS A DAY ANYWAY.
SHE'S BRAGGING THAT SHE DOESN'T SLEEP?!
USUALLY SLEEPS FOR EIGHT HOURS.
THAT DOESN'T SOUND VERY HEALTHY...
SO, WE'RE ALMOST IN SLOVIA, RIGHT? WHAT'S IT LIKE?
WELL, LIKE THE REPUBLIC OF ELIEL, THEY ARE A KINGDOM...
THAT THRIVES ON THE PRODUCTION OF IRON AND STEEL.
HUH?
IF SLOVIA AND ELIEL ARE NEIGHBORS AND THEY BOTH PRODUCE THE SAME THING, WHY DON'T THEY JUST FORM ONE COUNTRY?
SLOVIA AND ELIEL?
THAT WOULDN'T HAPPEN IN A MILLION YEARS.
SLOVIA IS A POWERFUL COUNTRY.
MORE POWERFUL THAN ANY WE'VE CROSSED HROUGH YET. SNEAKING HROUGH IT WON'T BE EASY.
THERE'S A GOOD CHANCE E'LL HAVE TO FIGHT OUR WAY HROUGH.

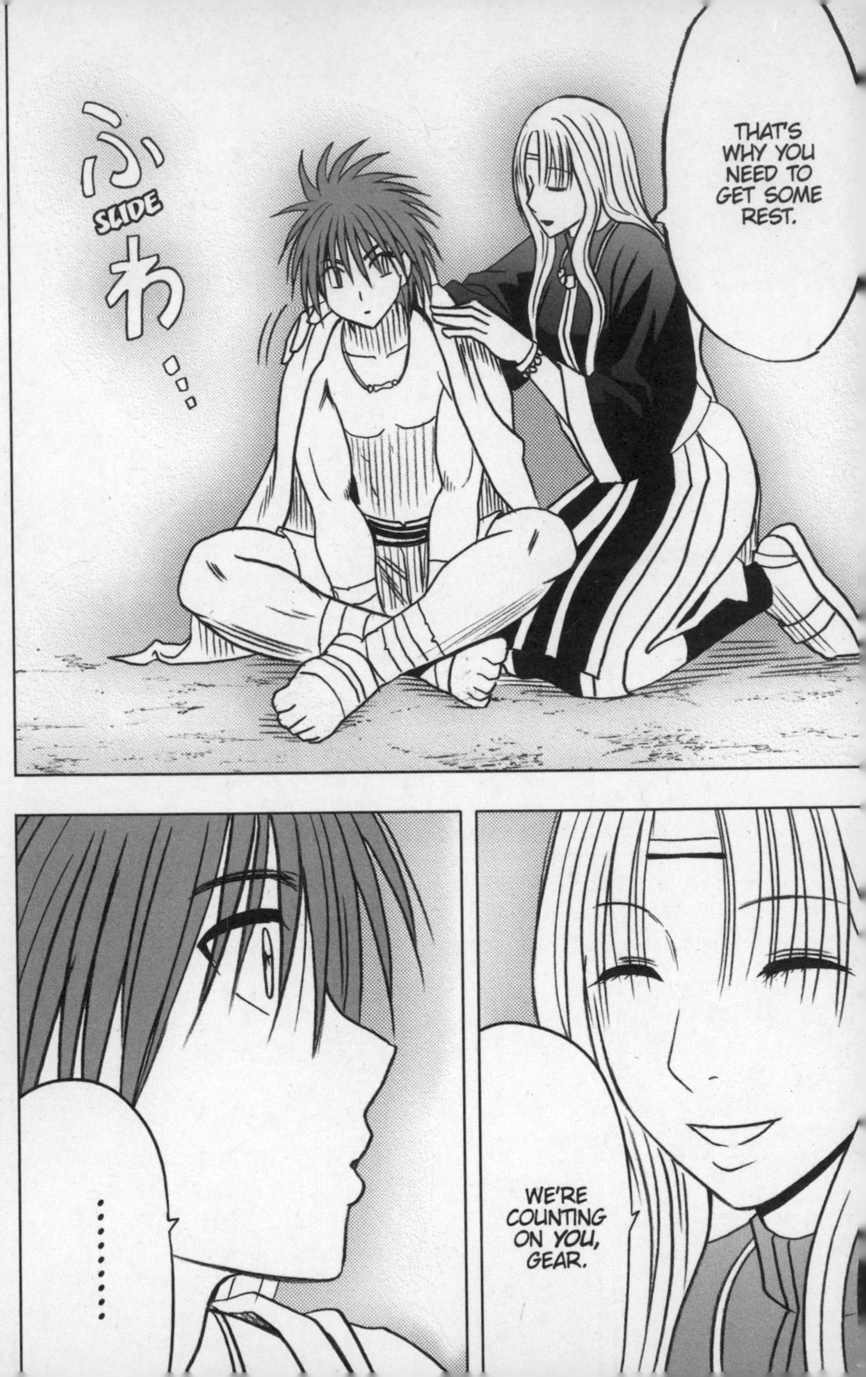
ふわ…
SLIDE
THAT'S WHY YOU NEED TO GET SOME REST.
WE'RE COUNTING ON YOU, GEAR.
……

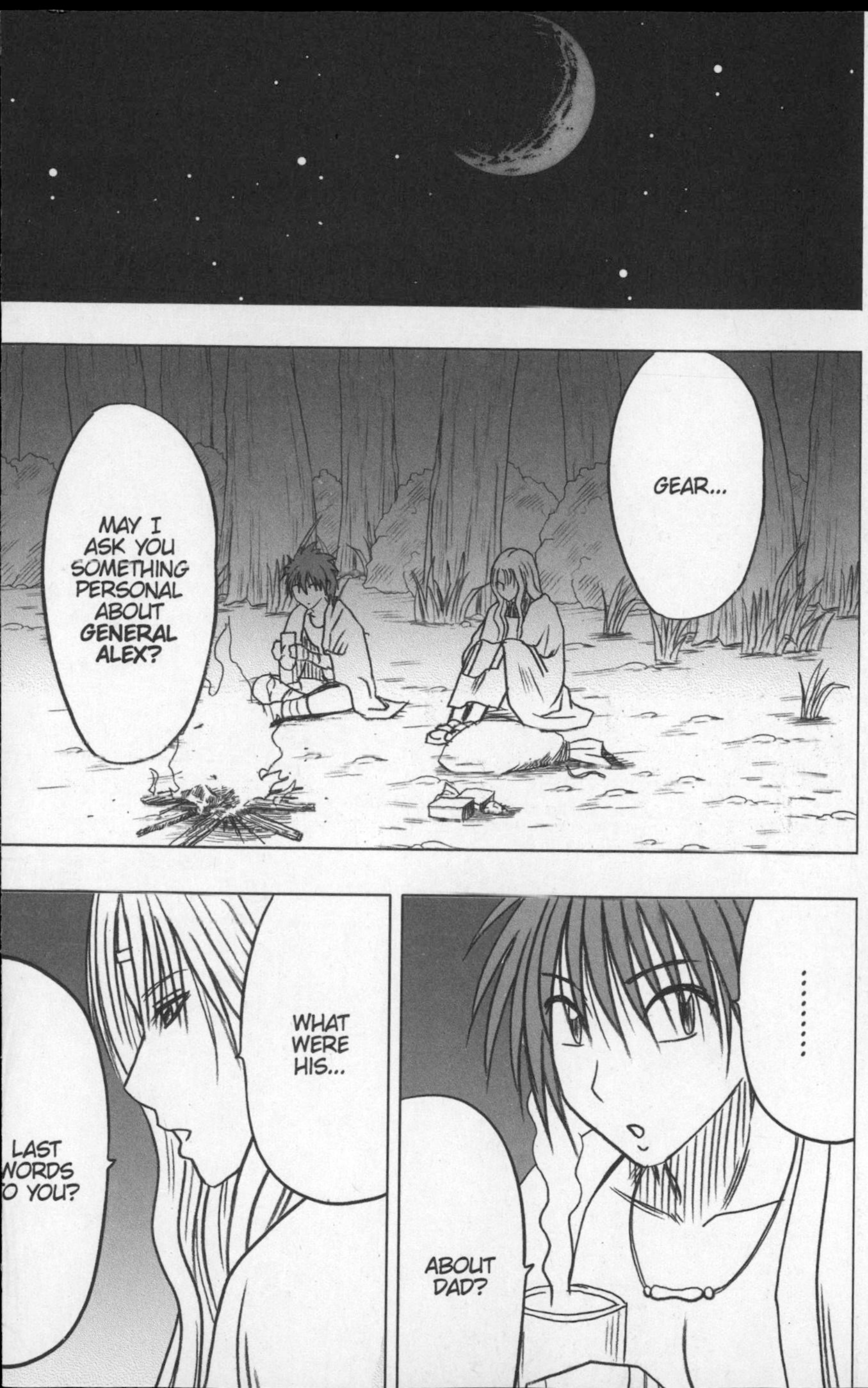
GEAR...
MAY I ASK YOU SOMETHING PERSONAL ABOUT GENERAL ALEX?
....
ABOUT DAD?
WHAT WERE HIS...
LAST WORDS O YOU?

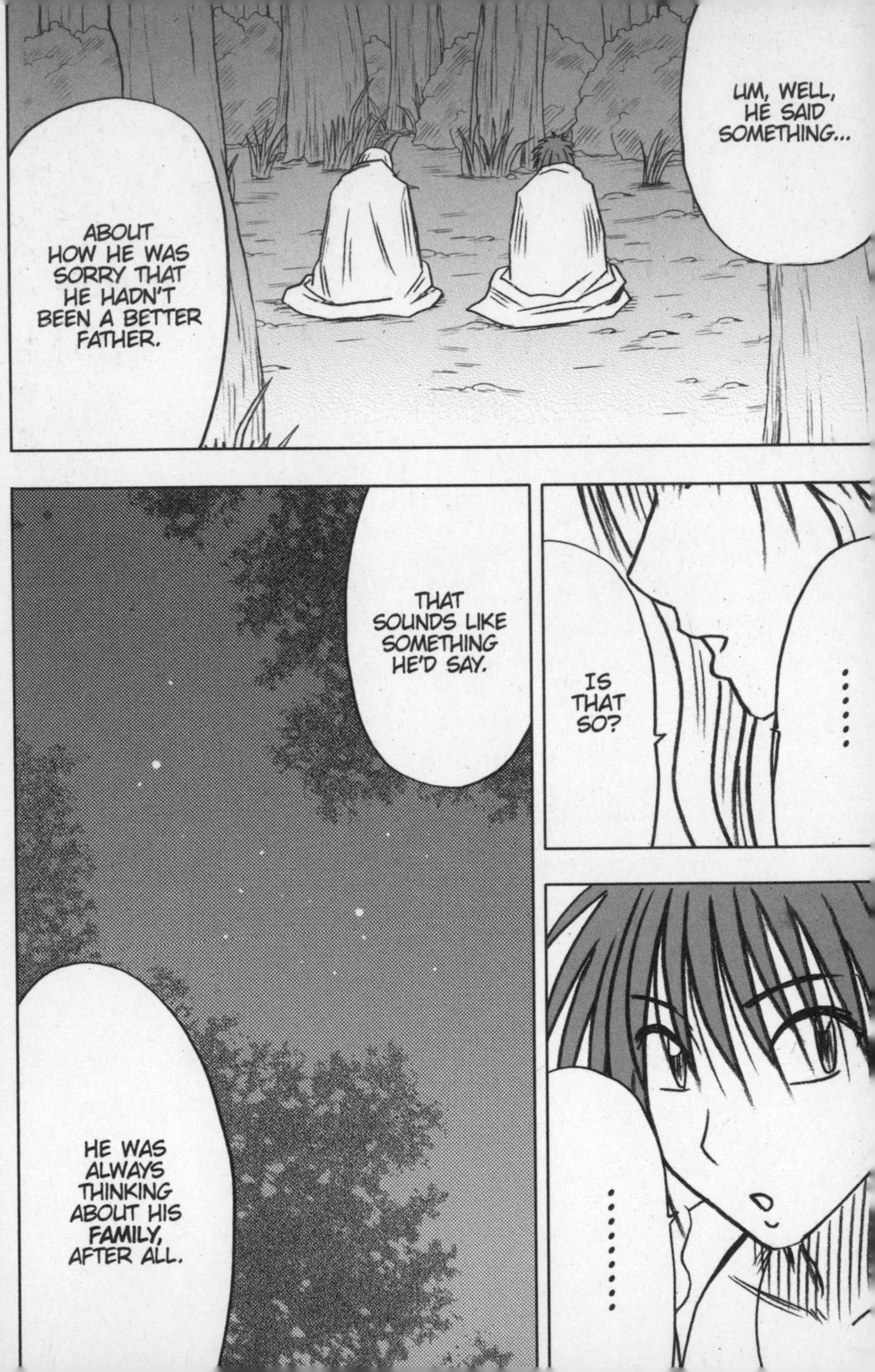
UM, WELL, HE SAID SOMETHING...
ABOUT HOW HE WAS SORRY THAT HE HADN'T BEEN A BETTER FATHER.
......
IS THAT SO?
......
THAT SOUNDS LIKE SOMETHING HE'D SAY.
HE WAS ALWAYS THINKING ABOUT HIS FAMILY, AFTER ALL.

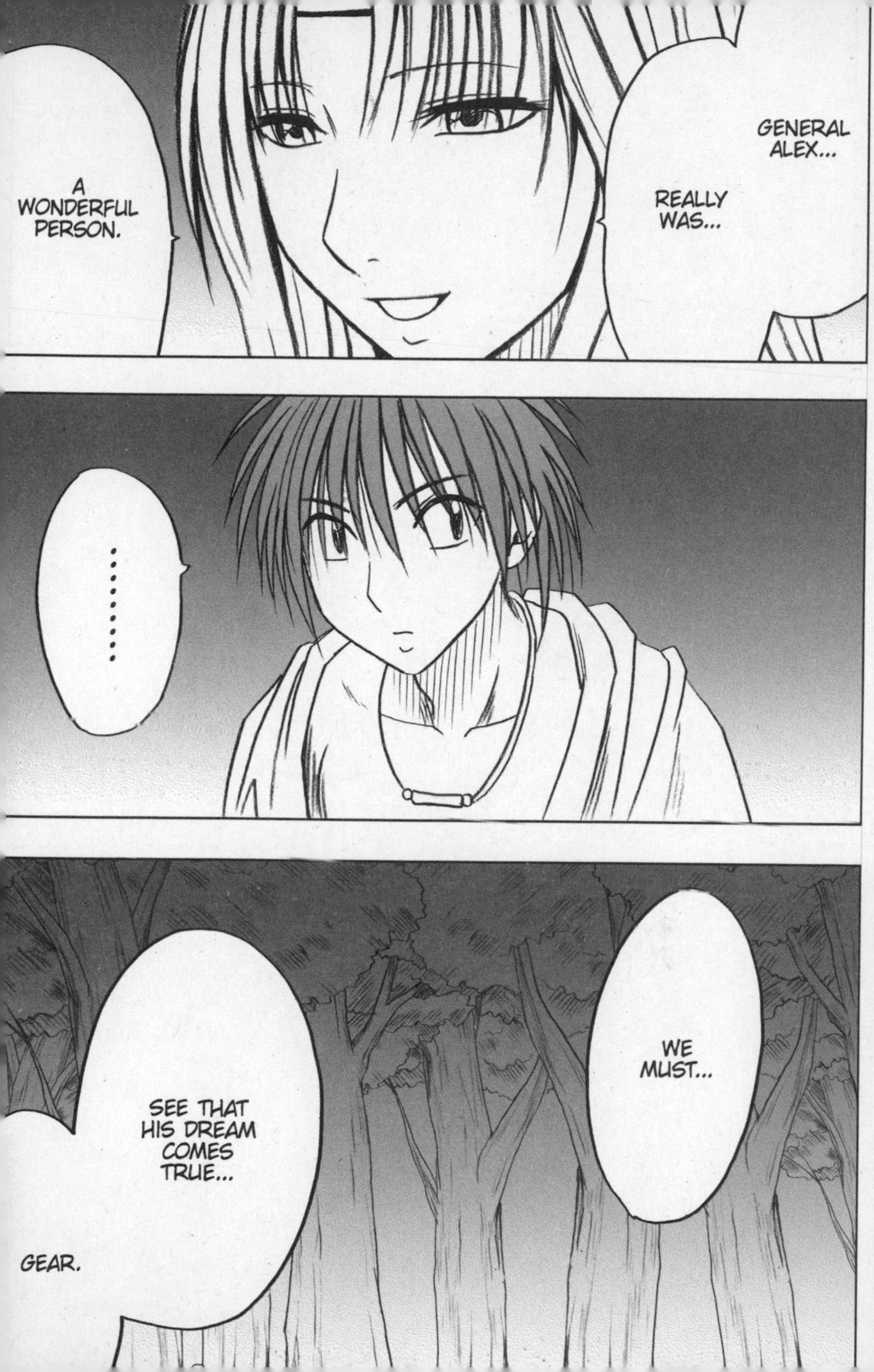
GENERAL ALEX...
REALLY WAS...
A WONDERFUL PERSON.
......
WE MUST...
SEE THAT HIS DREAM COMES TRUE...
GEAR.

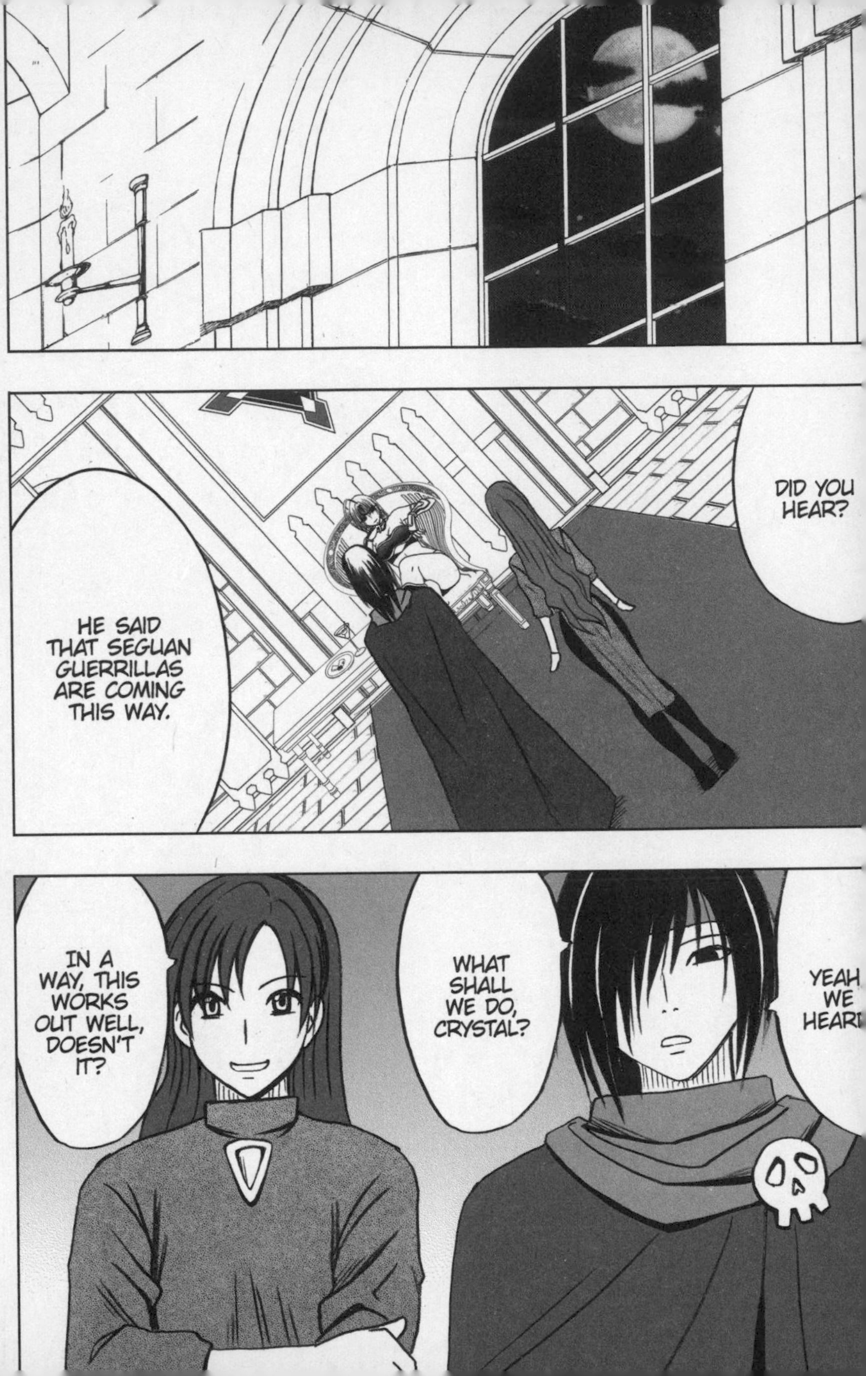
DID YOU HEAR?
HE SAID THAT SEGUAN GUERRILLAS ARE COMING THIS WAY.
YEAH WE HEAR
WHAT SHALL WE DO, CRYSTAL?
IN A WAY, THIS WORKS OUT WELL, DOESN'T IT?

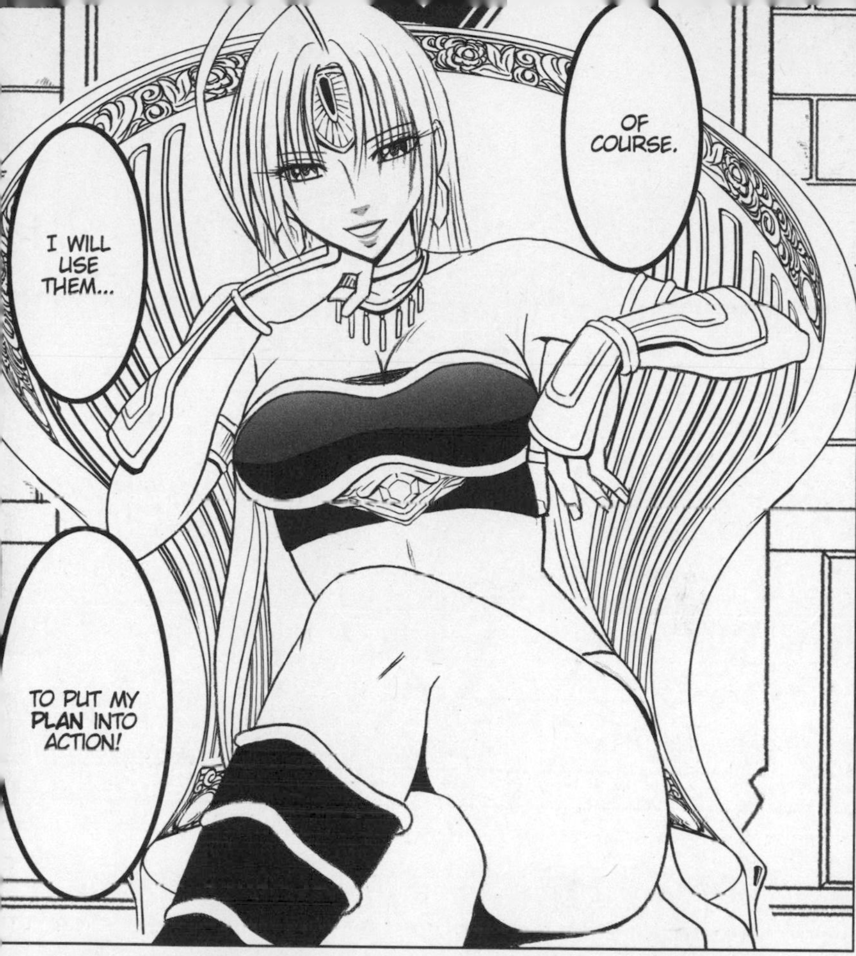
OF COURSE.
I WILL USE THEM...
TO PUT MY PLAN INTO ACTION!
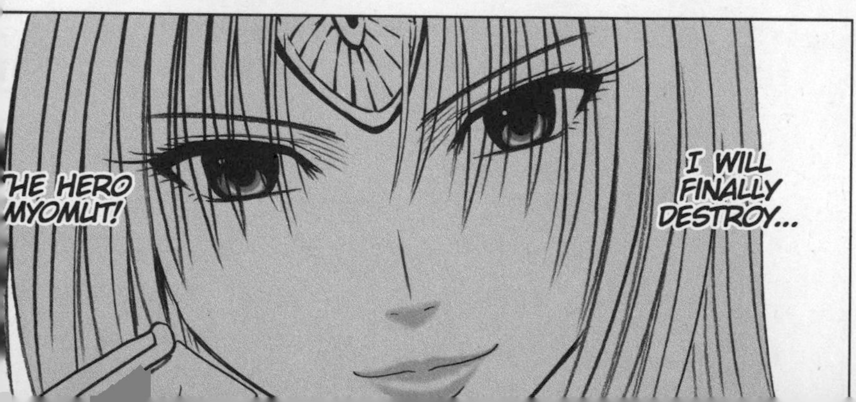
I WILL FINALLY DESTROY...
THE HERO MYOMUT!

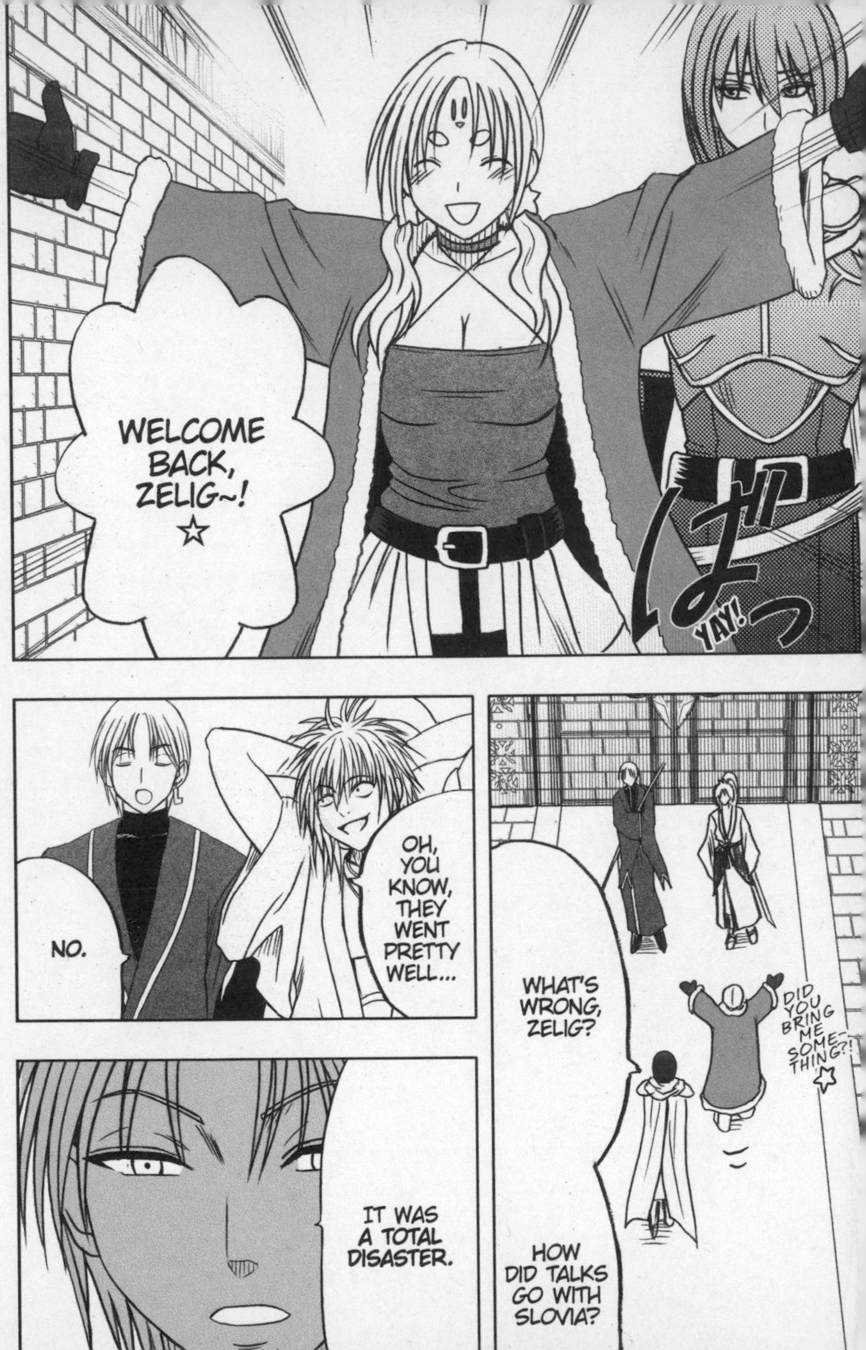
WELCOME BACK, ZELIG~! ☆
ぱっ
YAY!
DID YOU BRING ME SOME-THING?! ☆
WHAT'S WRONG, ZELIG?
HOW DID TALKS GO WITH SLOVIA?
OH, YOU KNOW, THEY WENT PRETTY WELL...
NO.
IT WAS A TOTAL DISASTER.

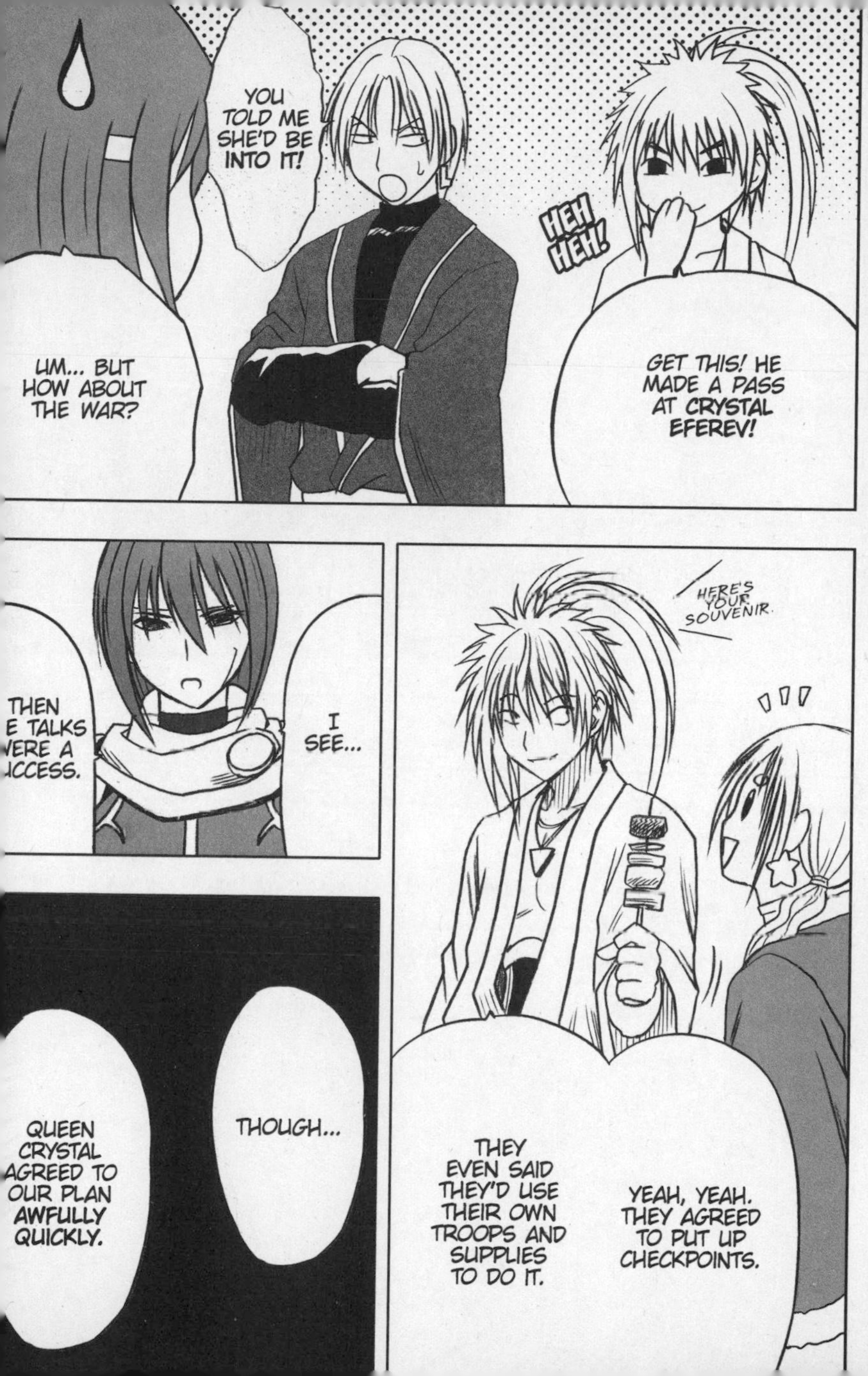
GET THIS! HE MADE A PASS AT CRYSTAL EFEREV!
YOU TOLD ME SHE'D BE INTO IT!
HEH HEH!
UM... BUT HOW ABOUT THE WAR?
YEAH, YEAH. THEY AGREED TO PUT UP CHECKPOINTS.
THEY EVEN SAID THEY'D USE THEIR OWN TROOPS AND SUPPLIES TO DO IT.
HERE'S YOUR SOUVENIR.
I SEE...
THEN E TALKS VERE A ICCESS.
THOUGH...
QUEEN CRYSTAL AGREED TO OUR PLAN AWFULLY QUICKLY.

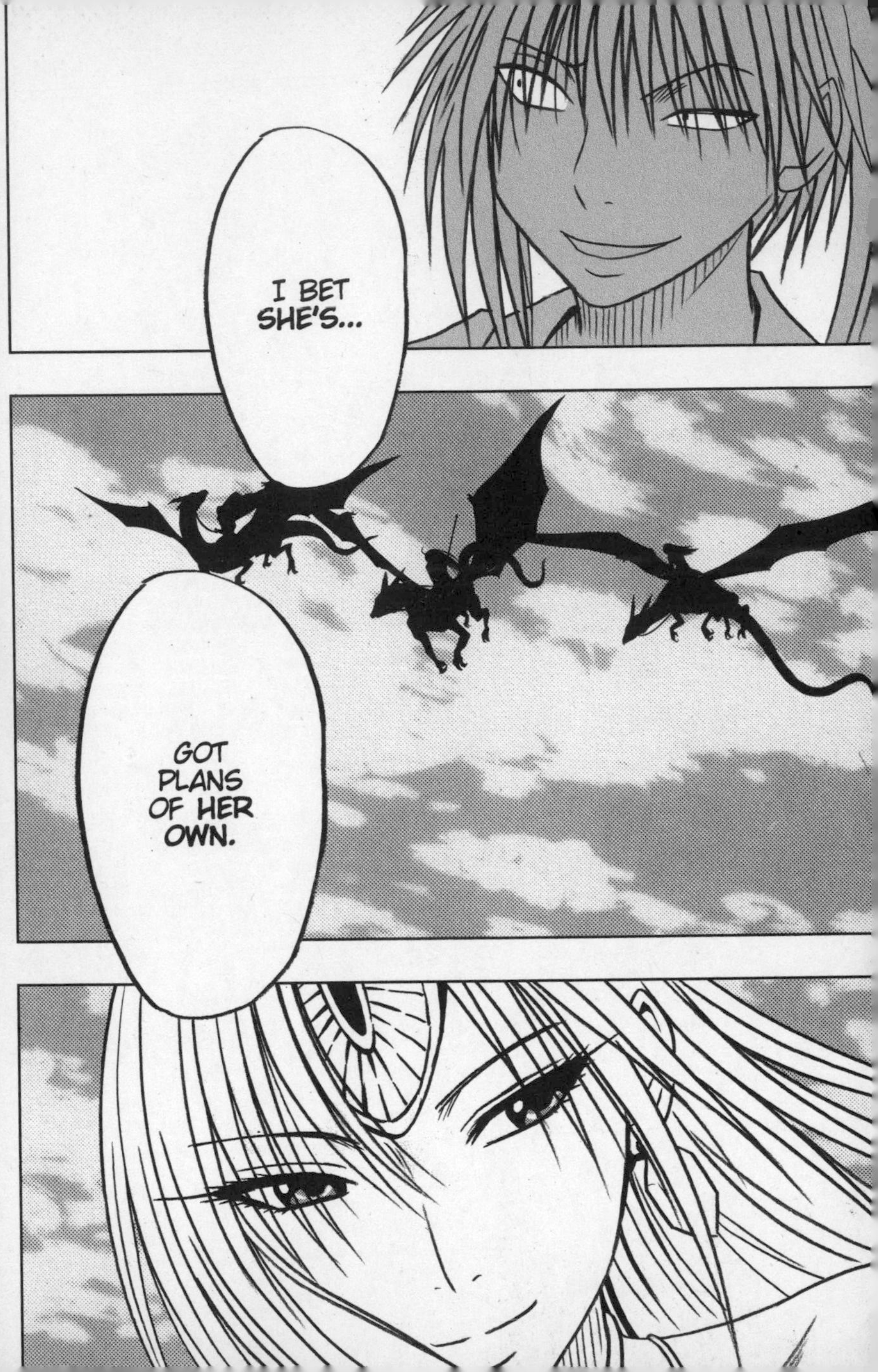
I BET SHE'S...
GOT PLANS OF HER OWN.

HOISTING LIGHT AND DARKNESS

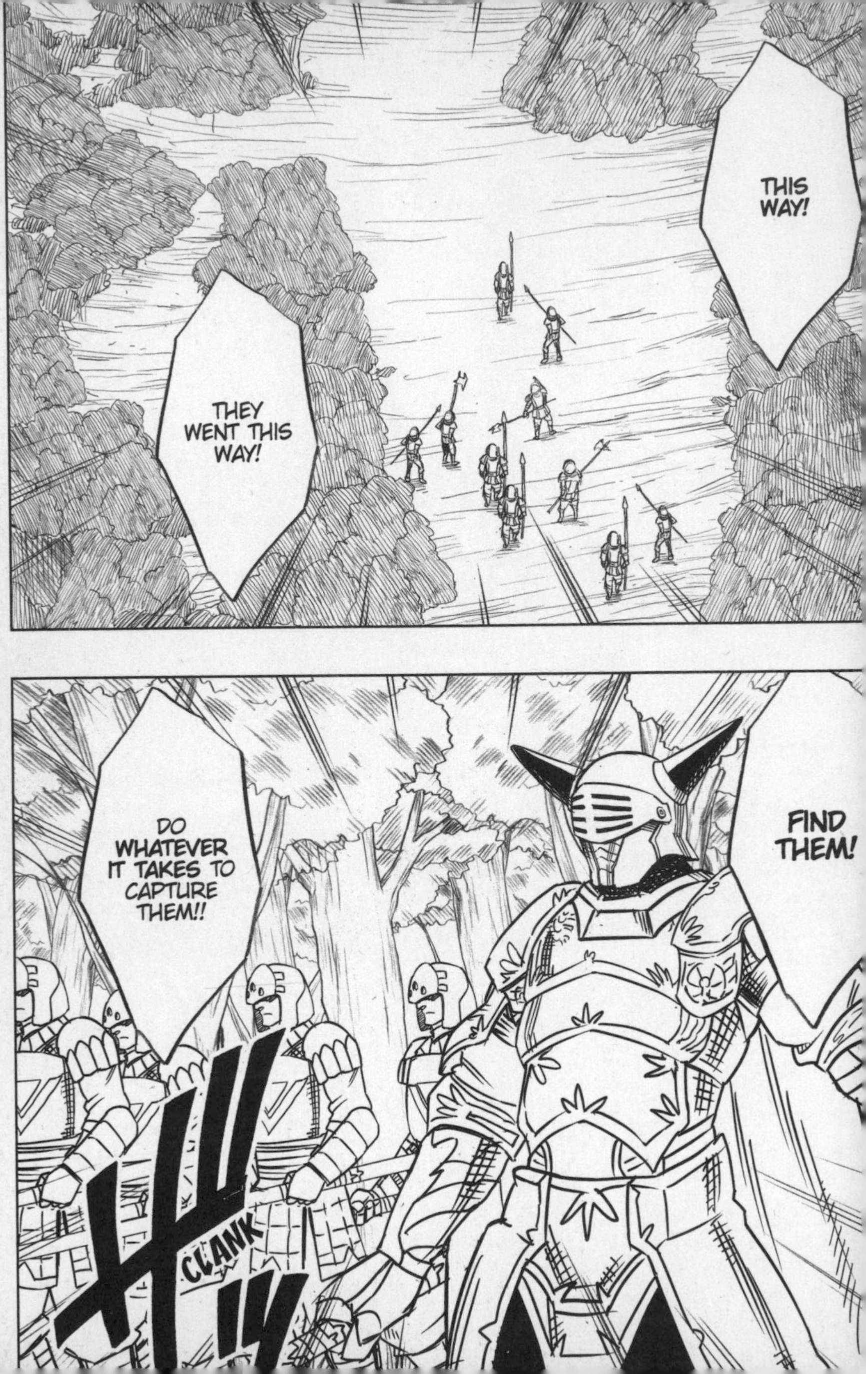
THIS WAY!
THEY WENT THIS WAY!
FIND THEM!
DO WHATEVER IT TAKES TO CAPTURE THEM!!
CLANK

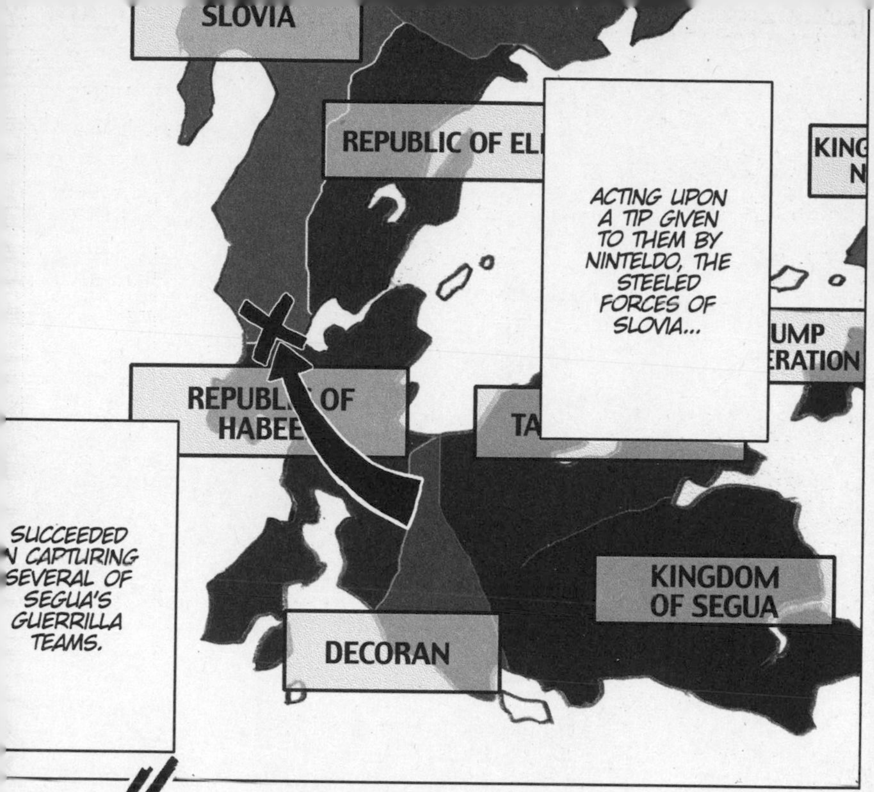
ACTING UPON A TIP GIVEN TO THEM BY NINTELDO, THE STEELED FORCES OF SLOVIA...
SLOVIA
KINGDOM OF SEGUA
DECORAN
SUCCEEDED IN CAPTURING SEVERAL OF SEGUA'S GUERRILLA TEAMS.
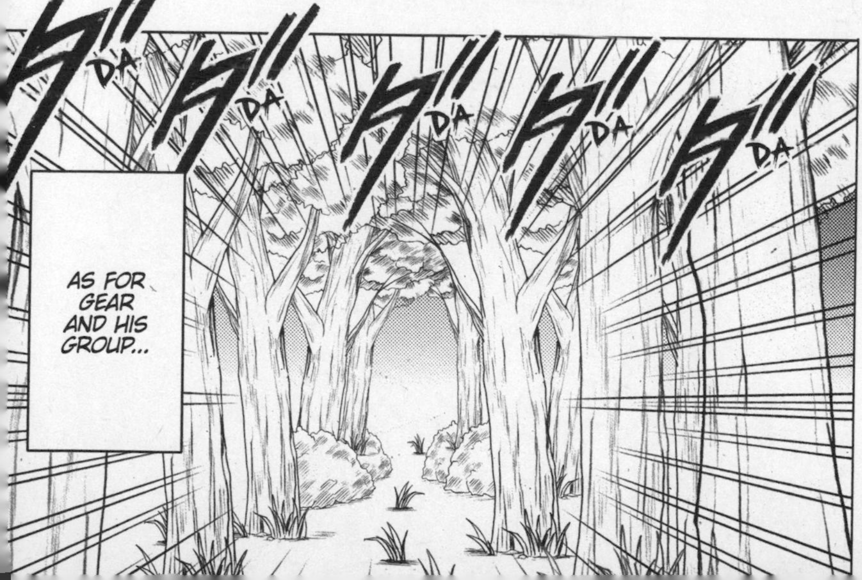
DA
DA
DA
DA
DA
AS FOR GEAR AND HIS GROUP...

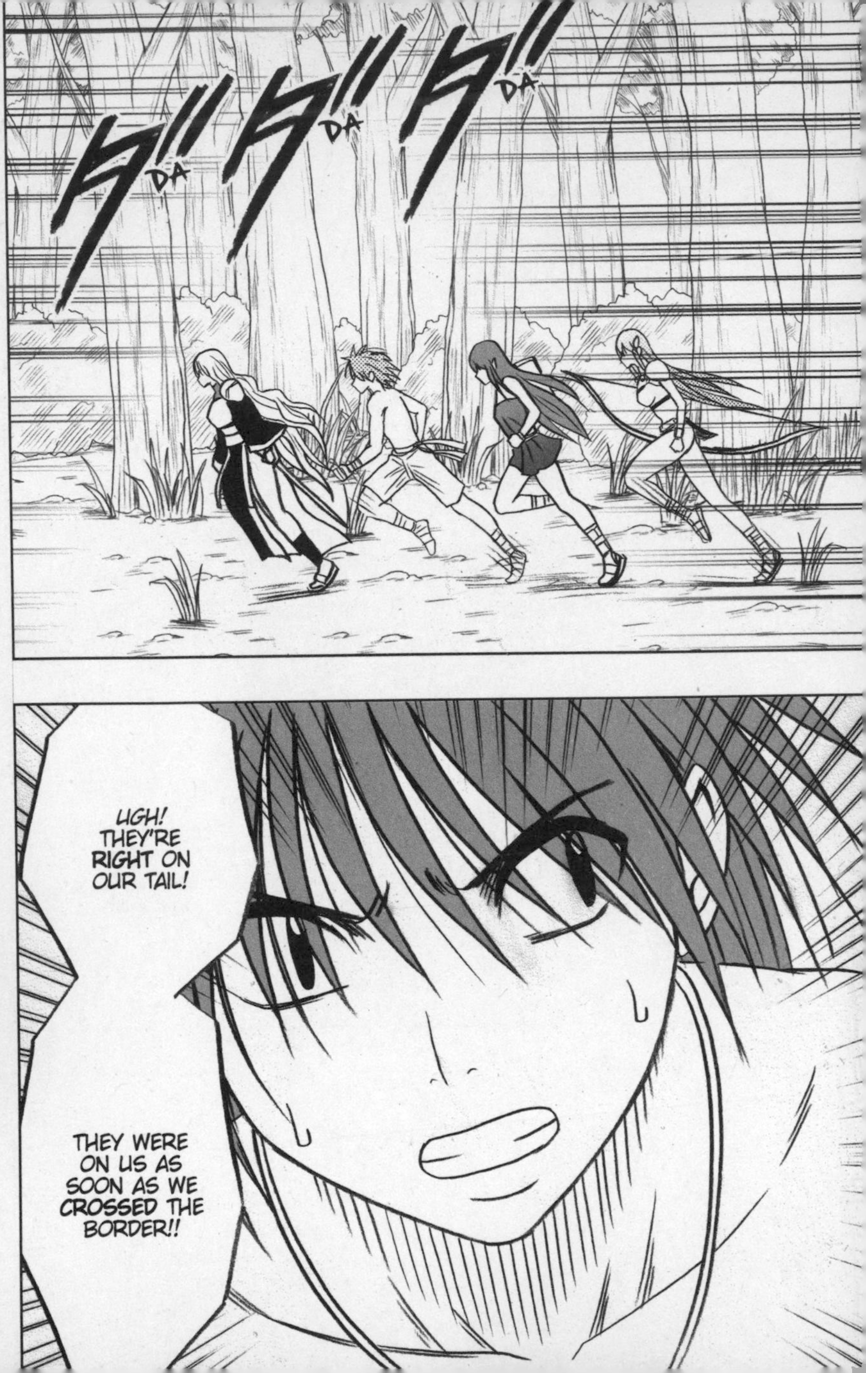
DA
DA
DA
UGH! THEY'RE RIGHT ON OUR TAIL!
THEY WERE ON US AS SOON AS WE CROSSED THE BORDER!!

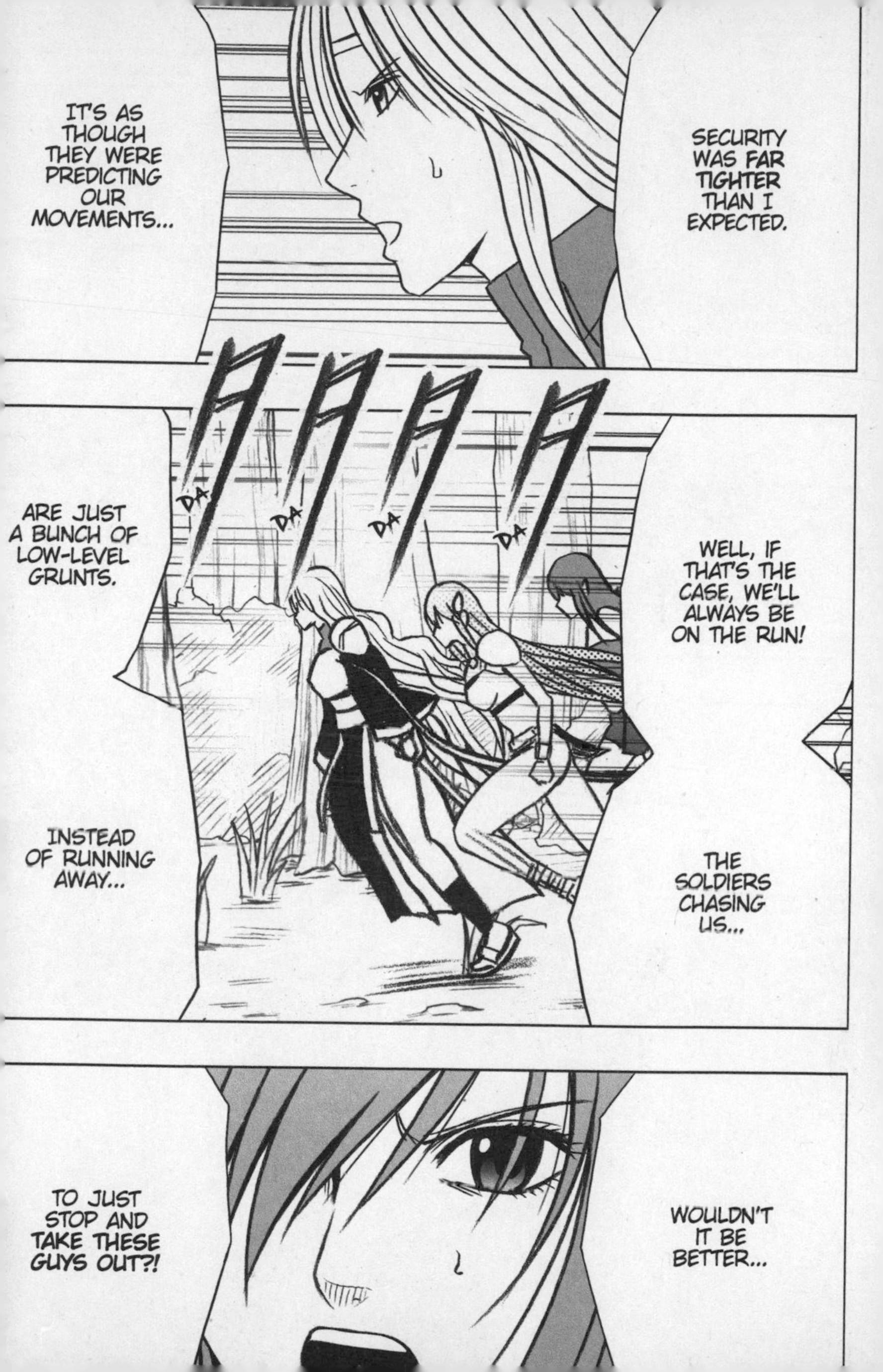
SECURITY WAS FAR TIGHTER THAN I EXPECTED.
IT'S AS THOUGH THEY WERE PREDICTING OUR MOVEMENTS...
WELL, IF THAT'S THE CASE, WE'LL ALWAYS BE ON THE RUN!
THE SOLDIERS CHASING US...
DA
DA
DA
DA
ARE JUST A BUNCH OF LOW-LEVEL GRUNTS.
INSTEAD OF RUNNING AWAY...
WOULDN'T IT BE BETTER...
TO JUST STOP AND TAKE THESE GUYS OUT?!

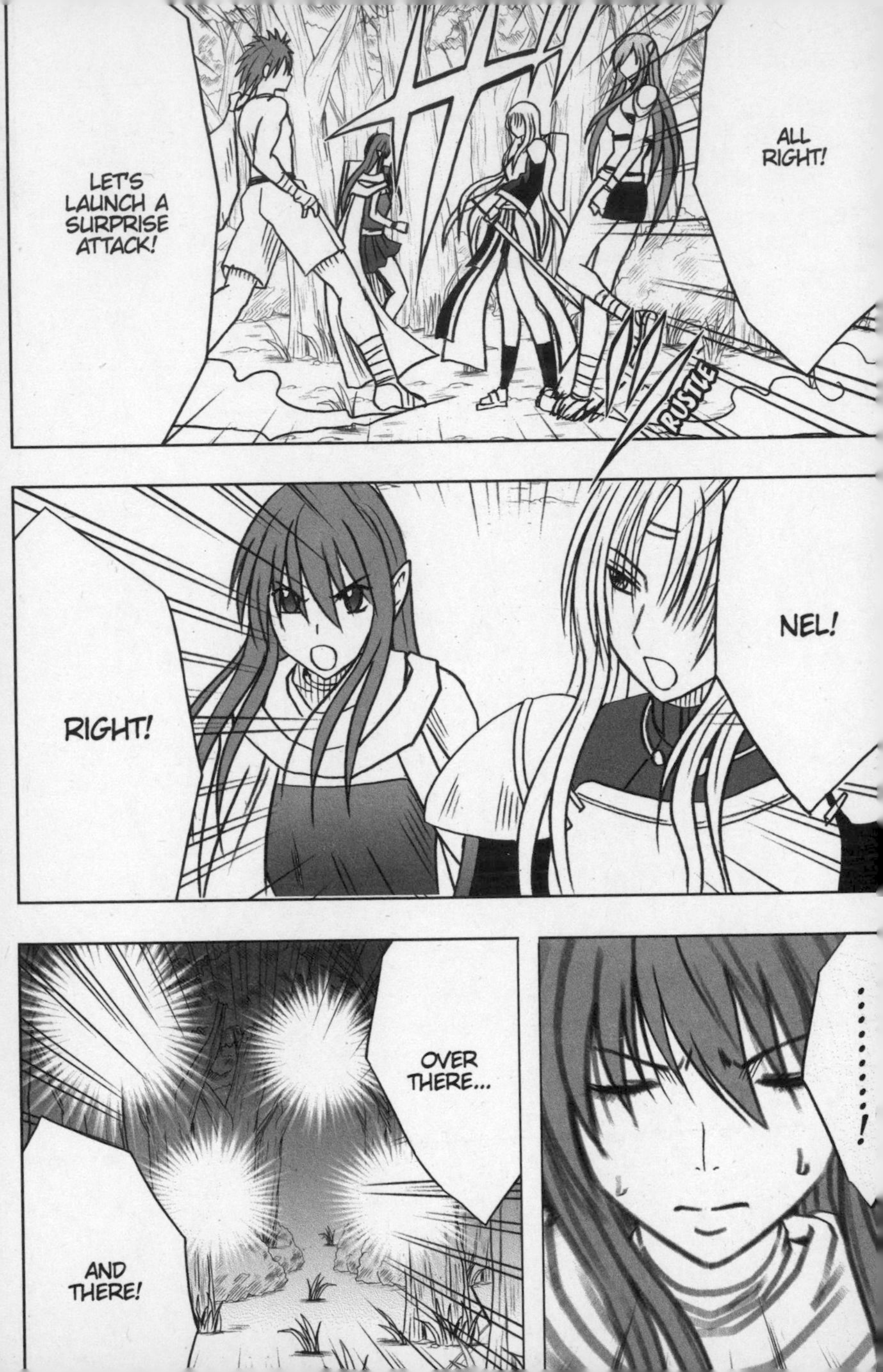
ALL RIGHT!
LET'S LAUNCH A SURPRISE ATTACK!
RUSTLE
NEL!
RIGHT!
.........!
OVER THERE...
AND THERE!

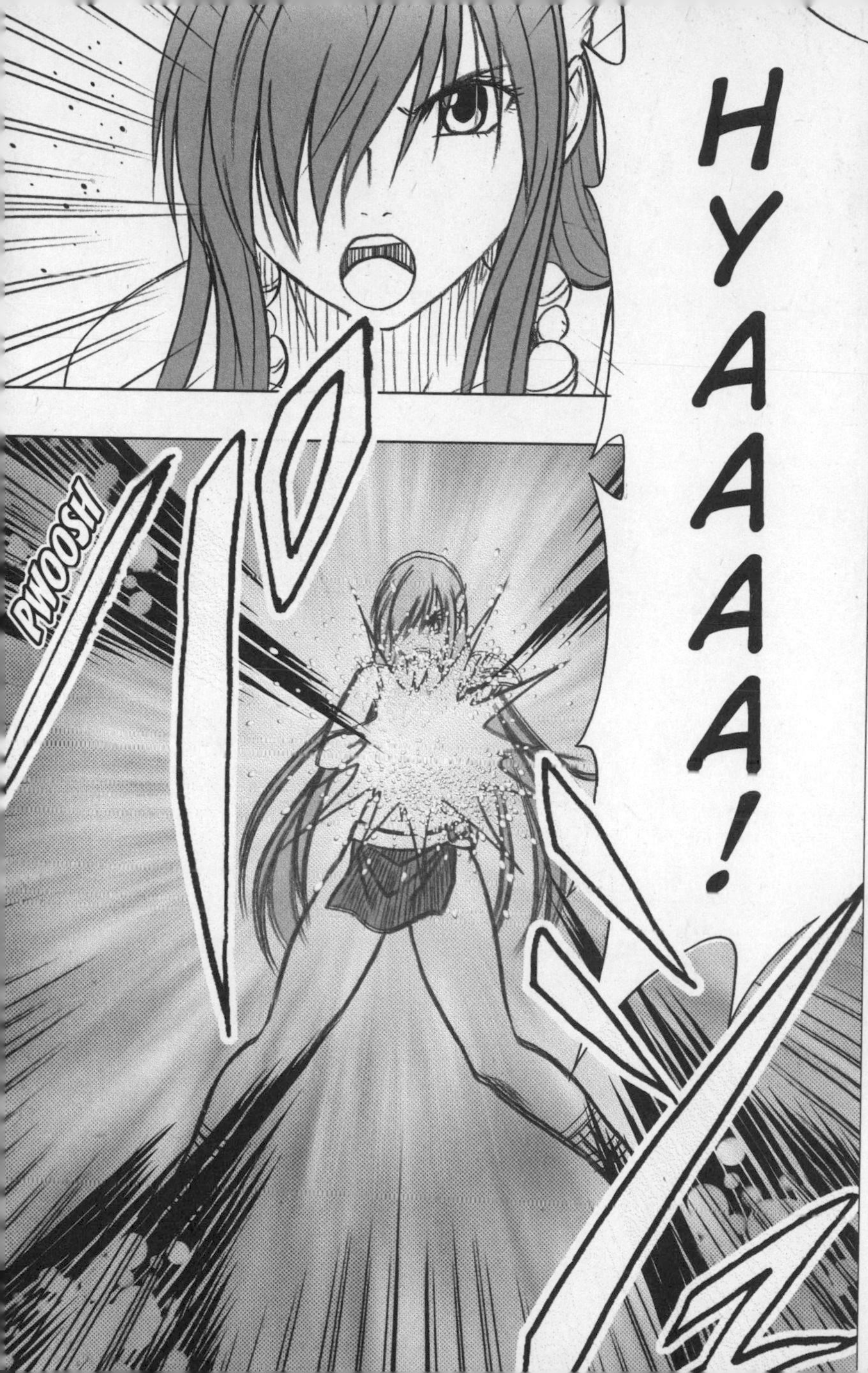
HYAAAAA!
PWOOSH

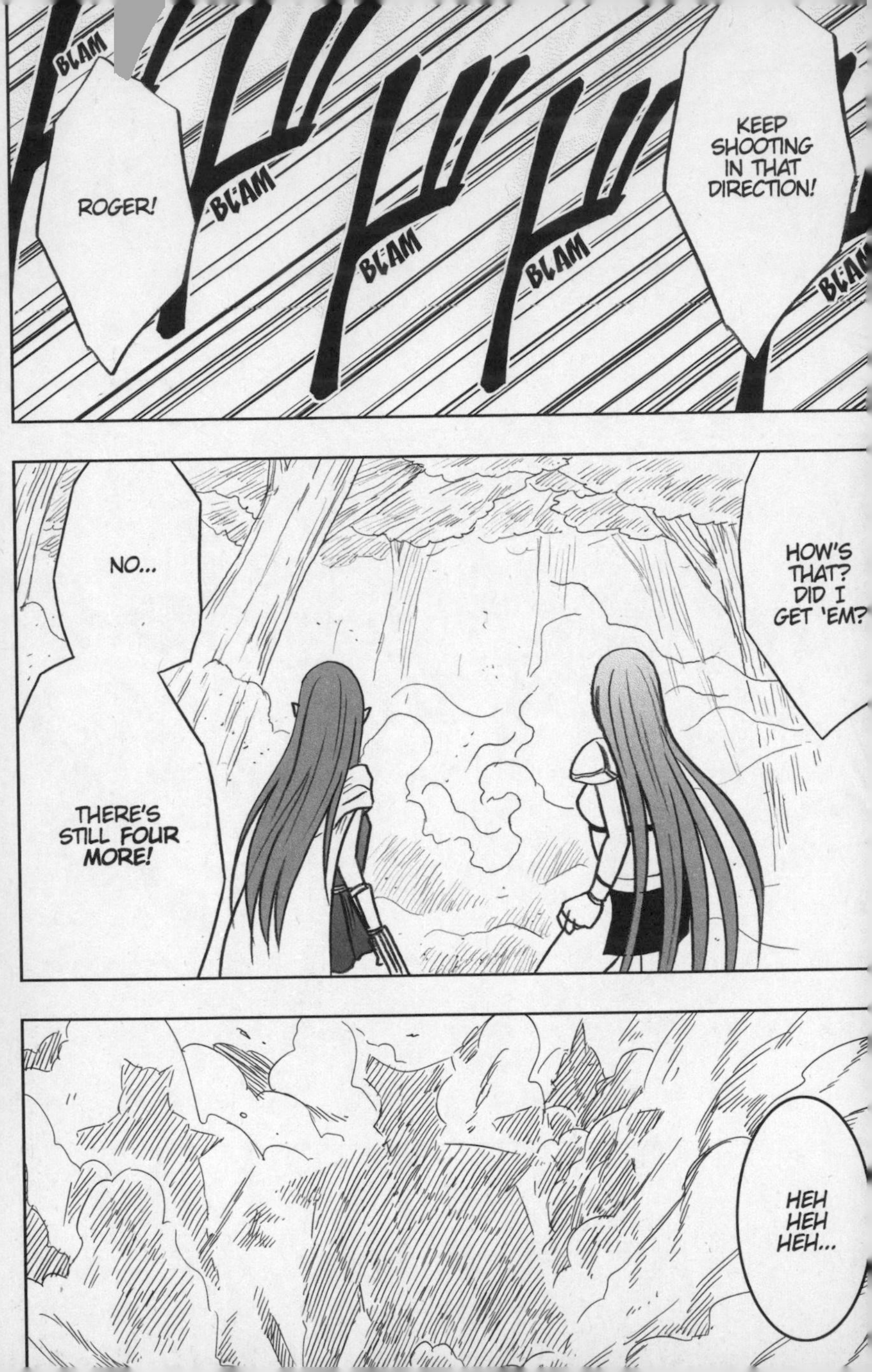
KEEP SHOOTING IN THAT DIRECTION!
BLAM
BLAM
BLAM
BLAM
ROGER!
BLAM
HOW'S THAT? DID I GET 'EM?
NO...
THERE'S STILL FOUR MORE!
HEH HEH HEH...

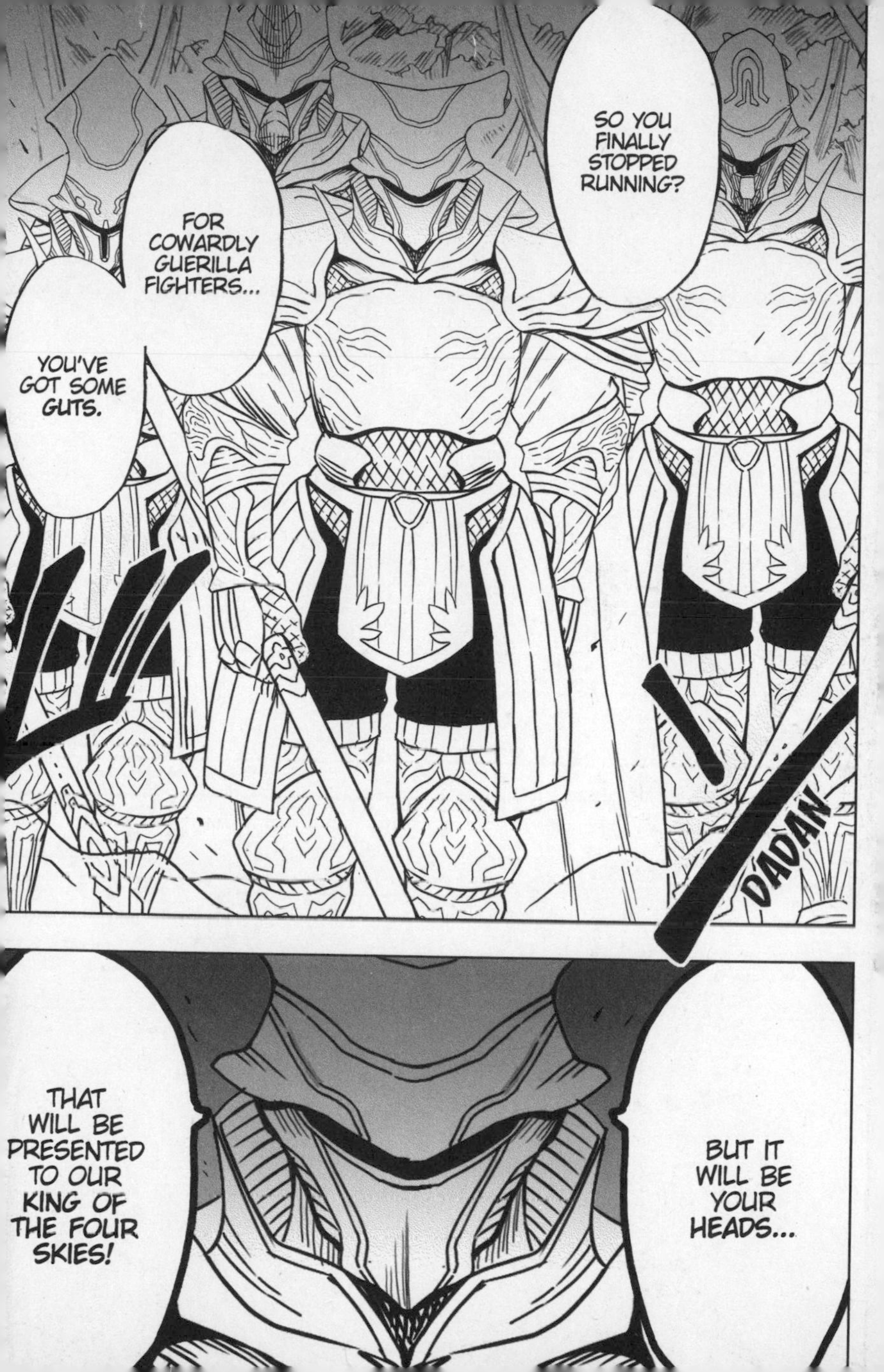
SO YOU FINALLY STOPPED RUNNING?
FOR COWARDLY GUERILLA FIGHTERS...
YOU'VE GOT SOME GUTS.
DADAN
BUT IT WILL BE YOUR HEADS...
THAT WILL BE PRESENTED TO OUR KING OF THE FOUR SKIES!

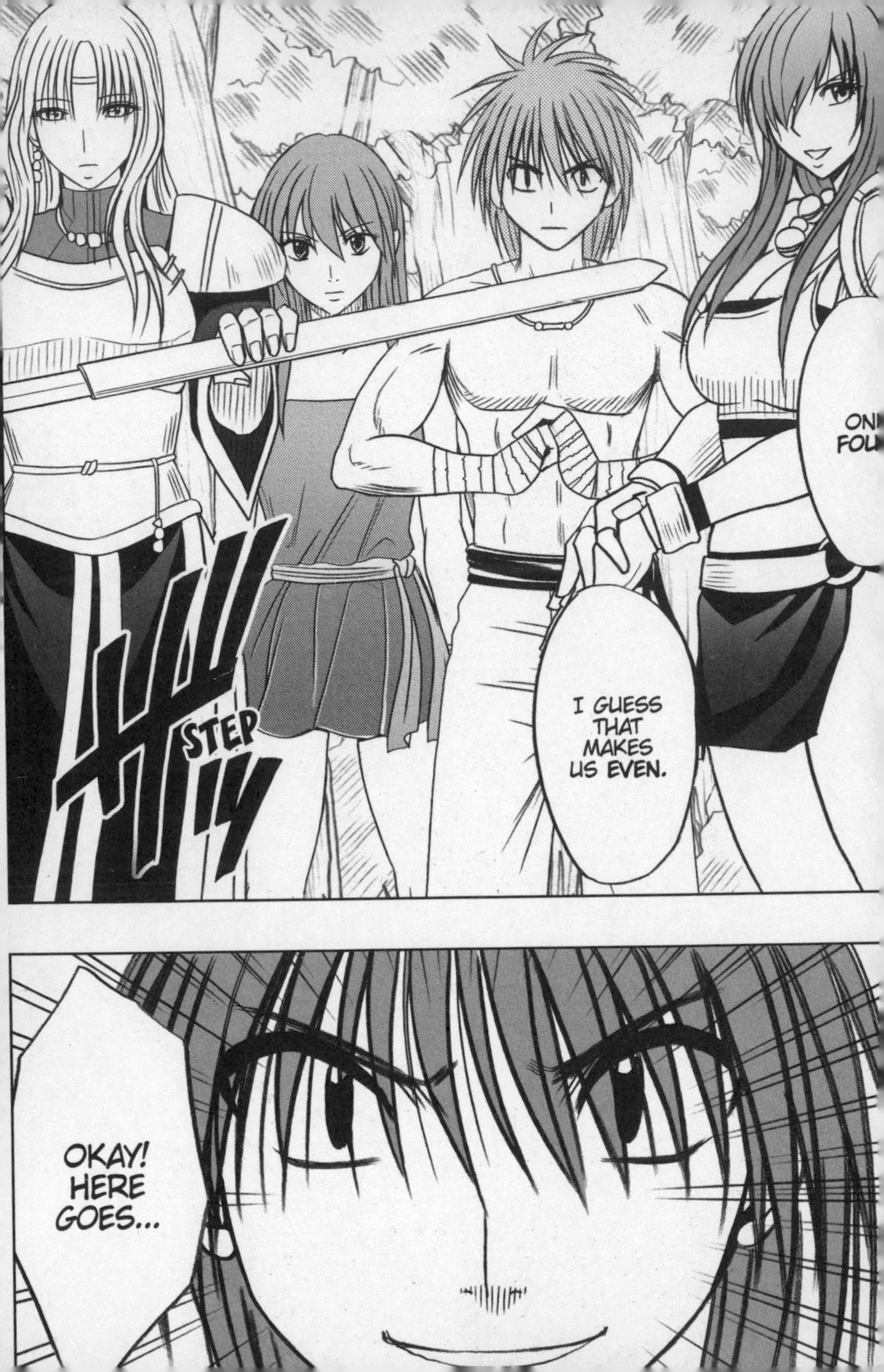
I GUESS THAT MAKES US EVEN.
STEP
OKAY! HERE GOES...

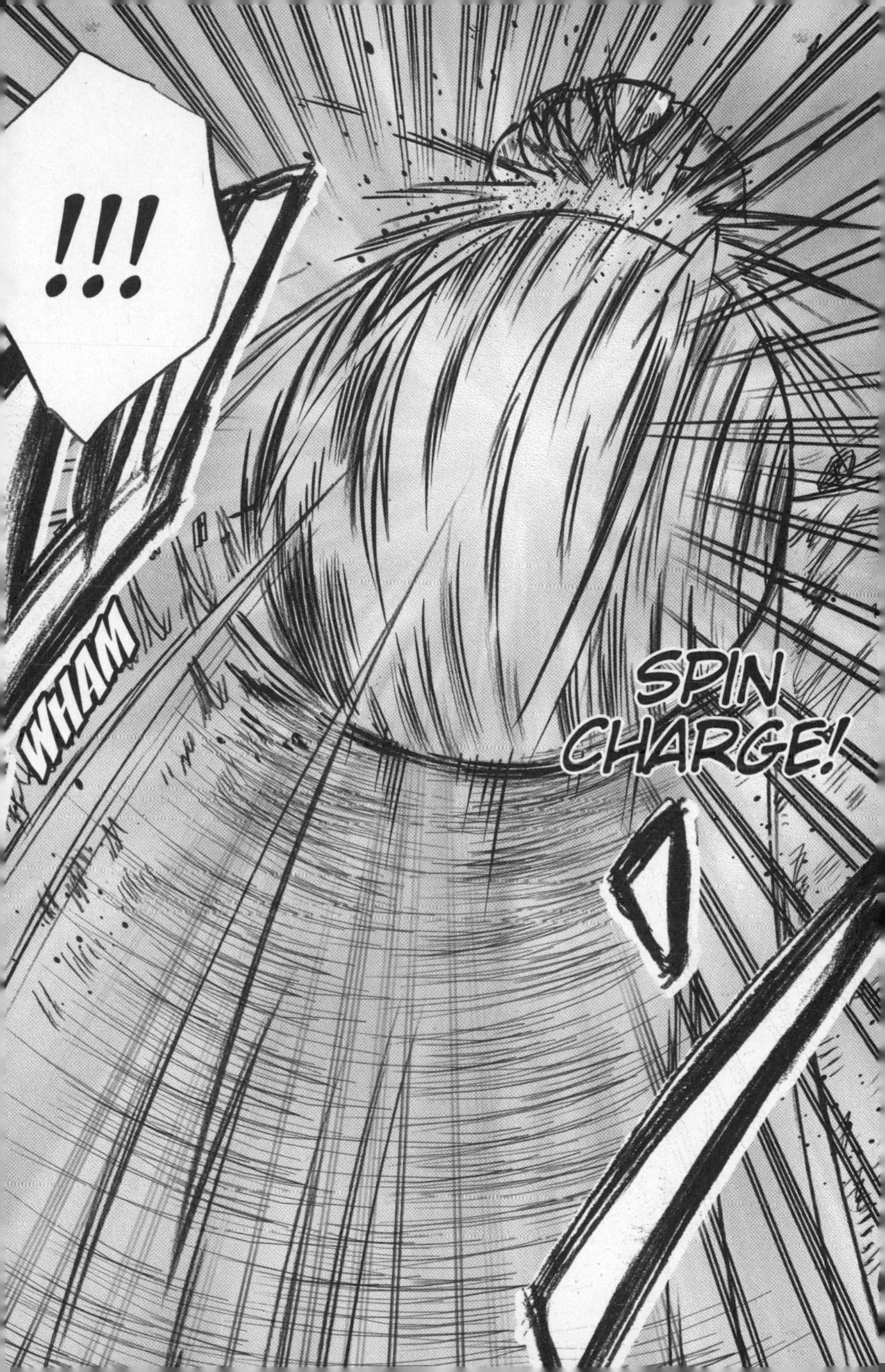
!!!
SPIN CHARGE!
WHAM

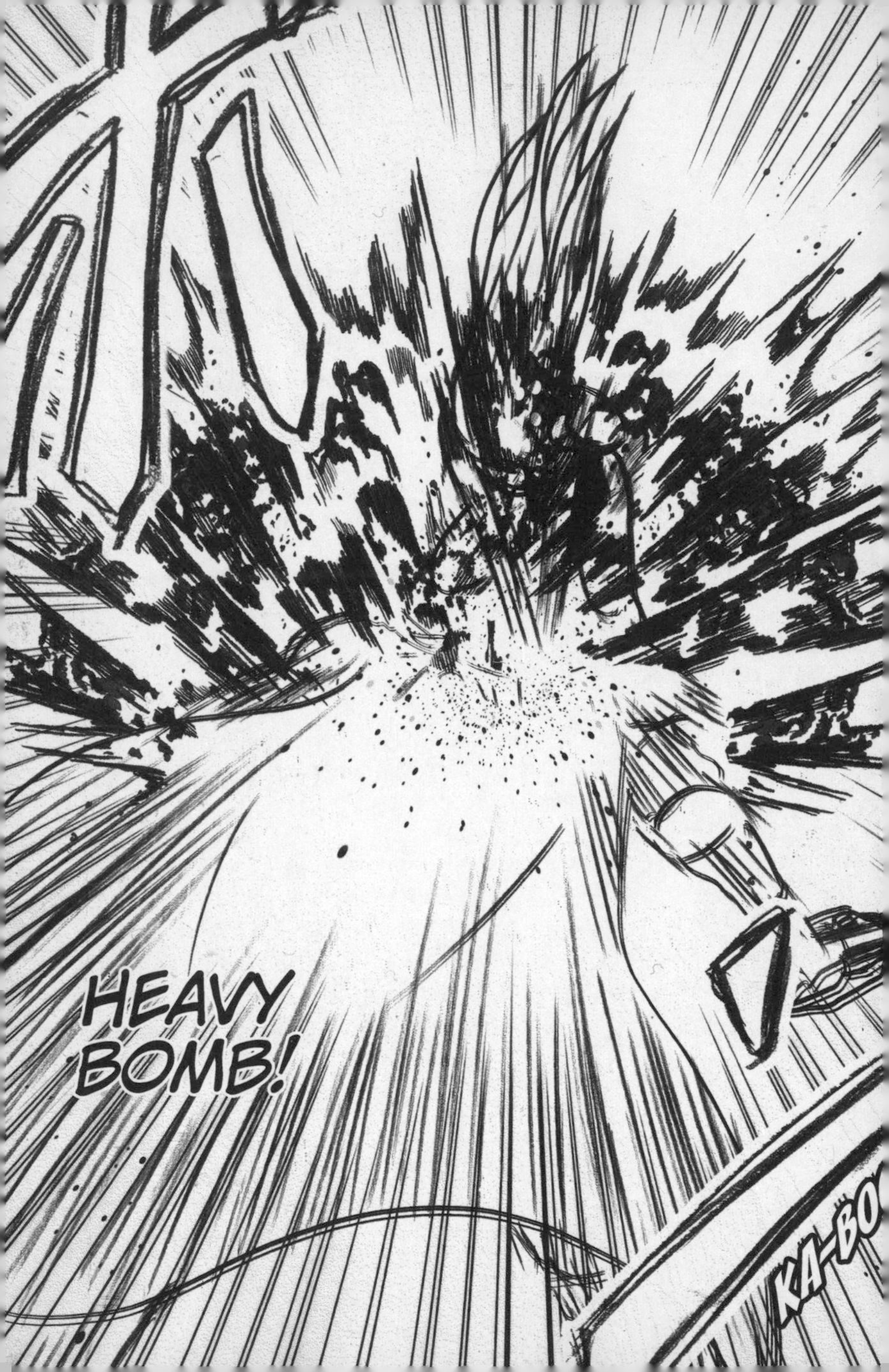
HEAVY BOMB!
KA-BO

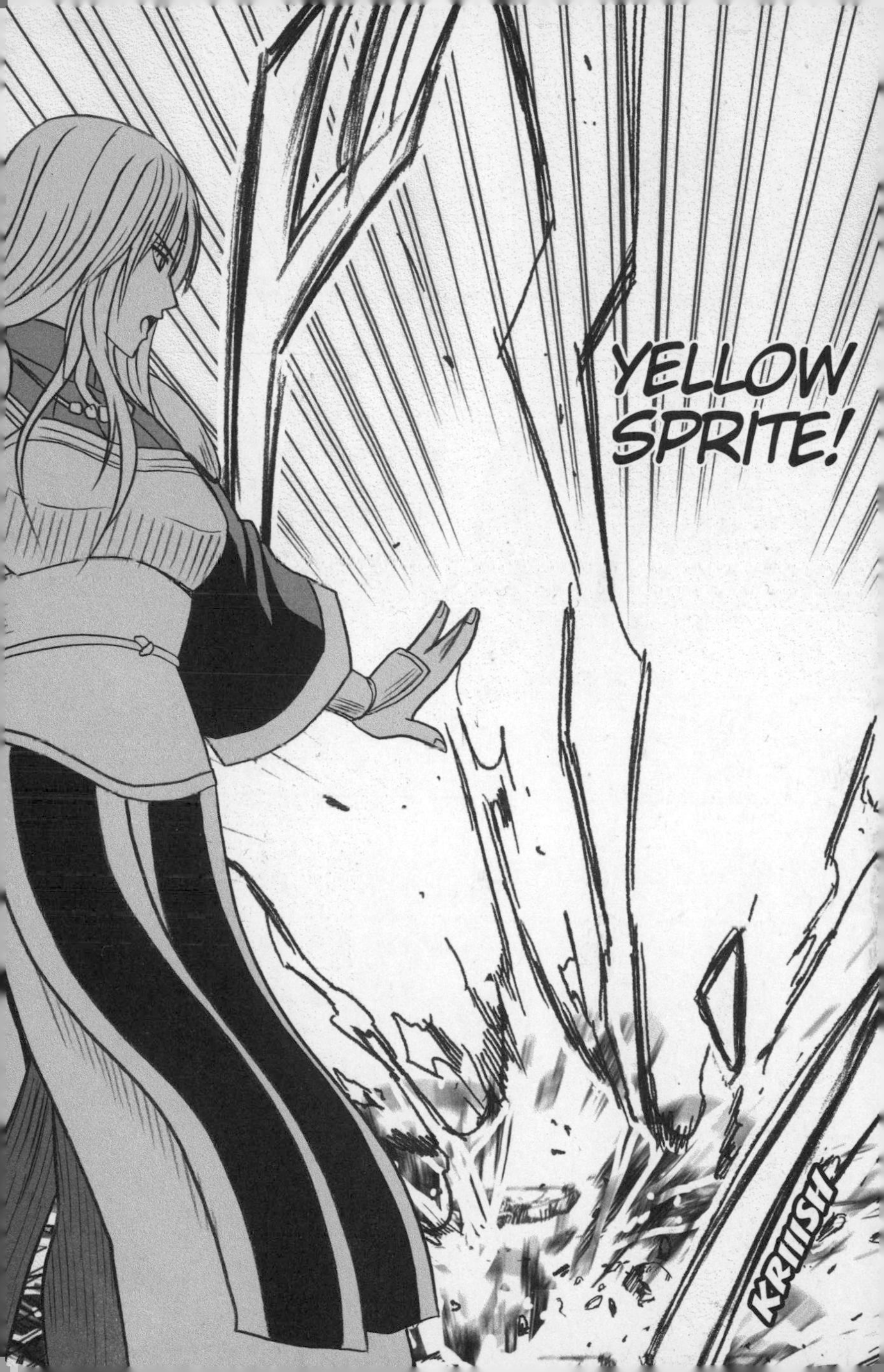
YELLOW SPRITE!
KRIIISH

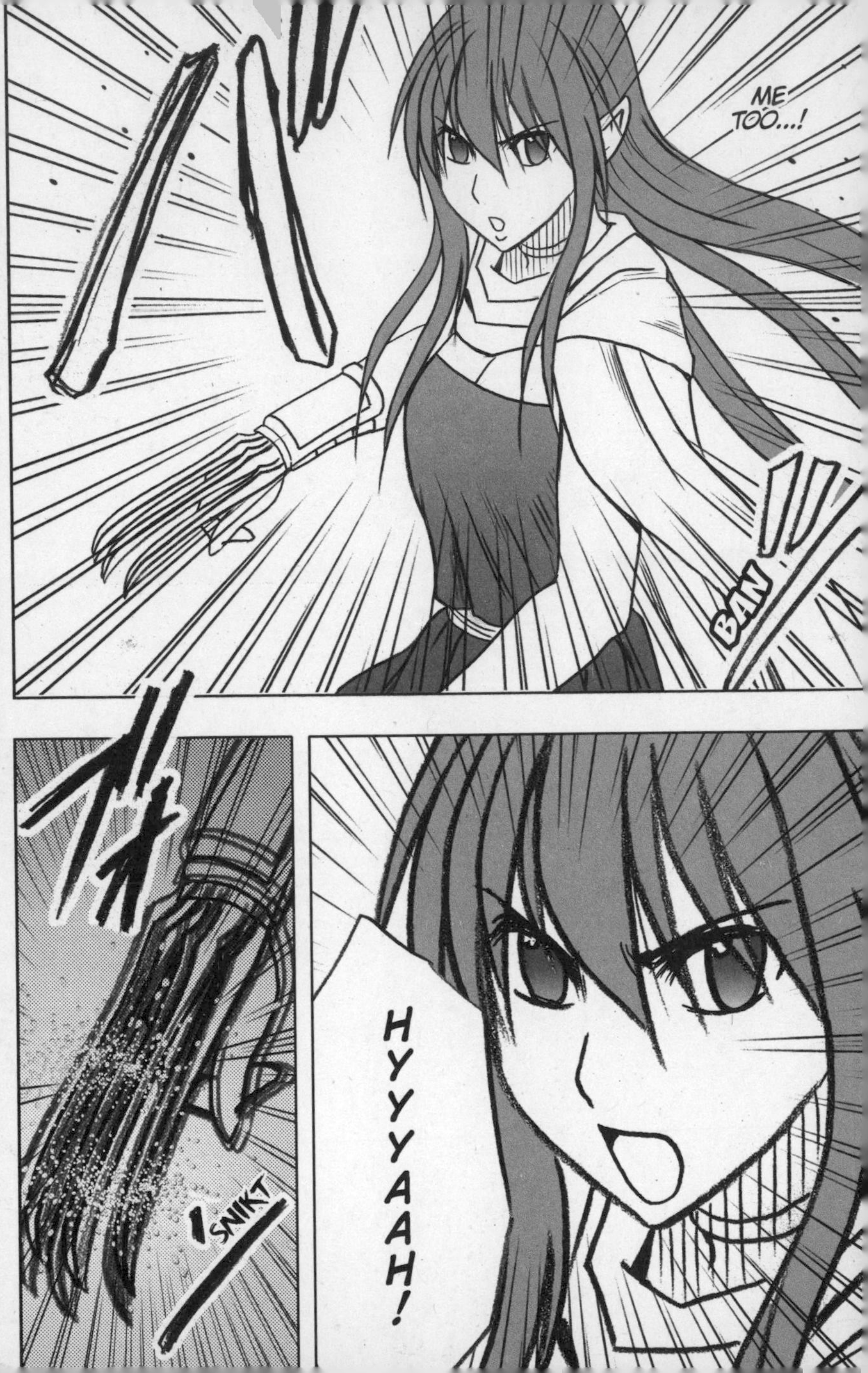
ME TOO...!
BAN
HYYYAAAH!
SNIKT

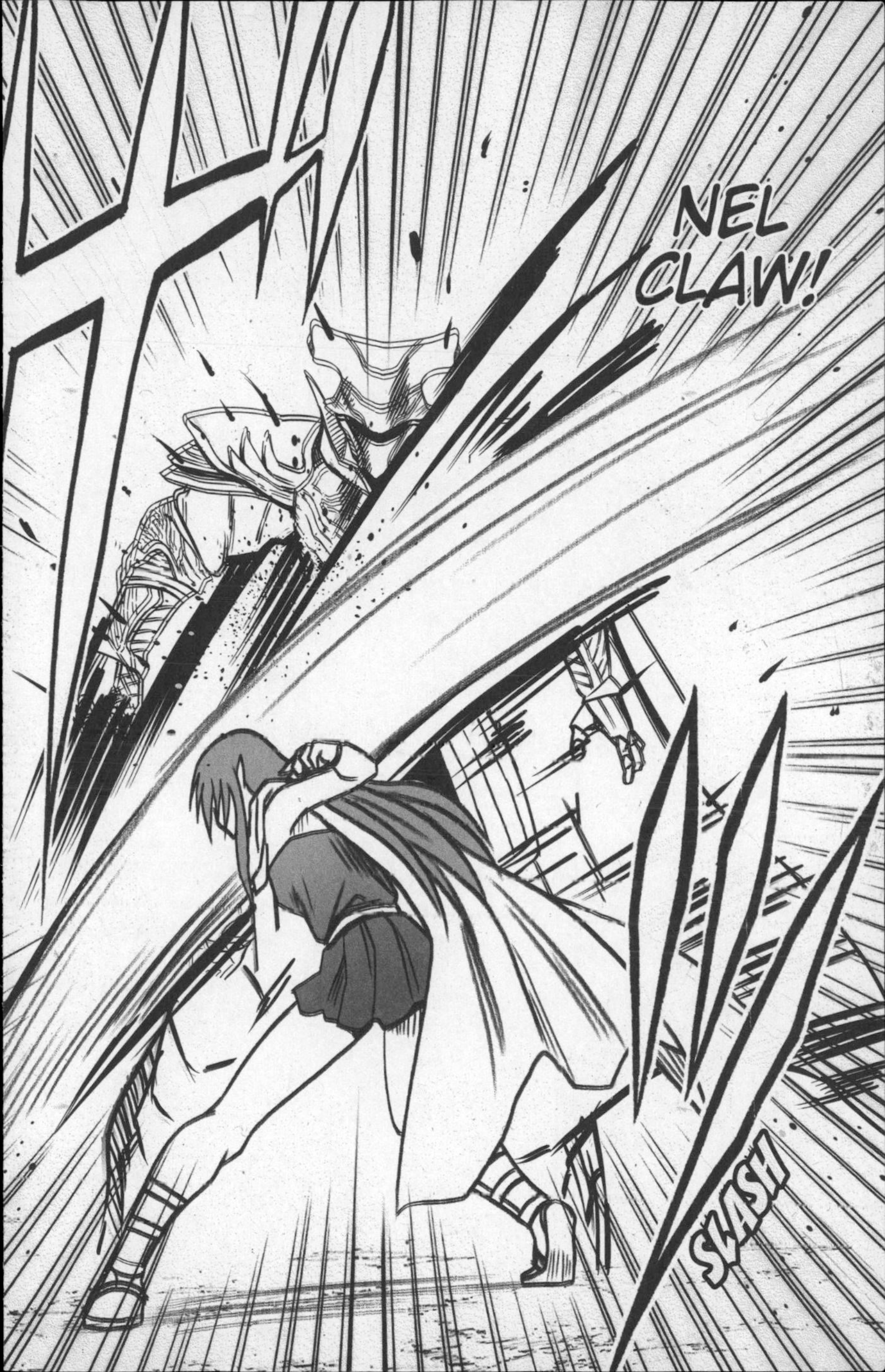
NEL CLAW!
SLASH

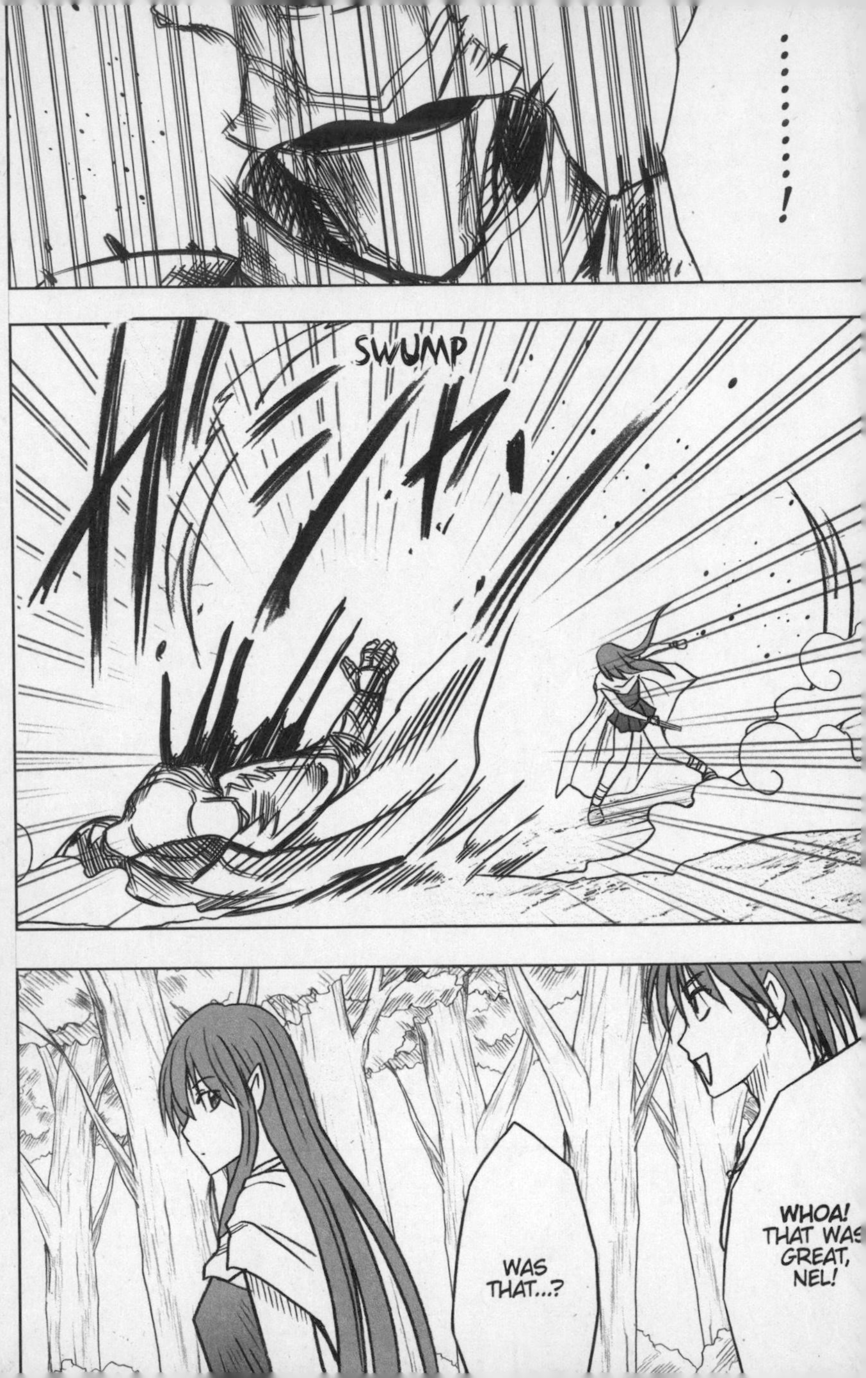
......!
SWUMP
WHOA! THAT WAS GREAT, NEL!
WAS THAT...?

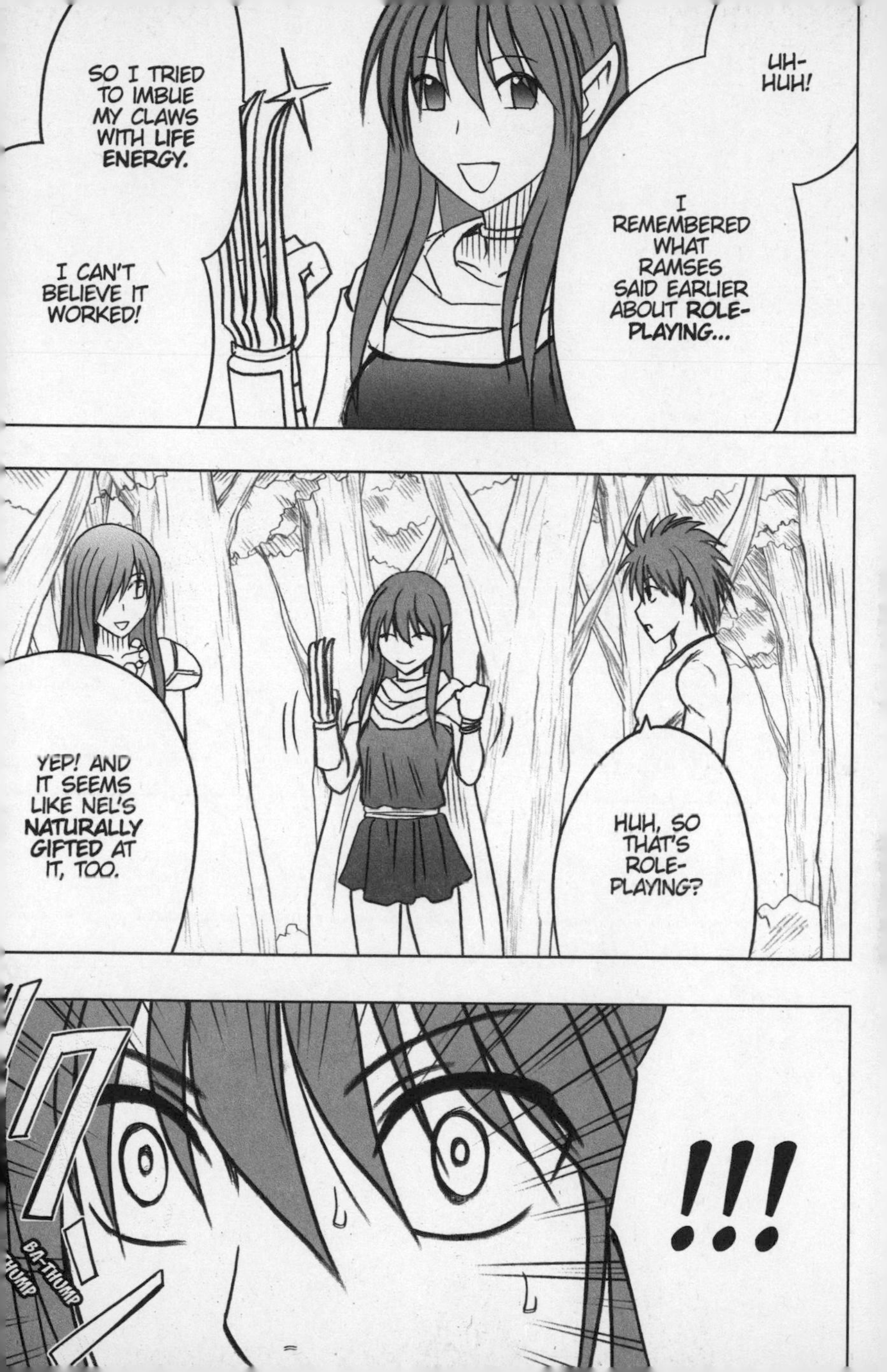
UH-HUH!
I REMEMBERED WHAT RAMSES SAID EARLIER ABOUT ROLE-PLAYING...
SO I TRIED TO IMBUE MY CLAWS WITH LIFE ENERGY.
I CAN'T BELIEVE IT WORKED!
HUH, SO THAT'S ROLE-PLAYING?
YEP! AND IT SEEMS LIKE NEL'S NATURALLY GIFTED AT IT, TOO.
!!!
BA-THUMP
THUMP

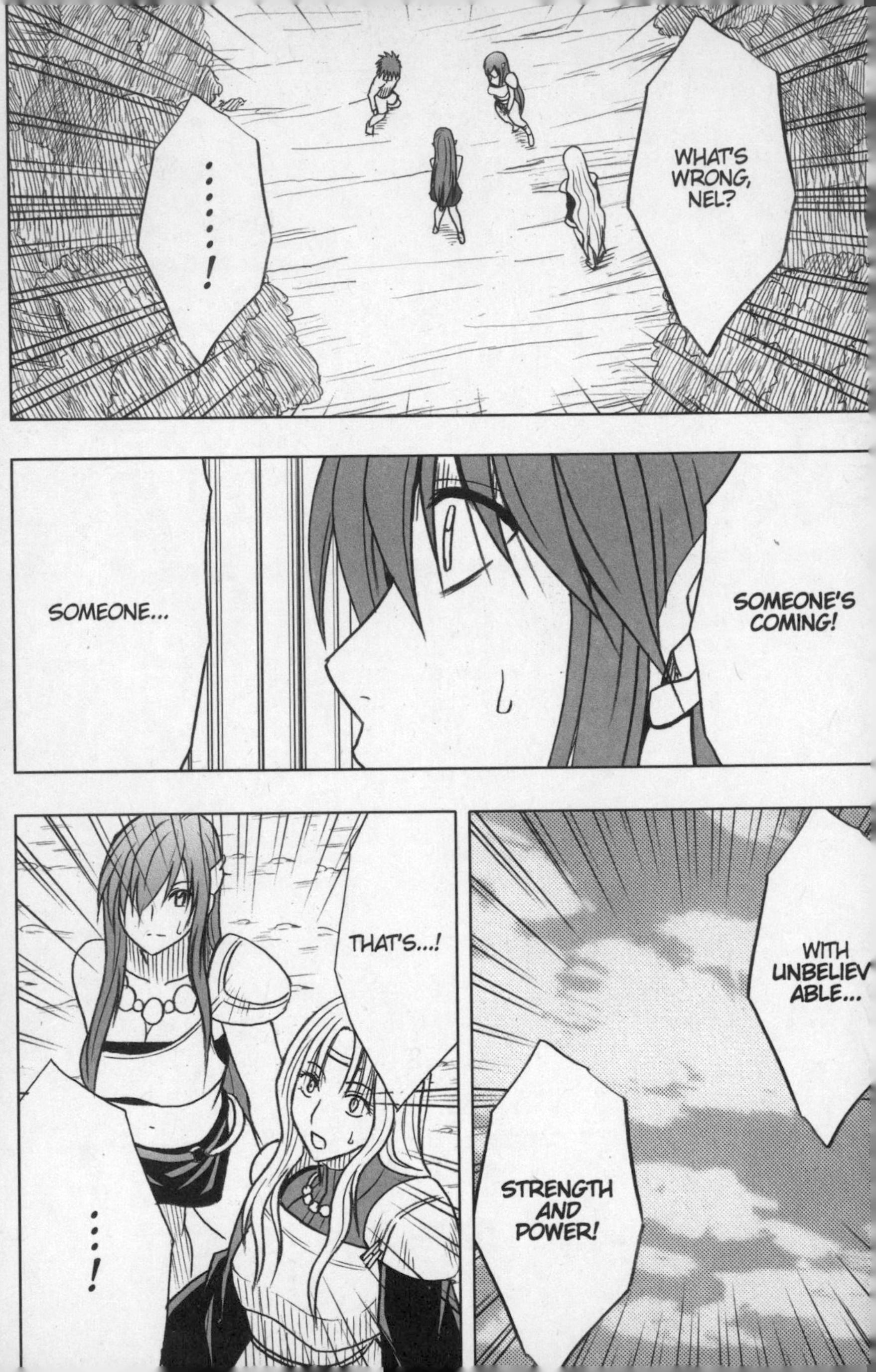
WHAT'S WRONG, NEL?
......!
SOMEONE'S COMING!
SOMEONE...
WITH UNBELIEV ABLE...
STRENGTH AND POWER!
THAT'S...!
...!

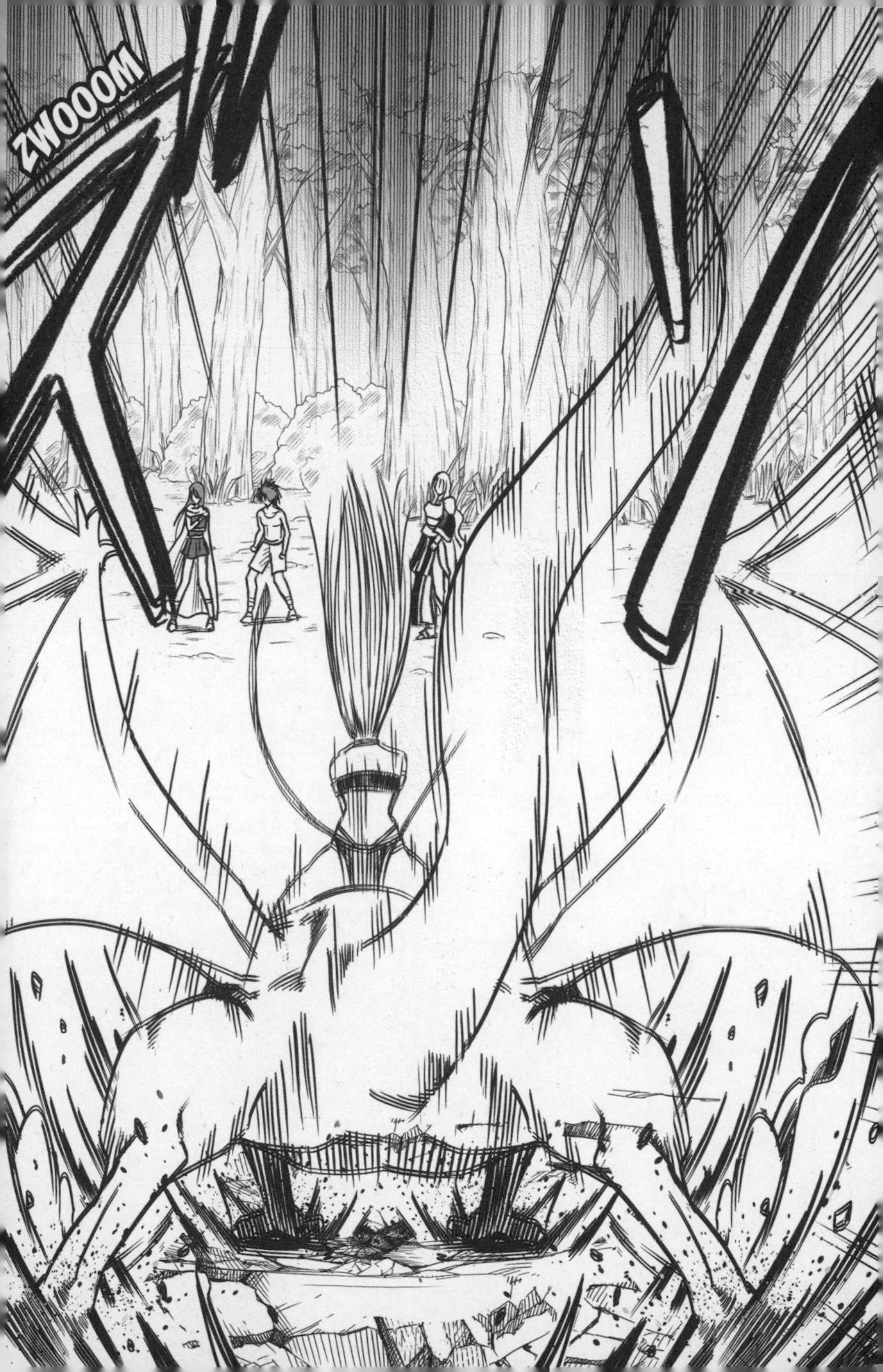
ZWOOOM

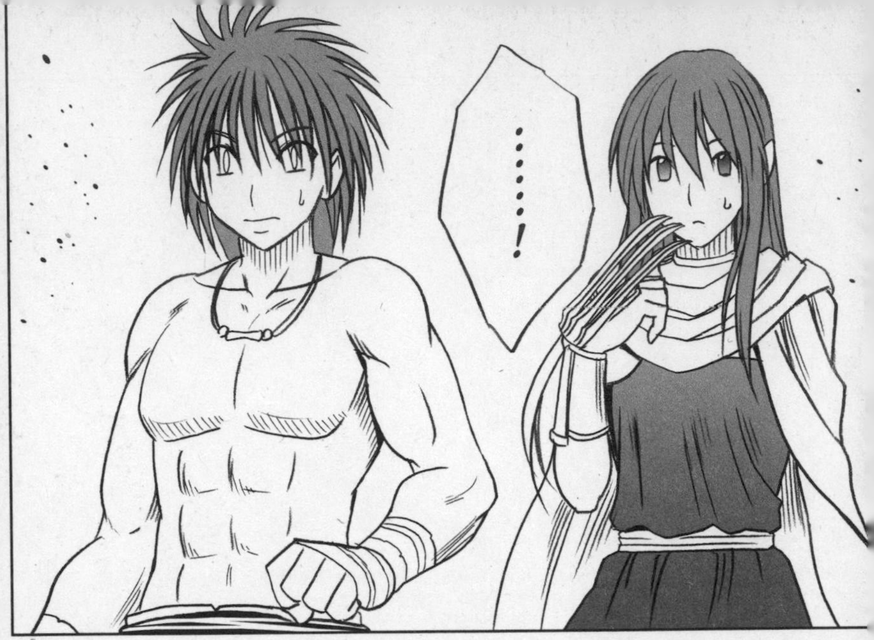
……!

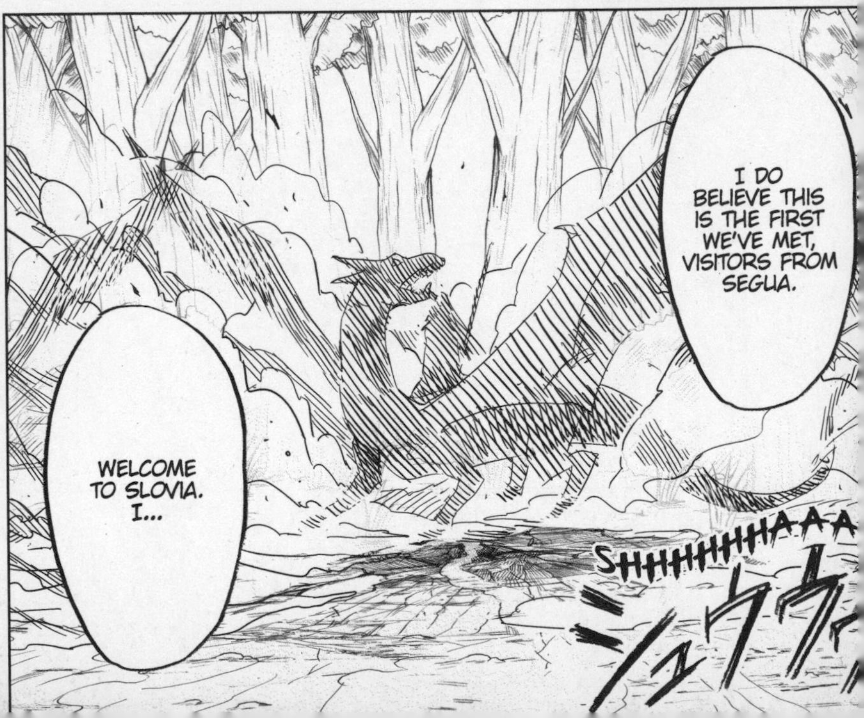
I DO BELIEVE THIS IS THE FIRST WE'VE MET, VISITORS FROM SEGUA.
WELCOME TO SLOVIA. I...
SHHHHHHHAAA
シュウウ

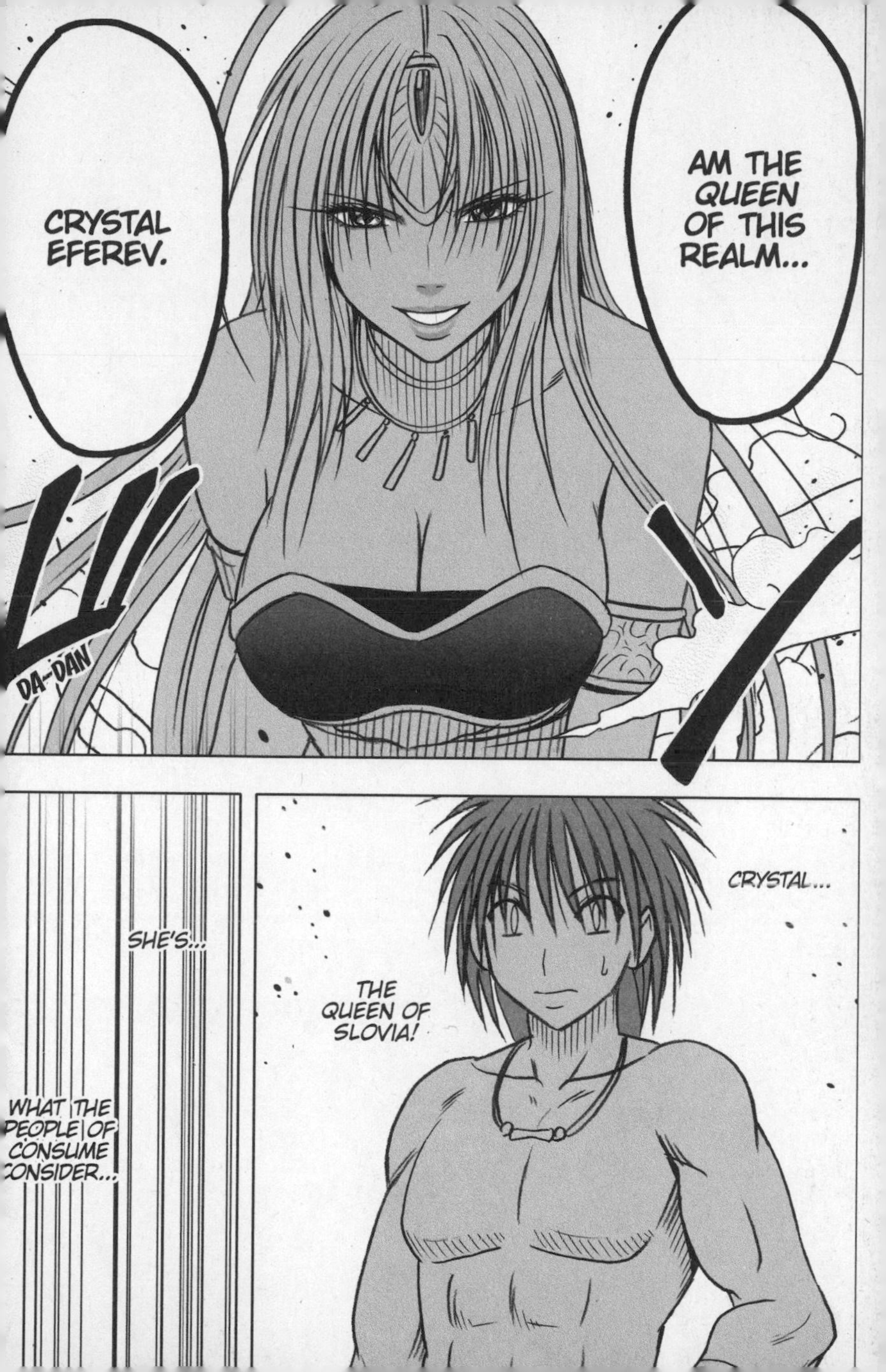
AM THE QUEEN OF THIS REALM...
CRYSTAL EFEREV.
DA-DAN
CRYSTAL...
THE QUEEN OF SLOVIA!
SHE'S...
WHAT THE PEOPLE OF CONSUME CONSIDER...

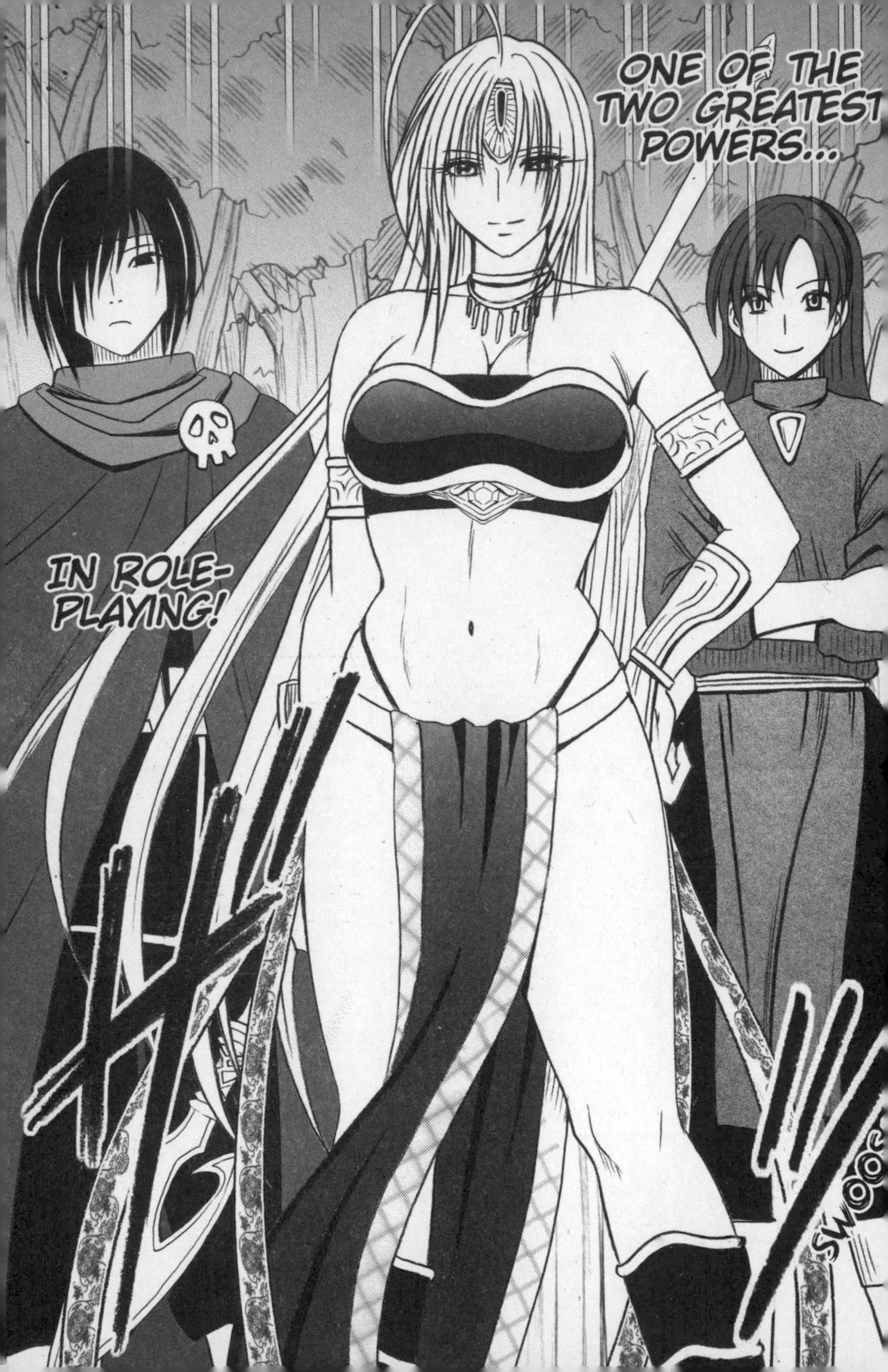
ONE OF THE TWO GREATEST POWERS...
IN ROLE-PLAYING!
SWOOP

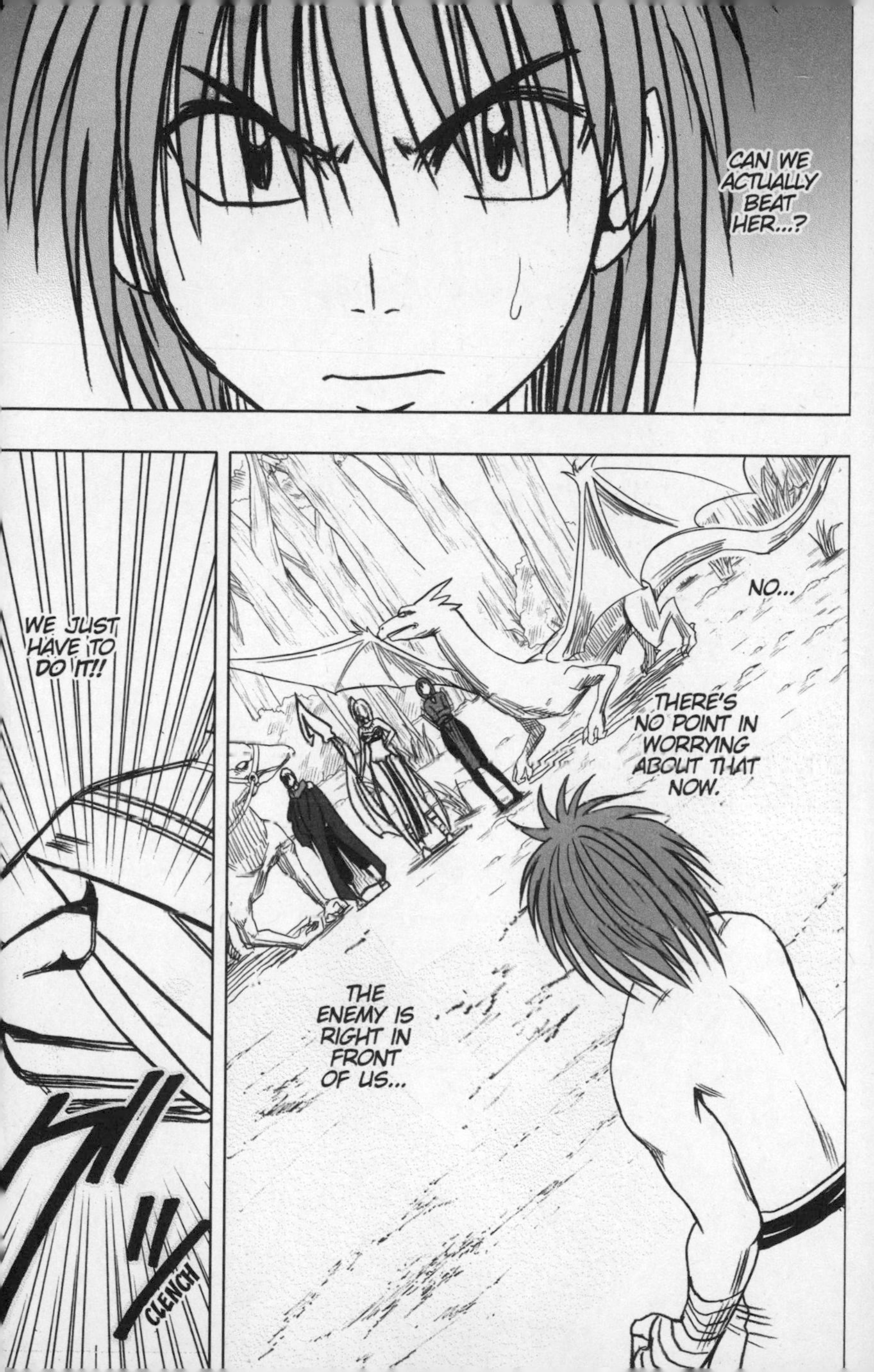
CAN WE ACTUALLY BEAT HER...?
NO...
THERE'S NO POINT IN WORRYING ABOUT THAT NOW.
THE ENEMY IS RIGHT IN FRONT OF US...
WE JUST HAVE TO DO IT!!
CLENCH

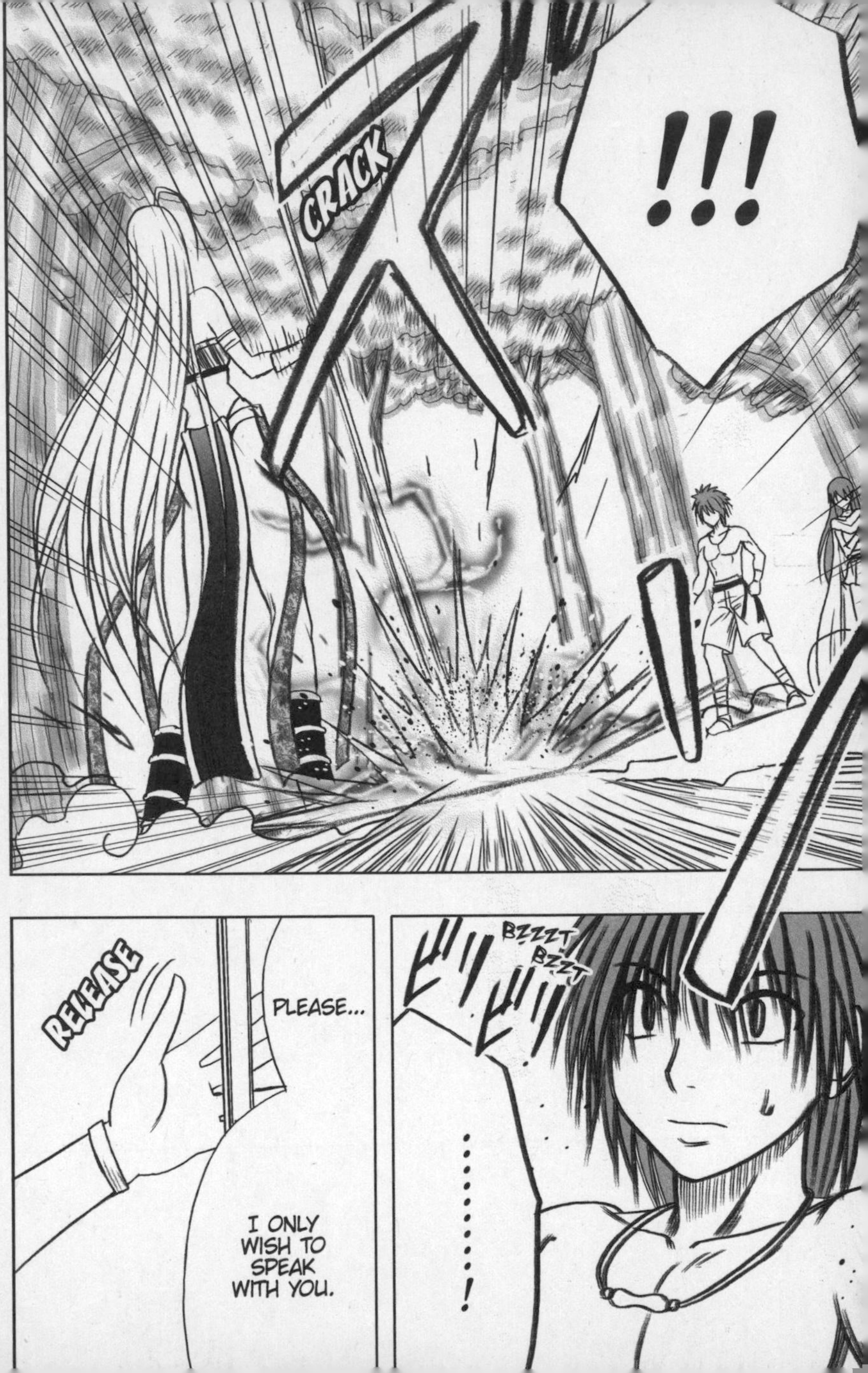
!!!
CRACK
BZZZT
BZZZT
........!
RELEASE
PLEASE...
I ONLY WISH TO SPEAK WITH YOU.

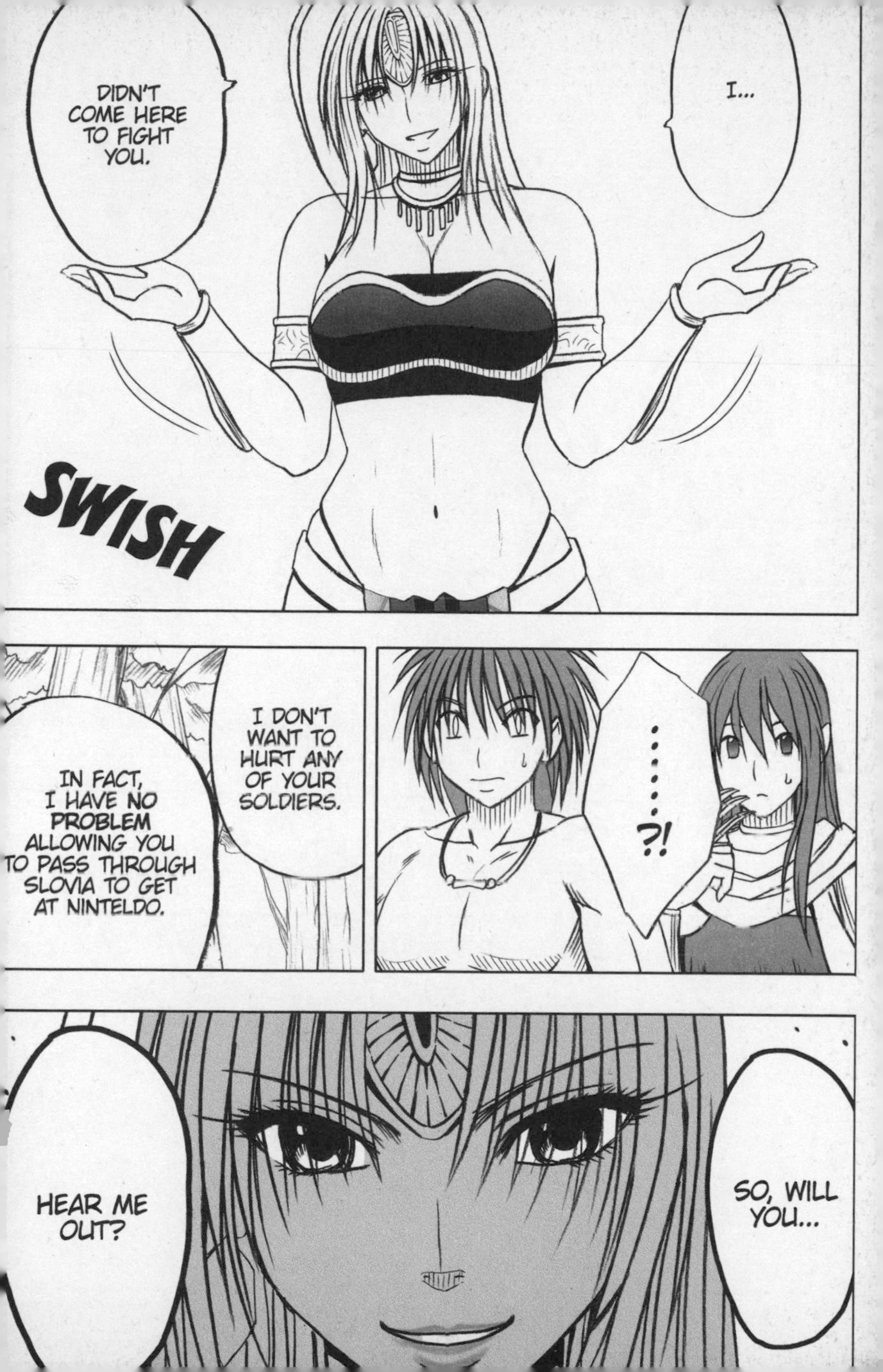
I...
DIDN'T COME HERE TO FIGHT YOU.
SWISH
......?!
I DON'T WANT TO HURT ANY OF YOUR SOLDIERS.
IN FACT, I HAVE NO PROBLEM ALLOWING YOU TO PASS THROUGH SLOVIA TO GET AT NINTELDO.
SO, WILL YOU...
HEAR ME OUT?

Bonus Comic

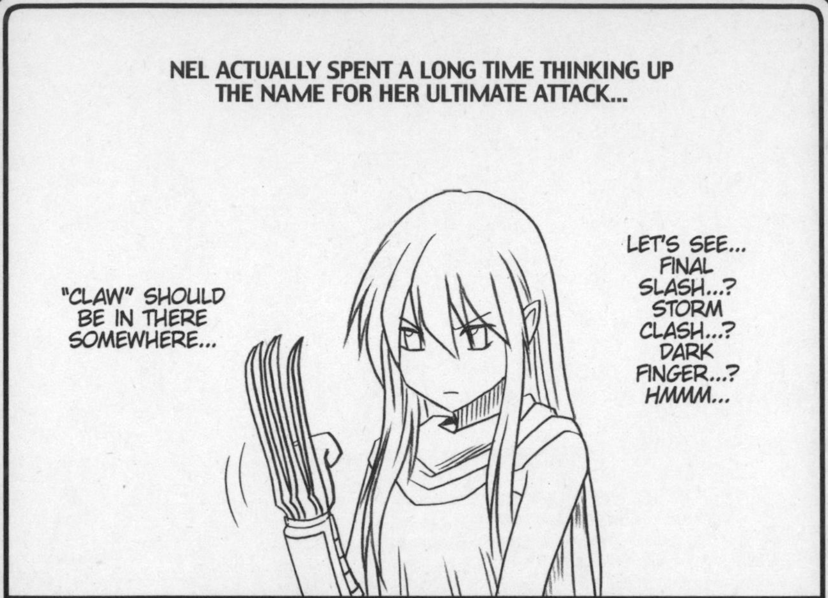
NEL ACTUALLY SPENT A LONG TIME THINKING UP THE NAME FOR HER ULTIMATE ATTACK...
LET'S SEE... FINAL SLASH...? STORM CLASH...? DARK FINGER...? HMMM...
"CLAW" SHOULD BE IN THERE SOMEWHERE...

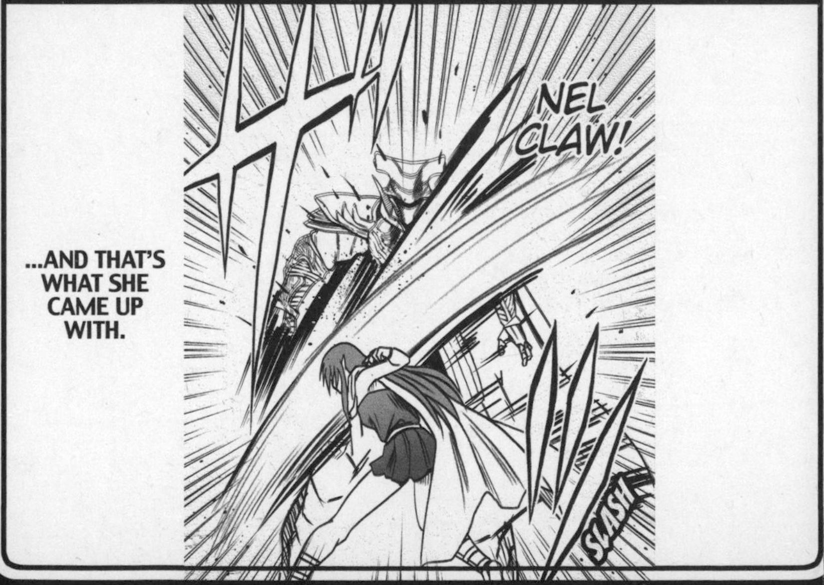
NEL CLAW!
...AND THAT'S WHAT SHE CAME UP WITH.
SLASH

Bonus Comic

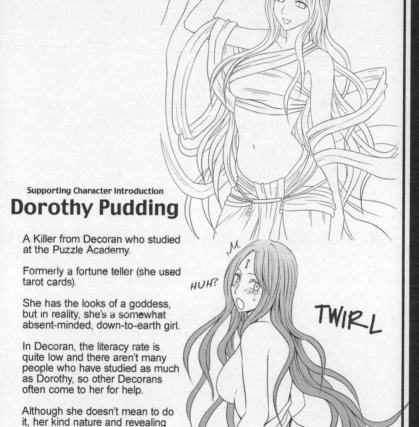

Supporting Character Introduction

Dorothy Pudding

A Killer from Decoran who studied at the Puzzle Academy.

Formerly a fortune teller (she used tarot cards).

She has the looks of a goddess, but in reality, she's a somewhat absent-minded, down-to-earth girl.

In Decoran, the literacy rate is quite low and there aren't many people who have studied as much as Dorothy, so other Decorans often come to her for help.

Although she doesn't mean to do it, her kind nature and revealing outfits often draw men to her.

She's had more than a few wardrobe malfunctions.

Perusing Video Game History

ON THE EDGE OF THE BLUE WORLD

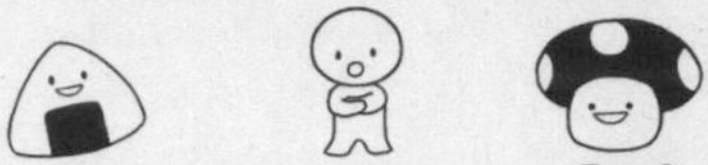

Dr. Onigiri   Mr. Why   Prof. Mushroom

Today's Topic

FINAL FANTASY

Mr. Why: It's finally here! Our talk on RPGs! So... What's an RPG?

Prof. Mushroom: Thanks for asking!

Dr. Onigiri: RPG is an acronym for Role-Playing Game. You play the part of a hero, or a warrior, or a mage, or some other type of character and live your life within the world the game provides you. Most of them take place in a fantasy setting.

Prof. Mushroom: Initially the genre was very popular for games on the PC, so there are a lot of famous PC RPGs out there. When it comes to console games though, you really only have two big heavy hitters: *Dragon Quest*, which was developed by Enix, and *Final Fantasy* from Square/Squaresoft.

Dr. Onigiri: Hey! There's the *Phantasy Star* series from Sega, too!

Prof. Mushroom: Who cares? I'm talking about the **two big ones** here.

Mr. Why: Whoa, calm down! Calm down!

Prof. Mushroom: Onigiri, why don't you go get some tea or something?

Dr. Onigiri: I'm just saying, Sega made RPGs too...

Mr. Why: Of course.

Prof. Mushroom: Yeah, but with their games, Enix and Squaresoft created social phenomena.

Mr. Why: Social phenomena?!

Prof. Mushroom: Indeed. On the day before *Dragon Quest* would go on sale, huge snake-like lines would form in front of game shops and electronic stores. People would camp out all night to get a copy of the game. It became so popular that people started packaging other games along with Dragon Quest as a combo deal. With so many excited people in one place, it felt almost like a festival.

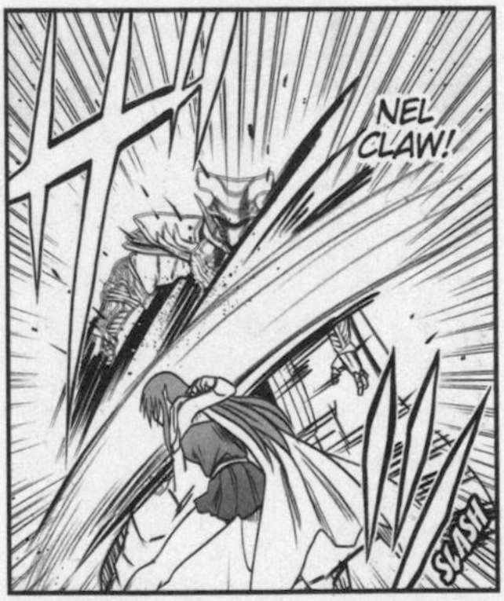
NEL CLAW!
SLASH

In *Phantasy Star Online*, there was a well-known weapon called Nel's Claw. It was a favorite weapon of the Newman.

Dr. Onigiri: It was the work of Yuji Horii, who went under the penname of "Yuutei"

Mr. Why: So what's the other big game?

Prof Mushroom: *Final Fantasy*, sometimes called *FF*. That's another awesome series.

Dr. Onigiri: We touched a bit on this in volume 2, but *Final Fantasy* really had some incredible graphics. Each installment looked more amazing than the last!

Prof. Mushroom: The programming was always top-notch, too. With *Final Fantasy's* quick scrolling and smooth animations, it really raised the bar for other games.

Dr. Onigiri: The stories revolved around these crystals that housed various elemental powers. For example, in *Final Fantasy III* for the Famicom, the rogue Gutsco steals the Crystal of Fire and attacks the party.

Prof. Mushroom: It had places with difficult to pronounce names such as Bostaunieux Oubliette, interesting vehicles such as airships, and writing that sounded like it could be from a fantasy novel, with lines like this one from *Final Fantasy IV*: *"One born of a dragon bearing darkness and light, shall rise to the heavens over the still land."* All this made *Final Fantasy* a little more stylish and grown up, compared to *Dragon Quest*.

Dr. Onigiri: In the next volume we'll go a little more in-depth about these two great RPGs!

To Be Continued...

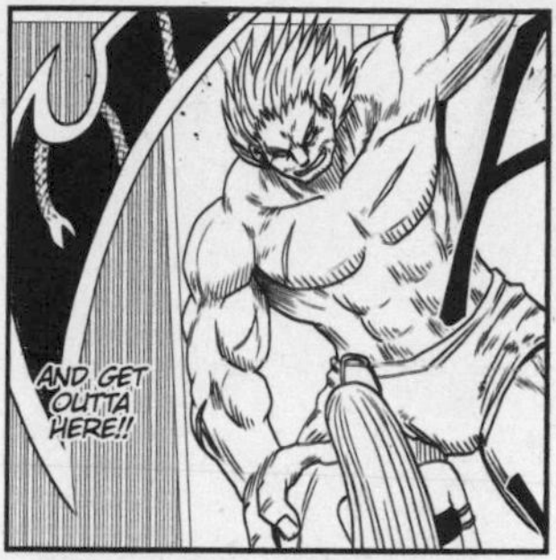
AND GET OUTTA HERE!!

In the DS version of *Final Fantasy III*, there was a secret boss that looked kind of like a sword at first but when you came closer, it became a giant called the Iron Giant. It was really powerful.

Dr. Onigiri: Today in Japan, we can buy games online or at convenience stores, but back then, if you wanted the newest game, you had to stand in line and wait.

Prof. Mushroom: The music used in the games was incredible. They even sold orchestral versions on CD.

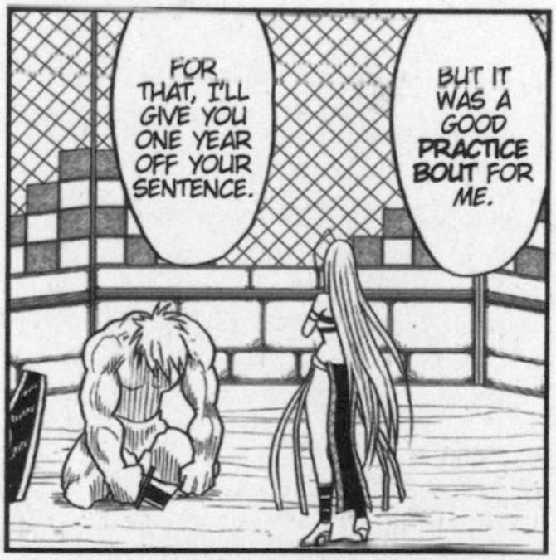
BUT IT WAS A GOOD PRACTICE BOUT FOR ME.
FOR THAT, I'LL GIVE YOU ONE YEAR OFF YOUR SENTENCE.

Crystal giving an inmate one year off his sentence. Not that it means much to a prisoner on death row...

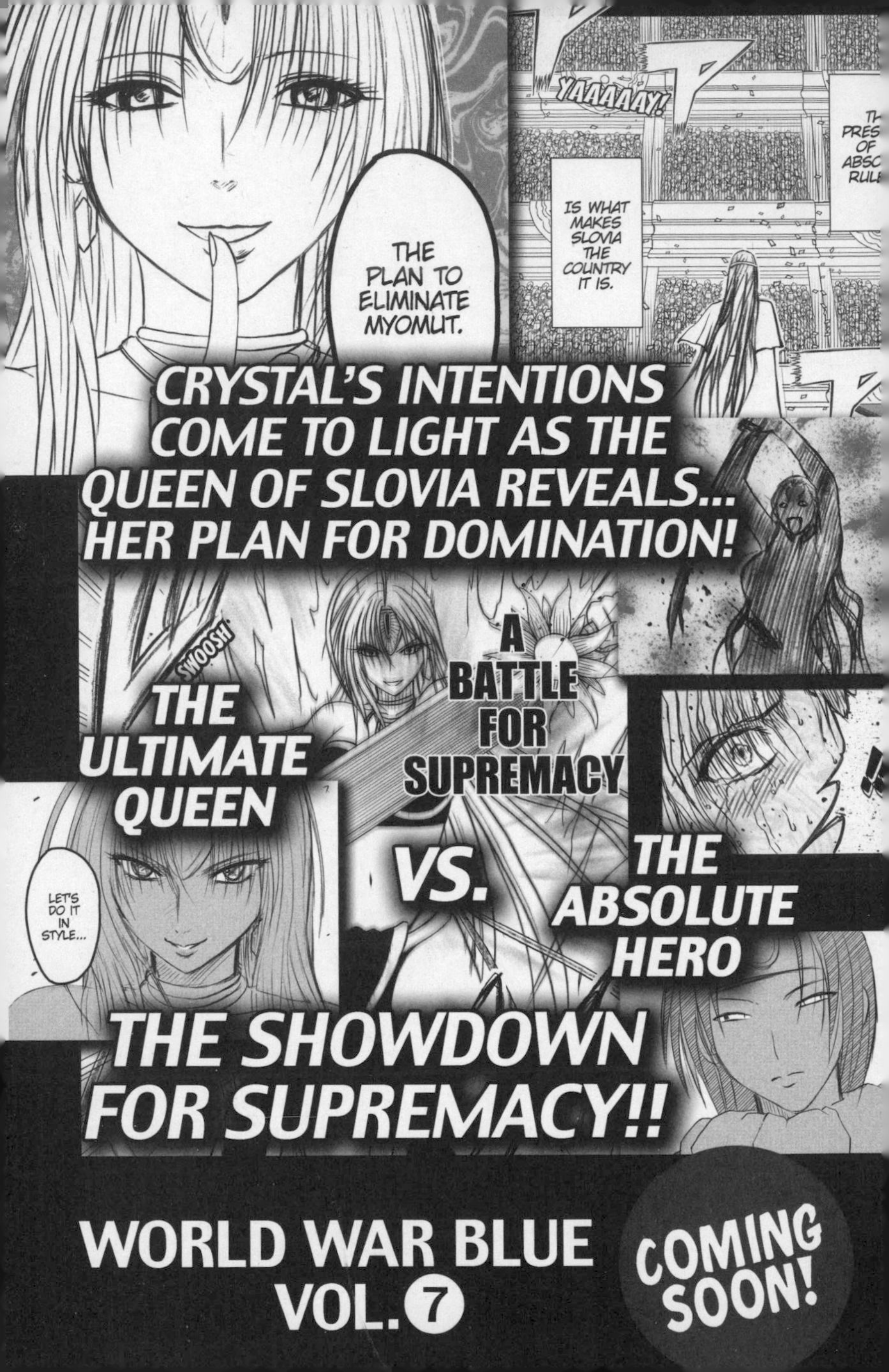
YAAAAAY!
TH PRES OF ABSC RUL
IS WHAT MAKES SLOVIA THE COUNTRY IT IS.
THE PLAN TO ELIMINATE MYOMUT.
CRYSTAL'S INTENTIONS COME TO LIGHT AS THE QUEEN OF SLOVIA REVEALS... HER PLAN FOR DOMINATION!
!!
A BATTLE FOR SUPREMACY
SWOOSH
THE ULTIMATE QUEEN
VS.
THE ABSOLUTE HERO
LET'S DO IT IN STYLE...
THE SHOWDOWN FOR SUPREMACY!!
WORLD WAR BLUE VOL. 7
COMING SOON!

WORLD WAR BLUE

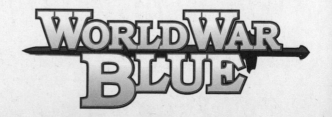

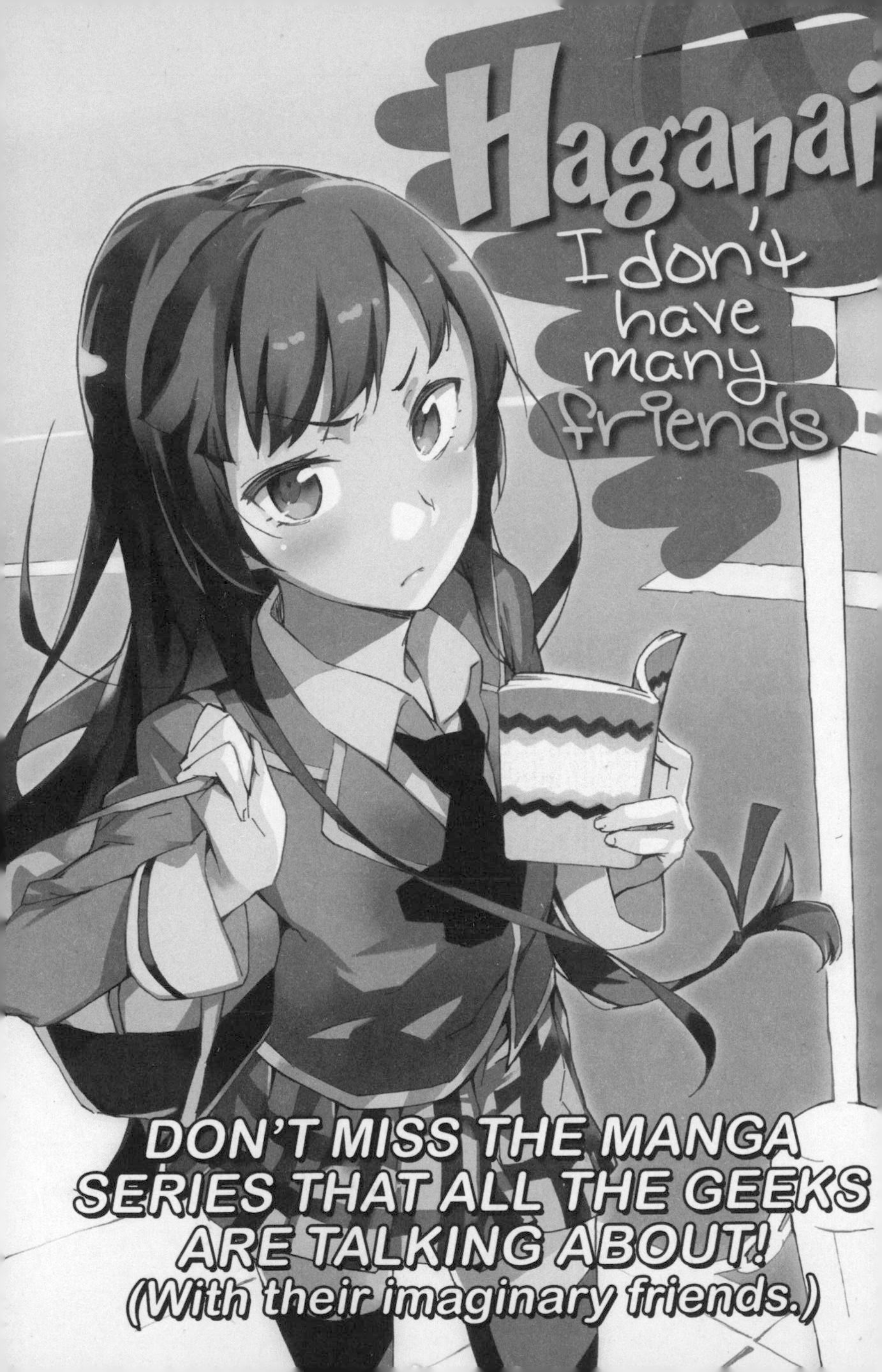
Haganai
I don't have many friends
DON'T MISS THE MANGA SERIES THAT ALL THE GEEKS ARE TALKING ABOUT!
(With their imaginary friends.)

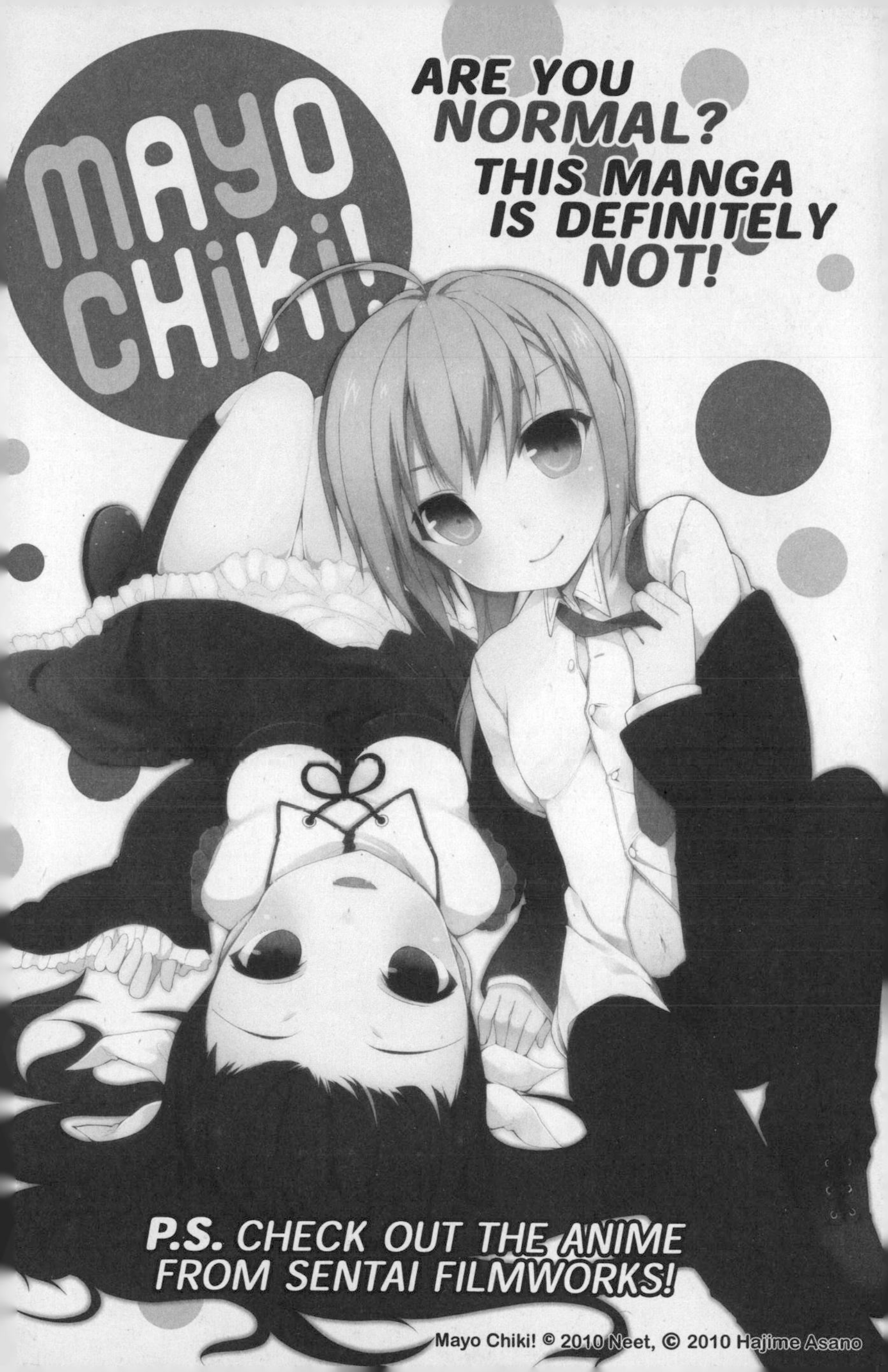
MAYO CHIKI!
ARE YOU NORMAL?
THIS MANGA IS DEFINITELY NOT!
P.S. CHECK OUT THE ANIME FROM SENTAI FILMWORKS!
Mayo Chiki! © 2010 Neet, © 2010 Hajime Asano

Experience all that
SEVEN SEAS has to offer!

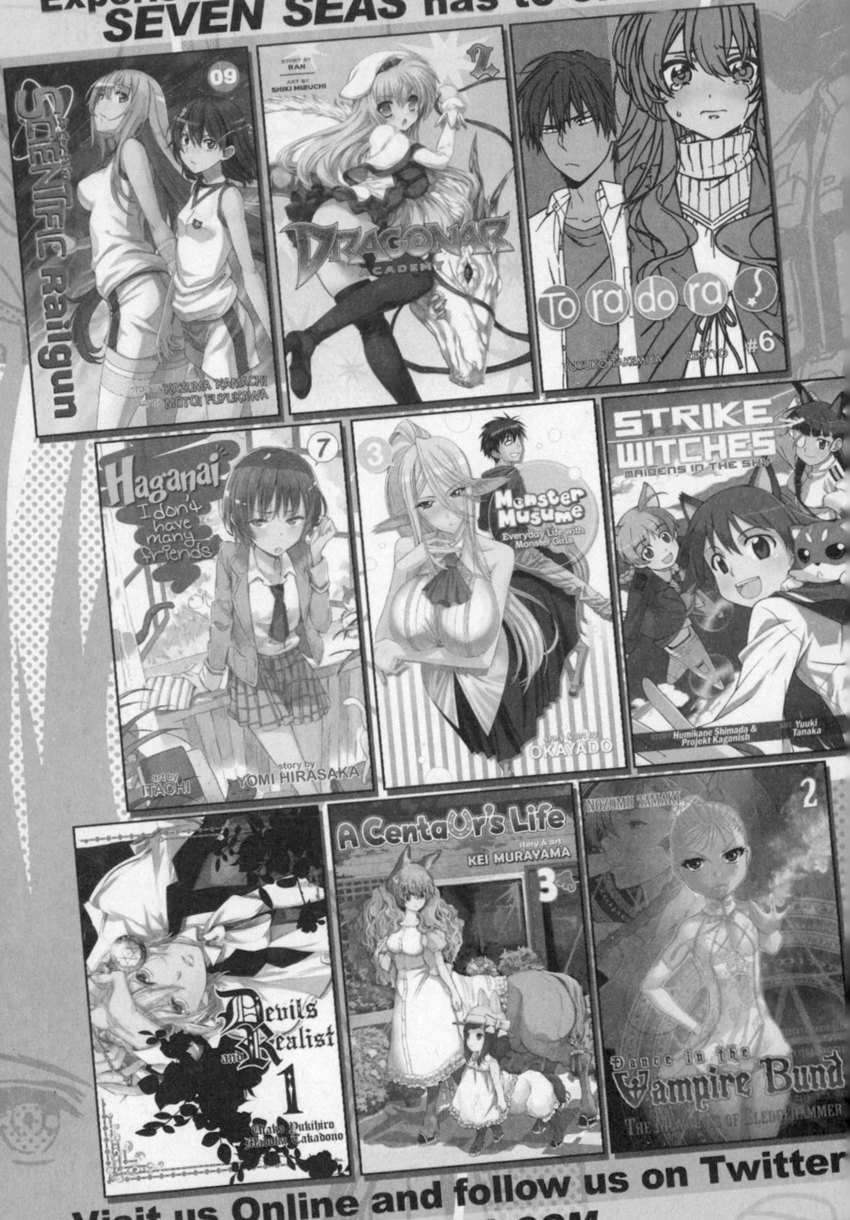

Scientific Railgun
09
story by KAZUMA KAMACHI
art by MOTOI FUYUKAWA
STORY BY RAN
ART BY SHIKI MIZUCHI
2
DRAGONAR ACADEMY
Toradora!
#6
YUYUKO TAKEMIYA
ZEKKYO
STRIKE WITCHES
MAIDENS IN THE SKY
Humikane Shimada & Projekt Kagonish
Yuuki Tanaka
3
Monster Musume
Everyday Life with Monster Girls
OKAYADO
7
Haganai
I don't have many friends
art by ITACHI
story by YOMI HIRASAKA
NOZOMU TAMAKI
2
Dance in the Vampire Bund
A Centaur's Life
story & art KEI MURAYAMA
3
Devils and Realist
1
Utako Yukihiro
Madoka Takadono

Visit us Online and follow us on Twitter

WWW.GOMANGA.COM

WWW.TWITTER.COM/GOMANGA

SEVEN SEAS ENTERTAINMENT PRESENTS

WORLD WA

art by **CRIMSON** / story by **ANASTASIA S**

D0546488

TRANSLATION
Wesley Bridges

ADAPTATION
Shannon Fay

LETTERING AND LAYOUT
Laura Scoville

LOGO DESIGN
Courtney Williams

COVER DESIGN
Nicky Lim

PROOFREADER
Janet Houck
Conner Crooks

MANAGING EDITOR
Adam Arnold

PUBLISHER
Jason DeAngelis

AOI SEKAI NO CHUSINDE KANZENBAN VOL. 6
© 2011 ANASTASIA SHESTAKOVA / © 2011 CRIMSON
This edition originally published in Japan in 2011 by
MICROMAGAZINE PUBLISHING CO., Tokyo. English translation rights
arranged with MICROMAGAZINE PUBLISHING CO., Tokyo through
TOHAN CORPORATION, Tokyo.

Seven Seas books may be purchased in bulk for educational, business, or
promotional use. For information on bulk purchases, please contact Macmillan
Corporate & Premium Sales Department at 1-800-221-7945 (ext 5442)
or write specialmarkets@macmillan.com.

Seven Seas and the Seven Seas logo are trademarks of
Seven Seas Entertainment, LLC. All rights reserved.

ISBN: 978-1-626920-59-0

Printed in Canada

First Printing: July 2014

10 9 8 7 6 5 4 3 2 1

FOLLOW US ONLINE: *www.gomanga.com*

3 3132 03640 4319

READING DIRECTIONS

This book reads from *right to left*, Japanese style.
If this is your first time reading manga, you start
reading from the top right panel on each page and
take it from there. If you get lost, just follow the
numbered diagram here. It may seem backwards at
first, but you'll get the hang of it! Have fun!!

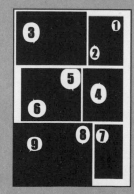